INDIVIDUAL DIFFERENCES IN COGNITION
Volume 1

Individual Differences in Cognition

VOLUME 1

Edited by

Ronna F. Dillon

Department of Guidance and Educational Psychology
Southern Illinois University
Carbondale, Illinois

Ronald R. Schmeck

Department of Psychology
Southern Illinois University
Carbondale, Illinois

With a Foreword by Robert Glaser

1983

ACADEMIC PRESS

A Subsidiary of Harcourt Brace Jovanovich, Publishers
New York   London
Paris   San Diego   San Francisco   São Paulo   Sydney   Tokyo   Toronto

ACADEMIC PRESS, INC.
111 Fifth Avenue, New York, New York 10003

United Kingdom Edition published by
ACADEMIC PRESS, INC. (LONDON) LTD.
24/28 Oval Road, London NW1 7DX

Library of Congress Cataloging in Publication Data

Main entry under title:

Individual differences in cognition.

Includes bibliographical references and index.
1. Cognition. 2. Individuality. I. Dillon,
Ronna F. II. Schmeck, Ronald R.
BF311.15 1983   153   82-22788
ISBN 0-12-216401-6

PRINTED IN THE UNITED STATES OF AMERICA

83 84 85 86   9 8 7 6 5 4 3 2 1

Contents

7. Individual Differences in the Solving of Social Science Problems
James F. Voss, Sherman W. Tyler, and Laurie A. Yengo

8. Learning Styles of College Students
R. R. Schmeck

9. Individual Differences in Children's Play: Selected Theoretical Analyses
Thomas D. Yawkey

Contributors

Numbers in parentheses indicate the pages on which the authors' contributions begin.

Diane J. Briars[1] (181), Department of Psychology, Carnegie-Mellon University, Pittsburgh, Pennsylvania 15213

John B. Carroll (1), Department of Psychology, University of North Carolina at Chapel Hill, Chapel Hill, North Carolina 27514

Susan R. Goldman (137), Department of Education, University of California at Santa Barbara, Santa Barbara, California 93106

James W. Hall (35), Department of Psychology, Northwestern University, Evanston, Illinois 60201

Michael S. Humphreys (35), Department of Psychology, Northwestern University, Evanston, Illinois 60201

Patrick C. Kyllonen (105), School of Education, Stanford University, Stanford, California 94305

David F. Lohman (105), School of Education, University of Iowa, Iowa City, Iowa 52242

Mary Jean Lynch (35), Department of Psychology, Northwestern University, Evanston, Illinois 60201

James W. Pellegrino (137), Department of Education, University of California at Santa Barbara, Santa Barbara, California 93106

Charles A. Perfetti (65), University of Pittsburgh Learning Research and Development Center, Pittsburgh, Pennsylvania 15260

William Revelle (35), Department of Psychology, Northwestern University, Evanston, Illinois 60201

[1]Present address: Department of Mathematical Sciences, Northern Illinois University, Dekalb, Illinois 60115.

R. R. Schmeck (233), Department of Psychology, Southern Illinois University at Carbondale, Carbondale, Illinois 62901

Sherman W. Tyler (205), University of Pittsburgh Learning Research and Development Center, Pittsburgh, Pennsylvania 15260

James F. Voss (205), Department of Psychology and Learning Research and Development Center, University of Pittsburgh, Pittsburgh, Pennsylvania 15260

Thomas D. Yawkey (281), Early Childhood Faculty, The Pennsylvania State University, University Park, Pennsylvania 16802

Laurie A. Yengo (205), University of Pittsburgh Learning Research and Development Center, Pittsburgh, Pennsylvania 15260

Foreword

The study of individual differences in cognition is as old as the beginnings of scientific psychology and, as this volume testifies, as new as modern cognitive psychology. As the editors indicate in their preface, the study of individual differences and the analysis of basic mental processes were not separable forms of investigation at the turn of this century. Differences among individuals were pervasive aspects of human behavior and were acknowledged as fundamental characteristics of psychological knowledge. The work of Darwin, the French studies of abnormality and feeblemindedness, and the new German empirical psychology of the elements of mental activity all nurtured attempts to investigate differences in mental processes. Measurement was a prerequisite to theoretical investigation; Galton, the father of mental ability tests, based his work on the experimental research of the German laboratories. Binet attempted to do the same, but found himself limited by the inability of the new science to analyze complex aspects of human cognition. In his practical task of predicting school success, he was forced to shun theoretical investigation of individual differences in favor of an atheoretical determination of relevant measures. Binet's success shifted the search for individual differences from elementary to complex processes and in so doing worsened the schism between experimental psychologists and psychologists who studied individual differences.

Based on the measures and correlational evidence that evolved in the growth of the testing movement, the methodology of factor analysis attempted to define and organize the knowledge that was emerging. The early pioneers, Spearman and Thurstone, were quite clear in characterizing their work as "prescientific," by which they meant that they were identifying classifications of human performance that would need to be explained by theories of mental processes. Nevertheless, over the past 50 years, the scientific study of individual differences has centered around factor analysis. Factor analysis has continued to work toward the identification of factors as the end products of research but has been less fruitful in explaining factors in terms of psychological processes. Test theory has centered on technological applications and has promoted models for accurate measures of individual differences with little consideration of the nature of the psychological performance being assessed.

The important purpose of this book is to establish connections between psychometrics, theories of individual differences, and modern cognitive psychology. Its excellent contributors are shaping current interest in applying the knowledge and methods of cognitive psychology to the understanding of individual differences. This book takes a wide view, highlighting many areas of psychology that are affected by this new influence. Its chapters cover the potential articulations between factor analysis and current cognitive theory; individual differences in short-term memory; verbal processes that influence differences in reading ability; process models of spatial and verbal aptitude, as measured on psychological tests; the relationship between developmental and individual differences; underlying information-processing abilities that contribute to differences in mathematical competence; and individual differences in problem-solving expertise and in learning styles, including children's play. This is, indeed, a broad and inclusive collection for those interested in new developments in the psychological bases of individual differences.

The chapter by Carroll makes a major statement about the possibilities for integrating the methodologies of test theory and factor analysis with the paradigms developed by cognitive psychologists for studying human information processing. Keenly aware that factor analysis is a method appropriate chiefly at an early stage in the investigation of a behavioral domain, Carroll considers many questions that go beyond factor analysis to further theoretical and practical understanding of individual differences in cognition.

Humphries, Lynch, Revelle, and Hall review theory, methods, and models in the study of short-term memory. They suggest a variety of components that may be responsible for individual differences. They particularly consider relationships between short-term memory and intelligence, arousal, and performance deficits such as dyslexia. They emphasize the mutual benefit for psychometrics and experimental psychology. Understanding models of memory should enable individual difference psychologists to apply their methodologies to cognitive functioning; and the individual-difference approach should encourage experimental psychologists to become more concerned with issues of reliability and validity in measurement.

Perfetti discusses in detail verbal processes that might influence individual differences in children's and adults' reading and verbal ability. He considers the processes of letter recognition, name retrieval, word decoding, and semantic access that patently contribute to reading performance. Of particular interest is his discussion of ways in which differences in ability in these simple verbal processes may contribute to the learning and performance of more complex verbal tasks.

Lohman and Kyllonen report the results of research on the factors involved with spatial ability. The hypothesis that they investigate and appear to confirm is that an important aspect of individual differences resides in the strategies used to solve spatial tasks. This is in contrast to previous research that has assumed uniform models of problem solving with variations in the parameters of these models. They point out the difficulties of identifying differences in spatial thinking because many spatial tasks can be solved, at least in part, by nonspatial strategies, and they emphasize that individual differences are manifested in the way people adapt their strategies.

Pellegrino and Goldman investigate developmental and individual differences in verbal and spatial reasoning in the kind of tasks that appear on aptitude test batteries. Of particular interest is their investigation of relationships between developmental and individual differences. In both verbal and spatial abilities, individual differences within an age group may parallel overall developmental trends. These authors emphasize the centrality of individual-difference data in understanding and identifying more general invariant processes of human information processing.

Briars discusses individual differences in mathematical ability. She asks why some people are "good" at mathematics whereas others are not, and she inquires about the underlying characteristics that may distinguish the two. To answer this query, she reviews studies that attempt to describe differences in mathematical ability in terms of the components of information processing models of cognition including: basic information-processing skills; content knowledge and its organization; and metacognitive knowledge, i.e., awareness and self-regulation of problem-solving performance.

Voss, Tyler, and Yengo consider problem-solving situations that are quite different from those encountered in mathematics, i.e., problems in the social sciences. Of special interest is the authors' attention to ill-structured problems in comparison to the more structured problems that have been generally studied in the cognitive psychology of problem solving. These authors investigate differences in novice and expert problem-solving strategies. Unlike novices, experts devote a large proportion of their time to developing a representation of the problem and to defining the initial state and the goal.

Schmeck reports on research about individual differences in learning strategies and style. The approach taken is that differences in learning strategy are a function of the information processing that occurs when students prepare for a test of memory. Learning style refers to predispositions to use particular strategies. The author emphasizes the necessity to study interventions and instructional procedures that can be used at early ages to influence the development of learning styles.

Yawkey defines play as the cognitive ability of children to experience themselves and things about them as other individuals, objects, or events through motoric and verbal activities. Although there is a long history of interest in children's play, psychological research on individual differences in this area is fairly recent. Both older and contemporary theories of children's play are described. Research on individual differences is reviewed in several dimensions including imaginativeness, symbolic modes and styles used in play, and differences between handicapped and nonhandicapped children in play behavior.

The chapters in this book show the recent progress and new interest in a science of individual differences. But in the context of the advances in modern psychology, a science of human differences is still in its early stages. It is fair to say that in the past 20 years, our knowledge about basic processes of human cognition in such fields as attention, memory, and problem solving has increased greatly. Rapid strides have also been made in the study of complex human knowledge and in skills such as language acquisition, reading and text comprehension, and mathematical understanding. Much less progress can be reported in our understanding of human differences. This book attempts to report the current state of that knowledge and to indicate the questions that are being investigated and that remain to be asked. In the present world scene, it is essential that our understanding of individual differences not be based on false ideas. Accurate information and understanding of human diversity is essential for the equitable treatment of individuals and for the effective development of human potential.

Robert Glaser
University of Pittsburgh
Learning Research and Development Center
Pittsburgh, Pennsylvania

Preface

The current trend of attempting to isolate fundamental processes in perception, learning, memory search, problem solving, and other cognitive activities through the study of variation in task performance began at least as early as the turn of the century. A. Binet, J. McK. Cattell, and others tried to measure intelligence through the assessment of simple processes such as sensory discrimination and choice reaction time. Our purpose in assembling this volume is to bring together a body of new material on individual differences in cognitive mechanisms underlying task performance.

Reflecting the benefits of a greatly refined technology of experimentation, elaborations in approaches to the study of cognitive processes are occurring in a host of cognitive abilities and performances. Topical coverage for this volume ranges from the study of individual differences in fundamental processes or components underlying variation in performance on IQ test-type tasks to investigations of the manner in which information processing differs among experts and novices as they solve problems in a given subject area. Also included are chapters centering on the relationship of individual differences in processes responsible for the acquisition of new information to variation in academic performance, as well as on individual differences in cognitive mechanisms contributing to variations in children's play.

In selecting areas to be represented, we have attempted to go beyond existing compilations of research on individual differences in information-processing components underlying performance differences in broad ability domains, to capture a sense of the depth and breadth of current interest in the study of individual differences in cognitive phenomena. We feel the work presented in this volume addresses the clear need to inform psychometrics and the theory of individual differences with the perspectives of cognitive psychology. Thus, this work moves us a step closer to under-standing the nature and determinants of cognitive processes and provides new foci and directions for individual differences among researchers and scholars.

We would like to express our appreciation for the assistance and support we have received from Harry O'Neil of the Army Research Institute for the Behavioral and Social Sciences and from the staff of Academic Press.

Studying Individual Differences in Cognitive Abilities: Through and Beyond Factor Analysis*

John B. Carroll

THE TASKS OF INDIVIDUAL DIFFERENCES RESEARCH

It is difficult—perhaps impossible—to find any domain or aspect of human responsiveness and performance in which individual differences are so small as to be negligible. Cognitive behavior, however one may define it, is not such a domain. Some respects in which wide individual differences—described in very general terms—are observed include the following: abilities to perceive aspects of the physical and social environment; abilities to notice and remember specific events, sequences of stimuli, similarities and differences among stimuli, and relationships; abilities to produce and comprehend speech and writing; abilities to form concepts, reason, make inferences, and arrive at decisions to achieve specific goals; abilities to learn to perform tasks requiring higher levels of complex information processing;

*This chapter is adapted from an address delivered at the Department of Psychology, University of Minnesota, April 15, 1981, as the annual Elliott–Paterson Lecture honoring the memory of Richard M. Elliott, founder and long-time chairman of that department, and Donald G. Paterson, a professor in the department for many years and a pioneer in the field of individual differences in both its theoretical and its applied aspects.

1

abilities to process information rapidly and to make quick and appropriate responses when such responses are required; knowledge of a wide range of information; competence in the use of information-processing procedures.

The study of individual differences is concerned with several basic and interrelated questions:

1. How can individual differences best be observed and described, and when appropriate, measured or put in quantitative terms?
2. What are the basic dimensions of these individual differences?
3. For each basic dimension, what are the dimensions and limits of variation and development in different populations and environments?
4. What are the sources and causes of this variation?
5. To what extent, and in what ways, if any, is this variation subject to modification by interventions of different kinds (e.g., giving practice, training, education, biomedical treatments)?
6. How does an individual's status with respect to different dimensions of individual differences impinge upon that individual's day-to-day activities and problems, education, career, and life history?

This is not the place to review psychologists' preoccupation with problems of individual differences in cognitive abilities, that is, in various kinds of "mental" or "intellectual" abilities (see Carroll, 1978b, pp. 1–106). The literature that has been produced along the way is vast, beginning as early as the nineteenth century and continuing with seemingly renewed vigor in recent years. The purpose here is to take a long view of this research effort and to put the work reviewed in this volume into a perspective that suggests the study of individual differences in cognitive abilities constitutes an important and integral part of psychological science.

Little will be said about particular methodologies of observing and measuring individual differences. It is taken for granted that the reader is reasonably familiar with a variety of psychological testing devices and observational techniques, and that he or she has some knowledge about problems of establishing the psychometric parameters of such instruments—their "reliability," various types and indices of "validity," and the like. The emphasis will be on techniques and results in establishing the dimensions of individual differences, for it is believed that questions of reliability and validity are secondary or subservient to basic questions of whether there is scientific utility in assuming that separate dimensions of individual differences exist, and if so, what these dimensions are, and what they mean in the context of psychological theory.

THE DEFINITION OF COGNITIVE ABILITY

What is a cognitive ability? At least a preliminary specification of this book's domain of interest needs to be given. It is useful to consider what is meant by a "cognitive task." One characteristic of a cognitive task is that it requires persons to act upon instructions (verbal or otherwise) given them by an experimenter or tester or that they themselves adopt, at least implicitly, when confronted with a challenge to achieve a certain outcome. Most items or subtests of psychometric instruments are cognitive tasks in this sense; part of the art of test construction has to do with framing effective instructions, practice exercises, and the like that convey to examinees a notion of their tasks. It is also the case that performance on cognitive tasks can usually be altered by giving different instructions, even when the stimulus materials and the total setting remain the same. For example, a digit span test will have different outcomes depending on whether the subject is asked to repeat digits in forward or backward order. The performance of cognitive tasks thus depends on the performer's having some prior notion of what kind of outcome is expected, and under what constraints the task is to be performed. Normally, when a cognitive task is used in testing cognitive abilities, it is assumed that subjects will attempt to display maximal performance—they will "do their best." Among other things, instructions are usually designed to motivate subjects to do just that.

Defining a task as "cognitive," however, requires further specification of the nature of the task. It is unlikely that we would say, for example, that an athletic performance such as running a mile is a cognitive task, although it is indeed a task that might be performed in response to instructions and there are undoubtedly cognitive elements in performing it. A cognitive task is one that critically requires the processing of information—information from the outside world that can be perceived by the individual and placed in some kind of memory, and/or information derived from previous experiences and retrieved from memory. There are many ways that such information may be processed: it may be stored in memory, compared with other information, retrieved from memory, transformed, or manipulated by complex procedures or algorithms. There are many possible types of cognitive tasks, varying in the type of information processing involved, the types of content operated on, and the types of response expected.

Tests of cognitive abilities often consist of a series of cognitive tasks. Sometimes the tasks are quite homogeneous. In the extreme case, they are simply repeated trials of the same task (e.g., a tapping test requiring the subject to place pencil marks in a series of circles printed on a piece of paper as rapidly as possible). In a less extreme case, the tasks might be repeated trials of the same process but with varying content or parameters (e.g., one requiring the subject to perform a series of additions of different pairs of numbers, or one requiring the subject to repeat series of digits, with different series lengths). At the opposite extreme are tests presenting a wide variety of cognitive tasks: the "omnibus" intelligence tests that present a series of verbal, mathematical, and figural items that may require quite different mental processes in their performance.

Depending on the nature of the tasks, performance may be observed in terms of the speed or rate at which the tasks are attempted or responded to, and/or the correctness or adequacy of the responses according to predetermined criteria. When tasks vary in such attributes as the likelihood that subjects are familiar with the properties of the stimuli (e.g., words of different degrees of familiarity in a vocabulary test), or the complexity of the information processing necessary for their performance, performance on the test may be interpreted as reflecting something about the subject's repertoire of responses or level of information-processing capabilities.

A cognitive ability may be defined as any of the one or more nonephemeral characteristics of an individual that determine the level of the individual's performance on a cognitive task when maximal performance is attempted. By "nonephemeral" we mean that the characteristic is one that changes, if at all, very slowly over time. A change, for example, would be detected only over months or years.

Exactly what cognitive abilities exist or can be differentiated has been—and continues to be—a matter for empirical determination, taking into account the possibility that any cognitive task may require more than one ability. The way in which psychological testing devices and procedures are designed may represent certain hypotheses about the cognitive abilities involved, and their number. A test composed of a series of identical or highly similar tasks, for example, is likely to be based on the assumption that one or a very small number of cognitive abilities are involved, whereas a test composed of heterogeneous tasks may be designed to obtain measurements that represent aggregations over many abilities, or, possibly, measurements that reflect "higher-order" abilities that account for correlations of narrowly defined abilities.

Historically, the method of choice in identifying dimensions of individual differences has been the use of correlations. Special developments and refinements of the correlational method that can be and have been used in these studies include the theory of mental tests, multiple regression, canonical correlation, certain types of analysis of variance designs, and factor analysis (especially the last of these). The basic idea, somewhat oversimplified, is that when any two variables of individual differences are found to be substantially correlated, there is the possibility that a single cognitive ability or a single set of cognitive abilities underlies these variables, whereas when two variables (each with established reliabilities) are found to be uncorrelated, it is probable that two different abilities or sets of abilities underlie them. When the variables are defined in terms of the range or levels of cognitive tasks they represent, it becomes possible to interpret the underlying abilities in terms of the characteristics of those tasks.

Recently, further methods of identifying individual difference dimensions have been introduced (e.g., R. J. Sternberg, 1977, 1980; Whitely, 1980a, 1980b), based on experimental designs that permit a stage analysis of cognitive tasks and the use of parameters describing task characteristics and stages. There is promise that these methods will usefully supplement traditional correlational procedures, such as factor analysis, in interpreting the nature of individual difference variables (see Carroll, 1980b). However, because the traditional methods are still not as widely and well understood as they might be, a substantial portion of this chapter must be devoted to these methods and the results obtained with their use, particularly the methods and results of factor analysis.

FACTOR ANALYSIS AS A METHOD OF CHOICE IN STUDYING INDIVIDUAL DIFFERENCES

Factor analysis has had a checkered career, one of ups and downs. When first introduced, it seemed to be the wave of the future, but in recent years it seems to have fallen on hard times. From outside this specialized field, it may appear that factor analysts cannot agree on their approaches and methods. Specialists in factor analysis methodology issue cautions about various problems inherent in the technique, such as indeterminacy (McDonald & Mulaik, 1979). Textbook presentations of factor analysis methodology do not give uniform advice. Users of factor analysis employ such a variety of methods—often without complete understanding of them when they rely on standard computer "packages"—that the results tend to be conflicting, difficult to interpret, and seemingly of little value in advancing knowledge. Models of mental ability structure offered by different factor analysts appear to disagree; there are endless quarrels, for example, between Guilford (1980) and Horn and Cattell (1982), Guilford criticizing "fluid intelligence" and "crystallized intelligence" as "fanciful concepts." Robert Sternberg (1977) devotes a chapter of his book to what he regards as the unsatisfactory features of factor analysis. Estes (1976) has these comments:

The perennial efforts to analyze intelligence tests in terms of theoretically based
ideas, and thus to arrive at purer measures of capacities, have never proven strikingly
successful. . . . The almost ubiquitous occurrence of positive correlations among
scores on various tests and scales led early to various conceptions of general ability,
ranging from Spearman's g to various systems of multiple factors. However, extensive and prolonged research efforts have not led to clear convergence on any one of
these systems, and on the whole there seems to be increasing disillusion with the
original idea that intercorrelations and factor analyses would lead to uncovering the
basic structures of the mind as determined by the underlying neural organization (pp.
295, 297).

Granted, there are limitations to factor analysis. One of its major limitations is its inability to deal readily with individual variation in the way
different abilities are used in the performance of tasks; its usual assumption
in this regard is that the abilities required for a task are the same for all
individuals in a sample. But in general, the limitations are not as serious as
they are often thought to be. Many of the difficulties with factor analysis
have come about because of the inappropriate design and selection of the
tests (and other variables subjected to factor analysis), improper design of
factor-analytic studies, unwisely chosen methods of computational analysis,
and unfortunate interpretations of results (Carroll, 1978a). Frequently, reanalysis of data from different studies can lead to much more convergence
and agreement in the findings than has appeared previously. Different factorial models of mental abilities can be translated into each other, and a
reasonable choice among models and methods can be made by the application of a number of principles of parsimony. Reasonable interpretations of
results can be made by appeal to general psychological theory.

Consider the basic equation of factor analysis, one form of which is
shown in Fig. 1a, with the terms identified and described. The equation
embodies a basic model similar to models in many other areas in psychology—indeed in many sciences. It seeks to account for variation over individuals in the observed variable y_{ji}, the standard score of individual i on
variable j. This is the term on the left side of the equation. On the right side
of the equation are various terms, as indicated: first, a series of terms with
weights w_{jp} for the individual's standard scores x_{pi} on m common factors
($p = 1, 2, \ldots, m$), and then terms for specific and error components that
together constitute the "unique" variance of a variable.

The principle of parsimony determines various aspects of this equation
and dictates a number of critical decisions about methods of performing
factor analysis. These decisions or criteria are as follows:

1. Parsimony constrains the equation to be linear rather than of a
higher order; in this way, the equation takes its simplest form. This implies
that the correlations from which a factor analysis is derived describe linear

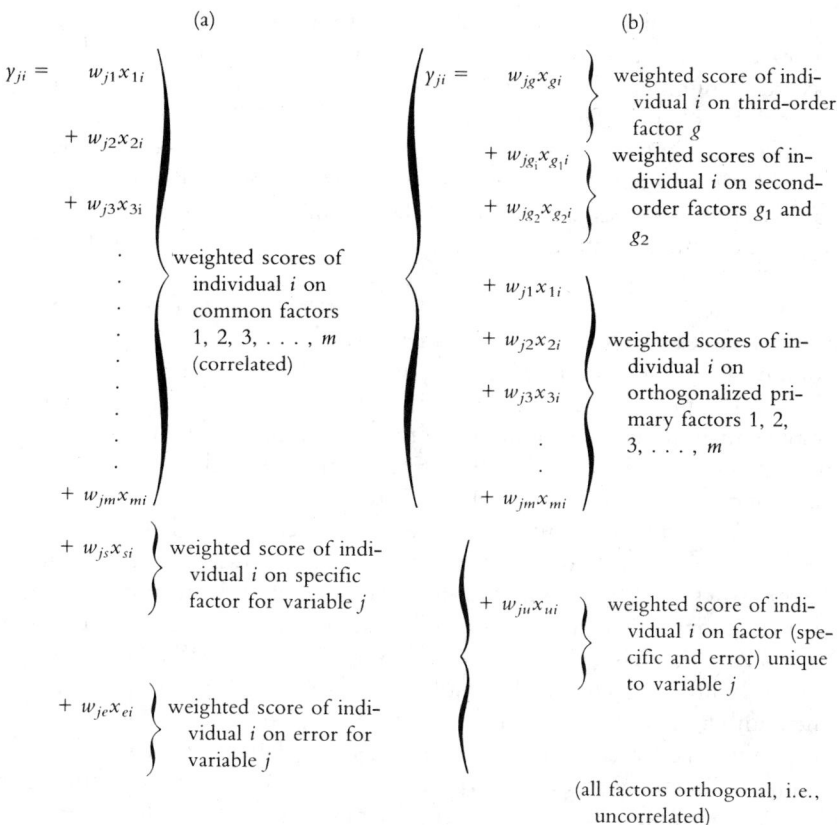

FIGURE 1. Alternative factor equations expressing composition of a manifest variable γ_j

rather than nonlinear relations, and makes certain requirements about the kinds of data and the kinds of correlations that can be subjected to factor analysis (Carroll, 1961).

2. The principle of parsimony recommends a clear distinction between common and unique variance. The common variance is that derived from the *co*variances of the variables and is properly the central focus of factor analysis. The method of factoring must preserve this distinction. Thus, a common factor model is to be preferred over the model implied by principal component analysis.

3. Parsimony recommends that a minimum number of common factors be identified to account for the covariances in a set of variables, at least to a reasonable approximation, laying aside chance covariance. In the initial computational analysis, this number refers to the number of factors in the

"primary" factor space, but in subsequent analysis, this number may be increased to account for correlations among primary factors. Finding the "correct" number of primary factors for a set of data is one of the more difficult problems in factor analysis, but usually, a defensible solution can be reached. Currently, the most useful preliminary criterion seems to be that offered by Montanelli and Humphreys (1976), since it takes account of sample size, whereas the popular Kaiser–Guttman (Kaiser, 1960) unity-eigenvalue rule does not. The ultimate criterion is probably to be found in the pattern of loadings in a rotated solution. Normally, the number of primary factors can be taken to be the largest number of factors such that there are at least two dominant or salient loadings on each factor in a rotated solution (e.g., by Kaiser's [1958] Varimax criterion).

4.   The principle of parsimony further suggests that for any variable, a minimum number of weights be zero or negligible. This is the primary justification for Thurstone's (1947) simple-structure criterion; it also justifies oblique rotations and correlated factors when necessary.

5.   The principle of parsimony justifies successive higher-order analyses of correlations among factors and orthogonalization of the resulting factor structure. Orthogonalization of factors makes them simpler because they are independent sources of variance. This can be accomplished by the Schmid and Leiman (1957) transformation—a procedure that has been used relatively little in factor-analytic studies. Parsimony also justifies increasing the number of common factors to allow the higher-order factors. In effect, one removes covariance from primary factors and places it in a higher-order domain. For many studies, a typical result is a hierarchical structure such that the common factors can be identified and classified as shown in Fig. 1b, still preserving the principle that the number of nonzero weights be minimal. It yields the simplest possible description of each variable; in practice, one no longer has to distinguish between reference vector, pattern, and structure matrices since they are all identical for uncorrelated factors. The Schmid–Leiman orthogonalization also provides a resolution between Thurstone (1947) solutions and those recommended by British workers such as Burt (1940) and Vernon (1961); these solutions are simple transformations of each other.

Unfortunately, relatively few studies in the factor-analytic literature have followed all the principles or criteria specified here, but with currently available computer facilities it is usually a simple matter to reanalyze their correlation matrices to do so. If this is done, we can expect that results will be much clearer and more convergent than has previously appeared to be the case. Experience thus far seems to bear out this expectation.

One or two further comments are in order:

1. The Guilford (1967, 1979) "Structure of Intellect" model must be rejected on several grounds: (a) the studies on which it is based do not generally conform to the methodological principles enunciated here: they are generally overfactored and rotated only orthogonally in dubious and questionable ways (Horn & Knapp, 1973; Merrifield, 1974); and (b) the categories in Guilford's system are vaguely defined and not well supported when Guilford's data are reanalyzed.

2. Models offered by Cattell, Horn, Hakstian, and their colleagues (Cattell & Horn, 1978; Hakstian & Cattell, 1978) are more likely to be in consonance with data and theory. One must prefer to let data speak for themselves rather than try to rotate factor configurations to fit any arbitrarily conceived set of operations, contents, and products. There is considerable evidence for the existence of higher-order factors such as what Cattell and Horn (1978) call "fluid" and "crystallized" intelligence. Furthermore, the several other higher-order factors identified by Hakstian and Cattell (1978) will probably hold up reasonably well in future analyses.

In sum, if factor analysis is given its due and used "correctly" and appropriately, researchers can arrive at a reasonable and confirmable picture of the structure of mental abilities. The main advantage of correlational and factorial methods is that they differentiate and sort out dimensions of individual differences. On the one hand, factor analysis can tell us that a series of variables have something in common or reflect some common influence; on the other hand, it is of value and interest when factor analysis indicates that variables can be classified and described in terms of distinctly different dimensions. Factor analysis provides an initial taxonomy of mental abilities.

AN EXAMPLE OF FACTOR ANALYSIS COMPUTATIONS

Because the factor-analytic literature and textbook presentations contain a great variety of factor analysis procedures—many of them less than desirable—it may be useful to present, as a tutorial, a factor analysis performed by procedures that meet the criteria set forth here. The example is based on data assembled by Wesche, Edwards, and Wells (1982), who administered four subtests of the Thurstone and Thurstone (1962) Primary Mental Abilities (PMA) battery and the five subtests of the Modern Language Aptitude Test (Carroll & Sapon, 1959) to 793 English-speaking Canadian public servants, average age 37, at various stages of intensive French language training in the Ottawa area. The object was to investigate the relation of general intelligence to foreign language learning aptitude. The essential data and factor analysis computations are shown in Table 1. The obtained Pearsonian correlations are given in the lower triangle of the first matrix; the variables are ordered in groups suggested by the eventual factor solution. (It is recommended that as a general procedure in publishing results, reordering of variables in matrices according to factor solutions will facilitate readers' understanding and appreciation of findings.) It may be presumed that the correlations reflect linear relations among the variables (although this is a matter that should always be checked), and thus that the data meet criterion 1 given above. All variables are oriented in a positive direction; that is, high scores imply more desirable performances. (As a general procedure, variables should be reflected if they are negatively oriented.)

In analyzing these data, the writer subjected the correlation matrix to three initial factoring procedures:

1.   A principal component (PC) solution, that is, a latent root analysis of the correlation matrix with unities on the diagonal. This procedure violates criterion 2 but is often used for determining the number of factors as the number of eigenvalues or latent roots that are greater than or equal to unity. As noted previously, this procedure is not generally recommended but its results are given here for illustrative purposes. The eigenvalues are given in the first row of a table of roots just below the correlation matrix. Only one eigenvalue is greater than unity and one might be tempted to conclude from this that there is only one "significant" factor in the data. Such a conclusion would be unwise, however, because other criteria suggest that the number of factors is greater than one. The unity-eigenvalue rule will often underestimate the number of factors when factors are oblique and substantially correlated (as will be seen to be true in the present case). There are also circumstances (e.g., when correlations are generally of low magnitude) when the unity-eigenvalue rule will suggest more than the correct number of factors. Normally, one can entirely dispense with the computation of the PC solution. (The fact that it is allegedly more elegant and often gives results very similar to those of other, more acceptable solutions is not a justification for using it.)

2.   A procedure involved in the use of the Montanelli–Humphreys (1976) "parallel analysis" criterion, that is, latent root analysis of the correlation matrix with squared multiple correlations (SMC's) on the diagonal. The resulting eigenvalues are given in the second row of the table of roots. They are to be compared with the corresponding values in the third row, which are the estimated eigenvalues expected to be yielded by purely random data with the given sample size ($N = 793$) and number of variables ($n = 9$). These values were computed with a formula developed by Tucker (Note 1) to provide convenient estimates of the values yielded by Mon-

TABLE 1

Factor Analysis of Scores on PMA and MLAT (N = 793 Canadian Public Servants)

	Correlations[a]								
	SC	VM	NF	R	SR	PA	NL	PS	WS
MLAT Spelling Clues (SC)	.451	.531	.394	.497	.248	.406	.341	.439	.515
PMA Verbal Meaning (VM)	.54	.407	.460	.509	.291	.280	.270	.349	.452
PMA Number Facility (NF)	.38	.46	.499	.654	.474	.271	.415	.322	.455
PMA Reasoning (R)	.49	.53	.63	.581	.476	.379	.489	.412	.536
PMA Spatial Relations (SR)	.28	.27	.48	.50	.309	.213	.339	.232	.322
MLAT Paired Associates (PA)	.41	.29	.25	.39	.22	.297	.408	.374	.400
MLAT Number Learning (NL)	.33	.28	.42	.49	.33	.42	.344	.362	.414
MLAT Phonetic Script (PS)	.46	.32	.32	.40	.25	.35	.36	.306	.411
MLAT Words in Sentence (WS)	.50	.44	.51	.53	.26	.40	.41	.44	.448

	Roots								
	1	2	3	4	5	6	7	8	9
Eigenvalues, 1's in diagonal	4.232	.995	.851	.655	.622	.514	.431	.365	.336
Eigenvalues, SMC's in diagonal	3.659	.381	.219	.023	−.021	−.117	−.124	−.180	−.199
Random data SMC eigenvalues	.177	.118	.081	.046	—	—	—	—	—

[a]Obtained, below diagonal; Reproduced from 3 factors, above diagonal; *SMCs, on diagonal.*

(continued)

tanelli and Humphreys' published procedures. Incidentally, this criterion assumes the data correlations are Pearsonian; caution should be observed in using it if, for example, the correlations are tetrachoric. In the present case, the correlations are Pearsonian and three SMC eigenvalues are found to be greater than the corresponding random data eigenvalues, tentatively suggesting three significant common factors in these data.

3. A principal factoring (PF) procedure, to iterate for communalities starting with SMC estimates on the diagonal of the correlation matrix. (The SMC values are given on the diagonal of the correlation matrix in Table 1.) This procedure fulfils criterion 2 in that it preserves the distinction between common and unique variance. Since the Montanelli–Humphreys criterion had suggested three factors, the PF solution was obtained for two, three, and four factors to examine the factor patterns produced by each solution. In each case, a Varimax (Kaiser, 1958) rotation was performed, and the largest value in each row of the rotated matrix was identified. For the four-factor solution (not shown here), one of these largest values was the only one in its column; this suggested that the fourth factor represented mainly

TABLE 1 *(Continued)*

	Unrotated principal factor orthogonal solution				Varimax-rotated factor matrix		
	I	II	III	h^2	A′	B′	C′
MLAT Spelling Clues (SC)	.693	.322	−.199	.623	.679	.174	.362
PMA Verbal Meaning (VM)	.641	.069	−.328	.523	.624	.340	.133
PMA Number Facility (NF)	.716	−.365	−.081	.653	.303	.729	.170
PMA Reasoning (R)	.808	−.203	−.015	.694	.385	.658	.336
PMA Spatial Relations (SR)	.514	−.302	.055	.359	.123	.555	.188
MLAT Paired Associates (PA)	.538	.258	.252	.420	.254	.130	.582
MLAT Number Learning (NL)	.605	−.026	.352	.491	.096	.395	.571
MLAT Phonetic Script (PS)	.562	.202	.077	.363	.362	.188	.443
MLAT Words in Sentences (WS)	.691	.111	−.004	.490	.450	.339	.415
Sum of squared loadings	3.770	.495	.351	4.616	1.514	1.743	1.359

	Varimax transformation matrix		
	A′	B′	C′
I	.576	.617	.536
II	.449	−.787	.423
III	−.683	.003	.730

unique variance and the four factors were more than could be supported by the data. In the three–factor solution (shown in Table 1 in both rotated and Varimax-rotated forms), each rotated factor had at least two (actually, three) largest values in their rows and it was decided the data could support three common factors. The two-factor solution (not shown here) was discarded. (It may be remarked that because of an idiosyncrasy of the algorithm used to compute eigenvectors, the computer reported the first unrotated factor coefficients with all negative values; since the orientation of a factor is arbitrary, like the sign of a square root, the values given here are reflected to all positive. As a general procedure, it is recommended that any column of a factor matrix should be reflected if the algebraic sum of its values is negative.)

The communalities for the three-factor PF solution are given, as well as the column sums of the squared loadings for both unrotated and Varimax-rotated solutions. Since the sum of the communalities, and the sum of the squared loadings over three factors is 4.616, the three PF factors account for

TABLE 1 (*Continued*)

	Oblique reference vector loadings			Orthogonalized simple structure matrix				
	A	B	C	g	a	b	c	h^2
MLAT Spelling Clues (SC)	.486	−.078	.209	.663	.374	−.065	.196	.622
PMA Verbal Meaning (VM)	.455	.099	−.050	.625	.350	.082	−.047	.523
PMA Number Facility (NF)	.047	.575	−.084	.643	.036	.480	−.079	.652
PMA Reasoning (R)	.095	.479	.083	.723	.074	.400	.078	.694
PMA Spatial Relations (SR)	−.080	.476	.005	.445	−.062	.397	.004	.359
MLAT Paired Associates (PA)	.042	.030	.484	.460	.032	.025	.455	.420
MLAT Number Learning (NL)	−.169	.333	.417	.496	−.130	.278	.393	.494
MLAT Phonetic Script (PS)	.166	.047	.321	.503	.128	.039	.302	.362
MLAT Words in Sentences (WS)	.217	.157	.240	.627	.167	.131	.226	.490
Sum of squared loadings:				3.070	.335	.655	.556	4.616

	Transformation matrix			Correlations among primary factors (obtained, below diagonal; reproduced, in and above diagonal)			
	A	B	C	A	B	C	g
I	.228	.373	.260				
II	.502	−.897	.569				
III	−.834	.238	.780				
A				.713	.680	.538	.845
B				.683	.648	.513	.805
C				.540	.509	.405	.637

4.616/9 = .513 or 51.3% of the total variance. This value might be regarded as somewhat small, but it should be noted that this analysis can be regarded as a higher-order analysis (analogous to that made by Hakstian and Cattell [1978] on 20 primary factor measurements) since most of the variables are measures of different, independent primary abilities. Thus, the uniquenesses of the variables may be thought of as composed, in part, of common factor variance at the first-order level.

It may be noted that the Varimax rotation redistributes the total common factor variance (4.616) into roughly equal portions for the three rotated factors. The correlations reproduced by either the unrotated or the Varimax-rotated factor matrices are shown in the upper triangle of the correlation matrix. Generally, they are very close to the original correlations, the largest residual being −.062. These results can be taken as fulfilling criterion 3; namely, that a minimum number of common factors be identified to account for the covariances "to a reasonable approximation." (Residuals would be considerably larger for a one- or two-factor solution.)

Pairwise plots of the Varimax factors suggested that a better simple structure would be attained through further, oblique rotations; therefore, graphical and other rotations were performed to produce the oblique reference-vector matrix shown in Table 1, with the associated correlations among the primary factors. These rotations were done while bearing in mind criterion 4; namely, that for any variable, a minimum number of weights in the factor equation should be nonzero or nonvanishing.

In view of the substantial correlations among the primary factors, Criterion 5 justified a factoring of those correlations and orthogonalization of the factors by the Schmid–Leiman (1957) procedure. The correlations among the primary factors were found to be very well accounted for by a single second-order factor, labeled g, as may be seen from the correlations reproduced by that factor. The orthogonalized simple structure matrix, with loadings on factor g and orthogonalized factors a, b, and c, is shown in the last portion of Table 1. This matrix gives reproduced correlations that are almost the same as those produced by the three-factor orthogonal matrices, and the communalities of the variables remain almost the same as previously. The sums of squared loadings show how the total common factor variance is allocated among the orthogonalized primary factors and the second-order factor g. A large portion (66.5%) of this variance is assigned to factor g, and all the variables have substantial loadings on this factor. The portions of common-factor variance remaining in the orthogonalized primary factors are relatively small but are, in part, a function of the number of variables having substantial loadings on these factors. (For example, if more variables measuring factor a had been present in the battery, the variance residing in this factor could have been larger.)

This completes the analysis. Evidently factor a is a verbal knowledge factor (MLAT subtest Spelling Clues is in part a disguised vocabulary test). Factor b, measured almost exclusively by PMA subtests, is probably some composite of the Gf (fluid intelligence) and Gc (crystallized intelligence) factors found in other studies using tests similar to those of the PMA battery. Factor c appears to represent a dimension of ability that is specific to the memory components of the foreign language aptitude tests. Factor g is apparently a general intellectual factor that enters into all the subtests of the batteries studied.

The example given here represents what this writer regards as appropriate methods of exploratory factor analysis, that is, factor analysis performed with the objective of identifying dimensions of individual differences. It does not claim to cover all the problems encountered in performing factor analyses of large data sets, but may nevertheless serve as a general guide. In recent years, "confirmatory" factor analysis procedures (Jöreskog, 1978) have been added to the methods available to the factor analyst. They permit testing the statistical significance of findings. The basic factor model, however, remains essentially the same. Generally, exploratory methods are to be preferred for establishing the probable factorial composition and structure of a set of variables; confirmatory methods can then be applied to establish or test their significance.

THE CLASSIFICATION OF MENTAL ABILITIES

The taxonomic task that can be undertaken with factor analysis is far from finished. Nevertheless, it is worthwhile to examine the rough approximation that can now be assembled from the available data. Table 2 presents a concordance of the factors of cognitive ability identified by French (1951) and in two successive "kits" of "factor-reference" tests assembled at Educational Testing Service (French, Ekstrom, & Price, 1963; Ekstrom, French, & Harman, 1976). The various primary factors are grouped in second-order domains; this grouping is very tentative because only recently have we begun to get a clear picture of these higher-order domains.

Two fundamental queries can be raised about the data represented in this concordance. One is that the variables studied are largely derived from printed, paper-and-pencil tests that involve written language and are affected by variations in subjects' reading abilities. A wide range of reading abilities is found in school populations—even at the college level. The factor structures both at primary and higher-order levels may thus be a function of these variations in reading abilities—or with the basic perceptual abilities associated with reading skills. New series of factor-analytic studies need to be designed and conducted with the specific aim of sorting out the effects of reading abilities, for these abilities themselves are apparently quite complex (Frederiksen, 1978; Jackson & McClelland, 1979). Many of the ETS factor-reference tests need to be redesigned to minimize effects of reading abilities; for example, the extent to which the vocabulary tests are measures of the Verbal Knowledge factor V is affected by the degree to which they may also be measures of ability to recognize printed words.

A second major concern is the role of speed in determining test scores. There is a moderately extensive literature (e.g., Baxter, 1941; Davidson & Carroll, 1945; Lord, 1956; Tate, 1948) that suggests that any time–limit scores taken from tests administered in the conventional manner are likely to be complex functions of separate speed and level of mastery components. This literature has been ignored by most researchers in factor analysis; it seems to have been neglected also in the development and construction of

TABLE 2
Concordance of Selected Cognitive and Cognitive-Related Factors[a]

Factor code	Factor name	French (1951) code, name (no. of studies)	1963 ETS kit code, name	1976 ETS kit code, name	Guilford factors[b]	Cattell univ'l index[c]
Gf ("fluid intelligence") factors[d,e]						
I	Induction	I:Induction (9)	I:Induction	I:Induction	(Several)	T5
RL	Logical reasoning	D:Deduction (37)	Rs:Syllogistic reasoning	RL:Logical reasoning	EMR?	T4
RG	General reasoning	—	R:General reasoning	RG:General reasoning	CMS	T34
IP	Integrative process	In:Integration (1)	—	IP:Integrative process	—	—
J	Judgment	J:Judgment (5)	—	—	—	—
PL	Planning	Pl:Planning (4)	—	—	—	—
Gc (crystallized intelligence) factors:						
V	Verbal knowledge	V:Verbal comprehension (46)	V:Verbal comprehension	V:Verbal comprehension	CMU	T13
N	Numerical facility	N:Number (35)	N:Number facility	N:Number facility	NSI,MSI?	T10
Gv (general visual perception) factors:						
—	—	S:Space (44)	—[f]	—[f]	—	—
SO	Spatial orientation	SO:Spatial orientation (4)	S:Spatial orientation	S:Spatial orientation	CFS	T11
VZ	Spatial visualization	Vi:Visualization (16)	Vs:Visualization	VZ:Visualization	CFT	T14
CS	Speed of closure	GP:Gestalt perception (2)	Cs:Speed of closure	CS:Speed of closure	CFU	T3
CF	Flexibility of closure	GF:Gestalt flexibility (1)	Cf:Flexibility of closure	CF:Flexibility of closure	NFT	T2
SS	Spatial scanning	—	Sa:Spatial scanning	SS:Spatial scanning	CFI	—
LE	Length estimation	LE:Length estimation (4)	Le:Length estimation	—	—	—
CV	Verbal closure	—	—	CV:Verbal closure	—	—
P	Perceptual speed	P:Perceptual speed (34)	P:Perceptual speed[g]	P:Perceptual speed	(ESU,EFU)	T12
PA	Perceptual alternations	PA:Perceptual alternations (1)	—	—	—	—
IL	Figure illusions	FI:Figure illusions (1)	—	—	—	—

Ga ("general auditory perception") factors:

AUI Auditory integration	AI:Auditory integration (1)	—	—	—	—
AUR Auditory resistance	AR:Auditory resistance (1)	—	—	—	—
LO Loudness	Lo:Loudness (1)	—	—	—	—
PQ Pitch quality	PQ:Pitch quality (1)	—	—	—	—

Gm ("general memory") factors:

MA Associative memory	M:Associative memory (16)	Ma:Associative memory	MA:Associative memory	MSR	T7
MS Memory span	Sm:Span memory (2)	Ms:Memory span	MS:Memory span	MSU,MSS?	—
MV Visual memory	VM:Visual memory (4)	—	MV:Visual memory	—	—
MMU Musical memory	MM:Musical memory (2)	—	—	—	—

Fluency and production factors:

FA Associational fluency	—	Fa:Associational fluency	FA:Associational fluency	DMR	—
FE Expressional fluency	FE:Fluency of expression (3)	Fe:Expressional fluency	FE:Expressional fluency	DMS	—
FI Ideational fluency	IF:Ideational fluency (4)	Fi:Ideational fluency	FI:Ideational fluency	DMU	T6
FW Word fluency	W:Word fluency (8)	Fw:Word fluency	FW:Word fluency	DSU	T15
XU Flexibility of use	—	Xs:Semantic spontaneous flexibility	XU:Flexibility of use	DMC	—
XF Figural flexibility	—	Xa:Figural adaptive flexibility	XF:Figural flexibility	DFT	—
NA Naming speed	Na:Naming (1)	—	—	—	—
FS Speech fluency	PS:Public speaking (1)	—	—	—	—
SA Speed of association	SA:Speed of association (2)	—	—	—	—
O Originality	—	O:Originality	—	DMT	—
RE Semantic redefinition	—	Re:Semantic redefinition	—	NMT	—
SEP Sensitivity to problems	—	Sep:Sensitivity to problems	—	EMI	—

Speed factors (not otherwise classified):

SD Speed	Sp:Speed (3)	—	—	—	—
SDJ Speed of judgment	SJ:Speed of judgment (1)	—	—	—	—

(continued)

TABLE 2 (Continued)

Factor code	Factor name	French (1951) code, name (no. of studies)	1963 ETS kit code, name	1976 ETS kit code, name	Guilford factors[b]	Cattell univ'l index[c]
Selected psychomotor factors:						
AIMG	Aiming	Ai:Aiming (7)	—	—	—	—
AMB	Ambidexterity	Am:Ambidexterity (2)	—	—	—	—
SDAR	Speed of articulation	Ar:Articulation (1)	—	—	—	—
FD	Finger dexterity	FD:Finger dexterity (11)	—	—	—	—
MD	Manual dexterity	MD:Manual dexterity (4)	—	—	—	—
PC	Psychomotor coordination	PC:Psychomotor coordination (10)	—	—	—	—
RT	Reaction time	RT:Reaction time (2)	—	—	—	—
TA	Tapping	Ta:Tapping (3)	—	—	—	—
Miscellaneous affective-cognitive factors:						
AT	Attention	At:Attention (4)	—	—	—	—
CA	Carefulness	C:Carefulness (6)	—	—	—	—
PE	Persistence	Pe:Persistence (2)	—	—	—	—
PN	Perseveration	Pn:Perseveration (1)	—	—	—	—

[a]Identified by French (1951) and in the 1963 and 1976 ETS kits of factor reference tests (Ekstrom, French, & Harman, 1976; French, Ekstrom, & Price, 1963).

[b]Designations of Guilford factors are those shown in the 1963 ETS kit manual. A key to these designations is as follows:
First character: C, Cognition; D, Divergent production; E, Evaluation; M, Memory; N, Convergent production (Process)
Second character: F, Figural; M, Semantic; S, Symbolic (Content)
Third character: C, Classes; I, Implications; R, Relations; S, Systems; T, Transformations; U, Units (Products)

[c]Designations of Cattell (1957) Universal Index codes are those shown in the 1963 ETS kit manual.

[d]The classification of factors into higher-order groups is tentative; it generally follows the Cattell and Horn model (see Horn, 1978, pp. 211–256).

[e]The two ETS kits distinguish two factors (Rs, RL; R, RG) derived from French's (1951) Deduction.

[f]French's (1951) Space appears as two factors SO (Spatial orientation) and VZ (Visualization) in the ETS Kits.

[g]The 1963 ETS kit notes that Perceptual speed may consist of several subfactors.

the ETS kits of factor-reference tests. Some of the information assembled in Table 2 is suspect in that somewhat different identifications and groupings of primary factors might appear if the speed–level distinction had been more rigorously observed in the design and analysis of factor studies. Recent demonstrations of the influence of speed on factor-analytic results have been made by Egan (1978, 1981), who found that separate and uncorrelated speed and accuracy components exist in the spatial-ability domain. Whereas previous literature had suggested two or three factors of spatial ability—a "true" spatial relations factor, a "visualization" factor, and a "spatial orientation" factor—it now appears that these factors are, in actuality, complex composites of speed and accuracy dimensions. Lohman (1979) has pointed out that tests of visualization (Factor VZ) are generally unspeeded (thus measuring primarily Egan's spatial accuracy factor), whereas tests of spatial relations (Factor SR) and spatial orientation (Factor SO) are generally speeded (and thus measure primarily Egan's spatial speed factor).

New studies of other domains, possibly carried out along the lines of Egan's methodology, would probably require the amendment of some of the findings presented in Table 2. Egan's methodology is interesting. He converted spatial ability test items to binary choice format and presented them individually in laboratory apparatus to obtain latency and accuracy data. The use of the customary multiple-choice format introduces a considerable amount of variance that is an unknown composite of error, visual scanning speed, and so forth.

It is hard not to conclude that, despite some 50 years of research, there is much that needs to be done within the methodology of factor analysis. In addition to exploring the role of reading abilities and separating speed and level of mastery components, it would be desirable to map more thoroughly the domain of auditory abilities. Most of the findings shown in Table 2 are based on visually presented stimuli. As yet, there are only a few studies of factors derived from auditory stimuli (Karlin, 1942; Stankov & Horn, 1980). Although it is probable that many factors will prove to be indifferent to modality of presentation, it is also likely that some dimensions of individual differences will be found to depend on the auditory modality. Various psychomotor and kinesthetic domains also need to be further investigated.

One can voice a further general concern about our present knowledge of the organization of mental abilities; namely, the failure to take adequate account of developmental aspects. The results embodied in Table 2 come largely from studies conducted with mature samples—high school and college students, military personnel, and the like—although some are derived from samples taken at younger ages, down to the preschool. Age factors have not always been properly controlled. Correlations among test scores or other variables obtained on samples that are heterogeneous in age may be spuriously inflated with age variance. This unwanted age variance is particularly likely to be present in higher-order domains, that is, in correlations among primary factors. The disputes about general, fluid, and crystallized intelligences may depend to an unknown extent on inadequate attention to the problem of spurious age variance. To give perspective on the problem, Fig. 2 attempts to represent, in an abstract way, the idea that different kinds of cognitive ability may have different courses of development over the age span from infancy to adulthood. Some types of functioning may reach asymptote early, others much later. Some types of mental functioning may not even begin to develop until late in childhood. What we would really like to know is what kinds of mental development are to be observed, and what their courses of development are. It seems reasonable to assume that if we can identify differently shaped growth curves for measurable cognitive functions, the fact of different growth curves demonstrates the existence of different cognitive functions. If we do a factor analysis of performances at any given age, and if a series of differentiable factors is obtained, these results would tell us that growth curves are differentially determined at that age. Thus far, little progress has been made in developing and applying factor-analytic models to longitudinal data to reveal differently shaped growth curves for different mental functions, but there is need for such work. The argument as to whether "Piagetian" intelligence is the same as, or different from, "psychometric" intelligence (Humphreys & Parsons, 1979; Kohlberg & DeVries, 1980) could probably be resolved with this research strategy.

Growth undoubtedly occurs as a function of both constitutional and environmental influences. Many of the primary factors of mental development are probably—to a considerable degree—reflections of environmental determinants. For example, the Verbal Knowledge factor V emerges from factorial studies not only because individuals vary in their ability to profit from their verbal environments but also because verbal environments differ markedly. Even though different aspects of language development are logically independent—for example, vocabulary knowledge and syntactical comprehension—tests of these aspects turn out to have high correlations because differences in verbal environments affect all of them in common. The second-order crystallized intelligence factor may reflect, similarly, the common environmental determinants of the primary factors—such as Verbal Knowledge and Numerical Facility, subsumed under crystallized intelligence.

Taking a developmental perspective should aid in clarifying the problem of a general intelligence or g factor as originally proposed by Spearman. A preliminary observation about this problem is that a general factor of intel-

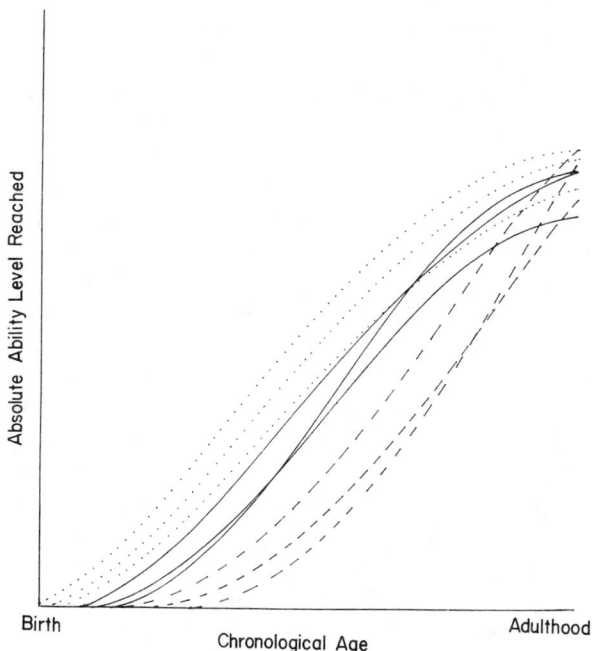

FIGURE 2. Hypothetical growth curves of three individuals on three abilities. (—) Ability A, (---) Ability B, (····) Ability C.

ligence should *not* be identified with a first principal component factor, contrary to Jensen's urgings in various writings (1979, 1980). A first principal component is nothing more than a mathematically constrained summarization of whatever variance is contained in a set of measures—even if some of the measures are totally uncorrelated, or even negatively correlated. A first principal component is more a measure of a person's versatility over the abilities measured than a measure of general intelligence. In appropriately analyzed studies, a general intelligence factor appears, if at all, in the higher-order factor space. Also, it usually appears only in a restricted set of primary factors—chiefly those covered by what Cattell and Horn (1978) call fluid and crystallized intelligence. It appears only weakly, if at all, in other sets of primary factors such as those in memory, verbal production, and speed domains. The general factor is not as general as might be thought. It represents some composite of constitutional and experientially acquired abilities. From a developmental perspective, it represents the average level of those abilities attained at any given age.

Just how much of the variance in a general factor is determined by genetic factors is a topic that can hardly be addressed here, except by pointing out that much of the evidence brought forth to answer this question is based on variables such as IQ or mental age, which are themselves based on composites of primary factors. To say that a certain percentage of IQ variance—somewhere between 0 and 80%, depending on whose conclusions one prefers—is attributable to genetics is more a comment on how IQ happens to be measured than on how much cognitive abilities are genetically or environmentally determined. From the multiple-factor viewpoint that is espoused here, the more useful way of looking at the nature–nurture issue is to seek to determine and specify the genetic and environmental proportions of variance associated with each of the possible primary and higher-order factors in their orthogonalized, uncorrelated versions. There is, as yet, little research information to permit such specification in any definitive way. One may surmise that variances in some factors are largely genetic, whereas variances in other factors are largely environmental. The evidence (Jones, 1949, 1954; Kaufman, 1975; Wright, 1939) that most popular measures of intelligence are actually composites of separate factors, linked only at higher-order levels, has been largely ignored by investigators of the nature–nurture problem. Even those who utilize a multifactor approach, like Vandenberg (1962), Martin (1975), DeFries, Vandenberg, and McClearn (1976), and Kuse (1977), have been handicapped—sometimes unwittingly so—by the complexity of the measures they employ. One example is the impurity of the Thurstone and Thurstone (1962) Primary Mental Abilities battery scores that are frequently employed in their research.

Although we have an almost staggering amount of knowledge about cognitive abilities and their origin and development, this information is complex, confused, incomplete, and often inaccurate, because of defects at many stages of investigation: the design of studies, the selection of subjects, the administration of tests and collection of data, and the analysis and interpretation of findings. It is worth reiterating the comment made previously that there is much to be done just within the established methodologies of test theory and factor analysis.

There is an urgent need to apply these methodologies in the domain of the paradigms developed by experimental cognitive psychologists for studying information processing behavior. Among these paradigms are the Posner (1978) mental comparisons tasks, the S. Sternberg (1966) short-term memory task, the Neisser (1967) visual search task, and the traditional reaction time tasks. Individual differences occur in the performance of these tasks, showing up in both latency and accuracy measures. What stable dimensions of individual differences do these tasks tap? Are any of these dimensions related to the dimensions identified in psychometric studies? Hunt (1978), one of the first experimental cognitive psychologists to ask this type of question, reports that performance on some of these tasks is related to performance on conventional psychometric tests. Jensen (1979, 1980) finds certain parameters of the choice reaction task to be substantially correlated with scores on certain intelligence tests, for example, the Raven Matrices test. Similar findings can be documented from other sources, for example, the work of Keating and Bobbitt (1978) and of Spiegel and Bryant (1978).

For the most part, these researchers considered limited sets of variables—rarely enough to permit performing a satisfactory factor analysis. Hunt, Lunneborg, and Lewis (1975) report a factor analysis of a number of cognitive-task variables along with certain psychometric variables, but their design and factoring procedures do not meet all the criteria cited. Hunt's (1978) data on a relationship between Posner (1978) task parameters and scholastic aptitude test scores do not permit a conclusion as to the components of scholastic aptitude test performance to which the relationship pertains: is it speed, level of accuracy or mastery, or some combination of these? Does it pertain to vocabulary knowledge, general verbal comprehension, reading ability, reasoning ability, some high-order factor of intelligence, or some unknown variable? Similar questions can be raised in connection with other studies mentioned.

Several years ago, I attempted to perform factor analyses, or reanalyses, of all the relevant data sets that could be found in recent literature on cognitive tasks. Not all these data sets were appropriate for factor analysis—whether because of small sample sizes, inadequate battery design, or other problems—but it seemed desirable to perform the analyses despite these problems, to take advantage of the summarizing and data reduction features of the technique. A summary of my findings (reported in more detail in a monograph, Carroll, 1980a) is presented in Table 3. The dimensions or factors are grouped into domains on an intuitive basis; no implication is intended that the factors within a domain are necessarily correlated. Sometimes they are correlated, as in the case of several factors in the memory domain identified in reanalysis of data from a study by Underwood Boruch, and Malmi (1978). In general, there is little information available about the overall structuring of the abilities identified in the table since it is rare that the variables grouped into a factor in a particular study can be satisfactorily matched with variables in another study. For example, the factor identified as "Slope of Choice Reaction Time re Bits of Information" from Jensen's (1980, Note 2) study (as I reanalyzed it) has no counterpart in variables included in other studies analyzed. Yet, it may be correlated with, or identical to, factors such as "Speed of Mental Comparisons" or "Slope of Visual and Memory Search."

There is need for further factor-analytically oriented correlational stud-

TABLE 3

A Sample of Possible Individual Difference Dimensions Identified in Recent Studies of Cognitive Tasks[a]

Suggested factor code	Domains and factors	Selected references	Remarks
	Perceptual domain		
VDT	Visual duration threshold	Jackson & McClelland (1979)	—
CS(?)	Speed of closure	Cory, Rimland, & Bryson (1977)	Probably same as CS (Table 1)
P(?)	Perceptual speed	Cory, Rimland, & Bryson (1977); Hunt, Lunneborg, & Lewis (1975)	Probably same as P (Table 1)
SPS	Spatial speed	Egan (1978)	A component of SO and/or VZ (Table 1)
SPA	Spatial accuracy	Egan (1978)	A component of SO and/or VZ (Table 1)
	Psychomotor and reaction time domain		
HMS	Hand movement speed	Jensen (1980); Rose (1974)	—
FMHC	Fine motor hand control	Lansman (1978)	Possibly same as AIMG (Table 1)
RT(?)	Simple reaction time	Robertson–Tchabo & Arenberg (1976)	Possibly same as RT (Table 1)
RTCS	Reaction time to complex sequential events	Robertson–Tchabo & Arenberg (1976)	
SCRT	Slope of choice reaction time re bits of information	Jensen (1980)	
	Accuracy of information processing domain		
IPA	Accuracy of complex information processing	Robertson–Tchabo & Arenberg (1976)	
IPSA	Accuracy of semantic information processing	Lansman (1978)	A component of V (Table 1)?

24

	Speed of information processing domain		
SDMC	Speed of mental comparisons	Chiang & Atkinson (1976) Jackson & McClelland (1979) Rose & Fernandes (1977)	A component of P (Table 1)?
SDSP	Speed of semantic processing	Lansman (1978)	Possibly same as SD (Table 1)
SVMS	Slope of visual & memory search	Rose & Fernandes (1977) Chiang & Atkinson (1976) Rose & Fernandes (1977)	A component of P (Table 1)?
	Response-to-Orthography Domain		
ORM	Encoding multiletter arrays	Frederiksen (1978)	A component of V? (Table 1)
ORP	Phonemic translation	Frederiksen (1978)	A component of V? (Table 1)
ORW	Depth of processing in word recognition	Frederiksen (1978)	A component of V? (Table 1)
AART	Automaticity of articulation	Frederiksen (1978)	Possibly related to SDAR (Table 1)
STRP	Stroop reading task	Rose (1974)	
	Memory domain		
MSR	Memory span (registration)	Berger (1977; Berger & Goldberger, 1979) Chiang & Atkinson (1976) Lansman (1978) Underwood, Boruch, & Maimi (1978)	A component of MS? (Table 1)
MSD	Memory span (delayed with interference)	Berger (1977; Berger & Goldberger, 1979)	
MSP	Memory span (proactive interference)	Berger (1977; Berger & Goldberger, 1979)	
FRS	Free recall (secondary memory)	Cory, Rimland, & Bryson (1977) Malmi, Underwood, & Carroll (1979) Robertson–Tchabo & Arenberg (1976) Underwood, Boruch, & Malmi (1978)	
FRP	Free recall (primary memory)	Robertson–Tchabo & Arenberg (1976)	
MA(?)	Paired–associate learning	Malmi, Underwood, & Carroll (1979)	Probably same as MA (Table 1)
VDL	Verbal discrimination learning	Underwood, Boruch, & Malmi (1978)	
MCE	Memory for complex events	Underwood, Boruch, & Malmi (1978)	

[a]In most cases, the factors and interpretations are those offered by Carroll (1980a) on the basis of reanalysis of correlational data.

ies that would explore selected domains of potential dimensions of individual differences in experimental cognitive tasks. Because of practical and logistic limitations, such studies might target small groups of possible dimensions—perhaps no more than three to five at a time. Furthermore, there is need for studies to determine correlates of these dimensions in psychometric tests. The psychometric tests need to be carefully constructed and administered in such a way that speed and level dimensions can be identified separately; they should also be as factorially pure as possible (although there are undoubtedly limits to which this can be the case). It may be pointed out, incidentally, that it is possible to include R. Sternberg's component scores in factorial studies that would also include external variables from psychometric tests (Carroll, 1980b; R. J. Sternberg, 1980).

To this point, individual differences have been considered from a factorial viewpoint. The question now to be addressed is What is to be done *beyond* factor analysis?

BEYOND FACTOR ANALYSIS

Thurstone (1947, p. 56) insisted that factor analysis is only an exploratory method that is appropriate chiefly at an early stage in the investigation of a behavioral domain. He believed that factor analysis is valuable only in the initial identification of important latent variables. Once such variables are identified, it would be possible to study them from many different perspectives. Many of these perspectives are implied in the following questions, many of them interrelated, that could be posed with regard to any underlying variable identified by factor analysis:

1. What is the nature of the factor in psychological, behavioral, or cognitive terms? To what range of behaviors does it apply? What psychological mechanisms, processes, or types of learning are involved in it?

2. What are the psychometric characteristics of the factor? Does it conform to the properties of a Guttman scale, or does it have to do with a set of behaviors that tend to be learned together because of the structure of cultural organization (as represented, for example, in the school curriculum)? If it has Guttman-scale properties, can the tasks in which the factor appears be arranged in order of "difficulty," "rarity," "complexity," or what? Can item difficulties be referred to physical or psychological parameters of the tasks? What are the lower and upper limits of the parameters that appear in human populations?

3. What is the status of the factor in terms of distinctions between primary, first-order factors and higher-order factors?

4. What are the developmental characteristics of the factor? What form of growth or decline curve is observable from infancy to adulthood and beyond? Are processes involved at different points or stages of this development uniform or diverse?

5. What are the relative influences of genetic, constitutional, and environmental (learning) factors on the development and/or decline of the ability? To what extent are environmental factors associated with particular cultures?

6. Are there meaningful group differences on the factor, associated with such demographic variables as sex, race, ethnic origin, or socioeconomic status, and if so, how can such differences be accounted for?

7. What physiological and/or neurological correlates of the factor can be identified? What are the effects or correlates of drugs, fatigue, and other constitutional alterations?

8. To what extent is an individual's status on the factor modifiable through training, practice, or other relatively short-term environmental manipulations? What are the limits, if any, of such modifications?

9. As an underlying factor of "cognitive" ability, what relations, if any, does it have to personality or other "noncognitive" variables, and how are such relations to be explained or accounted for?

10. For what kinds of "real-life" situations, if any, does the factor have some relevance, or influence on behavior and performance? Does such relevance or influence show up in measures of "validity" against measures of success in learning, job performance, and careers?

11. If the factor has influences on real-life situations that are in any way adverse, how can these influences be overcome or circumvented?

12. What does information about the factor (as represented in answers to the preceding questions) imply or suggest for psychological theory?

For each factor listed in Tables 2 and 3, to the extent that it can be firmly established, it would be desirable to have as much information as possible. For some factors, we have a considerable amount of such information; for others, we have little if any. Assembling the needed information requires both extensive compilations from the literature and large programs of new empirical research. Some of the chapters in this volume represent preliminary essays at compilation and analysis of available knowledge.

To make all this more concrete, I have attempted to sketch what we know and do not know about two dimensions of individual differences: one about which there is quite substantial information, Verbal Knowledge factor V, the other, about which very little information is available, Speed of Mental Comparisons (identified as factor SDMC in Table 3). Factor V is defined chiefly by psychometric variables, whereas speed of mental com-

TABLE 4
Characteristics of Two Mental Ability Factors[a]

	Verbal knowledge (V)	Speed of mental comparisons (SDMC)
Nature	Can appear in any task in which knowledge of the relevant language system is involved (especially lexical, syntactical, semantic aspects)	Appears in any cognitive task in which rapid comparison of stimuli or mental representations thereof is required
Psychometric characteristics	Weakly Guttman-scaled; competencies loosely interassociated & learned together due to organization and use-frequencies of language system; thousands of units to be learned; accuracy parameters a function of frequency, complexity, etc.	Strong Guttman-scaling of tasks as function of complexity or memory availability of elements to be compared; parameters are temporal (for accurate responses)
Status (primary–higher order)	Primary factor; substantial loadings on Gf, stronger on Gc	Primary; with strong loadings on a general speed factor(?)
Developmental aspects	Rapid early growth, slower later growth as elements have greater complexity & rarity; little decline until late senility	Negatively accelerated growth to maturity; considerable decline at older ages (?)
Etiology (genetic, maturational, environmental, cultural aspects)	Genetic–constitutional factors predict growth & ability to profit from environmental–educational–cultural opportunities	(no information)
Demographic aspects	No essential sex differences at maturity, but faster growth in females. Race/ethnic diff's a function of cultural opportunities	(no information)
Physiological–neurological correlates	Some involvement with hemispheric lateralization; subject to loss in certain types of aphasics	(no information)
Modifiability	Slow and difficult; probably limited by individual characteristics	Easily improvable with training and practice up to an asymptote characteristic of the individual (?)

TABLE 4 *(Continued)*

	Verbal knowledge (V)	Speed of mental comparisons (SDMC)
Relations with non-cognitive variables	Negligible or incidental	(no information)
Real-life relevance; (validity)	Highly relevant to academic education and professions requiring a high degree of language comprehension and production	Relevant to many types of clerical tasks and other real-life situations involving rapid comparisons of stimuli
Interventions to obviate adverse effects of low ability	Reduced cognitive load (e.g. simplified vocabulary, syntax)	Reduced speed requirements; training and practice
Implications for psychological theory	Learning theory re rate of item acquisition for long-term memory	Theories of perception, short-term memory, functioning of working memory. Relevant for possibly distinguishing this ability from speed of letter-name (etc.) retrieval

[a]Although much of the information given here can be documented, some of it is debatable, speculative, or not well supported. It is given to illustrate the type of information which should be sought by research.

parisons is defined chiefly through laboratory task variables, although it is possibly closely related to a factor derived chiefly from psychometric variables, the Perceptual Speed factor P.[1] Because of the volume of detail that might be imparted, the reader is referred to Table 4, which gives the information that can be recorded conveniently in a table of this kind. The caution must be issued, however, that a considerable amount of that information is actually speculative because the available information is not all well substantiated, even in the case of the Verbal Knowledge factor.

The task for research in individual differences in cognitive abilities is one of mapping a large territory. Some 350 years after the New World was opened up by Columbus, the British Admiralty, with the voyage of the *Beagle,* was still engaged in making more adequate maps to sail ships around

[1]It is only a matter of convenience to distinguish laboratory task variables from "psychometric" variables by applying the latter designation to variables derived from conventional psychological tests. Actually, laboratory task variables are also psychometric variables in the sense that all the traditional psychometric issues—reliability, validity, scaling, etc.—apply just as much to them as to variables derived from conventional psychological tests.

its waters; the task of mapping the terrain of the New World is still going on—using cameras in satellites, space shuttles, and other modern gadgetry. The task we have of mapping the terrain and the waters of cognitive individual differences is even more immense. If it is ever completed—even to a reasonable approximation—we will find that we have completed a large part of the task of psychological science itself.

REFERENCES

Baxter, B. J. An experimental analysis of the contributions of speed and level in an intelligence test. *Journal of Educational Psychology*, 1941, *32*, 285–296.

Berger, E. Field dependence and short-term memory. *Dissertation Abstracts International*, 1977, *38*(4-B), 1870.

Berger, E., & Goldberger, L. Field dependence and short-term memory. *Perceptual and Motor Skills*, 1979, *49*, 87–96.

Burt, C. *The factors of the mind.* London: University of London Press, 1940.

Carroll, J. B. The nature of the data, or how to choose a correlation coefficient. *Psychometrika*, 1961, *26*, 347–372.

Carroll, J. B. How shall we study individual differences in cognitive abilities?—Methodological and theoretical perspectives. *Intelligence*, 1978, *2*, 87–115. (a)

Carroll, J. B. On the theory-practice interface in the measurement of intellectual abilities. In P. Suppes (Ed.), *Impact of research on education: Some case studies.* Washington, D.C.: National Academy of Education, 1978. (b)

Carroll, J. B. *Individual difference relations in psychometric and experimental cognitive tasks* (Report No. 163). Chapel Hill: The L. L. Thurstone Psychometric Laboratory, University of North Carolina, April 1980. (NTIS Document AD-A086 057) (a)

Carroll, J. B. Remarks on Sternberg's "Factor theories of intelligence are all right almost." *Educational Researcher*, 1980, *9*(8), 14–18. (b)

Carroll, J. B., & Sapon, S. M. *Modern language aptitude test.* New York: Psychological Corporation, 1959.

Cattell, R. B. A universal index for psychological factors. *Psychologia*, 1957, *1*, 74–85.

Cattell, R. B., & Horn, J. L. A check on the theory of fluid and crystallized intelligence with description of new subtest designs. *Journal of Educational Measurement*, 1978, *15*, 139–164.

Chiang, A., & Atkinson, R. C. Individual differences and interrelationships among a select set of cognitive skills. *Memory & Cognition*, 1976, *4*, 661–672.

Cory, C. H., Rimland, B., & Bryson, R. A. Using computerized tests to measure new dimensions of abilities: An exploratory study. *Applied Psychological Measurement*, 1977, *1*, 101–110.

Davidson, W. M., & Carroll, J. B. Speed and level components in time-limit scores: A factor analysis. *Educational & Psychological Measurement*, 1945, *5*, 411–427.

DeFries, J. C., Vandenberg, S. G., & McClearn, G. E. Genetics of specific cognitive abilities. *Annual Review of Genetics*, 1976, *10*, 179–207.

Egan, D. E. *Characterizing spatial ability: Different mental processes reflected in accuracy and latency scores.* Murray Hill, N.J.: Bell Laboratories, 1978.

Egan, D. E. An analysis of spatial orientation test performance. *Intelligence*, 1981, *5*, 85–100.

Ekstrom, R. B., French, J. W., & Harman, H. H. *Manual for kit of factor-referenced cognitive tests.* Princeton, N.J.: Educational Testing Service, 1976.

Estes, W. K. Intelligence and cognitive psychology. In L. Resnick (Ed.), *The nature of intelligence*. Hillsdale, N.J.: Lawrence Erlbaum Associates, 1976.

Frederiksen, J. R. *A chronometric study of component skills in reading* (Report No. 3757). Cambridge, Mass.: Bolt Beranek & Newman, 1978.

French, J. W. The description of aptitude and achievement tests in terms of rotated factors. *Psychometric Monographs*, 1951, No. 5.

French, J. W., Ekstrom, R. B., & Price, L. A. *Manual and kit of reference tests for cognitive factors*. Princeton, N.J.: Educational Testing Service, 1963.

Guilford, J. P. *The nature of human intelligence*. New York: McGraw-Hill, 1967.

Guilford, J. P. *Cognitive psychology with a frame of reference*. San Diego, Calif.: Edits, 1979.

Guilford, J. P. Fluid and crystallized intelligences: Two fanciful concepts. *Psychological Bulletin*, 1980, *88*, 406–412.

Hakstian, A. R., & Cattell, R. B. Higher-stratum ability structures on a basis of twenty primary abilities. *Journal of Educational Psychology*, 1978, *70*, 657–669.

Horn, J. L. Human ability systems. In P. B. Baltes (Ed.), *Life-span development and behavior* (Vol. 1). New York: Academic Press, 1978.

Horn, J. L., & Cattell, R. B. Whimsy and misunderstandings of Gf-Gc theory: A comment on Guilford. *Psychological Bulletin*, 1982, *91*, 623–633.

Horn, J. L., & Knapp, J. R. On the subjective character of the empirical base of Guilford's Structure-of-Intellect model. *Psychological Bulletin*, 1973, *80*, 33–43.

Humphreys, L. G., & Parsons, C. K. Piagetian tasks measure intelligence and intelligence tests assess cognitive development: A reanalysis. *Intelligence*, 1979, *3*, 369–382.

Hunt, E. Mechanics of verbal ability. *Psychological Review*, 1978, *85*, 109–130.

Hunt, E., Lunneborg, C. E., & Lewis, J. What does it mean to be high verbal? *Cognitive Psychology*, 1975, *7*, 194–227.

Jackson, M. D., & McClelland, J. L. Processing determinants of reading speed. *Journal of Experimental Psychology: General*, 1979, *108*, 151–181.

Jensen, A. R. *g:* Outmoded theory or unconquered frontier? *Creative Science & Technology*, 1979, *2*(3), 16–29.

Jensen, A. R. *Bias in mental testing*. New York: Free Press, 1980.

Jöreskog, K. G. Structural analysis of covariance and correlation matrices. *Psychometrika*, 1978, *43*, 443–477.

Jones, L. V. A factor analysis of the Stanford-Binet at four age levels. *Psychometrika*, 1949, *14*, 299–331.

Jones, L. V. Primary abilities in the Stanford-Binet, age 13. *Journal of Genetic Psychology*, 1954, *84*, 125–147.

Kaiser, H. F. The varimax criterion for analytic rotation in factor analysis. *Psychometrika*, 1958, *23*, 187–200.

Kaiser, H. F. The application of electronic computers to factor analysis. *Educational & Psychological Measurement*, 1960, *20*, 141–151.

Karlin, J. E. A factorial study of auditory function. *Psychometrika*, 1942, *7*, 251–279.

Kaufman, A. S. Factor analysis of the WISC-R at 11 age levels between 6½ and 16½ years. *Journal of Consulting and Clinical Psychology*, 1975, *43*, 135–147.

Keating, D. P., & Bobbitt, B. L. Individual and developmental differences in cognitive processing components of mental ability. *Child Development*, 1978, *49*, 155–167.

Kohlberg, L., & DeVries, R. Don't throw out the Piagetian baby with the psychometric bath: Reply to Humphreys and Parsons. *Intelligence*, 1980, *4*, 175–178.

Kuse, A. R. Familial resemblances for cognitive abilities estimated from two test batteries in Hawaii. *Dissertation Abstracts International*, 1977, *38*(5-B), 2422.

Lansman, M. An attentional approach to individual differences in immediate memory. *Dissertation Abstracts International*, 1978, *39*(5-B), 2542–2543.

Lohman, D. F. *Spatial ability: A review and reanalysis of the correlational literature.* Stanford, Calif.: Aptitude Research Project, School of Education, Stanford University, October 1979.

Lord, F. M. A study of speed factors in tests and academic grades. *Psychometrika*, 1956, *21*, 31–50.

Malmi, R. A., Underwood, B. J., & Carroll, J. B. The interrelationships among some associative learning tasks. *Bulletin of the Psychonomic Society*, 1979, *13*, 121–123.

Martin, N. G. The inheritance of scholastic abilities in a sample of twins. II. Genetical analysis of examination results. *Annals of Human Genetics*, 1975, *39*, 219–229.

McDonald, R. R., & Mulaik, S. A. Determinacy of common factors: A nontechnical review. *Psychological Bulletin*, 1979, *86*, 297–306.

Merrifield, P. R. Factor analysis in educational research. *Review of Research in Education*, 1974, *2*, 393–434.

Montanelli, R. G., Jr., & Humphreys, L. G. Latent roots of random data correlation matrices with squared multiple correlations on the diagonal: A Monte Carlo study. *Psychometrika*, 1976, *41*, 341–348.

Neisser, U. *Cognitive psychology.* New York: Appleton, 1967.

Posner, M. I. *Chronometric explorations of mind.* Hillsdale, N.J.: Lawrence Erlbaum Associates, 1978.

Robertson-Tchabo, E., & Arenberg, D. Age differences in cognition in healthy educated men: A factor analysis of experimental measures. *Experimental Aging Research*, 1976, *2*, 75–86.

Rose, A. M. *Human information processing: An assessment and research battery.* Ann Arbor: Human Performance Center, Department of Psychology, University of Michigan, January 1974.

Rose, A. M., & Fernandes, K. *An information processing approach to performance assessment. I. Experimental investigation of an information processing performance battery.* Washington, D.C.: American Institutes for Research, November 1977.

Schmid, J., & Leiman, J. M. The development of hierarchical factor solutions. *Psychometrika*, 1957, *22*, 53–61.

Spiegel, M. R., & Bryant, N. D. Is speed of processing information related to intelligence and achievement? *Journal of Educational Psychology*, 1978, *70*, 904–910.

Stankov, L., & Horn, J. L. Human abilities revealed through auditory tests. *Journal of Educational Psychology*, 1980, *72*, 21–44.

Sternberg, R. J. *Intelligence, information processing, and analogical reasoning: The componential analysis of human abilities.* Hillsdale, N.J.: Lawrence Erlbaum Associates, 1977.

Sternberg, R. J. Factor theories of intelligence are all right almost. *Educational Researcher*, 1980, *9*(8), 6–13, 18.

Sternberg, S. High speed scanning in human memory. *Science*, 1966, *153*, 652–654.

Tate, M. W. Individual differences in speed of response in mental test materials of varying degrees of difficulty. *Educational & Psychological Measurement*, 1948, *8*, 353–374.

Thurstone, L. L. *Multiple factor analysis: A development and expansion of The Vectors of Mind.* Chicago: University of Chicago Press, 1947.

Thurstone, L. L., & Thurstone, T. G. *Primary mental abilities test.* Chicago: Science Research Associates, 1962.

Underwood, B. J., Boruch, R. F., & Malmi, R. A. Composition of episodic memory. *Journal of Experimental Psychology: General*, 1978, *107*, 393–419.

Vandenberg, S. G. The hereditary abilities study: Hereditary components in a psychological test battery. *American Journal of Human Genetics*, 1962, *14*, 220–237.

Vernon, P. E. *The structure of human abilities* (2nd ed.). London: Methuen, 1961.

Wesche, M., Edwards, H., & Wells, W. Foreign language aptitude and intelligence. *Applied Psycholinguistics,* 1982, *3,* 127–140.

Whitely, S. E. Latent trait models in the study of intelligence. *Intelligence,* 1980, *4,* 97–132. (a)

Whitely, S. E. Multicomponent latent trait models for ability tests. *Psychometrika,* 1980, *45,* 479–494. (b)

Wright, R. E. A factor analysis of the original Stanford-Binet scale. *Psychometrika,* 1939, *4,* 209–230.

NOTES

1. Tucker, L. R. Personal communication, April, 1979.
2. Jensen, A. R. Personal communication, October 1978.

2

Individual Differences in Short-Term Memory*

Michael S. Humphreys, Mary Jean Lynch,
William Revelle, and James W. Hall

INTRODUCTION

Central to the purposes of this book is the goal of understanding individual differences in intellectual achievement and performance. In this chapter, we hope to show how advances in both experimental and differential psychology can yield progress toward that goal through a focus on individual differences in short-term memory.

Intellectual differences traditionally have been the province of differential psychology, and early in this century impressive success was achieved in the assessment and prediction of individual differences in intellectual performance. That success, however, was not matched by efforts to account for such differences at the level of specific psychological mechanisms and processes. Short-term memory is a case in point. Memory has been seen as a

*Preparation of this manuscript was supported in part by a grant from the University of Queensland to Michael S. Humphreys, a grant from the National Institute of Mental Health (MH29209) to William Revelle, and a research contract from the Bureau of Education for the Handicapped, Office of Education (US HEW OE 300 770 493) for the University of Illinois' Chicago Institute for Learning Disabilities.

likely source of important individual differences in intellectual achievements for centuries. For example, Galton (1887) and others since provided empirical evidence from the memory-span task that individual differences in processes underlying short-term memory are probably important sources of individual differences in significant intellectual achievements. Yet over the next 80 years, there was little significant progress toward understanding just what those abilities are and how they relate to general intellectual achievement or to specific aspects of intellectual performance. A major reason for the lack of progress was the incomplete conception of the processes involved in short-term memory together with the absence of powerful techniques by which its components could be reliably identified and measured.

Not until the introduction of information-processing models (just over two decades ago) did short-term memory become a fashionable and productive area of study for experimental psychologists. Since then, significant advances have been made in the identification and description of components of short-term memory, in experimental paradigms and tools for the study of these components, and in the awareness of the role of these components in a variety of socially relevant intellectual skills (cf. LaBerge & Samuels, 1977, for an analysis of the role of short-term memory in reading). More recently, and perhaps not entirely independently, there has been a resurgence of activity directed toward the study of individual differences and substantial developments in methodology for that purpose. Cognitive psychologists have become interested in individual differences and individual-differences psychologists (including those whose main focus of interest has been the personality domain) have become interested in cognitive psychology. Our interest here is in exploring ways that these two disciplines can be brought to bear on the study of individual differences in short-term memory and intellectual performance.

The chapter contains two major sections. The first section provides a brief description of theoretical concepts and issues relating to short-term memory, with particular emphasis on various concepts and distinctions that may prove fruitful for the investigation of individual differences. In addition, considerable emphasis is placed on advances in experimental approaches and techniques that may be useful for this purpose, and some attention is given to potential measurement problems. The second section focuses on the application of theory and methodology in differential psychology.

Throughout this chapter, we observe the convention (Waugh & Norman, 1965) of using the terms "short-term memory" (STM) and "long-term memory" (LTM) for the empirical phenomenon of recall or recognition after short and long intervals, respectively. The terms "primary memory" (PM) and "secondary memory" (SM) are reserved for the theoretical constructs associated with STM and LTM, respectively. When we refer to theories of STM we mean theoretical explanations for the empirical phenomena.

CONTRIBUTIONS OF EXPERIMENTAL PSYCHOLOGY: THEORY AND METHOD

By the late 1960s, it had become widely—although not universally—accepted by experimental psychologists that memory performance at short (a few seconds to tens of seconds) and long (tens of seconds to years) intervals may require different explanations. The dominant theories during this period assumed that different structures were responsible for the differences between STM and LTM. These became known as "strength" and "capacity" theories of memory, and we begin this review with an examination of such models. In addition, we will examine how Baddeley and Hitch's (1974) integration of the concepts of STM and attention (working memory) can be used productively in individual-differences research. The differences between STM and LTM have also been explained in terms of process differences (see Craik & Levy, 1976, pp. 163–168). The processes that we will discuss include rehearsal, naming speed, and coding. The STM tasks may also be analyzed in terms of the cue used or type of information required to perform the task. Accordingly, the use of recency as a retrieval cue and the distinction between item and order information will be discussed.

STRUCTURAL MODELS

STRENGTH THEORY

Theory In strength theory, the presentation of an item for study results in the formation of a memory trace. In formal versions of the theory, this memory trace can be completely characterized by a value along a unidimensional continuum of strength. The stronger the trace of an item, the more likely it is to be recalled or recognized. In their model, Wickelgren and Norman (1966) assumed that while an item is being studied, two traces are formed, a short-term and a long-term trace. Performance is assumed to be a joint function of the strength of the two traces. If rehearsal after study is prevented, both traces start to decline, the short-term trace fading more quickly than the long-term trace. Various versions of the model have attributed the decline in trace strength to either interference or decay (cf. Wickelgren, 1974, pp. 225–231).

Methods of estimation In the Wickelgren and Norman (1966) model, each memory trace can be characterized by two parameters. One parameter is the amount of learning (the trace strength immediately after learning) and the other is the rate of loss or decay. The PM trace can be observed (estimated) once the contribution of the SM trace has been eliminated. The theoretical procedures for eliminating the SM contribution include the fitting of the formal model proposed by Wickelgren and Norman (1966) or the less formal procedure suggested by Waugh and Norman (1965). Experimentally, the SM contribution can be minimized by drawing the memory items from a limited set (e.g., digits) and repeatedly presenting them in different orders and combinations. Under such conditions of massive proactive interference, memory performance rapidly declines to an essentially zero asymptote. The zero asymptote permits the assumption that the contribution from the SM trace has been eliminated. One further point to be noted: in all these procedures, every effort is made to eliminate displaced rehearsals. That is, the subject is supposed to attend to each item as it is presented but to stop attending to that item as soon as the next item is presented.

A study which illustrates the role played by both parameters (the amount learned and the rate of loss) was reported by Wickelgren and Norman (1966). Their subjects studied lists of from one to seven three-digit numbers. These lists were presented auditorily at a rapid rate, and the subjects were instructed to, and trained so that presumably they could, attend to the presented item only. At the end of each memory string, a tone was sounded to signal the presentation of a probe item. The subject's task was to say whether the probe was the same as one of the items in the memory string. Since the strings varied in length, it was possible to probe the different positions in the string at the same lag (the number of items intervening between the target and the probe). For example, the lag would be the same for the first item in a three-item string and the fifth item in a seven-item string (in both cases, two items intervening between the target and the probe). Plots of d' as a function of lag were roughly linear. This finding was compatible with an exponential rate of loss proposed by the authors as the retention function. In addition, the plot for the first item in the series had the same slope as the plots for the other positions, but the intercept was higher. Given the assumptions of strength theory, it follows that, while forgetting rate was the same for all list positions, the degree of learning for the initial item was higher. This technique may not be ideal for examining individual differences in STM. It is a recognition procedure and doubts exist as to whether the same effects will be found with recognition and recall.

There are also some recall paradigms that estimate both the initial level of learning and the rate of loss, although the estimation is not accomplished in as rigorous a fashion as is permitted by the recognition paradigms. In the typical probe recall task, a short list is presented, followed by a probe from the list. The subject is to respond with the item which followed the probe in the list. (Short lists of pairs also can be used where one member of the pair is given as a cue for the recall of the other member.)

In the running memory-span paradigm, subjects are presented with lists of varying lengths so that they never know when a given list will end. When the list does end, they are required to recall the last k items (k is generally 3–8). This paradigm has been used frequently in investigations of the relationship between cognitive ability and STM. The reason for this pervasiveness is the general belief that running memory span provides less scope for the deployment of strategies (e.g., rehearsal, chunking) than does the traditional memory-span paradigm (Halford, in press). In any event, performance on the most recent items is a measure of how good learning is, and the slope of the lag curve provides a measure of the rate of loss. Although we have not been able to find an individual-differences study which has plotted data in this fashion, Hamilton, Hockey, and Rejman (1977, pp. 471–475) have done so in an investigation of the effects of noise on STM. Specifically, they found that in noise subjects were slightly better at the most recent items and slightly worse on the oldest items. Their data were very consistent over a wide range of presentation times, so study strategies appear not to have been important. However, a word of caution is in order. One would have to control and/or monitor output order to insure that retrieval strategies (e.g., recalling the most recent items and then guessing at the earlier items) were not responsible for these serial position effects.

CAPACITY THEORY

Capacity theory has been the most important theory of STM over the last two decades. The theory has not, however, had a substantial impact on differential psychology. Although the theory still deserves consideration in the study of individual differences, it should be noted that recently there have been substantial challenges to both its basic conception and methodology. These challenges will be discussed in subsequent sections.

Theory Although there are many variations on this general theory, enough similarities exist for a modal capacity model (Murdock, 1967) to be described. Generally, three stores are postulated: (1) a sensory store; (2) a short-term store; and (3) a long-term store. The sensory store is thought to hold uncategorized information (the raw sensory information). Although it is assumed to have a large capacity, the sensory store seems to be capable of holding information for only a very brief period (1–2 seconds in the case of auditory sensory memory).[1] The short-term store is assumed to have a limited capacity and items are assumed to be lost from it by all-or-none displacement; that is, if an item is in the short-term store and no additional information is entered into the store, then it will stay there. The role of rehearsal in these models is thus not to maintain or refresh the information that is in the short-term store; rather it is to transfer the information to the long-term store, which is viewed as being relatively permanent and having a very large capacity. The critical parameter to estimate for these models is the capacity of the short-term store. The problem is that, because items can be in both the short-term and the long-term stores at the same time, the performance of any individual in any given paradigm (e.g., digit span) will depend on the capacity of the individual's short-term store and on a contribution from the long-term store. In addition, for some situations, the probability of an item actually entering the short-term store has to be taken into account. Note that this latter parameter accounts for the same data accounted for by strength theory's assumption that initial learning is variable.

Methods of estimation   Some specialized paradigms have been developed to test aspects of the Atkinson and Shiffrin (1968, pp. 90–195) capacity model, and Murdock (1967) has proposed a method based on comparisons of immediate free recall across lists of varying lengths or of the same length presented at varying rates. Most of the work done within this general framework, however, has used some aspect of the recency portion of the free-recall curve to estimate the capacity of STM. In free recall with a single presentation of a list, the last few items typically are recalled first and are recalled with a higher probability than are the items from the middle of the list. This strategy is more characteristic of experienced than naive subjects, and it has been assumed to be deliberate. The subject is assumed to adopt a strategy of first recalling all the items which at that moment are in PM. The problem is to determine which items are recalled from PM and which from SM. Waugh and Norman (1965) and Raymond (1969) have suggested procedures whereby an estimate of the probability of recalling an item from SM is first obtained. This estimate then is used to correct the probability of recall in the recency portion of the curve for the contribution from SM. Other procedures have been suggested that are essentially rules of thumb and not derived in any formal fashion from an explicit theory of STM. For

---

[1]Recent work (cf. D. C. Watkins & Watkins, 1980) suggests that auditory sensory memory can persist in the absence of auditory interference for as long as 18 seconds. Such an effect complicates the interpretation of results from many paradigms. For example, the ability to recall one or two items from auditory sensory memory could provide a psychological floor below which performance on a digit span task would not fall. Such a psychological floor could explain why Torgesen and Houck (1980) find a much smaller difference in nonsense syllable span than digit span between learning disabled and control groups.

example, Tulving and Colotla (1970) suggested that if no more than seven input or output items separated the presentation of an item from its output, then that item could be considered as having been recalled from PM. M. J. Watkins (1974) has reviewed these and other estimation techniques and has evaluated them by looking at the consistency of the estimates obtained across various experimental conditions. He also reviews the assumptions underlying each method in more detail.

WORKING MEMORY

Theory The concept of working memory, as advanced by Baddeley and Hitch (1974, pp. 47–90), has both structural and process components and can be regarded as an extension of the existing models of STM. Specifically, they proposed that there were two components of PM, or in their terminology, *working memory*. One component was referred to as the *articulatory loop*, a system for the maintenance of verbal items in order. Such maintenance is disrupted by concurrent verbal activity and by phonemic similarity. The other component of PM was conceived of as a flexible *workspace* whose capacity could be devoted to storage, processing, or some mixture of both.

The concept of a working memory evolved from an investigation of performance on reasoning, sentence comprehension, and free-recall tasks as a function of a variety of loads on the PM system. Subjects were required to do these tasks while retaining three to six digits in memory or while counting repeatedly from one to six. Baddeley and Hitch (1974, pp. 47–90) found a modest impairment on all three tasks with a memory load of six digits but almost no impairment with a memory load of three digits. A major problem with this conception of STM, as acknowledged by the authors, is the imprecise and somewhat artificial distinction between storage and processing. Nevertheless, their notion of a trade-off between memory and performance appears to have important implications for individual differences research that can best be illustrated by considering a recent application.

Method Daneman and Carpenter (1980) were concerned with developing a memory test which would be more predictive of reading ability than were standard memory-span tests. Their approach was to embed a memory-span test within another task, increasing the processing demands on the subject. With this increase in processing requirements, presumably, there would be a decrease in storage capacity. It was hoped that the more demanding the processing task, the more sensitive it would be to individual differences in memory capacity. The first task the investigators developed was referred to as a reading-span task. Here subjects read sentences aloud at their own pace and then attempted to recall the last item from each sentence. To be scored as correct, each word had to be recalled in the correct order.

The first experiment compared performance on the reading span and conventional memory-span tasks as predictors of verbal ability and of reading comprehension. The results were unequivocal; correlations between the verbal ability and reading comprehension scores were substantially higher with the reading-span test than they were with the conventional memory-span test.

In a subsequent experiment, the reading-span test was modified so that both oral and silent reading span, as well as listening span, could be compared. Here the subject listened to or read a sentence and then verified that sentence as true or false. Again, the subject would then be required to recall the last word from a series of sentences, all of which had been read aloud by the subject (oral reading span), read silently by the subject (silent reading span), or read to the subject (listening span). The results were again quite impressive. The correlations between the three span tests and the verbal scholastic aptitude test scores ranged from .49 to .55 (df = 19) and the correlations with reading and listening comprehension tests ranged from .42 to .86.

Although this study is a promising initial step, it must be remembered that the object of this endeavor is not simply to find a task which correlates highly with measures of reading or listening comprehension but to find a task which explains why some individuals do well or poorly on the tests of reading or listening comprehension. We do not think it is enough to say that these individuals are doing poorly because they have a limited working-memory capacity, as Daneman and Carpenter (1980) conclude. Instead, it seems necessary to determine which aspect of working memory is responsible. As Daneman and Carpenter (1980) noted, subjects may perform poorly on these working memory tasks for one of two reasons. First, they could be deficient in memory capacity per se. This might involve a deficiency in the articulatory loop or might indicate a general limit on the resources available for storage. Alternatively, there might be nothing wrong with the memory, but rather difficulty with the processing task may be indicated. Given the two alternative explanations advanced for poor performance on any particular task, our preference would be to say that an individual has a memory problem or working-memory problem only if he or she does poorly across a wide variety of processing tasks.

PROCESSING EXPLANATIONS FOR THE STM/LTM DISTINCTION

REHEARSAL AND NAMING SPEED

Rehearsal as a process that delays the onset of forgetting has received a great deal of attention in several theories (Baddeley & Hitch, 1974, pp.

47–90; Broadbent, 1958; Shiffrin & Schneider, 1977). The basic ideas here can be explained with reference to memory-span experiments. The traditional conception of memory span is that it is the number of items that can be attended to simultaneously. According to these rehearsal models, subjects who are attempting to remember seven items are rehearsing them. As each item is rehearsed (attended to), it is reactivated or refreshed, but the strength of all other items declines. Memory span thus is seen as the product of a race between two processes: the speed with which the items can be rehearsed or recycled and the rate with which the strength of the items declines following each rehearsal.

The question then becomes: Which of these factors, speed of rehearsal or rate of loss, is primarily responsible for the individual differences observed in the STM paradigms? To solve this question requires the measurement of rehearsal speed. Baddeley, Thomson, and Buchanan (1975) have proposed that both articulation rate and reading rate may provide such a measure. To measure articulation rate, a set of known items (e.g., a subspan set or a highly learned set) is repeatedly articulated. Reading rate is measured by having a subject read aloud from a list of materials. A serious problem with both techniques concerns the possibility of a trade-off between quality and speed of pronunciation. Although subjects are instructed to pronounce each item accurately, this does not eliminate the possibility of such a trade-off. Nevertheless, interesting results have been obtained using these techniques. Baddeley et al. (1975) found a significant relationship between reading rate and memory span across words of different lengths and a significant correlation between reading rate and memory span across subjects, $r(13)$ = .685. The relationship between reading speed and rehearsal rate, however, may not be responsible for these correlations. Many authors have suggested (see Dempster, 1981, for a review) that reading rate, along with other measures, such as perceptual identification thresholds, are measures of naming speed. The idea here is that as naming becomes faster (more automatic), more resources will be available for temporarily storing information. Although the similarities and differences between the naming speed and rehearsal speed approaches have not been made clear, observations such as those by Cohen and Sandberg (1977) are perhaps best accommodated by the concept of naming speed. They observed that the correlations between IQ and the recall of the terminal items in nine-item strings increased as rate of presentation increased. Presumably, any rehearsal beyond simply naming the item was impossible with the fast rates.

As a final note, the magnitude of the correlations between reading rate or articulatory rate and memory span often need to be interpreted cautiously. For example, Standing, Bond, Smith, and Isely (1980) reported correlations between measures of reading rate and rehearsal speed. Those correlations ranged from .68 to .75. At the same time, the correlations between reading rate and IQ measures ranged from −.41 to .52. Although the partial correlations between the IQ measures and memory span with reading rate controlled did not reach statistical significance ($r = .28$ and .10), the best estimate of the reading rate–memory span relationship would be the partial correlation with IQ controlled. (In other studies, it would be sufficient to control for age.)

MEMORY CODES

The area of coding processes promises to be a fruitful place to look for individual differences in STM. We shall consider the nature of the codes employed in STM, the role played by strategic and nonstrategic processes in encoding, and the possibility that some individuals have a deficiency in the use of a particular code.

Theory In 1964, Conrad published a paper showing that the pattern of intrusion errors in a visual STM task is similar to the pattern obtained in an auditory identification task. For example, subjects asked to recall the letters "BPCT" were more likely to err with letters sounding like the correct items ("BPDV") than with letters sounding unlike the correct items ("MWKS"). The conclusion from this study and others which followed (cf. Hintzman, 1967; Wickelgren, 1965) was that subjects were transforming (recoding) the visual stimulus into an acoustic or perhaps articulatory code. These results suggested the possibility that PM could be characterized as exclusively acoustic–articulatory in nature. That view proved to be incorrect; visually based information (and possibly semantic information) is represented in PM. Nevertheless, it does appear that auditorily based information plays an especially prominent role in STM.

Craik and Lockhart's (1972) paper on levels of processing also stimulated interest in the codes and coding processes employed by subjects in both STM and LTM performance. Their general thesis was that rate of forgetting is determined by the characteristics of the codes laid down at the time of study; in turn, these codes are determined by the nature of the "perceptual analysis" performed by the subjects. Although there have been several changes in the original Craik and Lockhart (1972) position, this basic formulation has received considerable empirical support. The formulation, however, does lead to the idea that there is no fundamental difference between retention at short and long intervals; only the codes differ. To explain the differences requires only three assumptions. The first is that acoustic–articulatory codes are highly effective at short intervals (perhaps they are easier to form). The second assumption is that, on the average, one word is more similar to another in terms of its acoustic–articulatory characteristics than in terms of semantic characteristics. The third assumption is that forgetting is due to interference. If these three assumptions are correct, then we would expect acoustic–articulatory codes to be highly effective at short intervals but to be forgotten at a more rapid rate than semantic codes.

Encoding processes The nature of the codes formed when an item is studied appears to depend partly on processes that occur automatically and partly on strategies under the control of the learner. Thus, some sensory level as well as semantic level information generally appears automatically as a result of attending to an item. The extent of such coding varies with such factors as item familiarity, pronounceableness, and meaningfulness. The individual also may change the nature of the codes formed by the deliberate modification of the activities engaged in during study. Such variations, presumably, are in part a function of the individual's expectancies regarding the demands of the task. For example, Muter (1980) found that when subjects were led to expect that they would not have to recall items but, in fact, were tested shortly after presentation, their performance was much worse than ordinarily found when expectancies are accurate. This unusually low STM performance may be due to the employment of encoding operations which resulted in codes that were much less effective for STM than usual. An intriguing question is whether this ineffective encoding produced by an experimental manipulation may be similar to the encoding regularly employed by some individuals whose STM performance is poor. In any case, it seems plausible that some individuals are less effective strategists than others with respect to STM encoding.

A major source of individual and developmental differences relates to differential experience (Chi, 1976). Differences in item familiarity or meaningfulness arising from differential experience could be a major source of nonstrategic coding differences. This point can be grasped intuitively by comparing one's digit span for number words from one's native language and from a partially mastered foreign language. Huttenlocher and Burke (1976) have proposed such an explanation of age differences in digit span, having first reviewed and rejected the possibility that such differences are due to strategy differences. The presumed consequences of less experience or familiarity is to reduce the speed with which items can be identified and encoded (see the section on rehearsal and speed of encoding). Experience-related factors may also account for the observed superiority of digit span to word (noun) span, and of word span to nonsense word span. However, sheer familiarity or item frequency is not the whole story. Hall, Humphreys, and Wilson (Note 1) obtained very low estimates of memory span for function words such as "the." These words have a very high frequency of occurrence in the language and presumably are named very rapidly.

Differences in modality-specific encoding The possibility of modality-specific code differences has been discussed for many years, especially in the context of individuals presumed to have specific learning disabilities (LD). Frequently, LD children are characterized as deficient in visual STM or in auditory STM, and certain of the tests used in LD diagnosis contain subtests designed to detect such deficits. Although there may be modality-specific deficits or weaknesses, the situation is more complex than has been recognized.

One important distinction which has not been made consistently is between the *presentation modality* that results in unusually low performance and the *modality locus* of the deficiency. It appears that LD specialists tend to assume that the first of these situations implies the second; that is, if a child does poorly with visually presented information, the locus of the problem is in the visual memory system. For example, the problem might be that visual codes are degraded, slow to form or difficult to access, or especially subject to interference. Alternatively, while most individuals who are presented information visually code both visually and auditorily, this recoding from the visual to the auditory may be less efficient in some individuals. The locus of the difficulty with visual stimuli in such cases would not be in the visual system but in the mechanisms (including strategies) by which recoding occurs or in the auditory memory system.

Ceci, Lea, and Ringstrom (1980) have provided some evidence on the nature of the impairment for children who do poorly on the verbal and visual tests from the Detroit Test of Learning Aptitude (Baker & Leland, 1959), a commonly used test in the LD field. The investigators looked at the performance of four groups of children, three of which will be discussed here. In addition to a control group, there were two groups of LD children; one group was diagnosed with the Detroit Test as having a visual memory problem but no auditory memory problem, and the other group as having the reverse. Auditorily and visually cued recall tasks were used. These cued tasks are probably best considered to be LTM tasks, but the results obtained and the interpretation proferred are instructive for our purposes. In the auditory task, the cues employed were either the speaker's voice, rhymes, or the names of categories. In the visual task, the cues were either color, location, or category names. Surprisingly, with physical cues, the LD children had no difficulty with what was supposed to be their deficient modality. That is, those children who had been diagnosed as having an auditory memory deficit performed well on the auditory task when the cues were the speaker's voice or rhymes but did poorly when the cues were the category names. The visually impaired group likewise performed well on the visual task when the cues were color or location but performed poorly when they were category names. Ceci et al. interpreted their results as indicating a modality-specific deficit in semantic coding. Thus, those who had been diagnosed as having poor visual memories simply were not translating visual stimuli (pictures) into semantic codes or were not translating them into as good a code as they did with auditory presentation. A similar explanation applies for those who were diagnosed as having poor auditory memories.

The next series of experiments (see Kroll, 1975, pp. 156–158) are not primarily concerned with individual differences. However, they make some very provocative observations about individual differences, and the techniques used in them may be useful for the study of individual differences. Briefly, subjects were taught to shadow a series of letters presented auditorily at a rate of 2/second. The material to be recalled was also letters and was presented either visually or auditorily. When presented auditorily, the to-be-recalled material was presented in place of the to-be-shadowed material; when presented visually, it was presented concurrently with the to-be-shadowed material. The basic assumption was that the shadowing test is so demanding of attention that recoding normally will not occur. Thus, visual information will be stored about a visually presented letter but not about an auditorily presented letter, and auditory information will be stored about a letter presented auditorily but not about one presented visually. The results over a series of experiments provided very good support for this assumption and will now be summarized.

Tests immediately following the presentation of the auditory and visual letters showed that the letters were approximately equally likely to be perceived (learned). The auditory letters, however, were forgotten at a much faster rate, as would be expected if the verbal shadowing test were interfering with an acoustic–articulatory code. Based on this evidence, it seems possible that a visual code was used to store the visual letter, but we do not have to make this inference as more precise information was obtained. To get this information, patterns of intrusions were examined and the interfering effects of phonetic and visual similarity were investigated. This evidence also converged on the conclusion that auditory and visual codes were employed. Some casual observations by Kroll (1975) suggest that these procedures may be of some use in the study of individual differences. He noted that a few subjects reported subvocal rehearsal of the visual memory letter and did about as poorly on these letters as they did with the auditory memory letters. A few subjects also reported visualizing the auditory letters and these subjects typically did very well in this condition. The former subjects, who did not or could not maintain a visual memory trace, might indeed be candidates for a diagnosis of having a poor visual memory.

Methods for studying encoding modalities   The studies by Kroll (1975, pp. 156–158) and his associates illustrate the possibility of getting converging evidence on encoding issues. In summary, an experimenter may attempt to control encoding through the choice of materials or instructions, or by the use of a concurrent task which reduces the probability of recoding. The use of a materials variable has been by far the most popular in individual-differences research and a word of caution is in order. Using a picture does not guarantee that only a visual code will be employed. Subjects may name the picture and store this name. Using nonsense figures helps, but some subjects, and especially the bright ones, may still be able to create a label for some figures. Some investigators have used figures that have probably been impossible to label or encode verbally (see Cermak & Levine, 1971; Phillips & Baddeley, 1971). Unfortunately, such materials have not been used in individual-differences research. Use of a concurrent activity in addition to the materials variable is probably desirable with the materials generally employed. It should be noted that the success of an encoding manipulation can be confirmed in a variety of ways. For example, tasks can be designed to interfere with the presumed memory code and the kind of errors made can be analyzed. The types of cues employed to probe for the memory trace may also be varied, though this technique has received relatively little use (see Shulman, 1970).

The importance of converging lines of evidence is that they eliminate alternative explanations. Many reported studies (e.g., Liberman, Shankweiler, Liberman, Fowler, & Fischer, 1977, pp. 217–223) that have been interpreted as supporting a modality-specific encoding deficit have relied on only one type of evidence. When this evidence is in the form of an interaction in which the initially superior group is hurt more by a coding or materials manipulation than the initially inferior group, it is especially problematic. Performance on these paradigms is the result of a variety of factors. If one factor is affected by the manipulation while another is not, it is possible that the interaction is created by a floor effect. The effect is a psychological floor, not one that can be determined by comparing the obtained score with a theoretical minimum.

Training Studies In general, it is difficult to test a hypothesis about encoding differences that are due to differences in the way one responds to particular materials. To illustrate, is it just amount of familiarity or is it something else that causes the difference between digit span and word span? Training studies provide one method for examining these questions. In one study, Humphreys, Hall, Fuson, and Wilson (Note 2) looked at nonsense-syllable span as a function of practice. Two conditions were used. In one condition, subjects learned a serial list of 10 nonsense syllables. In a second condition, they learned a paired-associates list where 10 nonsense syllables served as responses. After a brief period of paired-associates learning, nonsense-syllable span was significantly better than after the same amount of serial learning. Of course, these results are preliminary, but they do raise questions about memory-span performance, especially among young children. That is, some children may have poor digit spans because they may have only learned the digits as a serial list; their word spans, however, may be normal because they have used the words in a variety of contexts, as illustrated by the paired-associates results.

Done and Miles (1978, pp. 554–560) also report a training study which sheds some light on individual differences in STM. They were investigating the hypothesis that dyslexics show a STM deficit when visual stimuli must be verbally encoded. First, they tested this notion by looking at a materials variable and then by using an interference paradigm. The final experiment was a training experiment where normal and dyslexic subjects learned to name nonsense shapes. After a fairly extensive amount of training, the normal subjects showed more improvement on the nonsense-syllable span test. The dyslexic subjects had considerably greater difficulty in learning the names of the nonsense shapes, but training had been carried out to a common criterion. Thus, although a considerable amount of evidence had been amassed for the verbal-labeling hypothesis, this was the first experiment which hoped to determine whether the difficulty with verbal labels was due to dyslexics not knowing the labels as well as normal subjects or to their not using them. To the extent that this training procedure brought dyslexics to the same level of learning, it provides evidence in favor of the latter explanation. Of course, equating for level of learning is a very difficult task (see Underwood, 1964) and more evidence is needed before this issue is resolved.

CUE AND INFORMATIONAL ANALYSES

This approach is based on an analysis of the information required and/or the cues utilized to perform an STM task. As such, it is at a very different level of discourse than that represented by the previous analyses.

RECENCY AS A RETRIEVAL CUE

Tulving (1968, pp. 2–36) was apparently the first investigator to suggest that the difference between STM and LTM might lie in the retrieval cues employed. This view has been clarified by Baddeley and Hitch (1974, pp. 47–90; 1977, pp. 199–241). Very briefly, they had observed that the recency portion of the free-recall curve was relatively unaffected by manipulations which should have filled or occupied PM. Specifically, subjects were required to learn a list of words and, at the same time, remember short lists of digits. In immediate free recall, a memory load of six digits depressed recall for the initial list positions but left recall for the final list positions largely unchanged. Baddeley and Hitch (1974) proposed that the recency effect in free recall was not due to PM but rather to the use of recency as a retrieval cue.

Also, a paradigm has been developed which provides additional support for this view. Bjork and Whitten (1974) had subjects study a list of word pairs where each pair was separated by distractor activity. They found a recency effect even when the final pair had been followed by as much as 30 seconds of distractor activity. This long-term recency effect has since been found in several studies, and alternative explanations such as output interference and displaced rehearsals largely have been eliminated (see Glenberg, Bradley, Stevenson, Kraus, Tkachuk, Gretz, Fish, & Turpin, 1980; Whitten, 1978). Thus, a retrieval explanation based on a temporal code seems the most plausible explanation.

The retrieval interpretation is relatively new and may face some serious problems. Grave doubts must remain as to what the recency portion of the free-recall curve measures. The Bjork and Whitten (1974) paradigm does, however, strike us as one that could be adapted to individual-difference and developmental research, although no one, as yet, appears to have done so. Such research might shed some light on this issue.

ITEM AND ORDER INFORMATION IN STM

Theory   Logically, it seems that serial recall and free recall require the use of different information. In free recall, one must remember only the items, whereas in serial recall, one must remember both the items and their order. Conrad (1964) has argued that order information is derived from item information. Thus, transposition errors are said to occur because of a loss of item information. The more widely accepted position, however, is that it is useful to distinguish between item and order information (cf. Murdock, 1976)

Martin (1978) has argued that digit span largely reflects order information and not item information. This suggestion is partially based on a logical analysis of the digit-span task; that is, since the set of items from which the to-be-recalled material is taken is small and known to the subject, it would appear that the primary problem is not remembering which items are presented but rather arranging them in order.

Martin (1978) also observed that digit span did not correlate with either immediate or delayed free recall (r (36) = .12 and .12, respectively). The correlations between digit span and four measures of capacity derived from the recency portion of the free recall curve also were small, being .11, .12, .18, and .20. The correlation with ordered recall was, however, significant and reasonably large, r = .66. In a second experiment, the correlation between digit span and the ordered recall of strings of 12 letters was $r(14) = .63$. When letter recall was rescored according to a free recall criterion, this correlation dropped to $r(14) = .28$, even though the correlation between the two scoring methods was substantial, $r(14) = .72$.

Method Given these findings and arguments, it would be of interest to look at individual-difference questions by getting separate estimates of the amount of each individual's item and order information. The problem is determining these estimates in light of the plethora of methods suggested. Perhaps, the simplest way is to ask subjects to recall in order and then score the protocols both for order recall (an item must be recalled in its input position in order to be counted as correct) and for free recall (an item is counted as correct even if it is not in its correct position). As the Martin (1978) study shows, this method may provide enough separation to produce interesting results. Although there are some obvious problems with this scoring system, the available evidence suggests that the estimate of item information is not seriously affected by the requirement that subjects recall in order (Detterman & Brown, 1974). Perhaps the most serious drawback is that subjects cannot exhibit order information unless they also have item information. To overcome this restriction, one can look at the probability of a correct ordering conditional on item recall (Murdock, 1968). This method also has several drawbacks, including: (1) a loss of reliability as the n on which the statistics are based is decreased; and (2) the possibility of item selection and subject selection artifacts.

Healy (1974) has proposed experimental procedures for getting independent estimates of item and order information in a recall paradigm. Four consonants were presented at a very rapid rate (400 milliseconds/item), followed by the presentation of 3, 8, or 18 digits at the same rate. Subjects were required to read aloud each consonant and digit as it was presented. To obtain estimates of order information, the same set of four consonants was used on every trial. In a similar manner, to obtain estimates of item information, only three consonants were permitted to occur at each serial position. Thus, if a subject knew which consonant had occurred, he or she would know where it had occurred. With both procedures, on each trial, subjects were asked to write down four consonants in their correct positions. Output order was not constrained. This procedure may prove to be useful if variables affecting one measure but not the other are found. However, it does not appear possible to either support it or reject it on purely logical grounds. Indeed, it seems possible to create models of the recall process for which this is an appropriate procedure and models for which it is not.

Recognition procedures have also been developed to look at both item and relational information (Donaldson & Glathe, 1969). These procedures have the advantage in that subjects are allowed the possibility of demonstrating that they have order information even if they do not have item information. A possible disadvantage is that it is not known whether processes which affect recall will also affect recognition.

At this point, we are in the unfortunate position of having many ways to assess item and order information, but we do not have any theoretical or empirical reason for choosing one over the other. We also have the suggestion, and it needs to be taken seriously, that digit span reflects primarily order and not item information. Given digit span's importance in the study of individual differences in STM, it seems important to verify this suggestion. As a first step, perhaps the relationships among the proposed measures could be assessed. Do the measures of order information correlate higher with other measures of order information than they do with measures of item information?

CONTRIBUTIONS OF INDIVIDUAL-DIFFERENCES PSYCHOLOGY

THEORETICAL CONTRIBUTIONS

The previous sections have suggested a variety of components which may be responsible for individual differences in STM—capacity, rate of loss, codes, and so forth. Although it may be that systematic individual differences will be found in many of these components, the more interesting question is whether there are systematic individual differences among people that manifest themselves in a variety of cognitive and behavioral processes, including STM performance. This is a question that differential psychologists can help to answer: they study differences between people; therefore, they can suggest the dimensions that may be relevant to the study of STM.

Three areas will be briefly discussed because they illustrate both the problems and promises associated with combining theoretical analyses of STM with the study of individual differences. Included are individual differences in intelligence and arousal, as well as the area defined by selecting individuals who have large discrepancies between different skills or abilities. The reader should note that these areas are not the only areas of interest. The study of brain-damaged individuals has been and should continue to be of considerable importance in our understanding of STM (Milner, 1966, pp. 109–133). The study of developmental differences also has had an impact, particularly through the conceptualization of strategic processes. This work has been extensively reviewed (Dempster, 1981; Halford, in press) and generally, the issues are similar to those encountered in the study of intellectual differences.

INTELLIGENCE

Intelligence and STM have been linked for decades, mainly through the memory-span task. As early as 1887, Jacobs noted that increases in the length of the "span of prehension" (digit span) paralleled the rankings of students in class. At the same time, Galton (1887) demonstrated that the memory-span task accurately distinguished normal persons from "idiots" (mental retardates). An early review of memory-span research (Blankenship, 1938) indicated that developmental increases in memory span were documented before the turn of the century. In addition, the Stanford–Binet IQ test included a digit-span task by 1905. Modern IQ tests, such as the Stanford-Binet, the Wechsler Intelligence Scale for Children (WISC), and the Wechsler Adult Intelligence Scale (WAIS), still include the task.

Even from this very brief review, it is obvious that the memory-span task has had a long history of use by differential psychologists. Although it is clear that the task is not a pure measure of any theoretical construct, an interesting consensus has been emerging from the theoretical work on STM and the empirical work on individual differences in memory span. In an extensive review of the literature, Dempster (1981) examined 10 possible sources of individual and developmental differences in performance. Although strategic processes (such as rehearsal, grouping, chunking, and retrieval strategies) have often been implicated as the source of individual differences in memory-span performance, Dempster concluded that the evidence does not provide strong support for this implication. Dempster's list of nonstrategic variables included item identification, item ordering, capacity, susceptibility to interference, search rate, and output buffer. His conclusion was that only item identification appeared to be a major source of individual and developmental differences, although ordering and susceptibility to interference may also be involved.

Hunt and his colleagues (Hunt, 1978; Hunt, Lunneborg, & Lewis, 1975) have been interested in whether those people who do well on psychometric tests also do well on cognitive tasks. Dismissing intelligence as too global a term for their purposes, Hunt et al. (1975) examined the information-processing capabilities of students classified as high or low verbal according to the Washington Pre-College Test (WPCT), a standardized exam similar to the Scholastic Aptitude Test (SAT) of the Educational Testing Service. Although they examined a number of cognitive tasks, we will only discuss the experiment in which a variation of the Brown–Peterson distractor task was employed.

Subjects were shown four letters—one at a time—at a rate of 400 milliseconds per letter. Immediately after the fourth letter, they were asked to shadow 1–36 visually presented digits and then to recall the letters. The retention functions for both groups were nearly parallel. That is, although the high-verbal subjects retained more information than the low-verbal subjects, the rate of loss from STM for the two groups was virtually identical. Hunt (1978) also rejected a strategic encoding explanation for his results, basing his arguments on much of the same evidence that Dempster (1981) had used. Instead, Hunt suggested that cognitive tasks, which are said to measure STM capacity, actually measure the availability of attentional resources.

If the Dempster (1981), Hunt (1978), and Baddeley and Hitch (1974, pp. 47–90) papers are examined together, an interesting picture of individual differences in STM emerges. For the high-verbal, high-intelligent, or older subject, such functions as item identification are relatively automatic and little attention (or working memory) must be directed to these processes in order to complete them. Attentional resources then are freed for other functions, such as the short-term storage of items. For the low-verbal, low-intelligent, or young subject, however, many attentional resources must be devoted to such processes as item identification, leaving fewer resources available for other functions. Several aspects of this theory, however, remain unspecified. For example, what are these other functions and what is the relationship between rehearsal and naming speed? Why in the Hunt et al. (1975) experiment was there a difference in initial learning but no difference in rate of loss? This lack of specification remains a major weakness of this approach. Another weakness lies in the limited number of STM tasks studied. Most of the work cited by Dempster (1981) has employed tasks with a substantial recall component; yet explanations in terms of speed of encoding should apply equally well to probe and recognition tasks. If, however, rehearsal speed is related to output or recall speed, and not to encoding speed, these explanations cannot be extended to probe or recognition tasks. In fact, it seems unlikely that much more progress can be made in this area until a larger variety of paradigms is employed and the results are analyzed from a variety of theoretical perspectives. Nevertheless, because the relationship between STM and intelligence has proven so robust, intellectual differences (along with developmental differences) can provide a major testing ground for the theoretical constructs and measures used in STM research.

AROUSAL

Some authors have suggested that performance differences between extraverts and introverts (H. J. Eysenck, 1967, 1981) or high and low impulsives (Revelle, Humphreys, Simon, & Gilliland, 1980) may be understood in terms of differences in basal arousal or in terms of phase differences in the diurnal arousal rhythm. Furthermore, it generally is maintained that arousal hurts STM (Craik & Blankstein, 1975, pp. 389–417; M. W. Eysenck, 1976). Unlike the work on intelligence, however, the work on arousal has proceeded largely independently of theoretical work on STM. In discussing this work, it is important, for historical reasons, to consider Walker's (1958) theory relating arousal to STM. According to Walker, a memory trace of an item is laid down during study. Because formation of the trace is not instantaneous, a period of consolidation follows during which the trace can be accessed only with difficulty. This consolidation period implies that the probability of immediate recall after study is low. Furthermore, arousal was thought to increase inhibition during the period of consolidation, with the result that a stronger secondary trace is formed. Thus, according to Walker, arousal hurts short-term recall but facilitates long-term recall.

One of the studies most often cited in support of this hypothesis was conducted by Kleinsmith and Kaplan (1963). Subjects were shown a list of eight paired associates in which the stimuli were words and the responses were digits. During study, GSR recordings were made for each pair and the pair assigned to a high- or low-arousal category. Recall was requested after intervals varying between 2 minutes and 1 day. The results showed that pairs associated with large GSR's were remembered poorly after short intervals and well at long intervals; the reverse occurred for pairs associated with small GSRs. Thus, arousal, as indexed by GSRs, appeared to hurt STM but facilitated LTM. There have been several other studies consistent with this hypothesis, perhaps the best of which was Geen's (1973) use of social facilitation as a between-groups arousal manipulation (cf. Deffenbacher, Platt, & Williams, 1974; Geen, 1974).

In spite of the apparent support, this work has been largely ignored by memory theorists. There are, perhaps, four reasons for this oversight. First, the physiology behind the action decrement theory has been regarded as too speculative. Second, there are a variety of methodological and interpretive problems associated with these studies. For example, when items are assigned to high- and low-arousal categories on the basis of GSR differences (cf. Kleinsmith & Kaplan, 1963), it is possible that the items differ in other ways (such as concreteness, meaningfulness, or even serial position) that may contribute more to their recall than does arousal (see M. W. Eysenck, 1976). Third, the results are inconsistent, as witnessed by failures to replicate (cf. Saufley & LaCava, 1977). Fourth, the shortest retention interval employed in these studies (2 minutes) is longer than that employed in the rest of STM research.

This last objection may not be appropriate. As Keppel and Underwood

(1962) have shown, there is essentially no forgetting on the first trial in a Brown–Peterson experiment. Most of the studies following the Kleinsmith and Kaplan (1963) tradition have used a single trial of a relatively short list. It is possible that retention after 2 minutes in the absence of proactive interference will require the same explanation as retention after 20 seconds in the presence of proactive interference. Nevertheless, the Kleinsmith and Kaplan (1963) task is neither readily interpretable nor robust and thus has very little to recommend it.

Other evidence primarily based on memory-span performance supports the idea that some aspect of STM is hurt by high arousal (Revelle & Humphreys, Note 3). The results, however, are frequently inconsistent and it is clear that if an effect exists, the correct paradigms to identify it are not being used. It is imperative in this area to explore alternative paradigms and theoretical conceptions. Because of the apparent existence of large individual differences in arousal level, it is also probable that any study attempting to demonstrate these effects will have to include both arousal variables and individual-difference variables.

SPECIFIC-PERFORMANCE DEFICITS

For many years, psychologists have been intrigued by individuals with severe specific-performance deficits, as in classic cases of dyslexia. In addition to the challenge of providing more effective instructional programs for these individuals, it has been hoped that the careful examination of such cases would shed light on the nature of specific components of intelligence and their role in various kinds of intellectual performance. Hundreds of thousands (perhaps millions) of school children have been labeled "learning disabled" (LD), and hundreds of investigations of the nature of the "disabilities" have been conducted. Prominent among processes in which deficiencies have been proposed (and sometimes reported) are those relating to STM. Unfortunately, enormous conceptual and methodological problems characterize this body of research, and it has yielded little (if any) reliable information for psychology (see, for example, critiques by Coles, 1978; Morrison & Manis, in press; Hall & Humphreys, Note 4).

One requirement in this area is to be very precise and analytical about the presumed source of the processing deficits. Since remedial teachers often base their instructional programs on these analyses (diagnoses), the practical consequences can be severe. To illustrate, consider a child who is diagnosed as having a poor visual memory but who, in reality, simply does not verbally label pictures. If a teacher assumes that the child cannot learn in the visual modality, most of that child's lessons might be given auditorily. Alternatively, the teacher might try to remedy the supposed deficiency and provide the child with a variety of visual-memory tasks. None of those, however, may require the child to provide verbal labels, so the remediation may be irrelevant as far as child's deficiency is concerned.

Although increased precision in the use of information processing constructs is necessary in this area, by itself, it is not enough. An adequate taxonomy of the subject population is frequently lacking. Such a taxonomy would include a detailed analysis of the school-achievement tasks (as well as other cognitive tasks) with which these children have difficulties. That is, in planning a research program one must know the likely number of reading-disabled students having difficulty due to word decoding as opposed to comprehension problems. One also needs to know more about developmental trends in these abilities or skills. Does the poor second-grade word decoder still have difficulties in the sixth grade? Without this detailed descriptive work on the subject population and on the school achievement tasks, no degree of precision on the information-processing constructs will be sufficient.

METHODOLOGICAL CONTRIBUTIONS

Individual-differences psychology can make two contributions to the study of cognitive processes. One of these, the identification of dimensions of individual differences, has already been discussed. This is the procedure which has been used in studying intelligence, in relating the various dimensions of personality to differences in cognitive processing, and in studying specific-performance deficits. This view is perhaps the traditional one of individual-differences psychology.

The other contribution of individual-differences psychology is the development of methods for studying individual differences. Other than the development of the correlation coefficient itself, perhaps the most useful contribution has been the development of exploratory and, more recently, confirmatory factor analysis. Although the use of factor analysis has a long tradition in test construction and personality research, it has been only recently applied to the study of cognitive processes in general, and to STM in particular. Earlier applications of factor analysis were concerned with the identification of "dimensions of the mind," but were not particularly helpful in testing hypotheses about cognitive processes. Two recent exceptions to this general statement can be found in the research of Carroll (Note 5) and of Woodward and his associates (cf. Geiselman, Woodward, & Beatty, 1982).

Carroll's recent work (see Chapter 1 in this volume) on dimensions of cognitive processes is an example of what can be done with exploratory factor analysis. In an earlier review and reanalysis of published studies,

Carroll (Note 5) summarized most of the published factor-analytic studies of cognitive abilities. His findings with respect to individual differences in STM are complicated; in general, the findings reflect the limitations of the studies he reviews. That is, Carroll is forced to consider the data from a variety of different paradigms; most have only a limited number of variables; and many have few subjects (median = 60). In addition, few studies had "marker" variables which could help identify the factors obtained. In general, Carroll finds it possible to find at least one STM-like factor (memory span) in the studies he reviews.

Perhaps a more important problem found in the reanalysis (as in the original studies) was that the factor analyses were exploratory. That is, the number of factors to extract and the rotations to apply were not based on particular hypotheses, but were merely convenient ways to describe the data. The number of factors extracted was not determined on the basis of hypothesized structures, but rather on rules of thumb and experience. Similarly, the rotations were to "simple structure" which, although an appealing criterion, does not necessarily reflect underlying structure. The consequences of this procedure are that the solutions are more a product of the analyst's sophistication and taste than a reflection of the underlying structure of the data. Such exploratory analyses are a useful means of hypothesis generation, and Carroll's review should be required reading for all cognitive scientists interested in individual differences. However, exploratory analyses can never be a substitute for hypothesis testing or confirmatory analyses.

A recent study by Geiselman et al. (1982) is a demonstration of the powers of using *confirmatory factor analysis* and *structural modeling* to test hypotheses about cognitive functioning. Rather than be concerned about individual differences per se, Geiselman et al. used the techniques developed in the individual-differences area to resolve theoretical issues in cognitive psychology. In three separate experiments, they examined the structural relationships between measures of rehearsal strategy and indices of STM and LTM.

To apply structural-equation modeling, Geiselman et al. needed to specify the models of memory they wished to test. One model, based upon Melton's (1963) theory, predicted that the intercorrelations between various measures of memory at short periods of time and at long periods of time could be explained in terms of one latent variable (overall memory functioning). The other model, based on the work of Atkinson and Shiffrin (1968, pp. 90–195), predicted that two separate latent variables (PM and SM) would be needed to explain the observed covariances.

In each of their three studies, Geiselman et al. examined how various measures of rehearsal and encoding strategy (based on eye movements and self-reports) related to measures which purport to measure short- and long-term components. Thus, indicators of a latent PM variable were number of acoustic confusions, number of words recalled on an immediate recall task before a 2-second pause in the verbal report, and number of items recalled in the immediate test corrected for the SM component (estimated from a delayed test). Indicators of the latent SM variable included recall on a delayed test, number of words recalled on an immediate test after a pause in the verbal report, and the number of semantic confusions. Through careful experimental control, these measures were kept experimentally independent (measures were derived from different trials). Although the STM and LTM variables were negatively correlated, Geiselman et al. were able to show that the best-fitting model was one that represented a rote rehearsal strategy as positively affecting PM and negatively affecting SM. That is, the correlations between the STM and LTM measures could be explained best in terms of the common effect that rehearsal strategy had on the latent PM and SM variables.

The important advantage of the use of confirmatory factor analysis and of structural-equation modeling is that, in addition to requiring specification of theoretical relationships, they provide an index of goodness of fit for each competing model. Although the significance values associated with a particular model should be interpreted with caution, the relative magnitude of fit is a useful index. Another important advantage of using factor analysis (especially confirmatory factor analysis) is that, by requiring at least two (and preferably more) measures of the same theoretical (latent) construct, the investigator is forced to specify how the theoretical concepts are to be measured. That is, multiple operationalizations of each construct are required. The failure of these multiple measures to correlate in the predicted manner is a strong indictment of the theoretical adequacy of a particular model. It is probably too early to tell how important the contribution of structural modeling will be, but it has the capability of greatly advancing our understanding of the relationships between various components of cognitive functioning.

CONCLUSIONS

We began this chapter with a discussion of reasons for the importance of individual differences in short-term memory. Partly reflecting our own biases, but also reflecting recent developments in the field, we have placed primary emphasis on experimental contributions to the study of STM. Only recently have individual-differences psychologists become interested in the *processes* which lie behind phenomena such as digit span. We can only hope that by better understanding experimental models of memory functioning, individual-differences psychologists will be able to apply their sophisticated methodologies to the issue of cognitive functioning.

In considering these experimental contributions, we have outlined a variety of theoretical positions on the differences between STM and LTM. These positions have included the structural approaches of strength, capacity, and working memory; the processing approaches which emphasized rehearsal, speed of encoding, and type of encoding, as well as the cue and information analyses. What task then is the individual-differences psychologist to choose? No easy response to this question is available, as the answer depends on the purpose of the investigation.

If the primary purpose of a study is prediction, then digit span or the more complicated working-memory paradigms might be the most appropriate. Digit span is a complex task, and it is possible that it is this complexity that is responsible for its robust relationship with intelligence and development. However, if the task is to understand why a relationship exists, then one of the more analytical paradigms would seem to be the most appropriate choice. When, as in the case of arousal, digit span yields small and inconsistent results, it is possible that some of the more analytic techniques will produce larger and more consistent results.

Both the study of individual differences and the techniques developed for this study can help the memory theorist. We have noted several areas where no compelling argument exists for selecting one memory measure over another. In some areas it is uncertain whether one or more aspects of memory are involved. The techniques derived from individual-differences psychology, and in particular confirmatory factor analysis, can help to determine the best measure (or best set of measures) and help to decide which constructs go together. A major advantage of the individual-differences approach is that it forces the experimental or cognitive psychologist to become more concerned with issues of reliability and even validity.

REFERENCES

Atkinson, R. C., & Shiffrin, R. M. Human memory: A proposed system and its control processes. In K. W. Spence & J. T. Spence (Eds.), *The psychology of learning and motivation* (Vol. 2). New York: Academic Press, 1968.

Baddeley, A. D., & Hitch, G. Working memory. In G. Bower (Ed.), *Advances in learning and motivation* (Vol. 8). New York: Academic Press, 1974.

Baddeley, A. D., & Hitch, G. Commentary on "Working memory." In G. Bower (Ed.), *Human memory: Basic processes.* New York: Academic Press, 1977.

Baddeley, A. D., Thomson, N., & Buchanan, M. Word length and the structure of short-term memory. *Journal of Verbal Learning and Verbal Behavior*, 1975, *14*, 575–589.

Baker, H. J., & Leland, B. *Detroit tests of learning aptitude.* Indianapolis, Ind.: Bobbs-Merrill, 1959.

Bjork, R. A., & Whitten, W. B. Recency-sensitive retrieval processes in long-term free recall. *Cognitive Psychology,* 1974, *6,* 173–189.

Blankenship, A. B. Memory span: A review of the literature. *Psychological Bulletin,* 1938, *35,* 1–25.

Broadbent, D. E. *Perception and communication.* Oxford: Pergamon, 1958.

Ceci, S. J., Lea, S. E. G., & Ringstrom, M. D. Coding processes in normal and learning-disabled children: Evidence for modality-specific pathways to the cognitive system. *Journal of Experimental Psychology: Human Learning and Memory,* 1980, *6,* 785–797.

Cermak, L. S., & Levine, R. Encoding as a function of the presentation-rehearsal interval in short-term memory. *Psychonomic Science,* 1971, *23,* 423–424.

Chi, M. T. H. Short-term memory limitation in children: Capacity or processing deficits? *Memory & Cognition,* 1976, *4,* 559–572.

Cohen, R., & Sandberg, T. Relation between intelligence and short-term memory. *Cognitive Psychology,* 1977, *9,* 534–554.

Coles, G. S. The learning disabilities test battery: Empirical and social issues. *Harvard Educational Review,* 1978, *48,* 313–340.

Conrad, R. Acoustic confusion in immediate memory. *British Journal of Psychology,* 1964, *55,* 75–84.

Craik, F. I. M., & Blankstein, K. R. Psychophysiology and human memory. In P. H. Venables & M. J. Christie (Eds.), *Research in psychophysiology.* New York: Wiley, 1975.

Craik, F. I. M., & Levy, B. A. The concept of primary memory. In W. K. Estes (Ed.), *Handbook of learning and cognitive processes* (Vol. 4). Hillsdale, N.J.: Lawrence Erlbaum Associates, 1976.

Craik, F. I. M., & Lockhart, R. S. Levels of processing: A framework for memory research. *Journal of Verbal Learning and Verbal Behavior,* 1972, *11,* 671–684.

Daneman, M., & Carpenter, P. A. Individual differences in working memory and reading. *Journal of Verbal Learning and Verbal Behavior,* 1980, *19,* 450–466.

Deffenbacher, K. A., Platt, G. J., & Williams, M. A. Differential recall as a function of socially induced arousal and retention interval. *Journal of Experimental Psychology,* 1974, *103,* 809–811.

Dempster, F. N. Memory span: Sources of individual and developmental differences. *Psychological Bulletin,* 1981, *89,* 63–100.

Detterman, D. K., & Brown, J. Order information in short-term memory. *Journal of Experimental Psychology,* 1974, *103,* 740–750.

Donaldson, W., & Glathe, H. Recognition memory for item and order information. *Journal of Experimental Psychology,* 1969, *82,* 557–560.

Done, D. J., & Miles, T. R. Visual information processing in dyslexic children. In M. M. Gruneberg, P. E. Morris, & R. N. Sykes (Eds.), *Practical aspects of memory.* New York: Academic Press, 1978.

Eysenck, H. J. *The biological basis of personality.* Springfield, Ill.: Thomas, 1967.

Eysenck, H. J. *A model for personality.* Berlin/New York: Springer-Verlag, 1981.

Eysenck, M. W. Arousal, learning, and memory. *Psychological Bulletin,* 1976, *83,* 389–404.

Galton, F. Notes on prehension in idiots. *Mind,* 1887, *12,* 79–82.

Geen, R. G. Effects of being observed on short-term and long-term recall. *Journal of Experimental Psychology,* 1973, *100,* 395–398.

Geen, R. G. Effects of evaluation apprehension on memory over intervals of varying lengths. *Journal of Experimental Psychology,* 1974, *102,* 908–910.

Geiselman, R. E., Woodward, A. E., & Beatty, J. Individual differences in verbal memory performance: A test of alternative information-processing models. *Journal of Experimental Psychology: General*, 1982, *111*, 109–134.

Glenberg, A. M., Bradley, M. M., Stevenson, J. A., Kraus, T. A., Tkachuk, M. J., Gretz, A. L., Fish, J. H., & Turpin, B. M. A two-process account of long-term serial position effects. *Journal of Experimental Psychology: Human Learning and Memory*, 1980, *6*, 355–369.

Halford, G. S. *The development of thought.* Hillsdale, N.J.: Lawrence Erlbaum Associates, in press.

Hamilton, P., Hockey, R., & Rejman, M. The place of the concept of activation in human information processing theory: An integrative approach. In S. Dornic (Ed.), *Attention and performance* (Vol. 6). New York: Academic Press, 1977.

Healy, A. F. Separating item from order information in short-term memory. *Journal of Verbal Learning and Verbal Behavior*, 1974, *13*, 644–655.

Hintzman, D. L. Articulatory coding in short-term memory. *Journal of Verbal Learning and Verbal Behavior*, 1967, *6*, 312–316.

Hunt, E. Mechanics of verbal ability. *Psychological Review*, 1978, *85*, 109–130.

Hunt, E., Lunneborg, C., & Lewis, J. What does it mean to be high verbal? *Cognitive Psychology*, 1975, 7, 194–227.

Huttenlocher, J., & Burke, D. Why does memory span increase with age? *Cognitive Psychology*, 1976, *8*, 1–31.

Jacbos, J. Experiments on prehension. *Mind*, 1887, *12*, 75–79.

Keppel, G., & Underwood, B. J. Proactive inhibition in short-term retention of single items. *Journal of Verbal Learning and Verbal Behavior*, 1962, *1*, 153–161.

Kleinsmith, L. J., & Kaplan, S. Paired-associate learning as a function of arousal and interpolated interval. *Journal of Experimental Psychology*, 1963, *65*, 190–193.

Kroll, N. E. A. Visual short-term memory. In D. Deutsch & J. A. Deutsch (Eds.), *Short-term memory*. New York: Academic Press, 1975.

LaBerge, D., & Samuels, S. J. *Basic processes in reading: Perception and comprehension.* Hillsdale, N.J.: Lawrence Erlbaum Associates, 1977.

Liberman, I. Y., Shankweiler, D., Liberman, A. M., Fowler, C., & Fischer, F. W. Phonetic segmentation and recoding in the beginning reader. In A. S. Reber & D. Scarborough (Eds.), *Toward a psychology of reading: The proceedings of the CUNY conference*. Hillsdale, N.J.: Lawrence Erlbaum Associates, 1977.

Martin, M. Memory span as a measure of individual differences in memory capacity. *Memory & Cognition*, 1978, *6*, 194–198.

Melton, A. W. Implications of short-term memory for a general theory of memory. *Journal of Verbal Learning and Verbal Behavior*, 1963, *2*, 1–21.

Milner, B. Amnesia following operation on the temporal lobes. In C. M. W. Whitty & O. L. Zangwill (Eds.), *Amnesia*. London: Butterworths, 1966.

Morrison, F. J., and Manis, F. R. Cognitive processes and reading disabilities: A critique and proposal. In C. J. Brainerd & M. Pressley (Eds.), *Advances in cognitive development* (Vol. 1). New York: Springer-Verlag, in press.

Murdock, B. B. Auditory and visual stores in short-term memory. *Acta Psychologia*, 1967, *27*, 316–324.

Murdock, B. B. Serial order effects in short-term memory. *Journal of Experimental Psychology Monograph*, 1968, 76 (4, Pt. 2).

Murdock, B. B. Item and order information in short-term serial memory. *Journal of Experimental Psychology: General*, 1976, *105*, 191–216.

Muter, P. Very rapid forgetting. *Memory & Cognition*, 1980, *8*, 174–179.

Phillips, W. A., & Baddeley, A. D. Reaction time and short-term visual memory. *Psychonomic Science*, 1971, *22*, 73–74.

Raymond, B. Short-term storage and long-term storage in free recall. *Journal of Verbal Learning and Verbal Behavior*, 1969, *8*, 567–574.

Revelle, W., Humphreys, M. S., Simon, L., & Gilliland, K. The interactive effect of personality, time of day, and caffeine: A test of the arousal model. *Journal of Experimental Psychology: General*, 1980, *109*, 1–31.

Saufley, W. J., Jr., & LaCava, S. C. Reminiscence and arousal: Replications and the matter of establishing a phenomenon. *Bulletin of the Psychonomic Society*, 1977, *9*, 155–158.

Shiffrin, R. M., & Schneider, W. Controlled and automatic human information processing. II. Perceptual learning, automatic attending, and a general theory. *Psychological Review*, 1977, *84*, 127–190.

Shulman, H. G. Encoding and retention of semantic and phonemic information in short-term memory. *Journal of Verbal Learning and Verbal Behavior*, 1970, *9*, 499–508.

Standing, L., Bond, B., Smith, P., & Isely, C. Is the immediate memory span determined by subvocalization rate? *British Journal of Psychology*, 1980, *71*, 525–539.

Torgesen, J. K., & Houck, D. G. Processing deficiencies of learning-disabled children who perform poorly on the digit span test. *Journal of Educational Psychology*, 1980, *72*, 141–160.

Tulving, E. Theoretical issues in free recall. In T. R. Dixon & D. L. Horton (Eds.), *Verbal behavior and general behavior theory*. Englewood Cliffs, N.J.: Prentice-Hall, 1968.

Tulving, E., & Colotla, V. A. Free recall of trilingual lists. *Cognitive Psychology*, 1970, *1*, 86–98.

Underwood, B. J. Degree of learning and the measurement of forgetting. *Journal of Verbal Learning and Verbal Behavior*, 1964, *3*, 112–129.

Walker, E. L. Action decrement and its relation to learning. *Psychological Review*, 1958, *78*, 103–106.

Watkins, D. C., & Watkins, M. J. The modality effect and echoic persistence. *Journal of Experimental: General*, 1980, *109*, 251–278.

Watkins, M. J. The concept and measurement of primary memory. *Psychological Bulletin*, 1974, *81*, 695–711.

Waugh, N. C., & Norman, D. A. Primary memory. *Psychological Review*, 1965, *62*, 89–104.

Whitten, W. B. Output interference and long-term serial position effects. *Journal of Experimental Psychology: Human Learning and Memory*, 1978, *4*, 685–692.

Wickelgren, W. A. Acoustic similarity and intrusion errors in short-term memory. *Journal of Experimental Psychology*, 1965, *70*, 102–108.

Wickelgren, W. A. Strength/resistance theory of the dynamics of memory storage. In D. H. Krantz (Ed.), *Contemporary developments in mathematical psychology* (Vol. 1). San Francisco: Freeman, 1974.

Wickelgren, W. A., & Norman, D. A. Strength models and serial position in short-term recognition memory. *Journal of Mathematical Psychology*, 1966, *3*, 316–347.

NOTES

1. Hall, J. W., Humphreys, M. S., & Wilson, K. *High frequency words do not always produce good serial recall: Implications for theories of memory span.* Unpublished manuscript, Northwestern University, 1980.

2. Humphreys, M. S., Hall, J., Fuson, K., & Wilson, K. *The effect of paired-associate and serial learning on memory span.* Unpublished manuscript, Northwestern University, 1980.

3. Revelle, W., & Humphreys, M. S. *Personality, motivation, and performance: A theory of*

individual differences and information processing. Unpublished manuscript, Northwestern University, 1981.

4.   Hall, J. W., & Humphreys, M. S. *Problems in conduction and interpreting learning disabilities research.* Unpublished manuscript, Northwestern University, 1980.

5.   Carroll, J. B. *Individual difference relations in psychometric and experimental cognitive tasks* (Tech. Rep. 163). Chapel Hill: L. L. Thurstone Psychometric Laboratory, University of North Carolina, 1980.

3

Individual Differences in Verbal Processes

Charles A. Perfetti

INTRODUCTION

Some persons read well, have large vocabularies, and score high on verbal intelligence tests. Others read with difficulty, have smaller vocabularies, and score lower on verbal intelligence tests. What processes underlie such pervasive differences in verbal ability? Are the processes that underlie differences among children in reading skill the same as those that underlie differences among adults in reading skill or in verbal intelligence? These are the general questions addressed by this chapter.

The outline of the chapter and my main conclusions are as follows: The first section argues for a heuristically useful distinction between simple verbal processes, complex verbal processes, and verbal knowledge as three components of general verbal ability. The remaining sections examine the extent to which four simple verbal processes—letter recognition, decoding, name retrieval, and semantic access—can account for differences in reading ability of children and adults, as well as in adult verbal intelligence. A major conclusion is that across different verbal domains and different ages, the hallmark of skilled verbal processing is efficient word retrieval from *inactive* memory. What varies across different verbal domains and verbal skill levels is the extent to which one or the other of these simple processes is rate limiting for an individual. Among children, the rate-limiting process is word decoding, whereas among college adults it is general name retrieval. In addition, verbal knowledge makes a contribution to general verbal ability that is not easily reduced to simple verbal processes. Knowledge of both linguistic forms and concepts is as characteristic of verbal ability as speed of name retrieval. The final section briefly suggests how complex verbal processes can be affected by, but not reduced to, simple verbal processes.

VERBAL PROCESSES: A DEFINITION AND THEORETICAL FRAMEWORK

For present purposes, *a verbal process* is any cognitive activity that (by reasonable inference) involves the recognition, retrieval, or understanding of linguistic forms. Thus, recognizing a word is a verbal process and recognizing a face is not. Furthermore, a *simple verbal process* is a verbal process that relies mainly on access and retrieval of linguistic elements stored in a memory system.[1] In its simplest form, it is access to a specific memory location, whereas in its more elaborate form, it also includes simple decoding operations. Thus recognition of a letter and recognition of a word are both simple verbal processes, even if recognition of a word involves retrieval of decoding rules and decoding operations. By contrast, a *complex verbal process* is one which requires multiple memory access and manipulations of accessed units. Thus, comprehension of even a two-word sentence is a complex verbal process. The distinction between simple and complex verbal processes becomes difficult for certain cases. For example, the decoding of a rare word, (e.g., *rogation*) or even a relatively common morphological compound (e.g., *nonsexist*) may involve multiple access and manipulation more than the understanding of the two-word "sentence" *No Smoking*. Such cases are interesting just because they suggest that decoding may sometimes be complex and comprehension may sometimes be simple. As a general case, however, letter and single-word processes are simple and comprehension, even sentence comprehension, is complex.

In addition to simple and complex verbal processes, verbal abilities rely on *verbal knowledge*. Verbal knowledge is the information in permanent memory that is accessed and manipulated by verbal processes. Again, it is useful to assume more than one level. *Word-form* knowledge includes infor-

---

[1] I refer to such processes as *simple* rather than *elementary* to avoid confusion with *elementary information processes* (Newell & Simon, 1972; also Chase, 1978, pp. 19–90). The latter are more *general* and more *elementary*. I assume that simple verbal processes are describable, in principle, in terms of those elementary processes; at present, the research on individual differences cannot, by and large, support a discussion at such a level.

mation about specific word forms, irrespective of word meanings, stored at specific memory locations. Thus knowledge that *fact* is a word in English and that it is pronounced /faekt/ is word-form knowledge. Closely related, but of a slightly different kind, is *verbal-rule* knowledge, of which rules of grapheme–phoneme correspondence, phonotactic rules, and orthographic rules are salient examples. Grammatical rules are also part of the knowledge system. A third type of permanent memory verbal knowledge is *word-concept* knowledge (vocabulary). It is the meaning of words, including a network of relationships among word concepts. Finally, higher level *schema* knowledge is represented in permanent memory. The difference between word-concept and schema knowledge is essentially one of organization. *Schemata* are parts of a conceptual network that acquire, through experience, some status as higher order concepts.[2]

What would it mean to characterize individual differences in terms of these processing and knowledge components? In fact, these components are interrelated aspects of an information-processing system. There is no reason to believe that there is independence between processing and knowledge components. Indeed, principles of system design include trade-offs between stored information (knowledge) and data-handling procedures. Instead, the knowledge–process distinction is simply a useful organizing device for considering complex cognitive processes. Thus, the characterization of individual differences in verbal ability will be in forms of simple and complex verbal processes and verbal knowledge.

The focus will be on general verbal abilities rather than specific ones: For example, as Hunt, Lunneborg, and Lewis (1975) put the question, What does it mean to be high verbal? What does it mean to be a skilled reader? What is involved in vocabulary differences? How does verbal ability in elementary school years relate to verbal ability of college students? These are the topics discussed in the remaining sections.

INDIVIDUAL DIFFERENCES IN READING SKILL

Reading encompasses a wide range of verbal processes that must be considered a pervasive part of what we ordinarily think of as verbal ability. In a nonliterate culture the concept of "verbal ability," were it to occur at all,

[2]The contents of the verbal memory system are representative of theories of semantic memory. Thus, *word-concept* knowledge is represented by semantic networks (Collins & Loftus, 1975; Lindsay & Norman, 1977) and schema knowledge is represented as elaborated conceptual networks (Rumelhart & Ortony, 1977, pp. 99–135).

would have a distinctly different flavor. An individual valued for his story-telling or some other oral talent could be expected not to show verbal ability, even orally, in the tasks devised by literate and technological societies (e.g., Cole & Scribner, 1974). Although some (e.g., Neisser, 1976, pp. 135–144) have taken this to argue against psychology's concept of intelligence, it is more to the point, in the present discussion, simply to note that literacy is likely to be a prerequisite for the sort of verbal abilities that this chapter is concerned with whether the particular research in question is on reading or oral language processing.

The range of reading talents is very wide. Roughly put, they range from children and adults who can barely read isolated common words to individuals who can read several hundreds of words per minute with some comprehension. The question is how can we account for this wide range of talent, or at least characterize it usefully? A related question is whether being skilled in reading at college age is roughly the same as being skilled in elementary school. Can ability differences among third-graders be described in the same processing terms as ability differences among college students?

ELEMENTARY SCHOOL READING ABILITY

Children begin formal reading instruction in the United States at age 6, although most have had considerable reading-relevant experience before then, at least in the form of "readiness" curricula offered in kindergarten. From the first day of instruction, there is a wide range of reading talent. As reading increases in comprehension demands, the contrast between high- and low-ability readers increases. Considering reading comprehension as the ability to be accounted for, what components of verbal processing are responsible?

SIMPLE VERBAL PROCESSES

The elementary reading activity is word *decoding*. Word decoding is the transform of a printed input into one or more of its corresponding linguistic forms. Thus, *lead* is decoded as /led/ or /lid/. In principle, the fact that the two forms are connected with different semantic structures is irrelevant. Because decoding, *prima facie,* is the essential simple reading process, the question is not so much whether it is a source of individual differences, but whether such differences reduce to other simple processes. One such process is *letter* or *letter pattern recognition*. Another is *name retrieval*.

Letter recognition is a simple verbal process which is some part of decoding. In general, recognizing constituent letters of a word mediates recognition of the word. This is not to say that reading is a letter-by-letter process (see Brewer, 1972, pp. 359–364; Gough, 1972, pp. 331–358) but rather that detailed process models of word recognition include some early state of letter recognition (e.g., Massaro, 1975). By an interactive model of word recognition, letter identification is facilitated by word recognition as well as vice versa (McClelland & Rumelhart, 1981; Rumelhart & McClelland, 1981, pp. 37–60). A good deal of letter processes for skilled readers involve using knowledge about letter patterns (Gibson, 1971) or constraints on permissible orthographic patterns (Venezky, 1970). Specific higher order letter patterns can be thought of as being accessible in memory as a function of learning (e.g., LaBerge & Samuels, 1974). Thus, pattern processes are not necessarily just recursively applied single-letter processes. The letter-pattern processes and letter processes are grouped together only by distinction from word decoding.

Another simple verbal process closely related to word decoding is name retrieval. Given any input which corresponds to a location in permanent memory, name retrieval is the process of accessing the location and producing the name. Thus name retrieval is patently part of decoding when oral reading is involved and implicitly part of decoding during silent reading. However, some decoding tasks, particularly lexical decisions, do not have to involve name retrieval, at least in principle. Note also that in some tasks letter recognition can involve retrieval of letter names.

A fourth simple verbal process is *semantic access*. Semantic access occurs when meaning components stored with a word in memory are activated. Reading comprehension, unlike decoding, cannot occur without semantic access. One of the individual-differences questions is whether ability differences exist in semantic access when differences in decoding are accounted for.

In summary, there are four simple verbal processes to consider. Two of these, decoding and semantic access are independent in principle. Decoding is the linguistic translation of a grapheme string which may or may not have a semantic entry in memory. Letter recognition is part of decoding. Name retrieval is also part of decoding, but it is a general process operating on name information in memory.

The question to be pursued is whether simple verbal processing differences are adequate to account for general reading-ability differences. Complex verbal processing differences are present, almost by definition: the ability measure in question is measured reading comprehension. The question is whether such differences can be characterized in terms of simple verbal processes. Furthermore, since decoding includes letter processes and general name retrieval processes, we want to know whether these last two are more basic to individual differences.

DECODING AND NAME RETRIEVAL

Given an ordinary printed word, a high-ability reader identifies it more rapidly than a low-ability reader. Among third-, fourth-, and fifth-grade subjects, we have found the mean difference in latency to vocalization ("naming time" as it is usually called) to be as high as 400 milliseconds (Perfetti, Finger & Hogaboam, 1978), although smaller differences are more typical (e.g., 200 milliseconds [Perfetti & Hogaboam, 1975], and 120 milliseconds [Hogaboam & Perfetti, 1978]). The magnitude of the difference is a function of word frequency and word length. The difference is less for high frequency words than low frequency words (Perfetti & Hogaboam, 1975) regardless of word length (Perfetti, Goldman, & Hogaboam, 1979) and higher for two-syllable words (Hogaboam & Perfetti, 1978) and especially large for three-syllable words, when frequency is controlled (Perfetti et al., 1978). As a general characterization, the magnitude of the ability difference is a linear function of average naming time; the more difficult the word-decoding process is, the greater the ability difference.

Decoding measured by naming time clearly involves name retrieval. Is general name retrieval a verbal-processing component that differentiates high- and low-ability readers? Perfetti et al. (1978) required subjects to name a variety of visually presented stimuli—colors, digits, and pictures as well as words. High-ability subjects were significantly faster than low-ability subjects only for word stimuli. Among other stimulus types, color-naming speed was completely unrelated to reading ability and digit-naming speed was significant only in a correlation using the full-ability range and not in the contrast between reader groups. For picture naming even the correlation of speed with reading ability ($r = .29$) was of no more than marginal reliability.

One of the comparisons obtainable from Perfetti et al. (1978) is especially useful for understanding any potential name-retrieval factor. In digit naming, there were two conditions, one in which the set of numbers that could occur was small and known to the subject. In the second condition, the set of numbers that could occur was large (100). The comparison between small-set and large-set performance can be considered a difference between *activated* memory and *inactive* memory. With a small set, all three digits can be kept active by the subject. When one is present, the response is mainly a matter of (1) encoding the digits; and (2) producing their name. Both the digit representation and its name are presumably already active in memory, so there is no retrieval in the ordinary sense. Under such a condition, the results were that there was no ability factor. In the large-set condition, by contrast, there is a third process, namely, *retrieving* the name of the digits of memory. The names are not active because the set is too large.

Under these conditions, there was a subject verbal-ability difference, detectable as a small correlation ($r = .38$) but not as a group contrast.

A related comparison from Perfetti et al. (1978) was between closed sets of words that were small and predictable (e.g., names of the four seasons) and open sets that were large and unpredictable (proper names). Unlike the case with the digits, ability differences were found regardless of set size. However, differences were much larger for open large sets than closed small sets. Again, the key seems to be whether retrieval from permanent memory is required (open sets) or whether the items to be produced are already active; hence, retrieval is not involved.

In addition to the name-retrieval factor, it is clear that a factor specific to linguistic forms is involved. Thus, for word identification, ability differences interacted with set size but even small closed sets produced significant differences. For digits, no differences were present for closed sets. In a multiple regression analysis of these data, Perfetti et al. (1978) found that even when the correlations between ability and all other variables were removed, verbal ability correlated significantly with times to name words from a closed set ($r = .33$) and times to name open-set words ($r = .42$). Perfetti et al. (1978) suggest that the various tasks can be ordered to reflect the following components: (1) name retrieval from permanent (inactive) memory; (2) large-memory search space; and (3) alphabetic inputs. Reading unpredictable words has all three components.

Based on the studies cited, the present conclusion is that name retrieval is one of the simple verbal processes that produce ability differences in reading. However, it is not the core component. Word decoding is an important process beyond name retrieval. This conclusion may not apply to the entire range of individual differences. Denckla and Rudel (1976), for example, have shown striking name-retrieval differences between normal readers and severe dyslexics. However, these studies have not ruled out the possibility that there is a decoding difference remaining when name retrieval is accounted for. In any case, the normal range of reading talents seems to require at least two factors—verbal decoding and general name retrieval from inactive memory.

There are tasks other than vocalization latency that can be used to index decoding. Three that have been used in my research are same–different judgments on simultaneously presented words (Hogaboam & Perfetti, 1978), same–different judgments on successively spoken and visually presented words (Perfetti, Hogaboam, & Bell, reported in Perfetti & Lesgold, 1979, pp. 141–183), and lexical decisions (unpublished, summarized in Perfetti, Note 1). All of these tasks are performed without the subject producing the word and the first two tend to produce smaller ability differences than tasks requiring word vocalization. For example, Hogaboam and Perfetti (1978, Experiment 2) presented subjects with word pairs for same–different judgments. Although high-ability readers performed these judgments more quickly than low-ability readers, the difference was not significant (in contrast to vocalization latencies of the same subjects). In a task in which a word is spoken and then immediately followed by a printed word for a same–different judgment, a similar unreliable difference was observed (see Perfetti & Lesgold, 1979, pp. 141–183). Lesgold and Curtis (1981, pp. 329–360) also found performance on this task to be somewhat less related to reading ability than is vocalization latency. These task differences can be related to the observation concerning retrieval and activation above. When a printed word is preceded by its oral equivalent, there is an activation of the word's memory location. Upon seeing the word, retrieval demands are minimal.[3] A related (but more complex) argument can be made for simultaneous word–word judgments. Such an account might help explain why lexical decisions for words *are* reliably related to ability (e.g., Perfetti, Note 1). Although naming is not involved, neither is prior activation of the word.

So far, all the tasks have involved a response to a single word. Thus, the decoding and retrieval processes are inferable as part of a single-response latency that includes other components. The reaction-time methodology of multiple stimulus arrays (Sternberg, 1969) provides a separation of the reaction time into processes (and error measurement) that accompany each trial (intercept components) and processes that are uniquely associated with processing rate (slope components). If word-decoding rate is a critical ability difference, it should be reflected in slope parameters of linear functions that relate reaction time to display size (e.g., number of words). There are two tasks of interest. A visual word-scan task provides information concerning word decoding rates. A memory scan task (Sternberg, 1966) provides information concerning rates for scanning memory for verbally stored items.

Visual Scan   Two experiments by Perfetti and Bell (Perfetti, Note 1) provide relevant data because they involved a population totally comparable to the one sampled in the studies cited above. Because the study is unpublished, a brief description is in order: Twenty-four third-grade subjects formed groups of high-ability and low-ability readers based on the reading subtest of the Metropolitan Achievement Test, with the high-group mean in the seventy-seventh percentile and the low-group mean in the nineteenth percentile. Two subgroups of eight each provided an IQ match, based on

---

[3]By this account, greater ability differences might be expected for a "different" word because its memory location has not been activated. Unfortunately, comparisons of same and different judgments are lacking.

second-grade scores. In Experiment 1, subjects participated in three visual search tasks: words, pseudowords, and category instances. In Experiment 2, subjects search for consonant bigrams. In the word-search task of Experiment 1, a target word was presented followed by a visual display containing one, three, five, or seven words which contained the target on half the trials. The word target remained constant for a block of eight trials, in order to minimize encoding and memory demands of the target stimulus. (For the other two tasks, the procedure was the same.) The data of interest are the functions relating search time to display size, particularly whether differences are to be found in intercept, slope, both, or neither.

For word search, there were significant differences between high- and low-ability readers in both intercepts and slopes. These data are shown in Figure 1 for the subgroups matched on IQ. For positive trials (target present), the intercepts were equal. This is consistent with the *activation* hypothesis described above: There are minimal decoding differences when the presentation of a target can prime the word about to be seen. This effect is maximum when display size is 1 and it is the target. However, there is an increasing ability difference as the set size increases to 7; this is reflected in a small—but significant—slope difference of about 100 milliseconds. When the target was absent (right panel of Figure 1), the situation might be slightly different. Even at set size 1, high-ability readers were faster, although this was not reflected in different intercepts, and low-ability readers were especially slow at the largest set size. Again, there was a significant slope difference. Thus, whether one considers strictly the data (a significant set size × ability interaction) or the best fit straight lines, the conclusion is that for this sample, low-ability readers have a slow *rate* of word decoding, not just a slower composite of the processing factors that are present in any trial. The rate parameter in this case can be interpreted as the time to identify a word in the display and compare it with the target word in memory.

There is at least one study that did not find slope differences between high- and low-ability readers. Katz and Wicklund (1971) had subjects search either a two- or three-word display for a word target. There were main effects of ability (intercept differences) but no interaction of ability with set size (slope differences). It is possible that population differences are responsible for the differences (Katz and Wicklund's subjects were two years older). However, it is also possible that larger display sizes are necessary in order to detect slope differences. For example, it is clear from the negative trials shown in Figure 1, that slope differences would not have been observed for set size one through five; the lines would have been parallel. It is conceivable that with a large set size, some less able readers change their scanning strategies and the rate difference includes some additional variance

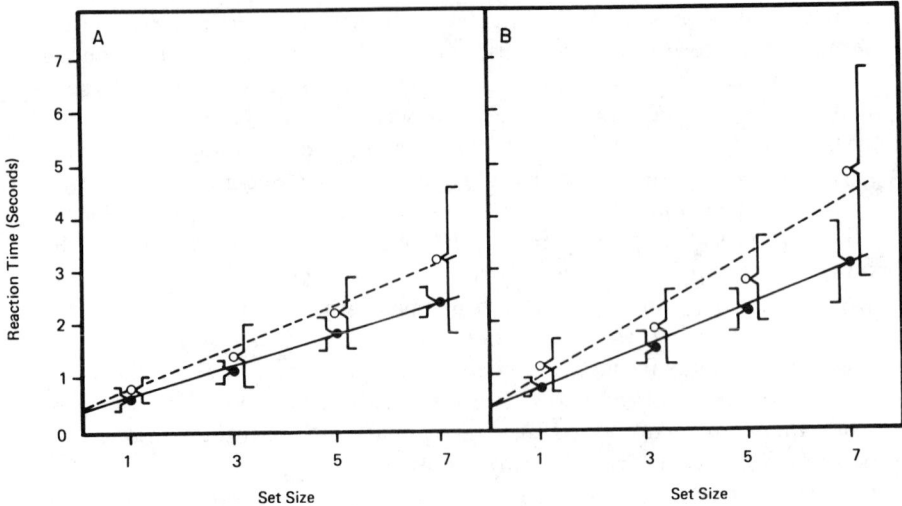

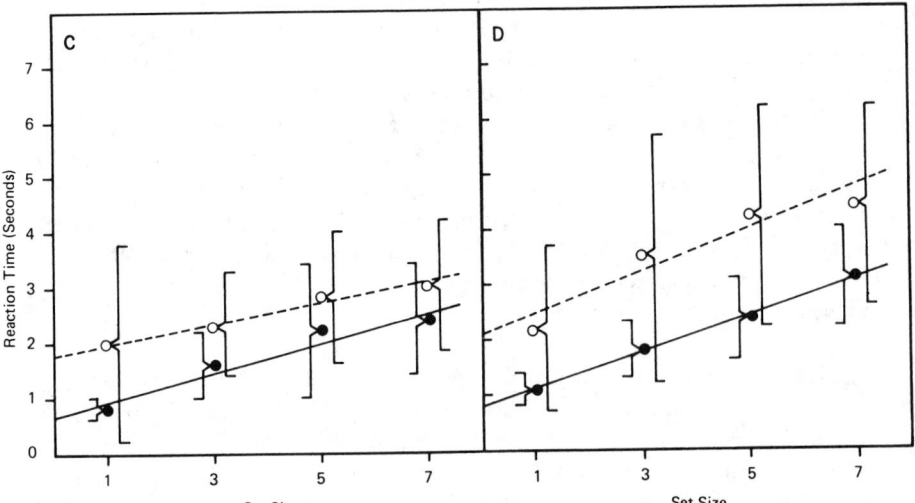

FIGURE 1. Word search and semantic category data for skilled and less skilled third grades. (**A**) Target-present word search data. ●————● Skilled (RT = .24 + .31 S). ○---○ Less skilled (RT = .23 + .41 S). (**B**) Target-absent word search data. ●————● Skilled (RT = .38 + .40 S). ○---○ Less Skilled (RT = .36 + .58 S). (**C**) Target-present semantic category data. ●————● Skilled (RT = .71 + .26 S). ○---○ Less skilled (RT = 1.8 + .18 S). (**D**) Target-absent semantic category data. ●————● Skilled (RT = .78 + .33 S). ○---○ Less skilled (RT = 2.1 + .37 S). Data points are means of subject medians.

possibly due to rescanning. On the other hand, the positive trials (Figure 1) do not show this possibility, but rather seem to reflect a constant slope effect. Nevertheless, it is easy to imagine that had the data shown in Figure 1 been restricted to sets of sizes two and three, statistically parallel lines might have been obtained. It is difficult to be confident about linear functions based on two points. In any case, such comparisons point to the difficulty of making individual difference comparisons across procedures and subject samples that differ even slightly.

Memory Scan In visual scan, rate (slope) differences include two elementary components: decoding and memory comparison. Thus, a rate difference could mean that reading ability is associated with either or both of these elementary components. By contrast, in backward memory search, the main component of the scan rate seems to be the rate of mental comparison. The subject is presented first with a list of items to be stored in memory followed by a probe item. The measure is the time to decide that the probe item is or is not in the memory set and the key variable is the size of the memory set; that is, the number of items presented to the subject. Differences in slope are taken to be differences in the rate of item comparison in memory. This task has been used as an individual-difference measure among college students (Chiang & Atkinson, 1976; Hunt, Frost, & Lunneborg, 1973, pp. 87–122). Data comparing high- and low-ability readers of the sort under discussion are scarce. However, Keating and Bobbitt (1978) compared 9-, 13-, and 17-year-olds on a digit-memory search task. The ability measure was not reading, but performance on the nonverbal Raven's Matrices. The groups can be characterized as superior and average (not below average) in ability. Keating and Bobbitt found significant intercept and slope differences between superior and average subjects, although only intercept values were related to age. The 9-year-old group, which is most comparable to the samples in the reading-ability studies, showed a clear slope difference of about 60 milliseconds. The 17-year-old group did not show a clear slope difference.

Kail, Chi, Ingram, and Danner (1977) and Kail and Marshall (1978) have reported results of memory-scan experiments more relevant to the subjects under consideration. However, their tasks tapped complex verbal processes, rather than simple verbal processes. Kail and Marshall (1978) varied set size by having third- and fourth-grade subjects read either one, two, or three (unrelated) sentences and then answer a yes–no question. While "yes" answers were generally unaffected by set size, latency to answer "no" questions increased as set size increased from one to three, especially for low-skill readers. Kail and Marshall suggest that skilled and less skilled readers differ in their memory search rates. Especially interesting, in light of the present hypothesis concerning retrieval, is that Kail and Marshall found no ability difference in a situation where the necessary information was already activated. This was a situation (Kail & Marshall, 1978, Experiment 4) in which subject response time was measured to verify an answer following a statement and question, exemplified as follows:

1. The man drank the milk.
2. What did the man drink?
3. Milk/water

The measure taken was the time to verify (or falsify) number 3 after the first two have been read. This suggests, consistent with the activation hypothesis offered above, that when the information is already *activated*, reader ability differences are reduced. In the Kail and Marshall experiment, asking the question has activated the answer.

The memory-scan data, considering both Keating and Bobbitt (1978) and Kail and Marshall (1978), is inconclusive because the former did not compare children of average and below average reading ability and the latter used a complex verbal processing task rather than a simple one. This latter difference is nontrivial insofar as memory capacity differences might be involved. That is, when subjects have to search memory for as many as three *unrelated* sentences, there is reason to doubt that the memory load is within capacity limits. The sort of memory-scan processes under discussion are those that take place safely within the limits of short-term memory. Complex verbal processes may or may not lie within the limits of memory capacity, but simple verbal processes must by definition. At this point, although there is evidence to suggest simple memory search rate differences related to reading ability, there is little reason to suppose such differences are a matter of simple verbal comparison processes.

SEMANTIC ACCESS

A second simple verbal process is obtaining relevant semantic information from a single word. If word decoding is a part of *semantic access*, then it is possible that semantic access differences between high- and low-ability readers are accounted for by decoding differences. Evidence from my research group indicates that semantic access time is a source of ability differences beyond decoding. In the Perfetti and Bell (Note 2) experiments referred to previously, one of the tasks required semantic-category decisions. Subjects were provided with a category name and, for a block of eight trials, had to decide whether a given display contained an instance of the category. The decision latencies are shown in Figure 1 as a function of set size. High-ability readers were faster than low-ability readers at all set sizes.

Figure 1 shows that the function relating set size to semantic decisions was quite linear with low variance for high-ability readers and not-so-linear with large variance for low-ability readers. The lines for high ability and low ability are relatively parallel, implicating intercept differences and not slope differences. However, the poor linear fit for low-ability readers makes any linear comparison suspect. In order to minimize any anomalies due to nonlinearity, a comparison of categorization and word search for set size = 1 is useful. Less skilled subjects, on this measure, show a marginal increase in decision time.

An index of semantic processing, beyond decoding, is obtained by subtracting, for each subject, the word-decision (WD) time from the semantic-decision (SD) time for set size 1, SD–WD. SD–WD can be taken as an index of semantic-processing time controlled for word-decoding time. The mean SD–WD for low-ability readers was 1050 milliseconds and the mean SD–WD for high-ability readers was 209 milliseconds. Keep in mind that a set size of 1 includes general task components as well as rate components of decoding and comparison. Nonetheless, it appears that differences between high- and low-ability readers for single-word comparisons go beyond simple decoding. As set size increased, this SD–WD difference is maintained for size 3 (950 milliseconds) and 5 (1000 milliseconds) and disappears for size 7. At the largest set size, both ability groups had essentially zero SD–WD scores. Thus, semantic-access differences, as measured by this difference between category- and word-level decisions, do seem to exist between some high- and low-ability readers. Unlike word processing, however, they seem to reflect mainly intercept rather than slope components.

Given these results, one could characterize the ability differences in semantic access *rate* as accounted for by word identification. However, low-ability readers do exhibit additional semantic processing difficulties in some task-specific components reflected in intercept. Such components are usually assumed to include orientation and response-execution components that occur once (regardless of display size). Since these intercept differences were so much smaller for word decisions than semantic decisions, it is possible to conjecture that response execution and display orientation are not responsible for the semantic-access difference. What component is in the intercept of a semantic decision but not in the intercept of a word decision? One possibility is the activation of the relevant semantic-category links, or the initiation of a search process for semantic attributes. Once initiated, there are no rate differences for semantic comparisons, but the initial activation of the relevant semantic attributes is subject to an inertia that is not present when simple decoding (word decision) is required. Of course, there are other possibilities, and the difficulty of drawing solid conclusions on the semantic-access question is apparent. More data that eliminate the uncertainty of intercept interpretations and processing models that enable more precise interpretations of semantic access are needed.

LETTER AND LETTER-PATTERN RECOGNITION

To the extent that decoding processes are a part of reading-ability differences, the processes by which letters and letter patterns are recognized are candidates for individual differences. The letter-recognition processes are not the simple form and shape perception that have been the subject of dyslexia theories (e.g., Orton, 1925). When the evidence is examined critically, such strictly perceptual factors do not seem to be significant ability factors as Vellutino (1979) has shown. The letter-recognition processes that make a difference in reading ability presuppose the elementary ability to discriminate letter forms and the ability to retrieve letter names; instead, these include the speed and efficiency with which letters can be identified and assembled into word-decoding units. By assumption, these units are something less than a word (the units, when assembled, add up to a word).

It is unwarranted and unnecessary to suppose that these units correspond to generalized units such as syllables (Spoehr & Smith, 1973), or to morphemic boundaries (Taft, 1979), or orthographic patterns (Venezky & Massaro, 1979, pp. 85–107). However, the assumption that strings of letters that are permissible and familiar achieve some status as higher-order units is pervasive across both perceptually described (Gibson, 1971) and information-processing theories (e.g., LaBerge & Samuels, 1974; Massaro, 1975). It is difficult to describe such units without referring to knowledge of orthographic patterns as well as processing. However, as Glushko (1981, pp. 61–84) demonstrates, it is necessary only to assume that the reader's memory stores the letter patterns of words. Thus orthographic knowledge can be inferred rather than stored directly. In any event, a particular "unit" of recognition does not have to be stated. The critical processing event converts a decodable letter string into its speech form or performs some other task on a letter string that tests the ability to take advantage of the structure of the letter pattern. Pseudowords and nonword syllables have such structure. The questions of interest include the following: Are there ability differences in processing pseudowords? Are there ability differences in processing letter strings that are not pseudowords? Do differences in the latter account for differences in the former?

We know that reader ability differences in vocalization latency are larger for pseudowords than for words (Hogaboam & Perfetti, 1978). However, comparisons of pseudowords with nonwords are what is needed. In the Perfetti and Bell (Perfetti, Note 1) search experiments described, there was a task in which subjects search for pseudowords in display sets of varying size. Pseudoword targets were one- or two-syllable and display words were varied accordingly. Again, the same target was searched for eight consecutive trials to eliminate any memory-for-target problem. The results: skilled readers were faster than less skilled readers, but more interesting their speed advantage was greater for two-syllable than one-syllable words and greater for multiple displays than for single-item displays. The syllable effect supports the assumption that decoding multiple units (of syllable size) is extra processing work for the less able reader. The set size effect, which can be seen in Figure 2, suggests a processing *rate* difference. The slopes for both positive and negative trials were larger for less able readers. That slope differences rather than just intercept differences were obtained strongly suggests that the process of decoding an orthographically regular letter pattern and comparing it with a memory target is a source of reading-ability difference.

In a separate experiment, these subjects performed a consonant bigram search task. The consonant bigrams were random (unstructured) pairings, thus allowing an index of processing much more akin to simple visual scanning. For example, the target WP was searched in one five-item display of MQ, WT, TL, WP, XP. Although this experiment has a few minor design differences from the previously described search tasks (most notably, blocks of 32 trials instead of eight) it can offer a useful comparison: Are slope differences found for this task as well as the pseudoword task? The search functions are shown in Figure 2. They reveal small intercept and slope differences for positive trials, although it is clear that with set size 1, there is no ability difference. For negative trials, presumably the fair test for an exhaustive search assumption, there are also small intercept and slope differences but with a better linear fit. The 70-millisecond slope difference for negative trials is only marginally significant.

To examine whether small ability differences in bigram search could account for large ability differences in pseudoword search, a "decoding" score was derived for each subject by subtracting bigram search time from pseudoword search time. This P–B score is analogous to the SD–WD score discussed previously, but it does *not* have the same interpretation because, unlike SD and WP, pseudowords and bigrams did *not* differ in the level of decision required. Instead, the difference score represents the same decision level (identity match) for two different types of letter strings. One short, unpronounceable, and unpredictable by orthography; the other longer, pronounceable, and orthographically regular. The results of this analysis were that less skilled readers had larger difference scores than skilled readers, but the difference was significantly longer for multiple-item displays than for single-item (set size = 1) displays. This is consistent with the following interpretation: there are genuine pseudoword processing-rate differences

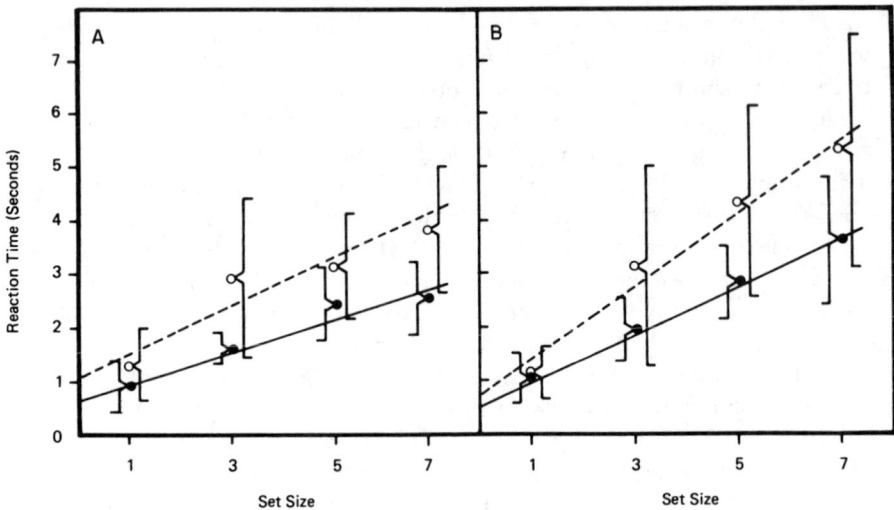

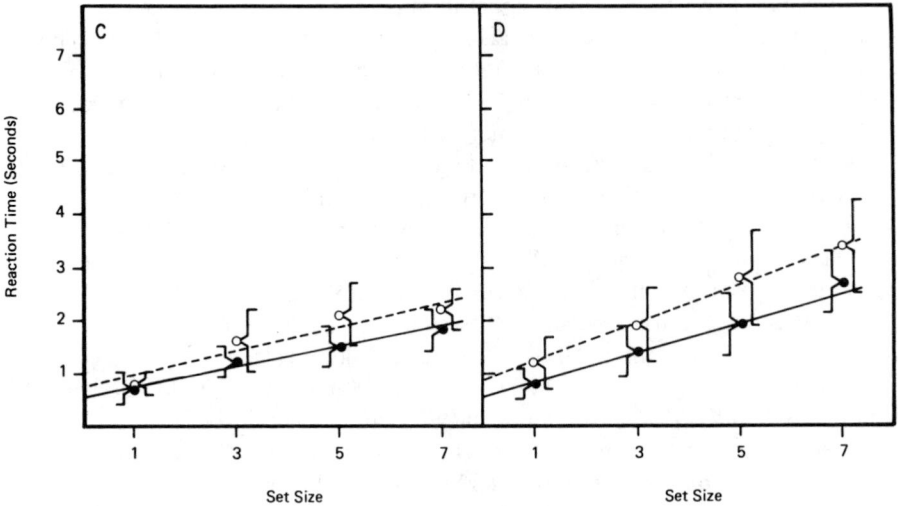

FIGURE 2. Search data for pseudowords and bigrams for third-grade subjects. (**A**) Target-present pseudoword data. ●———● Skilled (RT = .75 + .28 S). ○---○ Less skilled (RT = 1.12 + .42 S). (**B**) Target-absent pseudoword data. ●———● Skilled (RT = .52 + .45 S). ○---○ Less skilled (RT = .72 + .69 S). (**C**) Target-present bigram data. ●———● Skilled (RT = .56 + .19 S). ○---○ Less skilled (RT = .79 + .22 S). (**D**) Target-absent bigram data. ●———● Skilled (RT = .56 + .28 S). ○---○ Less skilled (RT = .92 + .35 S).

that do not seem to be accounted for by simple encoding of constituent letters. Decodable letter strings show the ability difference most clearly and this difference is seen in rate of processing (slope) both directly and in a difference measure that takes consonant bigram search time into account.

A related letter-recognition ability may be the use of serial position structure. Mason (1975) found that high-ability readers were better than low-ability readers at taking advantage of the positional predictability of a letter. For example, in a six-letter word, *F* is more likely to occur in Position 1 and less likely to occur in Position 5, whereas the reverse is true for *N*. However, when Massaro, Venezky, and Taylor (1979) replicated these search experiments controlling for orthographic regularity, they found that letter position was a relatively minor ability factor.

In some related experiments by Perfetti and Bell (Note 2), subjects performed either forward search (target first, then display) or backward search for target letters. Although high-ability readers showed a general speed advantage in forward search, the advantage was unrelated either to letter position or orthographic structure. In agreement with Massaro et al. (1979), they found search time to be mainly a function of visual-feature overlap between target and display. In backward search (display first, then target), Perfetti and Bell (Note 2) found that the orthographic regularity of the string did influence search accuracy and that its effect was greater for skilled readers. Letter position predictability had only a slight effect. Overall, the studies of Mason (1975), Massaro et al. (1979), and Perfetti and Bell (Note 2) suggest that orthographic structure may provide a significant ability factor for tasks of letter search. This effect is independent of a smaller and less reliable effect of position information.

The source of word-decoding superiority may be traced to letter-pattern recognition, that is, knowledge and use of letter-concurrence constraints. This, in turn, may reflect the ability to rapidly activate reliable phonetic codes associated in memory with these units. In a modification of the experiments of Perfetti and Bell (Note 2), encoding time for the letter string and the memory interval between the letter string and the probe letter were varied independently. An important result was that when low-ability readers were given more encoding time (1.5 seconds) they performed comparably to high-ability readers given less encoding time (.33 seconds) and they took advantage of orthographic structure. Low-ability readers with less encoding time did not take advantage of structure. Moreover, regardless of encoding time, low-ability readers were more affected by an increased memory interval between letter string and probe (4 seconds compared with .5 second). Low-ability readers appear vulnerable to a decoding problem that can show itself when either encoding or memory demands are present.

The exact source of ability differences in recognition and decoding of multiletter patterns remains in need of further research. There seems to be little reason to suppose that these ability differences are traceable to initial stages of visual processing (see Vellutino, 1979; and experiments by Mason & Katz, 1976). The ability to recognize individual letters in isolation is probably not sufficient to account for decoding differences, although this conclusion is less clear. More research that allows separation of processing-rate factors from other response-time factors would be helpful. For now, the Perfetti and Bell data (Figure 2) suggest that rate differences in letter scanning may not account for rate differences in decoding.

DIFFERENCES AMONG OLDER READERS

It is not necessarily the case that individual talents in reading are attributable to the same factors among older readers as younger ones. Children in the second through sixth grade have recently completed formal reading instruction. Adolescents and adults may have mastered the sort of simple processes that are implicated in ability differences among young readers. Indeed, since adult studies typically involve college students, we may expect individuals who represent below average or less skilled fourth-graders to be selected out of the sample. For such a group, so apparently different, the question of whether simple verbal processes can account for general differences in verbal comprehension is especially interesting.

COLLEGE STUDENTS

Jackson and McClelland (1979) carried out a series of experiments with college undergraduates as subjects. Reading ability was defined by performance on passages designed especially for the research. Subjects' reading times for the passages and the accuracy of their answers to short-answer comprehension questions were both taken into account in deriving a measure of "effective reading speed," the arithmetic product of reading speed and comprehension. In addition, there was a listening comprehension test based on the same paragraphs and verbal and quantitative college aptitude scores. Laboratory tasks tapping several processes were given to high- and low-ability subjects. Unlike early research by Jackson and McClelland (1975), which contrasted superior individuals with average ones, the sample of this study could be characterized as high and low reading ability, *relative* to college freshmen and sophomores in the population. High-ability readers were in the top quartile of effective reading speed and low-ability readers were in the bottom quartile.

One important result is that reading ability was not related to performance on simple letter identification, measured either by single letter report thresholds or double letter ("letter separation") report accuracy. This result, agreeing with Jackson and McClelland (1975) clearly indicates that simple single letter recognition is not a primary ability factor for college readers.

What about simple decoding processes? One set of tasks involved same–different decisions for single letters, synonyms, and homonyms, and nonletter patterns (two-item sequences of plus and square). Ability differences were found in all tasks, even the ostensibly nonlinguistic pattern matching task and the simple letter-matching tasks. Thus, Jackson and McClelland's (1979) subjects cannot be characterized as differing only in decoding ability, insofar as the matching paradigm is concerned.

A multiple display task, similar to the one previously described, was also used by Jackson and McClelland (1979). Targets and displays were single letters and set size was two, four, or six letters. Ability differences were found only in intercept and not in slope. Thus, high-ability college readers can be characterized as differing from low-ability college readers in some component independent of display size, for example, response speed, display orientation, but not rate of letter processing per se.

One other task of Jackson and McClelland (1979) was an auditory memory-span task. Similar to a standard digit-span task, it required subjects to recall—in order—a string of auditorially presented letters following a 1-second interval. Fast readers recalled significantly more than slow readers.

Taking all tasks into account, Jackson and McClelland (1979) report correlations that support the following conclusions. Listening comprehension (measured on the same paragraphs) is the strongest correlate of reading speed. Controlling for listening comprehension, a significant correlation remains between matching performance and reading speed. The task that contributes most to this correlation is "letter match." The contribution of this factor is interpreted as a name retrieval factor since all patterns in the matching task were nameable and performance did not correlate with the letter-threshold tasks. The importance of the naming component was supported by a second experiment that showed no ability difference in matching dot patterns. In an additional experiment with this population, Jackson (1980) found that high- and low-ability readers did not differ in time to match nonsense figures but did differ when the matches were based on names arbitrarily associated with the figures. Such results strongly support the assumption that adult ability differences do not lie in immediate perceptual processes that occur prior to contact with names in memory.

Jackson and McClelland (1979) concluded, on the basis of a multiple regression analysis of their data, that three ability differences were tapped by their tasks. The most important correlate of reading ability was listening comprehension. A second major component was access to letter codes from print, tapped mainly by the letter-matching task. Although there were significant correlations between ability and tasks of homophone matching (Experiment 1) and pseudohomophone matching (Experiment 2) that might be taken to reflect decoding ability, Jackson and McClelland (1979) did not suggest a separate decoding factor. Rather, the letter-access factor could account for all the correlation between ability and pseudohomophone matching times.

Jackson's (1980) experiments, at least in part, point to a similar conclusion. There are two major ability factors, a general language factor and a general visual-access factor. The visual access factor is general rather than alphabetic because Jackson (1980) found that reading ability was related to the speed of matching categories of drawings of objects as well as to letter name match. Thus, taken together, the Jackson and McClelland (1979) and Jackson (1980) experiments suggest that a major ability difference lies in the speed of access to a name-referenced memory location. The ability does not depend on alphabetic inputs but it does depend on memory access, as opposed to simple perception. Thus, in the terms of the framework offered in this chapter, decoding is not, but name retrieval (access) is, a major ability factor. Letter recognition is not a factor independent of name access. A general language-ability factor (reflected in language comprehension) is independent of this name-access factor.

Part of this picture is consistent with the results for elementary school readers, but some suggest different ability factors in older readers. The identification of a general language factor is consistent. Among children, reading ability is highly associated with memory for *spoken* language (Perfetti & Goldman, 1976) as well as memory for written language (Goldman, Hogaboam, Bell, & Perfetti, 1980). Furthermore, Berger and Perfetti (1977) found that differences between high- and low-ability sixth-grade readers both in the recall of a text and in the answers to comprehension tests were as large when subjects heard the text as when they read it. Curtis (1980), in a thorough multiple-task experiment, found that listening comprehension contributed unique variance to reading ability measures; further, for older readers (fifth grade), the contribution of listening comprehension was greater than for younger readers (second grade). Correspondingly, decoding factors accounted for less unique variance among older readers, although there remained large ability group differences. There is fairly clear evidence that reading ability depends on language ability in a general way. This relationship is seen strongly among young readers and adults, at least for readers beyond the second grade.

However, there appears to be an ability factor that is not continuous across this age range. Jackson and McClelland (1979; Jackson, 1980) conclude that ability differences in decoding can be accounted for by differences in visual name access. By contrast, studies in my laboratory suggest ability differences in decoding exist and are not reducible to more elementary processes. It is possible, of course, that these different conclusions reflect genuine age-related differences. Adult readers are not children and, in the college population, have probably been selected from the average and above average elementary school population. However, the *direction* of the children–adult differences does not encourage this conclusion. College-age readers show differences at the name-retrieval level, a more fundamental process than decoding. If the development of higher level abilities build on lower level abilities, we might expect differences to become negligible at lower levels and noticeable at higher levels. In other words, we might expect letter recognition or name retrieval to be a more important factor for younger readers than for adult readers. Instead, the data seem to say the opposite. Decoding differences do not depend on letter recognition or name retrieval for young readers as they do for adults.

It is quite possible that ability factors for children and adults are not different. The tasks used by Jackson and McClelland (1979) did not include naming tasks, whereas these were the basis of the Perfetti et al. (1978) conclusion that naming time independent of alphabetic input was not the only factor. Similarly, Jackson and McClelland (1979) concluded that letter-processing rate was not an ability factor; however, they did not test units larger than letters in multiunit displays. Thus, the conclusion that rate of processing differences occur at orthographic pattern levels may prove valid for adults as well as for children. In that light, it is possible that adult readers (and children) differ in a number of components that would be reflected in intercept values quite independent of material. The fact that Jackson (1980) found differences in RT to line drawings and letters in single displays is consistent with this. It would be interesting to see whether rate (slope) differences in object categorization were found. Without comparable tasks, it is difficult to compare research on younger and older readers.

HIGH-SCHOOL READERS

Intermediate in age to the two groups under discussion are the high-school subjects of Frederiksen (1978a, pp. 153–169; 1978b; 1981, pp. 361–386). Frederiksen's sample of 20 high-school students was divided into four quartile groups, based on their Nelson–Denny reading test scores. Although the sample size per group ($N = 5$) may seem rather small, there are some interesting results for ability differences. Frederiksen (1978a, 1978b) found that higher ability readers had faster letter-scan rates than lower ability readers. The task was not comparable to either the bigram search task of Perfetti and Bell (Perfetti, Note 1) or to the letter-search task of Jackson and McClelland (1979). Instead, slope values were inferred from the serial position occupied by two adjacent letters within a briefly presented four-letter array. Simultaneous masking of the other two letter positions enabled this comparison. Thus rate differences are the slopes of the function relating letter identification latency to position within a four-letter display. It is not clear whether such slope differences represent letter-scan rate differences or limitations on memory readout imposed by the task. The latter possibility arises because subjects had to report what they saw from a brief exposure. Accuracy results, which are not reported, are necessary in this respect. More straightforward is the finding that high- and low-ability readers differed in vocalization latency to words and pseudowords. Interestingly, the word differences are mainly due to the lowest group contrasted with the others whereas pseudoword latencies appear to distinguish among all groups.

In Frederiksen (1978b), the data from these same 20 subjects are correlated with individual reading scores and interpreted within a structural model that assumes five component skills. On the basis of the structural model analysis, Frederiksen concludes that multiple-letter encoding is a major predictor of general reading ability.[4] This refers to slope differences on the bigram scan task (described above) plus differences in name level, same–different letter judgments (*Aa* versus *Ad*), and facilitation due to bigram probabilities in the bigram scan task. This factor is one which reflects the ability to encode letter strings without facilitation of one sort (letter-sequence redundancy) or another (letter-category facilitation).

Whether there are differences between this analysis of high-school ability and either the college-level ability (Jackson & McClelland, 1979) or the elementary-level ability is again problematic—partly a question of the particular tasks used and the choice of models to test the intertask correlations. Frederiksen's analysis does not allow a general name-retrieval (access) factor nor a general language factor, and Jackson and McClelland (1979) do not allow a multiple letter-encoding factor. Still, it is possible to attempt a tentative characterization of reading ability across the three age levels, based on the work discussed along with some inferring.

In the elementary-school years, general reading ability has a strong decoding component that is a result of processing efficiency for alphabetic materials. This efficiency includes a general name-access-and-retrieval component, such that digits, pictures, and other nonalphabetic stimuli may produce differences in processing time. However, such differences are smaller and less reliable than alphabetic input differences. Whereas *some*

---

[4]A second major factor is referred to as "automaticity of articulation," essentially the *duration* of vocalization for pseudowords having extra-processing requirements (either two syllables instead of one or a complex vowel spelling instead of a simple one). As with most of Frederiksen's measures, these measures depend on difference scores. It is not clear whether we should think of this as a strictly speech-based skill or a decoding skill.

low-ability children have name-retrieval problems, there are many without such problems who nonetheless are less efficient processors of printed linguistic inputs. This factor seems to be more than single letter encoding and includes genuine rate differences for multiunit pronounceable pseudo-words. These factors continue to be important through high school and with adult readers.

For college adults, the population changes; hence, the range of abilities on the tasks in question changes. Those whose *only* or *main* problem in elementary school was decoding are either not in the college population or they have mastered decoding-related processes to an extent that the limiting performance factor lies elsewhere; that is, in name-code retrieval. In a sense, their reading ability matches their general intellectual ability and within the latter, there is a fairly narrow range—above average to superior. Along the way, high-school-level ability reflects both higher levels of skill than elementary-school-age ability and less selectivity than college-level ability. Decoding factors remain critical but they include more of the processing factors associated with simple processing rates and less (perhaps) with use of linguistic structure. At all levels, general language ability is a major limiting factor.

Thus, by this account, reading ability differences at the lower levels of skill are accounted for by simple verbal processes, including decoding and, apparently, semantic access. At higher levels, these factors remain only as they are associated with generalized processes that are perhaps less susceptible to training. It may be worth adding to this conjecture the apparent fact that at extremely low ability levels the generalized naming process is also seen independent of decoding (Denckla & Rudel, 1976). Thus decoding, over and above name retrieval, is not a critical ability factor for individuals whose general name retrieval ability is extremely low nor for individuals whose decoding *and* name retrieval abilities are very high.[5]

READING ABILITY AND MEMORY

I have referred to the processes under discussion as "simple verbal processes," although encoding multiple letter displays may or may not come under this category, depending on theoretical preferences as well as task and individual skill factors. The complex verbal processes are those in which (1) repeated access to a name in permanent memory is required; and (2) more

[5]There is at least one reservation I would add to this account. Studies of adult readers have seldom used sufficiently difficult decoding tasks. The sensitivity of the tasks thus are in question.

than one name must be retained. An ability difference in memory capacity is a good candidate for producing ability differences in reading.

Perfetti and Lesgold (1979, pp. 141–183) argued that an active verbal short-term memory is an ability factor in reading, whereas the storage capacity of a general short-term memory is not. Thus Perfetti and Goldman (1976) found that probe-digit performance, a paradigm short-term memory capacity measure (Waugh & Norman, 1965) did not distinguish high- and low-ability readers in the third and fifth grade who were comparable in IQ. However, they were distinguished by an analogous test of probe-discourse memory. In both tasks, output demands are minimal, the subject producing only the element following the probe, spoken digits in one case and words from spoken texts in the other. The critical difference may be the memory demands added by ongoing language processing. The latter would seem to test the operation of an active working memory (Baddeley & Hitch, 1974, pp. 47–89; Newell & Simon, 1972), and this is probably the memory function critical to reading ability. Perfetti and Lesgold (1979) also suggested that coding and storage processes would compete for functional working memory and for low-ability readers, for whom coding is less facile, functional working memory differences would become significant.

This general hypothesis has been given dramatic support by Daneman and Carpenter (1980). They tested adult subjects' working memory. The key test was to recall final words from sentences read aloud by subjects. A memory-span measure was derived which was analogous to digit-span measures; namely, the number of sentences read before ordered memory for the final word from each fell below criterion. This working memory-span measure correlated highly with comprehension accuracy on sort passages and with verbal SAT scores. Especially interesting was its correlation ($r = .90$) with performance on a pronoun reference test which varied the text distance between a referent and its later pronominal mention. Greater distance implies greater text demands on working memory, and correct pronoun identification did decrease as a function of text distance, except for readers with the highest working memory spans. A span measure involving word lists, rather than sentences produced smaller correlations, not significant, with comprehension measures. In a second experiment, Daneman and Carpenter (1980) found that their sentence-span measure correlated significantly with listening comprehension, although not quite as much as with reading comprehension. Interestingly, it did not matter whether the span test itself was written or aural. Given the difference between sentence-measured span and list-measured span, the degree to which working memory is actively taxed by processing demands seems important. The functional processing resources seem to be the limiting factor and they seem to be general factors, not print-specific ones.

These are adult data but they are quite consistent with ability differences among children (Kail & Marshall, 1978; Perfetti & Goldman, 1976). Working memory seems to be a limiting factor in complex verbal processes regardless of age. It seems unlikely, however, that a working memory factor is independent of the simple verbal processes discussed previously. More likely, there is a trade-off between speed of processing and memory ability (Lesgold & Perfetti, 1978). The modification of the backward letter-search experiment described previously (Perfetti & Bell, Note 2) demonstrated this tradeoff. Low-skill subjects given more encoding time performed as accurately on backward letter search as skilled readers with less encoding time. However, with a slightly longer (4 second) memory interval their processing difficulties were reflected in longer decision times. Skilled readers were unaffected by this increase in memory interval. Thus, encoding and memory factors both work against low-skill readers in such a situation.

Given an interest in simplifying explanations and results (such as those just described), a question arises as to whether our ability theories should handicap the low-ability reader with both working memory and decoding problems. Is there a single mechanism to account for both? The problem is that letter-recognition and word-recognition measures are clearly simple verbal processes that require, in most cases, a single access event to a name in memory. It is quite reasonable to say that in complex reading tasks the coding and memory requirements interact to produce ineffective verbal processing (cf. Perfetti & Lesgold, 1977, pp. 141–183). But this account can do little to explain memory-access differences of single decoding tasks. If there is any hope to discover a single mechanism rather than two, it would seem to require explaining memory limitations by coding inefficiency, rather than vice versa. There are suggestions in Lesgold and Perfetti (1978; Perfetti & Lesgold, 1977) along these lines, but a reasonably specific proposal is still lacking.

VERBAL INTELLIGENCE

A subject whose ability is measured on a reading-comprehension test is in a reading-ability experiment. A subject whose ability is measured on a verbal-abilities test is in a verbal-abilities experiment. Aside from such matters of definition, is being high verbal the same as being a high-ability reader? There is no answer to such questions in the absence of research with more attention to criteria-referenced ability tests. However, it seems likely that the verbal abilities important for verbal intelligence are the same as those that are important for reading. The difference, more often, will be one of level rather than type of knowledge. The college-level tests demand higher absolute verbal skill levels and are selectively taken by above-average readers. With that in mind, what simple verbal processes are involved in producing the wide range of general verbal abilities measured by college-level tests, such as the SAT?

The four simple verbal processes previously considered were letter recognition, decoding, semantic access, and name retrieval. Do these vary at the adult level as well? Name retrieval, for example, is a general performance-limiting factor that might be expected to have an effect even after letter recognition and decoding. Carroll (Note 3) summarized naming studies (Carroll, 1976; Carroll & White, 1973), concluding that picture-scanning speed is a parameter of individual differences. According to Carroll (Note 3), these differences in picture-naming were predictable from a set of psychometric tests, but mainly from a picture-naming test and not from other tests ostensibly more related to verbal ability (e.g., vocabulary).

A more typical procedure for examining name retrieval has been the letter-matching task first described by Posner and Mitchell (1967). The key ability question in this task concerns the difference between comparisons based on physical identities of printed letters (e.g., *AA*) and letter-name identities (e.g., *Aa*). Increasing differences between name identity (NI) and physical identity (PI) can be taken as a measure of name retrieval without name production. In the studies of Hunt and his colleagues, high- and low-verbal college students did not differ in PI match times although they did show small differences in NI match times (Hunt et al., 1973, pp. 87–122; Hunt et al., 1975). Hunt (1978), in summarizing studies of name matching and verbal ability, notes that such studies yield small but consistent correlations between verbal ability and the NI–PI difference in letter matching.

It appears from some of the data summarized in Hunt (1978), that ability differences in letter-name matching decrease with increasing abilities of the subjects. Nonuniversity adults show NI–PI differences of 110 milliseconds (Parkinson, Note 4) compared with 64 milliseconds for University of Washington high-verbal students, 190 milliseconds for 10-year-old children and 310 milliseconds for mildly mentally retarded children (Warren & Hunt, Note 6). A general picture emerging is that verbal ability, over a wide range, is associated with the time to perform a comparison based on the name of a letter. Importantly, since it is a difference score this name comparison controls the time to make comparison based on physical identity. Thus, while the complete lack of ability differences in physical matches reported by Hunt et al. (1975) is seldom found (see Carroll, 1976), the conclusion seems to be that, beyond mental comparisons based on shape identity, verbal ability differences are associated with speed of letter-name comparisons.

Carroll's (Note 3) discussion of data using the name-identity measures is informative. Although his review of studies measuring physical and name identity showed consistent physical identity differences, name identity provided a processing difference beyond physical identity, when task means for ability groups were compared. More interesting, perhaps, is Carroll's estimation of the NI–PI correlation of Jackson and McClelland's (1979) data on adult readers (discussed previously). The NI–PI difference was estimated to correlate .57 with short-passage, effective reading speed of Jackson and McClelland's (1979) subjects and nearly as highly with their verbal and quantitative aptitude scores, but nonsignificantly with listening comprehension. Certainly, reading ability and verbal ability arise from similar verbal processes, insofar as the retrieval of symbol names (at least letters) is important in both.

Note that in the letter-name-matching task, simple name retrieval is only one component. In fact, in a typical case, there are at least two name retrievals and a comparison process. In reading, it seems important to consider letter recognition (and decoding) processes as potentially independent of name-retrieval processes. The former, perforce, are components of reading; the latter, as general processes that are important in verbal tasks other than reading, are not. It is interesting that research on adult verbal intelligence has so exploited the letter-matching task and not picture or digit naming. The tacit assumption is that the process of interest is access to overlearned codes. Reading is the principle means for acquiring overlearned codes. College adults who differ in verbal ability may essentially represent the upper ranges of reading ability. Indeed, even the low-ability subjects are beyond the verbal ability of high-ability children, at least in terms of practice at simple verbal processes.

The question of rate of processing arises again in connection with adult verbal ability. Because the NI–PI difference is useful in controlling for subject preparedness and response execution, it is partly analogous to a name-processing rate measure. Thus, letter-scan tasks with multiple arrays should produce results comparable to NI–PI in the slope relating RT to set size. Apparently they do, although the relationship of slope to verbal ability is not striking (Chiang & Atkinson, 1976). Similarly, memory-search slopes appear to be related to verbal ability and to visual-scanning slopes (Chiang & Atkinson, 1976).

What of word decoding, aside from name retrieval and letter recognition? The effects reported by Perfetti and Hogaboam (1975) for children of different reading abilities have been found also for college students distinguished by vocabulary tests (Butler & Hains, 1979), as well as high-school students differing in reading ability (Frederiksen, 1978b). Moreover, Butler and Hains (1979) found that word length was a less significant factor for high-ability subjects, in agreement with the results of Hogaboam and Perfetti (1978) for reading ability.

In the case of children's reading ability, I suggested that differences in decoding ability seemed to go beyond both letter recognition and name retrieval. In the case of adult verbal ability, especially college students, this seems less tenable. Although studies using tasks appropriate for all three processes seem not to have been done, the studies on letter comparison and letter search implicate letter- and/or name-retrieval processes. Decoding differences, that is, processes of lexical access and retrieval from print, may depend on these.

Consider semantic access. In the case of children's reading ability, there remains some question as to whether or not access to semantic information stored with words is accounted for completely by word name access. Goldberg, Schwartz, and Stewart (1977) had college subjects classified as high and low verbal make same–different decisions for words based on physical identity (*deer–dear*), or category membership (*deer–elk*). The question is whether ability differences exist in category decisions beyond decoding (name identity). The answer from Goldberg et al. (1977) seems to be "no." Although ability differences in decoding were larger (363 milliseconds) than physical matches (136 milliseconds), category decision differences (360 milliseconds) were not greater than decoding differences. Hogaboam and Pellegrino (1978) used a category-decision task wherein single words and pictures were verified according to a prior semantic category. They report no correlation between verbal ability (SAT) of college subjects and speed of semantic decision. In light of other research showing name-level differences, such null results are difficult to explain. (In fact, Hunt, Davidson, & Lansman [Note 6]) report data showing name-level and category-level differences among adult subjects.) However, the point is that ability differences are typically found at lower levels of code access (letter, word, name retrieval) whereas additional differences in category level are not.

Finally, consider working memory. Just as reading ability is associated with working-memory capacity, so too is adult verbal ability. For example, Hunt et al. (1975) compared high- and low-verbal subjects in their ability to recall four visually presented letters following digit-shadowing task that intervened between input and recall. Low-ability subjects uniformly recalled less regardless of the number of intervening digits. Memory differences related to verbal ability are found also in digit-span tasks (Lyon, 1977). Such results are consistent with those of Daneman and Carpenter (1980) for reading ability of adults. Since coding differences in verbal ability are clearly indicated, it is not possible to be sure whether working-memory processes represent an additional source of individual differences or whether initial coding difficulty leads to memory loss.

In summary, there is reason to assume that children's reading ability, adult verbal ability, and adult reading ability can be accounted for by a common set of simple verbal processes. Processes of name retrieval, letter recognition, word decoding, and semantic access have been examined because they are patently involved in reading. Name retrieval, as a general mechanism of locating symbols in memory, is a fundamental processing limitation that seems to account for some of adult verbal processing ability. The remaining three processes, each more specific than name retrieval in some way, may not be critical in adult verbal ability *beyond* their reliance on general name-retrieval processes. However, for children with less verbal experience, there are specific linguistic processes still being acquired. At a given level of skill, for example, third-grade average ability, name-retrieval processes may set general processing limitations. However, specific code processes set stronger limits because knowledge and processes relevant for linguistic coding are still being acquired. By the time an individual is in college, especially given the selection factor, word-specific skills have reached a high level and differences in name retrieval are seen. By this account, even letter-recognition differences are a matter of name-retrieval differences. A representation of this account is shown in Figure 3.

It is consistent with data on children's reading ability and adult verbal ability to suggest that decoding speed does not make a constant contribution to differences in verbal processing rate. As Figure 3 illustrates, the contribution of decoding speed, *relative* to name retrieval, is high for children, especially low-skill children. For college adults, decoding speed has increased nearer to the potential limit set by name retrieval. Thus, the latter makes more of a rate-limiting contribution to verbal processing speed.

VERBAL KNOWLEDGE

Together with the simple verbal processes discussed before, variations in verbal knowledge can be important for general verbal ability. Indeed, despite the attention given to these processes, it is quite possible that verbal knowledge is the fundamental ability factor for reading and verbal intelligence. Three kinds of verbal knowledge were suggested in the introduction: word-form knowledge, rule knowledge, and concept knowledge. It is clear that, especially for reading ability, knowledge of form and rules is critical. Especially insofar as decoding processes are an important source of ability, the question can be asked whether decoding processes are important independent of the knowledge of form and rules. Knowing the formal relationship between a printed word and its phonemic form is one kind of knowledge that can underlie decoding. Knowing that, depending on

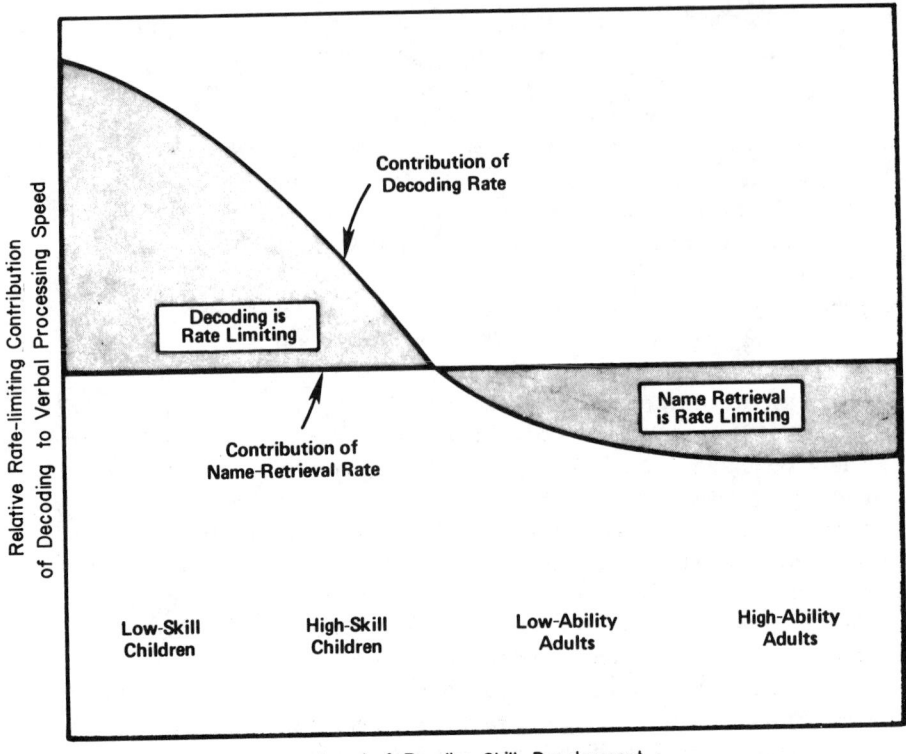

FIGURE 3. Schematic model of the relative contribution of decoding and name-retrieval rates to verbal processing with increasing reading skill development. Decoding is rate limiting at lower skill levels and name retrieval is rate limiting at higher skill levels.

orthographic environment, certain grapheme patterns map onto phonemic sequences, is a second kind of knowledge that can underlie decoding.

It is even possible, as Baron (1979; Baron & Strawson, 1976) has suggested, that individuals, at least children, differ fundamentally in whether their decoding processes are driven by form knowledge or rule knowledge; that is, whether an individual uses whole-word patterns or grapheme–phoneme translation as the basis of decoding. Baron and Strawson (1976) have referred to the former individuals as "Chinese" and the latter as "Phoenicians." There is, in fact, suggestive evidence that although verbal ability is supported by word-form knowledge, it is necessary to have rule knowledge to achieve high–ability levels. The children identified as Phoenicians tend to be better readers than those identified as Chinese. Indeed, encounters with unfamiliar words cannot be routinely successful without implicit rule knowledge, although it is possible to suggest otherwise (Glushko, 1981, pp. 61–84).

Rule knowledge is such a patently necessary part of decoding, at least as a backup system for word-form knowledge, that the debate should be shifted up one level: Are differences in word-decoding ability *only* a matter of word form and word-rule knowledge or are there additional differences in the processes that access such knowledge? In the earlier sections of this chapter, we assumed that there are processing differences over and above knowledge differences, in particular, that speed of decoding is critical. However, the evidence for this assumption is weak. It depends on decoding-speed differences in the absence of decoding-accuracy differences. More sensitive measures of knowledge might reveal knowledge differences. For example, does a low-ability reader know the orthographic rule relating syllable final *e* to vowel tenseness as well as the high-ability reader? Calfee, Venezky, and Chapman (Note 7) presented data showing that such knowledge differences were rather pronounced among younger readers. In general, sensitive tests of such knowledge among older readers have not been done, perhaps partly on the assumption that speed and automaticity are more critical.

Of course, this issue is difficult to decide fundamentally because it involves the trade-off between knowledge and process. To the extent that knowledge representation can be "slippery," there is a sense in which two knowledges that seem to be equivalent may not be. In other words, knowledge that is stable and context-free is not equivalent to knowledge that is labile and context-dependent, even though both sorts of knowledge may produce an accurate response in a given situation. How individual differences in verbal ability can be further understood as differences in the quality of verbal knowledge remains an important question deserving more attention than it has received.

Verbal Concept Knowledge

Access to word meanings is a central component of most verbal tasks, including reading. As in the case of decoding, there is again the question of whether individual differences in verbal ability include both knowledge and process. Unlike the case of decoding, however, process differences, over and above decoding and name retrieval, are less well established compared with knowledge differences. Even compared with decoding and name retrieval, concept knowledge is, on the face of it, a more important source of ability differences. Consider, for example, that the correlations between adult verbal ability and the speed of name retrieval (as measured by NI–PI) are typically about .3 (Hunt, 1978) whereas correlations between verbal ability and vocabulary are typically above .8 (Anderson & Freebody, Note 8). Indeed, tests of vocabulary knowledge directly and indirectly constitute a larger part of the SAT and similar standardized tests used to define verbal ability in individual-differences research. Thus, the question is not whether word–concept knowledge is an important component of ability, but rather, What is the nature of the relevant knowledge.

There are two general features of word-concept knowledge that are important for general verbal abilities. One is the number of word concepts familiar to a person and the other is the quality of the knowledge for a given word. These two aspects of meaning have been acknowledged in one form or another for some time; that is, breadth versus precision (Cronbach, 1942), and range versus precision (Kirkpatrick & Cureton, 1949), and simply richness of meaning (Dolch, 1927). Anderson and Freebody (Note 8) refer to *breadth* of word knowledge and *depth* of word knowledge, respectively, and those are the terms I will use here.

Several problems arise in assessing the breadth factor. As Anderson and Freebody (Note 8) point out, estimations of vocabulary knowledge are very sensitive to the form of the vocabulary test, and, in the case of a multiple-choice test, the nature of the foils. For these (and probably other) reasons, estimations of vocabulary size for a subpopulation vary over a vast range, with the highest estimate for college students being more than 12 times larger than the smallest estimate (Anderson & Freebody, Note 8). In any case, it is clear that the number of word concepts familiar to a person will play a role in his ability to read with understanding. Thus, vocabulary breadth is both a part of reading ability and a general verbal-ability factor.

In considering the relationship between breadth and depth and the role of each in verbal ability, a study by Curtis (Note 9) is informative. Curtis (Note 9) classified subjects as high or low in vocabulary knowledge on the basis of a multiple-choice test consisting of items from standardized tests. A second test was then composed, based on the difficulty and discriminability of the items: *known* words (95% of subjects correct), *discriminating* words (50% of subjects correct and discriminatory between high and low scorers) and *unknown* words (28% of subjects correct but not discriminating between high and low scores). In the second test, among other tasks, subjects were asked to define the words and were encouraged to provide any semantic association to an unfamiliar word. An interesting result of this second test was that low-knowledge subjects could provide little semantic information about discriminating and unknown words. They did *not* tend to produce vaguely related associations (e.g., "*desist* is like cease and desist," which was a response of a high-knowledge subject) but rather produced associations unrelated to the meaning of the word or no association at all.

This suggests, as Curtis (Note 9) observed, that low-knowledge subjects missed such items on the forced-choice vocabulary test, not from failure to evaluate semantic attributes of the foils, but because they were unfamiliar with the words. On the other hand, the low-knowledge subjects did produce relevant associations for the known words; however, half the time they could not give a synonym or correct explanation of the meaning, despite being able (twice) to chose the correct alternative in a multiple-choice test. A general conclusion, based on several analyses by Curtis (Note 9), is that vocabulary knowledge as measured by such tests is largely a matter of some minimal familiarity with the words and not a matter of deep semantic knowledge. This is interesting because of the ability implication: vocabulary ability, in the usual sense, includes a large component of very superficial semantic knowledge. Nevertheless, Curtis (Note 9) found that high and low subjects also differ in the depth of their semantic knowledge even when differences in semantic breadth (range) were taken into account. Low-knowledge individuals were not only familiar with fewer words—a fact sufficient to explain vocabulary score differences—they were also less precise in the knowledge of words with which they were familiar.

It was also possible in the Curtis (Note 9) study to relate performance on the vocabulary tests to ability scores based on the verbal SAT. Measures of decoding accuracy, based on identifying the vocabulary test words, semantic range (or breadth), and semantic depth, were all highly correlated with verbal SATs. In fact, the correlations of semantic range and semantic depth with verbal SATS were at least as high ($r = .92$ and $r = .91$, respectively) as they were with performance on the vocabulary test ($r = .88$ and $r = .83$, respectively). It is especially interesting that Curtis also found decoding accuracy to be highly related to verbal SAT scores of low-scoring subjects. Indeed, the results of multiple-regression and commonality analyses indicated that decoding accuracy accounted for more unique variance in the verbal-ability scores of low-ability subjects than did semantic depth (with range controlled). By contrast, high-ability subjects' scores were completely accounted for by the depth (with range controlled) of semantic knowledge. This fact seems to support the possibility, raised previously, that more sensitive measures of word-form and/or word-rule knowledge might well indicate significant ability differences among adults. In this case, the decoding weakness of low-verbal college students is seen in less-familiar words.

At the same time, high-vocabulary-knowledge subjects are faster at decoding, when accuracy is accounted for (Butler & Haines, 1979; Curtis, Note 9). Moreover, the word-identification times of high-vocabulary subjects are less affected by word length (Butler & Hains, 1979). Thus, part of what it means to be high verbal seems to be developing processes for word identification that are less sensitive to word length. And part of what it means is to acquire a passing familiarity with a large number of word concepts and a more refined semantic appreciation of a large percentage of those concepts. Understanding the relationship between these two abilities is a matter for future research.

BEYOND SIMPLE VERBAL PROCESSES

In this discussion, I have largely ignored complex verbal processes, exploring instead the role of simple verbal processes in verbal ability. A question to raise is whether, in general, differences in verbal ability can be reduced to these simple processes and conceptual knowledge. It is useful to consider what is involved in a complex verbal task such as understanding or writing a text. There are at least two ways that simple verbal processes may contribute to performance on these more complex verbal tasks. One way is that simple verbal processes may affect performance because they are *process-limiting* factors. A second possibility for such effects is that simple verbal processes are *learning-limiting* factors. The distinction between process-limiting factors and learning-limiting factors is that the former affect the *processes* occurring at the time of performance, whereas the latter have affected the prior acquisition of *knowledge* and *strategies* which are activated during the task.

One particular mechanism of process-limiting is that the overall rate of a complex verbal task is limited by the rate of execution of its elementary components. This does not necessarily imply that complex verbal processes are merely concatenations of simple ones. For example, a cascade model (McClelland, 1979) that makes weaker sequential assumptions about processes occurring together would imply that a low-level process would be rate-limiting for task performance. Even more completely interactive models (Rumelhart & McClelland, 1981, pp. 37–60) are consistent with the possibility that lower-level processes are rate-limiting. Applied to verbal ability differences, the rate-limiting hypothesis is that performance of a verbal task is limited by simpler component rates that vary with individuals. For example, this possibility has been demonstrated by Perfetti and Roth (1981, pp. 269–297) for the case of children's reading ability: In identifying words in context, low-ability readers are limited by their rate of basic context-free word decoding. It is possible to extend the rate-limiting principle to more complex text-processing tasks (e.g., Lesgold & Perfetti, 1978).

It is unlikely that this can account for all—or even most—of individual ability differences in more complex tasks. The learning-limiting factor is that any complex verbal performance will be limited by the prior acquisition of relevant conceptual knowledge and strategies for the task at hand. Evidence for the importance of knowledge is extensive over a range of tasks (Anderson, Reynolds, Schallert & Goetz, 1977; Bransford & Johnson, 1973, pp. 383–438; Dooling & Lachman, 1971; Spilich, Vesonder, Chiesi, & Voss, 1979). Any factor that inhibits activation of relevant knowledge during processing will limit performance. Thus, verbal ability differences are partly a question of individual differences in relevant knowledge. By the learning-limiting hypothesis, differences in such verbal knowledge arise in part because low-efficiency, simple processes have limited the acquisition of relevant knowledge. The fact that simple verbal-process-rate differences exist among adults can be taken as consistent with this possibility. At any given age, low-ability individuals have had less task-relevant verbal processing and have made less effective use of it. Hunt (1978) made a similar suggestion.

It is obvious that this is a "chicken or the egg problem" and that there is little reason to prefer the hypothesis that simple verbal processes limit acquisition of knowledge to the hypothesis that acquisition of knowledge allows simple verbal processes. Rather than making spurious arguments about what causes what, I suggest that we assume that simple verbal processes contribute to knowledge acquisition and that both simple verbal processes and knowledge acquisition contribute to verbal ability. Even if a stronger case could be made for reducing verbal-ability differences to simple processes, it may not be useful for deeper understanding of complex verbal performances. For example, consider the relatively simple knowledge involved in appreciating the difference in meaning between disinterested and uninterested. It is unlikely that such knowledge can be reduced to simple verbal processes. Similarly, the ability to write a coherent and stylish text seems to be more than simple verbal processes. Both these examples represent verbal abilities which are poorly understood. The former implies fairly simple but powerful semantic and morphological knowledge. The latter entails a number of complex verbal abilities producing very wide individual talents. Such abilities have to be examined in their own right by reference to their cognitive components and not only by reference to simple verbal processes. As such work progresses, there will be more to say about complex verbal abilities.

CONCLUSION AND SUMMARY

Individual differences in verbal processes may be traced, in part, to simple verbal processes. Although I have largely ignored complex verbal processes, this does not mean that differences in verbal ability can be reduced to the simple ones discussed here. It will be important for future research to establish individual differences in specific higher level verbal processes and examine other levels of explanation. Such differences in the ability to compose a text and to appreciate the distinctions between semantically related words are just two examples of the many verbal skills that differentiate individuals. That all these can be completely accounted for by simple verbal processes seems more than unlikely.

However, simple verbal processes appear to have some role in general verbal skill. Reading comprehension and related verbal skills, even at the college level, are related to the ability to perform simple verbal tasks. I have emphasized four verbal processes and three kinds of verbal knowledge. The latter are knowledge of word formation (including word form and rule knowledge) and the breadth and depth of word concepts. The processes are name retrieval, letter recognition, decoding, and semantic access. Name retrieval is fundamental in that the rate of other processes is set by the rate at which any over learned symbol is retrieved. It is perhaps rate-limiting for high levels of verbal skill. For lower levels of verbal skill, the other three processes, especially decoding and semantic access may be rate-limiting. Although memory processes also are part of verbal ability, I have suggested that efficient word retrieval from inactivated memory is a particular hallmark of skilled verbal processing.

REFERENCES

Anderson, R. C., Reynolds, R. E., Schallert, D. L., & Goetz, T. E. Frameworks for comprehending discourse. *American Educational Research Journal*, 1977, *14*, 367–381.

Baddeley, A. D., & Hitch, G. Working memory. In G. A. Bower (Ed.), *The psychology of learning and motivation* (Vol. 8). New York: Academic Press, 1974.

Baron, J. Orthographic and word-specific mechanisms in children's reading of words. *Child Development*, 1979, *50*, 60–72.

Baron, J., & Strawson, C. Use of orthographic and word-specific knowledge in reading words aloud. *Journal of Experimental Psychology: Human Perception and Performance*, 1976, *2*, 386–393.

Berger, N. S., & Perfetti, C. A. Reading skill and memory for spoken and written discourse. *Journal of Reading Behavior*, 1977, *9*, 7–16.

Bransford, J. D., & Johnson, M. K. Considerations of some problems of comprehension. In W. G. Chase (Ed.), *Visual information processing*. New York: Academic Press, 1973.

Brewer, W. F. Is reading a letter-by-letter process? In J. F. Kavanagh & I. G. Mattingly (Eds.), *Language by ear and by eye*. Cambridge, Mass.: MIT Press, 1972.

Butler, B., & Hains, S. Individual differences in word recognition latency. *Memory & Cognition*, 1979, *7*, 68–76.

Carroll, J. B. *Word retrieval latencies as a function of frequency and age-of-acquisition priming, repeated trials, and individual differences* (Res. Bull. RB-76-7). Princeton, N.J.: Educational Testing Service, March, 1976. (ERIC Document, ED 150 154)

Carroll, J. B., & White, M. N. Word frequency and age of acquisitions as determiners of picture-naming latency. *Quarterly Journal of Experimental Psychology,* 1973, *25,* 85–95.

Chase, W. G. Elementary information processes. In W. K. Estes (Ed.), *Handbook of learning and cognitive processes* (Vol. 5). Hillsdale, N.J: Lawrence Erlbaum Associates, 1978.

Chiang, A., & Atkinson, R. C. Individual differences and interrelationships among a select set of cognitive skills. *Memory & Cognition,* 1976, *4,* 661–672.

Cole, M., & Scribner, S. *Culture and thought.* New York: Wiley, 1974.

Collins, A., & Loftus, E. A spreading activation theory of semantic processing. *Psychological Review,* 1975, *82,* 407–428.

Cronbach, L. J. An analysis of techniques for diagnostic vocabulary testing. *Journal of Educational Research,* 1942, *36,* 206–217.

Curtis, M. E. Development of components of reading skill. *Journal of Educational Psychology,* 1980, *72,* 656–669.

Daneman, M., & Carpenter, P. A. Individual differences in working memory and reading. *Journal of Verbal Learning and Verbal Behavior,* 1980, *19,* 450–466.

Denckla, M. B., & Rudel, R. G. Naming of object drawings by dyslexic and other learning disabled children. *Brain and Language,* 1976, *3,* 1–15.

Dolch, E. C. *Reading and word meanings.* New York: Ginn & Company, 1927.

Dooling, D. J., & Lachman, R. Effects of comprehension on retention of prose. *Journal of Educational Psychology,* 1971, *88,* 216–222.

Frederiksen, J. R. Assessment of perceptual, decoding, and lexical skills and their relation to reading proficiency. In A. M. Lesgold, J. W. Pellegrino, S. D. Fokkema, & R. Glaser (Eds.), *Cognitive psychology and instruction.* New York: Plenum, 1978. (a)

Frederiksen, J. R. *A chronometric study of component skills in reading* (Tech. Rep. 2). Cambridge, Mass.: Bolt, Beranek & Newman, 1978. (b)

Frederiksen, J. R. Sources of process interactions in reading. In A. M. Lesgold & C. A. Perfetti (Eds.), *Interactive processes in reading.* Hillsdale, N.J.: Lawrence Erlbaum Associates, 1981.

Gibson, E. J. Perceptual learning and the theory of word perception. *Cognitive Psychology,* 1971, *2,* 351–368.

Glushko, R. J. Principles for pronouncing print: The psychology of phonography. In A. M. Lesgold & C. A. Perfetti (Eds.), *Interactive processes in reading.* Hillsdale, N.J.: Lawrence Erlbaum Associates, 1981.

Goldberg, R. A., Schwartz, S., & Stewart, M. Individual differences in cognitive processes. *Journal of Educational Psychology,* 1977, *69,* 9–14.

Goldman, S. R., Hogaboam, T. W., Bell, L. C., & Perfetti, C. A. Short-term discourse memory during reading and listening. *Journal of Educational Psychology,* 1980, *72,* 647–655.

Gough, P. B. One second of reading. In J. F. Kavanagh & I. G. Mattingly, (Eds.), *Language by ear and by eye.* Cambridge, Mass.: The MIT Press, 1972.

Hogaboam, T. W., & Pellegrino, J. W. Hunting for individual differences in cognitive processes: Verbal ability and semantic processing of pictures and words. *Memory & Cognition,* 1978, *6,* 189–193.

Hogaboam, T. W., & Perfetti, C. A. Reading skill and the role of verbal experience in decoding. *Journal of Educational Psychology,* 1978, *70* (5), 717–729.

Hunt, E. Mechanics of verbal ability. *Psychological Review,* 1978, *85,* 109–130.

Hunt, E., Frost, N., & Lunneborg, C. Individual differences in cognition: A new approach to intelligence. In G. Bower (Ed.), *The psychology of learning and motivation: Advances in research and theory* (Vol. 7). New York: Academic Press, 1973.

Hunt, E., Lunneborg, C. E., & Lewis, J. What does it mean to be high verbal? *Cognitive Psychology,* 1975, *7,* 194–227.

Jackson, M. D. Further evidence for a relationship between memory access and reading ability. *Journal of Verbal Learning and Verbal Behavior*, 1980, *19*, 683–694.

Jackson, M. D., & McClelland, J. L. Sensory and cognitive determinants of reading speed. *Journal of Verbal Learning and Verbal Behavior*, 1975, *14*, 565–574.

Jackson, M. D., & McClelland, J. L. Processing determinants of reading speed. *Journal of Experimental Psychology: General*, 1979, *108*, 151–181.

Kail, R. V., Chi, M. T. H., Ingram, A. L., & Danner, F. W. Constructive aspects of children's reading comprehension. *Child Development*, 1977, *48*, 684–688.

Kail, R. V., & Marshall, C. V. Reading skill and memory scanning. *Journal of Educational Psychology*, 1978, *70*, 808–814.

Katz, L., & Wicklund, D. Word scanning rates for good and poor readers. *Journal of Educational Psychology*, 1971, *62*, 138–140.

Keating, D. P., & Bobbitt, B. L. Individual and developmental differences in cognitive processing components of mental ability. *Child Development*, 1978, *49*, 155–167.

Kirkpatrick, J. J., & Cureton, E. E. Vocabulary item difficulty and word frequency. *Journal of Applied Psychology*, 1949, *33*, 347–351.

LaBerge, D., and Samuels, S. J. Toward a theory of automatic information processing in reading. *Cognitive Psychology*, 1974, *6*, 293–323.

Lesgold, A. M., and Curtis, M. E. Learning to read words efficiently. In A. M. Lesgold & C. A. Perfetti (Eds.), *Interactive processes in reading*. Hillsdale, N.J.: Lawrence Erlbaum Associates, 1981.

Lesgold, A. M., & Perfetti, C. A. Interactive processes in reading comprehension. *Discourse Processes*, 1978, *1*, 323–336.

Lindsay, P. H., & Norman, D. A. *An introduction to psychology*. New York: Academic Press, 1977.

Lyon, D. R. Individual differences in immediate serial recall: A matter of mnemonics? *Cognitive Psychology*, 1977, *9*, 403–411.

Mason, M. Reading ability and letter search time: Effects of orthographic structure defined by single-letter positional frequency. *Journal of Experimental Psychology: General*, 1975, *2*, 146–166.

Mason, M., & Katz, L. Visual processing of non-linguistic strings: Redundancy effects and reading ability. *Journal of Experimental Psychology: General*, 1976, *105*, 338–348.

Massaro, D. W. *Understanding language: An information-processing analysis of speech perception, reading, and psycholinguistics*. New York: Academic Press, 1975.

Massaro, D. W., Venezky, R. L., & Taylor, G. A. Orthographic regularity, positional frequency, and visual processing of letter strings. *Journal of Experimental Psychology: General*, 1979, *108*, 107–124.

McClelland, J. L. On the time relations of mental processes: An examination of systems of processes in cascade. *Psychological Review*, 1979, *86*, 287–330.

Neisser, U. General, academic, and artificial intelligence. In L. B. Resnick (Ed.), *The nature of intelligence*. Hillsdale, N.J.: Lawrence Erlbaum Associates, 1976.

Newell, A., & Simon, H. A. *Human problem solving*. Englewood Cliffs, N.J.: Prentice-Hall, 1972.

Orton, S. T. "Word blindness" in school children. *Archives of Neurology and Psychiatry*, 1925, *14*, 581–615.

Perfetti, C. A., Finger, E., & Hogaboam, T. W. Sources of vocalization latency differences between skilled and less skilled young readers. *Journal of Educational Psychology*, 1978, *70* (5), 730–739.

Perfetti, C. A., & Goldman, S. Discourse memory and reading comprehension skill. *Journal of Verbal Learning and Verbal Behavior*, 1976, *14*, 33–42.

Perfetti, C. A., Goldman, S. R., & Hogaboam, T. W. Reading skill and the identification of words in discourse context. *Memory & Cognition*, 1979, *7*, 273–282.

Perfetti, C. A., & Hogaboam, T. The relationship between single word decoding and reading comprehension skills. *Journal of Educational Psychology*, 1975, *67*, 461–469.

Perfetti, C. A., & Lesgold, A. M. Discourse comprehension and sources of individual differences. In M. Just & P. Carpenter (Eds.), *Cognitive processes in comprehension*. Hillsdale, N.J.: Lawrence Erlbaum Associates, 1977.

Perfetti, C. A., & Lesgold, A. M. Coding and comprehension in skilled reading and implications for reading instruction. In L. B. Resnick & P. Weaver (Eds.), *Theory and practice in early reading* (Vol. 1). Hillsdale, N.J.: Lawrence Erlbaum Associates, 1979.

Perfetti, C. A., & Roth, S. Some of the interactive processes in reading and their role in reading skill. In A. M. Lesgold & C. A. Perfetti (Eds.), *Interactive processes in reading*. Hillsdale, N.J.: Lawrence Erlbaum Associates, 1981.

Posner, M. I., & Mitchell, R. Chronometric analysis of classification. *Psychological Review*, 1967, *74*, 392–409.

Rumelhart, D. E., & McClelland, J. L. Interactive processing through spreading activation. In A. M. Lesgold & C. A. Perfetti (Eds.), *Interactive processes in reading*. Hillsdale, N.J.: Lawrence Erlbaum Associates, 1981.

Rumelhart, D. E., & Ortony, A. The representation of knowledge in memory. In R. C. Anderson, R. J. Spiro, & W. E. Montague (Eds.), *Schooling and the acquisition of knowledge*. Hillsdale, N.J.: Lawrence Erlbaum Associates, 1977.

Spilich, G. J., Vesonder, G. T., Chiesi, H. L., & Voss, J. F. Text processing of domain-related information for individuals with high and low domain knowledge. *Journal of Verbal Learning and Verbal Behavior*, 1979, *18*, 275–290.

Spoehr, K. T., & Smith, E. E. The role of syllables in perceptual processing. *Cognitive Psychology*, 1973, *5*, 71–89.

Sternberg, S. High speed scanning in human memory. *Science*, 1966, *153*, 652–654.

Sternberg, S. Memory-scanning: Mental processes revealed by reaction-time experiments. *American Scientist*, 1969, *57*, 421–457.

Taft, M. Lexical access via an orthographic code: The basic orthographic syllabic structure (BOSS). *Journal of Verbal Learning and Verbal Behavior*, 1979, *18*, 21–40.

Vellutino, F. R. *Dyslexia: Theory and Research*. Cambridge, Mass.: The MIT Press, 1979.

Venezky, R. L. *The structure of English orthography*. The Hague: Mouton, 1970.

Venezky, R. L., & Massaro, D. W. The role of orthographic regularity in word recognition. In L. B. Resnick & P. A. Weaver (Eds.), *Theory and practice of early reading* (Vol. 1). Hillsdale, N.J.: Lawrence Erlbaum Associates, 1979.

Waugh, N. C., & Norman, D. A. Primary memory. *Psychological Review*, 1965, *72*, 89–104.

NOTES

1. Perfetti, C. A. *The verbal part of reading difficulty*. Paper presented at the Seventh World Congress on Reading, Hamburg, Germany, August 1978.

2. Perfetti, C. A., & Bell, L. C. *Forward and backward letter search: Reading skill and the role of letter position and letter pattern*. Unpublished manuscript, University of Pittsburgh, Learning Research and Development Center, 1981.

3. Carroll, J. B. *Individual difference relations in psychometric and experimental cognitive tasks* (Tech. Rep. 163). Chapel Hill: University of North Carolina, April 1980.

4. Parkinson, S. *Information processing in the aged*. Paper presented at the Sandoz Conference on Aging, Batelle Memorial Institute, Seattle, Washington, 1977.

5. Warren, J., & Hunt, E. *Information processing in medically defined groups of retarded children*. Paper presented at the Gatlinburg Conference on Mental Retardation, University of Washington, Department of Psychology, 1976.

6. Hunt, E., Davidson, J., & Lansman, M. *Individual differences in semantic memory access*. Paper presented at the annual meeting of the Psychonomic Society, April 1980.

7. Calfee, R. C., Venezky, R. L., & Chapman, R. S. *Pronunciation of synthetic words with predictable and unpredictable letter-sound correspondences* (Tech. Rep. 71). Wisconsin Research and Development Center for Cognitive Learning, 1969.

8. Anderson, R. C., & Freebody, P. *Vocabulary knowledge* (Tech. Rep. No. 136). Urbana: University of Illinois, Center for the Study of Reading, August 1979.

9. Curtis, M. E. *Word knowledge and verbal aptitude*. Unpublished manuscript, University of Pittsburgh, Learning Research and Development Center, 1981.

4

Individual Differences in Solution Strategy on Spatial Tasks*

David F. Lohman and Patrick C. Kyllonen

INTRODUCTION

Although intelligence and other aptitude tests predict school learning, we have not yet developed good psychological models of individual differences in aptitude, scholastic learning, or the relationships between them. Recent advances in cognitive psychology have rekindled interest in the varieties of

*Most of the research reported in this chapter was supported by Office of Naval Research Contract No. N00014–79–C–0171 to Richard E. Snow. The views and conclusions contained in this document are those of the authors and should not be interpreted as necessarily representing the official policies, either expressed or implied, of the Office of Naval Research or the United States Government.

105

complex problem solving required by aptitude tests, and in the relationships between these problem-solving behaviors and other forms of meaningful learning. Understanding individual differences in the cognitive processes and structures shared by complex problem solving and scholastic learning would greatly facilitate efforts to adapt instruction to the relatively stable characteristics of the learner, or to directly train these characteristics.

CORRELATES AND COMPONENTS

Two research strategies have characterized attempts to identify the cognitive processes required by tests that define various aptitude constructs. Pellegrino and Glaser (1979) have called these approaches *cognitive correlates* and *cognitive components*. When using the correlates method, one attempts to explain aptitude constructs by correlating performance on aptitude tests with performance on a variety of other, presumably better understood cognitive tasks. Hunt (1980) has used this method extensively in his studies of verbal ability. In the components method, on the other hand, one focuses directly on the aptitude test and attempts to decompose this performance into a set of simpler, presumably univocal component processes. Sternberg (1977) has been the most ardent advocate of this approach, particularly as developed in a set of procedures he calls "componential analysis." Componential analysis results not only in a decomposition of the task, but also in a detailed specification of various ways the component operations might be combined when subjects actually solve the task. Alternate methods for solving a task may be tested by excluding particular components, combining them in different ways, specifying different orders of component execution, or altering the way in which components execute their various operations.

The most important difference between these two methods is the locus of psychological primitives: a correlates analysis presumes that external indices are more psychologically pure, whereas a components analysis presumes that psychologically pure indices can be identified within the target task. Correlates analysis resembles the older psychometric method of correlating—and then sometimes factor analyzing—various mental tests. The major difference is that parameters derived from well understood experimental tasks replace scores from some of the poorly understood tests. Since these task parameters are assumed to be more basic or better understood than the test scores, test scores are regressed on task parameters. However, individual differences in task parameters are not necessarily more fundamental than test scores, even though most experimental tasks are supported by some form of model whereas most mental tests are not (Snow, 1979).

More importantly, a correlates analysis provides a deeper understanding of aptitude constructs only if the "well understood" experimental tasks are, in fact, well understood for every subject. If subjects solve the experimental tasks in different ways, then correlations must be computed within strategy groups. Experiments by MacLeod, Hunt, and Mathews (1978) and Glushko and Cooper (1978) demonstrated that the well understood star-above-plus task of Clark and Chase (1972) was solved in different ways by different subjects. To complicate matters further, seemingly minor variations in the way items are administered can sometimes alter subjects' solution strategies (Cooper, 1980; Kyllonen, Lohman, & Snow, Note 1). Nevertheless, a cognitive correlates analysis is more revealing than a components analysis when individual differences in test performance are primarily a reflection of past processing. For example, individual differences in vocabulary test scores are primarily a reflection of the effectiveness of past attempts to infer the meanings of words from contexts rather than the effectiveness of retrieval and comparison processes required at the time of testing (Marshalek, Note 2). On the other hand, the components approach is more appropriate for "present process" tasks in which individual differences result primarily from the efficiency and effectiveness of processes executed at the time of testing. Fluid ability, reasoning, and spatial visualization tests are prime candidates for this type of analysis.

Sternberg has successfully applied the componential method to a wide variety of tasks, including analogies (Sternberg, 1977), linear syllogisms (Sternberg, 1980), and metaphors (Sternberg, Tourangeau, & Nigro, 1979). Nevertheless, even statistically successful componential models are sometimes psychologically bland, offering little new insight into the locus of individual differences in reasoning skills or other complex cognitive performances. Failure to obtain expected correlations between component parameters and scores on external reference tests has been a particular puzzlement. For example, componential models of analogical reasoning have included several component operations, such as *encoding* the terms of the analogy, *inferring* the relationship between the first two terms, *applying* this relationship to the third term of the analogy to generate an answer, and finally, *responding* to a test probe. One would expect the inference or application components to correlate highest with other measures of reasoning. Instead, these components frequently show no relationship with reference tests, whereas the "wastebasket" preparation–response parameter correlates significantly (e.g., Sternberg, 1977). These correlations would be of little interest if the componential models fit the data poorly. However, final componential models frequently appear to account for virtually all the reliable variance in the data, suggesting that the models are indeed psychologically valid. For these and other reasons, componential analysis has been subjected to increasingly severe criticism in recent years (e.g., Fredericksen, 1980).

THE IMPORTANCE OF VARIATION IN SOLUTION STRATEGY

Most psychological experiments tacitly assume that all subjects presented with a task will solve that task in the same way. Idiosyncratic variations in solution strategy are covered—or perhaps obscured—by the error of measurement blanket, even though data averaged over subjects may not represent the performance of all or even any of the subjects in the sample (Estes, 1956). Most correlational analyses assume that individuals differ only parametrically, whereas between-group analysis of variance relegates even these parameter differences to the error term.

Interpretations of test scores routinely presume knowledge of how subjects solved test items. For example, interpreting a total score on a figural rotation test as an estimate of spatial ability presumes that the subject did indeed perform mental rotation in order to solve items. However, we now know that this is frequently not the case. Subjects often shift strategies, particularly as they become more experienced with the test, or as items increase in difficulty (Barratt, 1953; Lohman, Note 3).

Thurstone (1938a) was one of the first to recognize that routine correlational analyses may obscure individual differences in solution strategy:

> When a test shows saturation with two or more factors we have no means of knowing by factorial analysis whether the several abilities enter into the test for every subject, or whether some subjects use one ability and other subjects use other abilities for the same performance. A study with individual subjects could reveal these differences, especially when the subjects indicate how they solve each problem (p. 8).

Unfortunately, Thurstone did not pursue these ideas experimentally, but, instead, tried to develop factorially "pure" measures of ability. However, tests that defined these univocal ability factors tended to be simple, speeded, and highly similar. Thus, the tenets of simple structure not only defined new criteria for the rotation of factor axes, but also resulted in a gradual change in the nature of the tests that were included in factorial investigations. Difficult, factorially complex tests were replaced by simple, factorially specific tests. Guilford's (1967) fractionalization of ability represents the endpoint of this tradition.

The attempt to find factorially pure tests that were solved in the same way by all test takers never really succeeded. French (1965) demonstrated that even simple, factorially pure tests such as the Cubes test were sometimes solved in different ways by different subjects. More importantly, factorially pure tests did not prove to be practically useful (e.g., Cronbach

& Snow, 1977; McNemar, 1964), and so secular psychologists continued to rely on factorially complex, but predictively more useful intelligence and achievement tests. Actually, the predictive validity of tests tends to drop as their factorial purity increases (Gheselli, 1966; McNemar, 1964). Thus, the search for factorially pure tests did more than merely rotate g into oblivion (Spearman, 1939); it led many investigators in the research community to rely on simple tasks that did not require within-task adaptation. But it is our contention that variations in solution strategy are not unwanted noise; rather, such flexible, within-task adaptation may be one of the central features of intelligent performance.

COMPONENTIAL ANALYSIS

Recognizing that different persons could obtain similar test scores by quite different methods, Sternberg (1977) expected that componential analyses would reveal major differences in solution strategies between subjects. However, he repeatedly found that, unless these alternative solution methods were artificially induced, one model fit everyone about equally well. There are at least three reasons for this failure.

1. Latency was the preferred dependent measure in these experiments, and since latencies for error responses are ambiguous, only relatively simple items were included in some experimental tasks. Between-subject variation in solution strategies tends to be small on simpler tasks; therefore, most of these studies found that people could not be grouped according to preferred solution strategy.

2. Most efforts to identify strategy differences between individuals have focused on differences in the self-terminating or exhaustive mode of component execution and ignored possible differences in the identity of the component processes employed or the order of component execution. Thus, the least interesting strategy difference—mode of component execution—has received the most careful scrutiny. Unfortunately, however, the regression models used to test the differences between self-terminating and exhaustive execution of a component do not allow for a proper comparison of models, at least as these models were originally formulated (Bethell-Fox, Lohman, & Snow, Note 4).

3. Most importantly, although subjects might differ from one another in solution strategy, previous componential analyses have assumed that each subject applied this same strategy to all items. This is particularly unlikely on complex tasks, such as those that define general reasoning skills. Skill in adapting problem-solving strategy to meet the changing demands of the items is one of the hallmarks of intelligent performance.

We will examine three sources of evidence for the hypothesis that subjects solve spatial problems in different ways. First, we will briefly outline some of the major dimensions of spatial ability. Second, we will examine attempts to document variation in solution strategies on spatial tests, usually by gathering introspective reports. Third, we will review a recent study in which we developed and tested componential models of strategy shifting on a complex spatial task. Finally, we will summarize our findings and their implications for attempts to estimate spatial abilities and, more generally, attempts to validate process models of complex problem solving.

VARIETIES OF INDIVIDUAL DIFFERENCES IN SPATIAL ABILITY

Every task that presents figural stimuli does not necessarily require spatial thinking. Nor does the absence of figural stimuli mean that the task does *not* require spatial thinking. Indeed, some of the better spatial tests present problems verbally and require subjects to generate their own images rather than decipher line drawings. Furthermore, there are substantial differences even among those tests that are commonly viewed as measuring some aspect of spatial thinking. The correlational literature is replete with tests that purport to measure different aspects of spatial ability and different factors that purport to tap a smaller set of source traits that underpin these various performances.

MAJOR SPATIAL FACTORS

Several years ago, Lohman (Note 3) set out to review and summarize the correlational studies of spatial ability before conducting some experimental investigations of spatial thinking. But in attempting to summarize this work, it quickly became apparent that there were as many endpoints as investigators. The only way to integrate the research was to reanalyze studies using a common methodological and theoretical perspective. Although complex hierarchical factor methods and multidimensional scalings were sometimes employed, the reanalyses were frankly more exploratory than confirmatory. Several hypotheses about the nature of spatial ability emerged from these analyses that, subsequently, we have subjected to more rigorous experimental test.

At the most basic level, spatial thinking requires (among other things) the ability to encode, remember, transform, and discriminate spatial stimuli. Factors such as Closure Speed (i.e., speed of matching incomplete visual stimuli with their long-term memory representations), Perceptual Speed

(speed of matching visual stimuli), Visual Memory (short-term memory for visual stimuli), and Kinesthetic Judgment (speed of making left–right discriminations) may represent individual differences in the speed or efficiency of some of these basic cognitive processes. However, these factors surface only when extremely similar tests are included in a test battery. Such tests and their factors consistently fall near the periphery of a scaling representation, or at the bottom of a hierarchical model.

Although the processes that these factors hypothetically represent are certainly spatial in nature, they are not usually the referent of the term "spatial ability." Only three of the many spatial factors that have been identified were consistently confirmed in the reanalyses (see Lohman, Note 3). All of the factors involve mental transformation. The factors are as follows:

1.   Spatial Relations. This factor is defined by tests such as Cards, Flags, and Figures (Thurstone, 1938b). These tests are all parallel forms of one another, and the factor emerges only if these or highly similar tests are included in the battery. Although mental rotation is the common element, the factor probably does not represent speed of mental rotation; rather, it represents the ability to solve such problems quickly, by whatever means.

2.   Spatial Orientation. This factor appears to involve the ability to imagine how a stimulus array will appear from another perspective. In the true spatial orientation test, the subjects must imagine that they are re-oriented in space, and then make some judgment about the situation. There is often a left–right discrimination component in these tasks, but this discrimination must be made from the imagined perspective. However, the factor is difficult to measure since tests designed to tap it are often solved by mentally rotating the array rather than reorienting an imagined self.

3.   Visualization. The factor is represented by a wide variety of tests such as Paper Folding, Form Board, Surface Development, Hidden Figures, Copying, and so forth (see French, Ekstrom, & Price, 1963 for these and similar tests). The tests that load on this factor, in addition to their spatial–figural content, share two important features: they are all administered under relatively unspeeded conditions, and most are much more complex than corresponding tests that load on the more peripheral factors. Tests designed to measure this factor usually fall near the center of a two-dimensional scaling representation, and are often quite close to tests of Spearman's g (such as Raven Matrices or Figure Classification) or Cattell's (1963) Gf.

UNDERLYING DIMENSIONS

This list of factors may be misleading, however, since it implies more conformity and exactness than really exist. There are potentially an infinite number of factors defined by what amounts to a parallel forms reliability coefficient between two simple, highly speeded tests. Complex spatial tests cluster loosely at the other end of the spectrum in the visualization factor, or may even become indistinguishable from general or fluid ability tests. Other distinctions between factors are hazy, and usually quite arbitrary. The important question is not What are the factors? but What are the dimensions along which factors are arrayed? Test speededness or complexity is clearly one of the most important dimensions in the correlation matrices of such tests. Nonhierarchical factor methods frequently obscure this dimension, although multidimensional scaling displays it clearly. Some tests correlate highly with many other tests whereas other tests correlate with only a few, highly similar tests. This implies that individual differences in speed of solving simple spatial problems are largely independent of individual differences in the ability to correctly solve difficult spatial problems. Therefore, models of error-free performance may explain little of the variance in spatial ability (see also Lohman, Note 5).

In addition to the speed–level dimension, there appear to be important differences in the type of mental transformations required on the more complex spatial tests. The first is mental movement. Reflecting, rotating, folding, or simply imagining that a stimulus is moved from one position in an array to another position are all varieties of mental movement. Shepard (1975) and Cooper (1980) have studied this type of transformation extensively.

The second type of mental transformation is construction or synthesis. At the simplest level, construction is represented in tests such as Thurstone's (1938b) Copying, where the subject must correctly copy a stimulus design. At the next level, it is represented by tests such as Graham and Kendall's (1948) Memory for Designs, where the design must be reproduced from memory. One important difference between these tests and those that load on more peripheral factors like Perceptual Speed or Memory Span is that the design must be reproduced, not just recognized. Retaining a veridical mental image of a design may be an important component of other complex spatial tasks, such as Hidden Figures (French et al., 1963).

In the more complex mental-synthesis tasks, however, the subject must actually construct a new mental image, usually by reorganizing the stimulus elements in a new way. The clearest examples of this sort of process are tests such as Form Equations (El Koussy, 1935) and Paper Form Board (e.g., French et al., 1963; Thurstone, 1938b). Mental construction is an important component of many complex spatial tests. For example, in Surface Development (French et al., 1963), the task is not simply to fold the sides of the figure mentally (i.e., mental movement), but rather to construct a three-dimensional figure from a two-dimensional drawing. Similarly, in Paper

Folding (French et al., 1963), the examinees must construct new holes as they mentally unfold the stimulus. Finally, mental construction may take the form of mentally deleting parts of a stimulus, as in match problems (Guilford & Hoepfner, 1971). This component may also be important in tests such as Embedded Figures (Witkin, Oltman, Raskin, & Karp, 1971) or Hidden Figures (French et al., 1963).

Experimental investigations of the synthesis transformation are virtually nonexistent. Palmer (1977) found that the time taken to synthesize a stimulus mentally was inversely related to the "goodness" of the component parts. However, there were important individual differences in discriminative reaction time to the test stimulus, indicating that some of the subjects may not have completely synthesized the component parts. Glushko and Cooper (1978) used a different paradigm to investigate mental construction. They asked subjects to construct a mental image of a composite figure on the basis of a verbal description of the component parts. Construction time increased with the number of component parts, but discriminative reaction time to a test figure was independent of complexity. We will describe a more extensive investigation of mental synthesis later in the chapter.

INTROSPECTIVE EVIDENCE FOR
STRATEGY SHIFTS ON SPATIAL TASKS

Only a few studies report attempts to examine variations in solution strategy on spatial tests and then test the implications of these differences for interpretations of test scores. Most of these studies remain buried in technical reports, research memoranda, research bulletins, and other obscure sources. The research community has occasionally acknowledged the problem of alternative solution strategies, but never really taken the possibility too seriously, since it would necessitate a serious rethinking of the meaning of test scores and, more generally, of all experimental tasks.

INTROSPECTIVE AND RETROSPECTIVE REPORTS

Early differential psychologists gathered evidence on solution strategies primarily to help them label or interpret factors. For example, El Koussy (1935) obtained introspective reports from some of his subjects on how they solved various tests in his battery. Many subjects reported using visual imagery to solve tests that loaded on his spatial factor; from this he concluded that the factor represented the ability to generate and use spatial imagery.

Much of the reluctance to investigate individual differences in solution strategies undoubtedly stemmed from the behaviorist taboo on introspective evidence. However, even those who recognized the possibility of strategic differences seemed to regard them as of only minor importance. There appears to have been a blind faith in the power of factor analysis to disentangle the multiple sources of individual differences in test performance. Perhaps the best example of this is a study by Michael, Zimmerman, and Guilford (1950). After careful exposition of several hypotheses about the possible psychological differences between the Spatial Relations and Visualization factors, they simply administered a battery of tests and factored the correlation matrix. Introspective reports were gathered, but again, they were used only to interpret and, at times, rationalize the results.

Although Bloom and Broder (1950) had previously gathered introspective reports from college students during problem solving, Barratt (1953) and Lucas (1953) were the first to report systematic analyses of verbal reports of solution strategy on spatial tests. Barratt (1953) administered seven spatial tests and three verbal tests to 84 college males. The spatial tests included three of Thurstone's (1938b) simple rotation tests (Cards, Flags, and Figures). The more complex Space Relations subtest of the Differential Aptitude Test, and three spatial orientation tests.

As in many other factorial investigations, Barratt's main objective was to use these retrospections to develop definitions for the three spatial factors he obtained in the factor analysis. In addition to these definitions—which are of little interest here—Barratt noted several contrasts for some of the tests. On the Figures test, 39 subjects reported that they rotated the whole figure, whereas 43 reported that they rotated only a part of the stimulus. Subjects who used the latter approach performed significantly better than those who attempted to rotate the entire figure. Additionally, those who used abstract symbols scored higher than those who attempted to relate the figure to some familiar or more concrete object.

Four subcategories of solution strategies were reported for the more difficult DAT Space Relations test. These strategies were used with different frequencies, depending on item difficulty. The categories were (1) subject spontaneously folded the pattern and then noted the relationships of the parts (57 subjects on the easier problems; 12 on more difficult items); (2) subject started with the alternatives first, and then looked at the stimulus figures (17 subjects on easy problems; 20 on hard problems); (3) subject did not fold or unfold the stimulus pattern or response figures, but looked for other cues such as angle intersections (7 subjects on easy problems; 44 on difficult problems); and (4) subject guessed (1 subject on easy problems; 8 on difficult problems).

Two distinct strategies were noted for the Guilford–Zimmerman Spatial Orientation and Industrial Aptitude Spatial Orientation tests. Some subjects imagined themselves being reoriented with regard to the stimulus. Only 26 subjects used this approach on the Guilford–Zimmerman Spatial Orientation test, whereas 58 used it on the Industrial Aptitude Spatial Orientation test. Other subjects mentally rotated the stimulus and response figures but did not imagine themselves being reoriented. This method was used by 58 subjects on the Guilford–Zimmerman Spatial Orientation test. Thus, subjects reported using different methods to solve the same test. Furthermore, on any given test, the number of reported strategies increased with item difficulty. More distinct strategies were reported for complex tests (e.g., DAT Space Relations) than for relatively simple tests (e.g., Figures), although subjects reported different problems-solving processes even on simple tests. Finally, Barratt discovered a tendency to shift from a direct mental manipulation strategy to a more "analytic" strategy as item difficulty increased.

Most attempts to gather introspective reports of subjects' solution strategies ask subjects to recall their problem-solving processes *after* solving the problem. Such reports are really retrospections rather than introspections. Retrospective reports tend to make the problem-solving process appear more systematic and rational than do play-by-play introspections (Bloom & Broder, 1950, p. 6). The subject is usually asked to solve only a few items that parallel those found in the test before giving a retrospective report, which is a reasonable procedure only if it can be assumed that items are homogeneous. A study by Lucas (1953) questions this assumption: He found that variations in solution strategy are more a function of item characteristics than of subject characteristics.

Lucas (1953) asked his 42 subjects to introspect while solving items from the relative movement test. Items on this test describe the maneuvers of one or more ships as they change direction or speed. The examinee is required to answer a question about the relative course, bearing, speed, or distance of ships without the aid of plotting or calculating on paper. The test appears to be factorially complex, since performance on it correlates with both mathematical reasoning and spatial tests (Lucas & French, 1953).

Six judges listened to the recorded introspections and wrote a description of the mental processes they thought were involved in each solution. Judges identified three groups of items: spatial, deductive, and mixed. Spatial items generally required course or bearing answers, whereas deductive items generally required relative-speed answers. The most important finding, however, was that solution processes varied more as a function of item than as a function of the subject. In fact, none of the subjects employed any one of the three basic strategies consistently.

Two reports by Myers (1957, 1958) suggest additional sources of difficulty and confusion on spatial tests. In the first study (Myers, 1957), four college students were administered Hidden Blocks and a surface development test. After the time limits had expired, students were given the answers and asked to discuss among themselves how they could best improve their scores on the tests. The experimenter than left the room and later analyzed the tape of their conversations. Myers felt that this procedure was more likely to yield an unbiased picture of how the students solved the problems than if they attempted to communicate their problem-solving processes to a psychologist.

In the second study, five college students were administered three spatial tests. During the following week, each subject participated in several hour-long interviews in which items from three spatial tests similar to those they had taken on the first day were presented. Observations on the verbal reports were similar in both studies.

1.   A number of the subjects failed to understand the test directions. A particularly common shortcoming was the tendency to overlook a key assumption about the nature of the task; for example, that all blocks were the same size or that the figures could only be folded in one way. Further, some subjects had difficulty deciphering how the numerical and alphabetical symbols were to be used to codify answer choices on the surface development test. Myers concluded: "With the large groups used in factor analysis, it is not safe to assume that all subjects are attempting to do the same thing" (1957, p. 6).

2.   Subjects reported difficulty in "reading" or understanding the line drawings. Also, there were apparently differences in the size of perceptual units between subjects: some subjects tended to see a block where others saw more molecular units such as lines or planes.

3.   Subjects reported using mental imagery to solve easy surface development items, but shifting to more analytic methods as the problems became more difficult. Barratt (1953) observed a similar shift in his study.

The most extensive study of the relationship between problem-solving styles and cognitive processes was reported by French (1965). He administered a battery of five pure factor tests and 10 factorially complex tests to 177 male high-school and college students. Students also completed a questionnaire about their background and general approach to the test problems. Then, they were asked to think aloud while they solved one to five items from each test in the battery. In addition, the interviewer asked specific questions when the student did not voluntarily report information needed to complete the interview form.

The tetrachoric correlation matrix of the questionnaire, interview, and test variables was factored by principal components with varimax rotation. This analysis produced 25 orthogonal factors, 17 of which were considered representative of psychologically distinct problem-solving styles or background characteristics. The factors were used to divide the subject pool into 17 pairs of subsamples.

An initial factoring of the 15-test correlation matrix for the entire sample indicated five factors. Tests that loaded highest on the first four of these factors were used as marker variables in the rotations of the 17 pairs of subsample factor analyses. Five factors were extracted in each of these subsample analyses. A targeted, quartimax rotation was then performed, using the four sets of marker tests. The first four of these factors were further rotated to a patterned oblimax criterion to bring the factors as close as possible to the marker tests. The fifth factor was kept orthogonal throughout these rotations.

Although dividing the sample according to whether subjects reported using rule for solving Cards items produced no noticeable differences in the factor loading or factor intercorrelations, the correlation between the Space-Visualization and Verbal-Comprehension factors *decreased* in 11 pairs of subsamples where some "systematic" (i.e., reasonably well defined) approach was used for a test. For example, although factor structures were about the same for those who said they used more or less visualization, factor intercorrelations were higher in the group reporting more visualizations, suggesting a stronger general factor. Thus, those who had well-defined strategies tended to show greater differentiation of abilities than those who had not developed such specific problem-solving skills. In one of the more dramatic changes, the loading of the Cubes test dropped from .52 to .07 on the Space-Visualization factor for those who used an analytic strategy to solve the items. Similarly, the Guilford–Zimmerman Spatial Orientation test loaded on a general ability, or Reasoning, factor rather than on the Space-Visualization factor for those who used a more analytic, reasoned approach on the test.

French concluded that the most pervasive strategic difference was "some kind of reasoned or systematic approach as contrasted to less orderly scanning and visualizing, with reliance on common sense" (1965, p. 26). He further observed that the systematic approach may work differently on different tests. A systematic approach could eliminate random behavior and increase both the reliability and factorial purity of a test. This may have been the case for the 11 contrasts in which a systematic approach decreased the correlation between the verbal and spatial factors, producing a sharper differentiation of abilities. On the other hand, especially on spatial tests, a systematic approach could enable a student to derive the correct answer by an entirely different set of processes than those intended by the test constructor. For such individuals, the expected factor loading of the test would decline or vanish altogether, as they did for those who used an analytic approach to the Cubes test.

Although this study suggests the type of strategy differences that may influence factor structures, there is no way of knowing what factor structure differences would have been produced by 17 random splittings of the sample. Further, the difference between systematic strategies and analytic, nonvisual strategies warrants more precise differentiation. Nevertheless, as French notes "even simple 'pure factor' tests . . . do not measure the same things for all people" (p. 26).

A recent investigation reported by Yalow and Webb (Note 6) further defines the major dimensions of reported solution strategies. Retrospective reports of solution strategy were obtained from 48 high-school students on a range of verbal, spatial, and reasoning tests. Eye fixations were recorded while students solved several items from each test. Students were then presented with three or four items from each test and asked to describe how they solved them. The experimenters completed a questionnaire for each test on the basis of these responses. Questionnaires had been developed during pilot investigations with more than 100 college students. Experimenters asked students additional questions only if it was not possible to complete the questionnaires from the students' first descriptions.

Yalow and Webb (Note 6) reported a preliminary analysis of 13 strategy indices computed across four tests: Vocabulary, Verbal Analogies, Paper Folding, and Paper Form Board. The score on each index was a ratio of the number of times the student reported using a particular strategy to total number of opportunities to report that strategy.

They reported that high-ability students usually knew the answer before looking at the alternatives, whereas low-ability students spent more time evaluating and eliminating alternatives. Further, low-ability students reported more internal verbalization while solving tasks, guessed more frequently, and had less confidence in their answers. Students of intermediate ability reported using specific spatial strategies more frequently than either high- or low-ability students.

With one exception, the correlations between particular strategy indices for right and wrong items were all positive. Further, the pattern of intercorrelations of the various indices were about the same for the right and wrong items, except much lower for the wrong items, suggesting that subjects did not drastically alter solution strategy on items they missed. Closer examination of these correlations suggested that there were three major dimensions in the 13 indices. The first dimension represented the tendency to analyze the response alternatives; the second dimension represented the tendency to construct a response from a careful analysis of the stimulus words or pictures before looking at the response alternatives; and the third dimension distinguished impressionistic, intuitive solutions from more analytic, well-articulated solutions. This dimension is similar to French's (1965) distinction between the reasoned–systematic approach and the scanning–visualization–common sense approach. However, the Yalow–Webb data also suggest that it is important to distinguish between a systematic analysis of the problem stem and response alternatives.

LESS INTRUSIVE MEASURES

Both introspective and retrospective reports are intrusive and may lead to the modification of the thought processes that are monitored. Some investigators have argued that this intrusiveness invalidates verbal reports (e.g., Nisbitt & Wilson, 1977), whereas others have pointed out that the amount of interference will depend on many factors, including the nature of the task, the method of gathering verbal reports, and the information reported (Ericsson & Simon, 1980).

But verbal reports are only one method for gathering evidence on the problem solver's thought processes. In addition to latency, error, and eye-fixation data, other less systematic, but also less intrusive measures are sometimes available. For example, examinees frequently make drawings or other marks on test items when attempting to solve them. In addition to the incomplete written record that they may provide, such drawings could relieve short-term memory burdens or signal an even more substantial shift in solution strategy, especially on spatial tests.

In a previous study (see Lohman, Note 3), we explored the nature of these drawings on several complex spatial tests, including Surface Development, Paper Folding, and Form Board (all from French et al., 1963). Although the tendency to draw did not generalize over tests, the number of items marked on the Paper-Folding test altered relationships between performance on that test and other tests. For those who made one or no marks on the test, total correct correlated higher with other spatial tests; whereas for those who marked two or more items, correlations were lower with other spatial tests but higher with reasoning and perceptual speed tests. The implication is that the Paper-Folding test was a poorer measure of spatial ability for those who used their pencils to help them solve items. Parenthetically, this study also found that the correlation between self-reported vividness of visual imagery was even more strongly negative in the no-marking group than the marking group. Thus, as Smith (1964) and others have suggested, extremely vivid visual imagery may actually inhibit abstract spatial problem solving.

Finally, a few investigators have manipulated task variables in an effort to directly alter solution strategies on spatial tasks. For example, Gavurin (1967) administered 10 anagram problems under two conditions. In the first condition ($N = 13$), letters could not be physically rearranged, and so subjects had to solve the anagrams mentally. In the second condition, another group of subjects ($N = 14$) was allowed to rearrange the tiles on which letters of each anagram were printed. The correlation between anagram solving and the Minnesota Paper Form Board test was .54 in the nonmanipulation, and $-.18$ in the manipulation condition. Thus, how the anagram test was administered dramatically affected correlations with a reference spatial test and, by implication, how items were solved.

A study by Frandsen and Holder (1969) provides further support for French's (1965) observation that having a systematic approach to a particular problem type makes a difference. They selected 18 pairs of students from a population of 146 undergraduate general psychology students. Pairs were matched on the DAT Verbal Reasoning test, but as disparate as possible on DAT Space Relations. One student from each pair was then randomly assigned to a treatment group, and the other to a control group. Those in the treatment group were taught specific diagrammatic techniques to represent syllogistic, time–rate–distance, and logical deduction problems. Venn diagrams were used to represent syllogisms; marked lines represented time–rate–distance problems; diagrams of the facts and conditions were adapted for the deduction problems. Only subjects low in spatial aptitude who had received the instruction showed significant improvement on a test containing these types of verbal problems. Those high in spatial ability were not affected by the treatment, although there were some ceiling effects for high-ability students on both pretest and posttest.

Other studies support the holistic versus analytic distinction in spatial-test-solution strategy. Snow (1978, 1980) investigated strategies for the Paper-Folding test using a retrospective questionnaire and eye-fixation records collected during item performance. Subjects appeared to use either a mental construction or a feature-extraction strategy while examining the stimulus figures, and either a template-matching or a distractor-elimination strategy while selecting an alternative. The most effective strategy appeared to combine a mental-image construction during stimulus analysis with a self-terminating match of the result to response alternatives.

Analyses of discriminative response latencies have resulted in a similar distinction. Cooper (1976) (see also Cooper & Podgorny, 1976) found that, for some subjects, "same" responses were, on the average faster than "different" responses. Further, the speed of "different" responses was not related to the similarity of the test stimulus to the standard. For other subjects, "different" responses were generally faster than "same" responses, and "different" reaction time decreased as the standard and test stimuli became increasingly dissimilar. Cooper (1980) argues that these patterns reflect different strategies. One strategy consists of a process of holistic, parallel comparison of a visual memory representation with a test shape; the other strategy appears to be a sequential, analytic comparison process. Kail, Carter, and Pellegrino (1979) used a similar approach to examine gender differences on a mental rotation task. Their data suggested that some subjects rotate an image holistically while others rotate certain features sequentially. A significant subset of females appeared to employ the latter strategy.

Finally, in an earlier study (Kyllonen et al., Note 1), we attempted to manipulate subjects' solution strategies on a paper-folding task by demonstrating alternate solution strategies and by systematically altering item characteristics and mode of item presentation. Training efforts were effective, but depended on subjects' aptitude profiles and the type of item presented. High-spatial-ability subjects performed best when they simply practiced solving items and received feedback on their performance. Subjects low in both spatial and verbal abilities performed best after a treatment that modeled the visualization process, whereas subjects low in spatial ability but high in verbal ability performed best after a treatment that modeled a nonvisual strategy. Thus, solution strategy is not an indelible characteristic of the person, although changes in solution strategy are much more difficult to induce on complex tasks than on relatively simple tasks (see, e.g., Glushko & Cooper, 1978; Hunt & MacLeod, 1979), and must be fit to the skill profile of the individual.

SUMMARY

In summation, individual differences in solution strategy are a major problem for both experimental and correlational studies of spatial thinking. Although some subjects solve verbal problems such as anagrams, syllogisms, and three-term series problems using a predominately spatial strategy, it is possible to construct verbal tasks where spatial strategies would be of little or no assistance (e.g., a simple vocabulary test). On the other hand, it is extremely difficult to devise spatial tasks that cannot be solved at least in part by some nonspatial strategy.

There are important differences in solution strategy both between subjects and within subjects over items. Tests often measure different abilities for different students, depending on how problems are solved. Further, complex, level tests elicit a wider range of alternative solution strategies than simple, highly speeded tests. Similarly, within a test, the more difficult items elicit a wider range of solution strategies than easy items.

High-ability students report studying the problem stem and constructing an answer before examining the alternatives. These subjects are usually able to give a coherent verbal report of how they solved the item, and they express confidence in their answers. Low-ability students, on the other hand, frequently report that they attempt to solve the item by analyzing the alternatives. Further, they report more internal verbalization, more guessing, and less confidence in their answers than do high-ability students.

Certain tests are particularly susceptible to alternative solution strategies. For example, many spatial orientation tests can be solved by mentally rotating the stimulus field rather than imagining how this stimulus would appear from a different perspective. On a more general level, multiple choice paper-and-pencil tests permit a number of alternative solution strategies that are not possible when the student must construct rather than select an answer. Students can also draw or mark on the test, thereby reducing the need to remember more than a single step in the solution of the problem. They can attempt to solve the problem by "working backward" from the alternatives to the stem, or by looking for clues in the alternatives that may reveal the correct answer or otherwise help them solve the problem.

Individual differences in solution strategy challenge a basic assumption of factor analysis. Factor structures obtained from analyses of such tests may be severely distorted. The most likely outcome is an overestimation of the factorial complexity of a test. The factorially complex test may be solved in different ways by different students, or, alternatively, students may switch strategies while solving different items. However, it is impossible to know whether the test measures two different aptitudes in any one individual, or whether it measures different aptitudes in different individuals. On a more general level, the presence of several tests in a battery that are amenable to alternate solution strategies seriously distorts the factor structure, so that the obtained factor structure may not apply to anyone in the sample. Factoring within strategy groups would undoubtedly produce cleaner factor patterns, but may be impossible if many tests are suspect.

Individual differences in solution strategy present a major stumbling block for both correlational and experimental investigations of spatial ability. Averaging data from subjects who solve a task in different ways produces a mean that can be as misleading as a factor analysis of a matrix that included these scores as a variable. The challenge for future research is to devise experiments that reveal solution strategy for each subject on each item type, or better still, on each item. Only by knowing how subjects solve items can the investigator know what it is that the task measures, or evaluate the generalizability of the processing models that are proposed to describe task performance.

Solution strategy is a function of both the person and the item. Attempts to sort people into typological categories assume strategy is a consistent feature of the person. Sorting items into categories assumes all people solve each item in the same way. Ultimately, we must model the full person by item-data matrix, and account for variations in strategy that are a function of both the person and the item. It is only in this way that we will be able to model within-item shifts in solution strategy.

COMPONENTIAL MODELS OF STRATEGY SHIFTS

Thus far, we have briefly reviewed the major dimensions of individual differences in spatial skills as they are represented in the correlational litera- ture. We noted the importance of the complexity or speed-level dimension and observed that truly generalizable models of spatial thinking must ac- count for individual differences in the ability to solve complex spatial tasks, and not simply account for error-free latency on necessarily simpler spatial tasks. We also suggested that two major types of mental transformation are required on complex tests; namely, movement and synthesis, and observed that although movement transformations have been studied extensively, research on mental synthesis is virtually nonexistent. Finally, we reviewed the evidence for strategy shifting on spatial tasks, and concluded that ty- pological classifications of persons or items cannot account for the type of flexible adaptation of solution strategy over items that appears to be re- quired on many complex spatial tests.

EXPERIMENTAL TASK

These concerns motivated the development of a spatial task in which items varied systematically in complexity in order to represent the full range of item difficulty typically observed in spatial tests, from simple perceptual speed and closure speed tests to the most complex mental rotation and mental synthesis tests, with a particular emphasis on the latter. Subjects were required to memorize, synthesize, rotate, and match various poly- gons. Exemplary items from this task are shown in Figure 1.

Each trial contained four to six slides. The first and last slides were a "ready" probe and a "confidence" request. The first stimulus was presented on the second slide and the test stimulus (signaled by a yellow background on the slide) immediately preceded the confidence slide.

The first column in Figure 1 shows the sequence of events for the

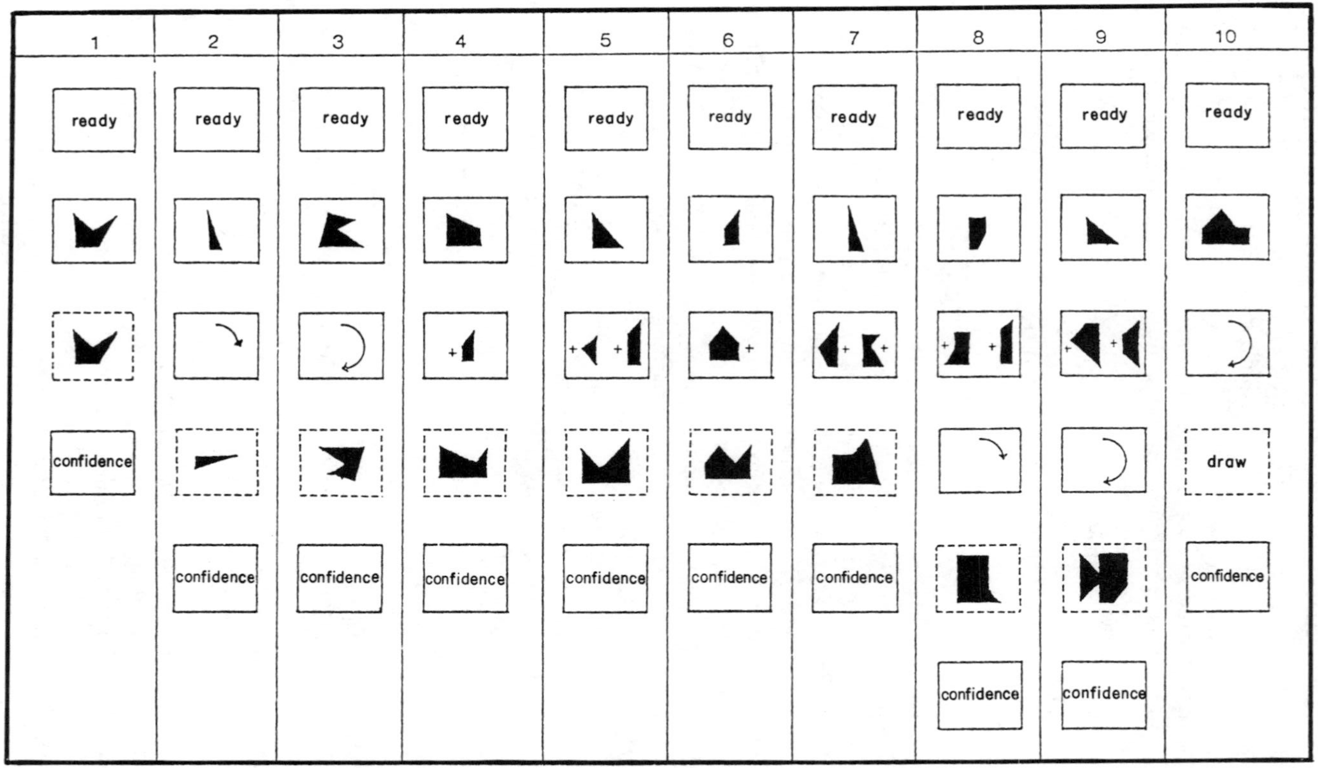

FIGURE 1. Examples of major trial types in the experimental task (from Lohman, Note 5).

simplest item, while simple 90 and 180° rotation trials are shown in columns two and three. One- and two-piece left-addition items are shown in columns 6 and 7. The plus sign indicates the location of the synthesis, and, on two-piece additions, subjects were instructed to work from left to right (e.g., columns 5 and 7). Stimulus complexity of both the stimulus pieces and to-be-constructed stimulus was varied systematically. Complex pieces could combine to form either a simple or a complex product image, and simple pieces could do the same. Finally, all types of addition could be followed by rotation, as shown in columns 8 and 9. The three levels of construction (zero, one, or two additions), three levels of rotation (0, 90, or 180°), three levels of stimulus complexity (low, medium, or high), and two types of discriminative response (correct or incorrect) were fully crossed. Additionally, location of addition (left or right) and complexity of the to-be-constructed image were crossed with each other and all other design facets for construction items. In addition to correctness and confidence, from two or four latencies were recorded for each item: encoding (time to memorize the first figure), construction (time to synthesize the separate stimuli), rotation (time to rotate stimuli), and comparison (time to accept or reject the test probe).

Thirty high-school and college males selected to represent a wide range of verbal and spatial abilities solved the 216 items in this task. Extensive reference aptitude information had been collected in a previous study and was available for each subject.

Initial analyses (see Lohman, Note 5) demonstrated the relative independence of speed of solving simple items and level or the ability to solve complex items. How fast subjects solved easy items allowed no prediction of how complex an item they could solve. Furthermore, although total errors were highly correlated with performance on reference spatial tests, increases in latency over the design facets were correlated with verbal reference tests. Thus, even though the task was a good measure of spatial ability, some subjects, particularly those who took much longer on difficult items than on easy items, appeared to be relying on nonspatial skills. But firm statements about process were not possible since these initial analyses relied on a statistical model, the analysis of variance, rather than a psychological model, as in later componential analyses.

STRATEGY-SHIFT COMPONENTIAL MODELS

Some descriptions of componential analysis emphasize the goal of isolating and validating component processes. We prefer to emphasize the value of the method for testing process models of task performance. The identifi-

cation of component processes is a secondary and, at best, tenuous procedure. It is usually difficult and sometimes impossible to keep the variables
that identify componential processes experimentally and statistically independent. Correlated predictors produced unstable beta weights or component score estimates. Further, validation of component latency scores
through correlations with reference measures requires the identification of
the same component operations over the same range of items for all subjects. It is virtually impossible to meet these conditions unless one model fits
every subjects' data, and items are kept simple so that all subjects can solve
all of the items. Simple items that are all solved in one way probably do not
require much of the intelligent performance we hope to understand.

But our purpose here is not to criticize componential analysis; rather, it
is to elaborate a particular type of componential model that predicts subjects
will solve different items in different ways. Previous componential analyses
have fit models which specify that all items are solved by the same set of
processes (e.g., Sternberg, 1977). Of course, every item or part of an item
does not require all processes specified in the model or equal "amounts" of
these processes, since independent variables that predict processes must
vary over items and covary with each other as little as possible. Further,
these models are not the same as "mixed" models (e.g., Sternberg, 1980),
which specify a fixed, nonshifting mixture of components, such as linguistic and spatial components.

RELATIONSHIPS BETWEEN APTITUDE AND STRATEGY

The goal of research on aptitude processes is to develop process theories
for families of related tests that usually define a particular aptitude construct
(Snow, 1981). What, then, is the relationship between solution strategy and
aptitude? At one extreme, differences in aptitude may be entirely a function
of differences in how subjects solve problems. Here, the strategy is the
aptitude. At the other extreme, strategy may be important for understanding task performance, but irrelevant for understanding aptitude. For example, individuals might differ in whether they can solve a task; how they
solve it is happenstance, or, at best, an indication of a stylistic preference.
They can solve the task other ways, and can easily do so upon request (e.g.,
MacLeod et al., 1978).

Kyllonen, Woltz, and Lohman (Note 7) distinguished three intermediate
relationships between aptitude and strategy. In a *Case I* relationship, aptitude limits strategy selection. In a *Case II* relationship, strategy choice is
unrelated to aptitude, but the effectiveness of implementing a strategy depends on aptitude. In a *Case III* relationship, aptitude both limits strategy

and predicts performance within strategy groups. We found evidence for all three of these relationships in the componential analyses of the mental synthesis task shown in Figure 1. Only an overview of the results is provided here; the reader is referred to Kyllonen et al. (Note 7) for additional details.

MEMORIZING THE INITIAL STIMULUS FIGURE

Three single-strategy models and two strategy-shift models were tested for the encoding step. These models specified different procedures for memorizing the initial stimulus figure. The single or consistent strategy models were feature analysis, figure decomposition, and verbal labeling. The feature-analysis model predicted that subjects stored each figure as a set of basic features. More complex figures contained more of these elementary features, and would take longer to memorize. The decomposition and labeling strategies represented attempts to reduce the number of independent features in the stimulus figure that had to be retained in active memory, either by decomposing the complex figure into simpler units such as triangles or rectangles, or attempting to apply a descriptive label to the figure as a whole. One shift model predicted that subjects would label some figures and decompose others, whichever was easier. Other shift models predicted that subjects would label 25, 50, or 75% of the figures and use the decomposition or feature-analysis strategy for the remainder.

Of the 30 subjects, 11 were best fit by the feature-analysis model, 14 were best fit by the decomposition model, and 9 were best fit by one of the label-feature analysis shift models (the remaining 6 were well fit by more than one model). Subjects best fit by either of the two complexity reduction models were significantly faster than those who were best fit by the feature-analysis model. Further, those best fit by the decomposition model obtained much higher scores than other subjects on reference spatial and closure speed tests. These findings suggest that an important aspect of spatial ability may be skill in using prior figural knowledge when attempting to remember new figural stimuli. Changes in strategy with practice provided further support for this hypothesis. Although 12 subjects changed from a feature-analysis strategy to one of the complexity-reduction strategies between the first and last block of items, none of the subjects showed the reverse pattern of starting with a complexity-reduction strategy and switching to feature analysis. This finding is precisely what one would expect if subjects were learning the stimuli used in the task and learning how to apply their knowledge of stimulus and task constraints to reduce processing burdens. There is a tendency to view individual differences in fluid and spatial abilities as process-based rather than knowledge-based, even though knowledge figures importantly in other aptitude constructs. Much of all problem solving—whether it is verbal, spatial, or symbolic—consists of making the unfamiliar, familiar, and the meaningless, meaningful. Perhaps it is the lack of a common spatial vocabulary—or even the ability to create one—that leads us to slight the role of figural knowledge in spatial problem solving.

MODELS FOR SYNTHESIS

Models for the construction step were more varied and complex than those for either encoding or comparison. The subject's task during the construction step was to imagine the synthesis of the two or three separate stimulus pieces into one shape, a problem akin to assembling a puzzle mentally. For explaining the strategies on this task step, we refer to the figure presented during the encoding step as the A figure, and the second and third stimuli as the B and C figures, respectively. Although items differed in several respects, the most important design facet for distinguishing the different componential models was complexity of the to-be-constructed (or product) image and the statistical independence between the complexity of this imaginary figure and the complexity of separate pieces. One simple hypothesis was that complexity of this imaginary product would predict the performance of subjects who synthesized the separate figures, whereas complexity of the separate stimuli would predict construction time for those who could not or did not synthesize the image. All construction models were built from a small set of cognitive operations: retrieval, synthesis, evaluation, and storage. Models differed in the sequence of operations and whether synthesized or separate figures were stored in memory.

Two consistent strategy models and four strategy-shift models were tested. The first consistent strategy model predicted that subjects always synthesized the separate A, B, and C figures into a single ABC unit, which they then stored in memory. The other consistent strategy model predicted that subjects never synthesized the separate figures, and instead stored them as individual units. The simplest shift model predicted that subjects synthesized only when the ABC product was simple, and reverted to storing the separate figures when this image was complex.

More complex shift models predicted that subjects would sometimes synthesize only intermediate products such as AB or BC when the ABC image was too complex. The first of these models—the forward synthesis strategy—predicted that subjects would attempt to synthesize pieces in the order in which they were instructed to synthesize: A with B, and then AB with C. If the AB image was complex, then A, B, and C would be retained as separate figures. Similarly, if the AB product was simple but ABC more complex, then AB and C would be retained as separate images.

The reverse or backward synthesis model predicted that subjects would attempt to synthesize the B and C figures first. We hypothesized that subjects who had difficulty remembering the A figure while looking at the B and C figures might resort to such a strategy.

Finally, the most complex model—the multiple-recovery strategy—predicted that subjects would first attempt to synthesize the A, B, and C figures into the ABC product image. But if the ABC image was too complex, then subjects would recover and attempt to synthesize A and B, and if this failed, try to synthesize B and C, and if all synthesis efforts failed, then store the separate A, B, and C figures.

Although no subject was best fit by the consistent no-synthesis model, four subjects were best fit by the consistent synthesis model. The aptitude profile for this group of subjects revealed high-spatial and visual-memory abilities, but lower skills in other areas. Two subjects best fit by the reverse synthesis model were at the other extreme. As predicted, these subjects were by far the lowest in spatial and visual-memory abilities. Thus, the subjects who performed much better on reference spatial and visual-memory tests than on other tests consistently synthesized figures, whereas those who showed the opposite profile on reference tests were apparently unable to remember the A figure once the B and C figure appeared and, instead, attempted to synthesize the B and C figures.

Ten subjects were best fit by the simple shift model, and 15 subjects were best fit by the multiple-recovery shift model. The latter subjects had the highest average-score profile on all aptitude measures, whereas those best fit by the simple shift model had the second highest ability profile. In other words, those who were generally the most able evidenced the most flexible adaptation on this task, while those who were on average less able (particularly in spatial skills) followed a much simpler model, but one that also required a strategy shift. Those subjects with the most extreme aptitude profiles followed more restricted routes, either always synthesizing or attempting to synthesize only those stimuli that remained in view.

MODELS FOR COMPARISON

Three strategies for comparing the products of the synthesis step with the test probe were tested. One strategy specified a serial, exhaustive comparison of features of the test probe and features of a properly synthesized image. A variant of this model allowed for quick rejection of radically discrepant test probes. The second model predicted that subjects would compare images of the A, B, and C stimuli with corresponding parts of the test probe. Each stimulus would be compared as a unit, with the number of comparisons required equal to the number of stimuli. Comparisons of stimulus features within a stimulus unit were performed in parallel in this model. A variant of this model used the predicted output of the construction step rather than the separate A, B, and C figures. Thus, if the construction model specified that the subject synthesized some or all of the figures, then the number of comparisons would be less than the total number of separate figures.

The third model predicted that subjects would shift between the previous models, depending on the output of the construction step. Here, we predicted that subjects would use the feature-comparison strategy if they synthesized the figures during construction, but would rely on the presumably less accurate unit-comparison strategy to compare nonsynthesized figures.

These comparison step models accounted for less variance than the encoding or construction models, possibly because the comparison latencies were shorter and less variable than latencies for the other steps. But a holistic, parallel comparison model predicts that comparison latencies would be independent of any of the predictors in the three models that were tested here (see, e.g., Cooper, 1980). Thus, we cannot reject a default holistic comparison model for the three subjects who were poorly fit by the other three models. And, in fact, it is possible that other subjects compared at least some stimuli in this manner.

Once again, the shift model appeared to fit more subjects than the other models. In all, 10 subjects were best fit by the shift model, 5 by the unit model, and 3 by the feature comparison model. Another 3 subjects were not well described by any of the models and the remaining 9 subjects were fit equally well by two different models, usually the shift and unit-comparison models.

Reference closure speed, visual memory, and spatial abilities were highly correlated with latency for seven subjects who were reasonably well fit by the feature comparison model, but the small sample size makes inference tenuous.

IMPLICATIONS

There are several substantive and methodological implications of these analyses. The most important conclusion must be this: We cannot ignore item-to-item variation in solution strategy and still hope to develop process theories of general aptitude constructs. We have cited evidence from intro-

spective and retrospective reports, eye fixation records, experimental manipulations, and componential shift models to support the hypothesis that
subjects often adapt their solution strategy to item demands. Averaging
over items or people will not eliminate the problem, since averaging assumes that deviations among the averaged elements are randomly dis-
tributed errors. Nor can we accept attempts to explain away poor-fitting
models by claiming either the raw data or components derived from these
data are unreliable. Data will appear unreliable when subjects shift strategy,
since items that are constructed to be parallel will not necessarily be solved
in the same way by any one subject. Increases in within-cell variability
mean decreases in internal consistency. But if the experiment is well controlled, then only a small subset of this variation between similar items may
be attributed to inattention, false starts, or other obvious "errors" of measurement. If the subject is actually solving items in the task, then there must
exist some model or models that would explain performance. Explaining
away poor-fitting models by claiming low reliability will not do. Performance may not generalize from item to item, but this does not mean that it
is errorful. Our analyses suggest that shifts in strategy may provide a more
likely explanation.

But are changes in strategy always substantively interesting? Our results, and those of other investigators (e.g., French, 1965), suggest that such
strategy shifts can either be irrelevant noise or an indispensable part of the
performance. Definitions of intelligence have long emphasized the role of
adaptation. Our results suggest that adaptations in strategy become more
critically important with increases in the difficulty of the task and, correspondingly, the generality of the aptitude construct. But whether strategy
shifts define the aptitude or obfuscate attempts to measure it, we must be
able to account for them before we will be able to develop generalizable
models of task performances. Componential shift models provide a
uniquely powerful method for accomplishing this task.

Finally, our studies have suggested some hypotheses about the nature of
spatial ability that warrant further consideration. There are two major explanations for individual differences in the ability to solve spatial tasks. The
first explanation emphasizes individual differences in system processes and
structures. In this view, the "size" of visual short-term memory or visual
buffer (Kosslyn, 1981)—the speed with which images can be generated and
refreshed—or other such system limitations determine variation in spatial
skills. For example, Smith (1964) has argued that the essence of spatial
ability is skill in retaining a veridical mental image. Our models also suggest
that subjects who were unable to retain an image of the first stimulus while
viewing additional stimuli were at a particular disadvantage. Although system limitations are a possible explanation, we suspect that subjects lose the

image of the previous figure primarily because the image is stored in an unelaborated form; thus, it is highly susceptible to interference from subsequent visual inputs. Some high-spatial subjects avoided this interference by decomposing unfamiliar stimuli into more familiar elements, thereby simultaneously reducing the attentional resources allocated to retaining images and increasing the probability that the figures could be successfully reconstructed at a later time. Therefore, one need not explain differences in the ability to retain an image by referring only to structural parameters of the system.

Additional evidence is provided by our finding that subjects were able to achieve high scores in this task in different ways. It appears that spatial ability is not simply the ability to generate visual images; rather, it is skill in reasoning with abstract visual images and with more concrete figural representations of these images. This reasoning aspect of spatial thinking is supported by our finding that those who were able to flexibly adapt their performance committed fewer errors on the experimental task and on most reference tests than those who followed a more rigid routine. Thus, the store of spatial knowledge and skill in using that knowledge may be more important in spatial thinking than some previous accounts have suggested.

REFERENCES

Barratt, E. S. An analysis of verbal reports of solving spatial problems as an aid in defining spatial factors. *Journal of Psychology*, 1953, *36*, 17–25.

Bloom, B. S., & Broder, L. J. *Problem-solving processes of college students*. Chicago: University of Chicago Press, 1950.

Cattell, R. B. Theory of fluid and crystallized intelligence: A critical experiment. *Journal of Educational Psychology*, 1963, *54*, 1–22.

Clark, H. H., & Chase, W. G. On the process of comparing sentences against pictures. *Cognitive Psychology*, 1972, *3*, 472–517.

Cooper, L. A. Individual differences in visual comparison processes. *Perception & Psychophysics*, 1976, *19*, 433–444.

Cooper, L. A. Spatial information processing: Strategies for research. In R. E. Snow, P.-A. Federico, & W. E. Montague (Eds.), *Aptitude, learning, and instruction* (Vol. 1). Hillsdale, N.J.: Lawrence Erlbaum Associates, 1980.

Cooper, L. A., & Podgorny, P. Mental transformations and visual comparison processes: Effects of complexity and similarity. *Journal of Experimental Psychology: Human Perception and Performance*, 1976, *2*, 503–514.

Cronbach, L. J., & Snow, R. E. *Aptitudes and instructional methods: A handbook for research on interactions*. New York: Irvington, 1977.

El Koussy, A. A. H. The visual perception of space. *British Journal of Psychology*, 1935, *20*. (Monograph supplement)

Ericsson, K. A., & Simon, H. A. Verbal reports as data. *Psychological Review*, 1980, *87*, 215–251.

Estes, W. K. The problem of inference from curves based on group data. *Psychological Bulletin*, 1956, *53*, 134–140.

Frandsen, A. N., & Holder, J. R. Spatial visualization in solving complex verbal problems. *Journal of Psychology*, 1969, *73*, 229–233.

Frederiksen, J. R. A Thrustonian's reaction to a componential theory of intelligence. *Behavioral and Brain Sciences*, 1980, *3*, 590–591.

French, J. W. The relationship of problem-solving styles to the factor composition of tests. *Educational and Psychological Measurement*, 1965, *25*, 9–28.

French, J. W., Ekstrom, R. B., & Price, L. A. *Kit of reference tests for cognitive factors*. Princeton, N.J.: Educational Testing Service, 1963.

Gavurin, E. I. Anagram solving and spatial aptitude. *Journal of Psychology*, 1967, *65*, 65–68.

Gheselli, E. E. *The validity of occupational aptitude tests*. New York: Wiley, 1966.

Glushko, R. J., & Cooper, L. A. Spatial comprehension and comparison processes in verification tasks. *Cognitive Psychology*, 1978, *10*, 391–421.

Graham, F. K., & Kendall, B. S. *Memory for designs test*. Seattle: Department of Neuropsychiatry, Washington University School of Medicine, 1948.

Guilford, J. P. *The nature of human intelligence*. New York: McGraw-Hill, 1967.

Guilford, J. P., & Hoepfner, R. *The analysis of intelligence*. New York: McGraw-Hill, 1971.

Hunt, E. The foundations of verbal comprehension. In R. E. Snow, P.-A. Federico, & N. E. Montague (Eds.), *Aptitude, learning, and instruction* (Vol. 1). Hillsdale, N.J.: Lawrence Erlbaum Associates, 1980.

Hunt, E., & MacLeod, C. M. The sentence-verification paradigm: A case study for individual differences. In R. J. Sternberg & D. K. Detterman (Eds.), *Human intelligence: Perspectives on its theory and measurement*. Norwood, N.J.: Ablex, 1979.

Kail, R., Carter, P., & Pellegrino, J. The locus of sex differences in spatial ability. *Perception & Psychophysics*, 1979, *26*, 182–186.

Kosslyn, S. M. The medium and the message in mental imagery: A theory. *Psychological Review*, 1981, *88*, 46–66.

Lucas, C. M. *Analysis of the Relative Movement test by a method of individual interviews* (ETS RM 53–08). Princeton, N.J.: Educational Testing Service, 1953.

Lucas, C. M., & French, J. W. *A factorial study of experimental tests of integration, judgment, and planning* (ETS RB 53–16). Princeton, N.J.: Educational Testing Service, 1953.

MacLeod, C. M., Hunt, E. B., & Mathews, N. N. Individual differences in the verification of sentence-picture relationships. *Journal of Verbal Learning and Verbal Behavior*, 1978, *17*, 493–507.

McNemar, Q. Lost: Our intelligence? Why? *American Psychologist*, 1964, *19*, 871–882.

Michael, W. B., Zimmerman, W. S., & Guilford, J. P. An investigation of two hypotheses regarding the nature of the spatial relations and visualization factors. *Educational and Psychological Measurement*, 1950, *10*, 187–243.

Myers, C. T. *Some observations and opinions concerning spatial relations tests* (ETS RM 57-7). Princeton, N.J.: Educational Testing Service, 1957.

Myers, C. T. *Some observations of problem solving in spatial relations tests* (ETS RB 58–16). Princeton, N.J.: Educational Testing Service, 1958.

Nisbitt, R. E., & Wilson, T. D. Telling more than we can know: Verbal reports on mental processes. *Psychological Review*, 1977, *84*, 231–259.

Palmer, S. E. Hierarchical structure in perceptual representation. *Cognitive Psychology*, 1977, *9*, 441–474.

Pellegrino, J. W., & Glaser, R. Cognitive correlates and components in the analysis of individual differences. In R. J. Sternberg & D. K. Detterman (Eds.), *Human intelligence: Perspectives on its theory and measurement*. Norwood, N. J.: Ablex, 1979.

Shepard, R. N. Form, formation, and transformation of internal representations. In R. Solso (Ed.), *Information processing and cognition: The Loyola Symposium*. Hillsdale, N.J.: Lawrence Erlbaum Associates, 1975.

Smith, I. M. *Spatial ability*. San Diego, Calif.: Knapp, 1964.

Snow, R. E. Eye fixation and strategy analyses of individual differences in cognitive aptitudes. In A. M. Lesgold, J. W. Pellegrino, S. D. Fokkeman, & R. Glaser (Eds.), *Cognitive psychology and instruction*. New York: Plenum, 1978.

Snow, R. E. Theory and method for research on aptitude processes. In R. J. Sternberg & D. K. Detterman (Eds.), *Human intelligence: Perspectives on its theory and measurement*. Norwood, N.J.: Ablex, 1979.

Snow, R. E. Aptitude processes. In R. E. Snow, P.-A. Federico, & W. E. Montague (Eds.), *Aptitude, learning, and instruction* (Vol. 1). Hillsdale, N.J.: Lawrence Erlbaum Associates, 1980.

Snow, R. E. Toward a theory of aptitude for learning. I. Fluid and crystallized abilities and their correlates. In M. P. Friedman, J. P. Das, & N. O'Connor (Eds.), *Intelligence and learning*. New York: Plenum, 1981.

Spearman, C. Thurstone's work re-worked. *Journal of Educational Psychology*, 1939, *16*, 1–16.

Sternberg, R. J. *Intelligence, information processing, and analogical reasoning: The componential analysis of human abilities*. Hillsdale, N.J.: Lawrence Erlbaum Associates, 1977.

Sternberg, R. J. Representation and process in linear syllogistic reasoning. *Journal of Experimental Psychology: General*, 1980, *109*, 119–159.

Sternberg, R. J., Tourangeau, R., & Nigro, G. Metaphor, induction, and social policy: The convergence of macroscopic and microscopic views. In A. Ortony (Ed.), *Metaphor and thought*. London/New York: Cambridge Univ. Press, 1979.

Thurstone, L. L. The perceptual factor. *Psychometrica*, 1938, *3*, 1–12. (a)

Thurstone, L. L. Primary mental abilities. *Psychometric Monographs*, 1938, *1*. (b)

Witkin, H. A., Oltman, P. K., Raskin, E., & Karp, S. A. *Embedded figures test*. Palo Alto, Calif.: Consulting Psychologists Press, 1971.

NOTES

1. Kyllonen, P. C., Lohman, D. F., & Snow, R. E. *Effects of item facets and strategy training on spatial task performance* (Tech. Rep. No. 14). Stanford, Calif.: Aptitude Research Project, School of Education, Stanford University, 1981.

2. Marshalek, B. *Trait and process aspects of vocabulary knowledge and verbal ability* (Tech. Rep. No. 15). Stanford, Calif.: Aptitude Research Project, School of Education, Stanford University, 1981.

3. Lohman, D. F. *Spatial ability: A review and reanalysis of the correlational literature* (Tech. Rep. No. 8). Stanford, Calif.: Aptitude Research Project, School of Education, Stanford University, 1979.

4. Bethell-Fox, C. E., Lohman, D. F., & Snow, R. E. *Componential and eye movement analysis of geometric analogy performance* (Tech. Rep. No. 16). Stanford, Calif.: Aptitude Research Project, School of Education, Stanford University, 1981.

5. Lohman, D. F. *Spatial ability: Individual differences in speed and level* (Tech. Rep. No. 9). Stanford, Calif.: Aptitude Research Project, School of Education, Stanford University, 1979.

6. Yallow, E., & Webb, N. *Introspective strategy differences reflecting aptitude processes*. Paper

presented at the meeting of the American Psychological Association, San Francisco, August 1977.

7.   Kyllonen, P. C., Woltz, D. J., & Lohman, D. F. *Models of strategy and strategy-shifting in spatial visualization performance* (Tech. Rep. No. 17). Stanford, Calif.: Aptitude Research Project, School of Education, Stanford University, 1981.

5

Developmental and Individual Differences in Verbal and Spatial Reasoning*

James W. Pellegrino and Susan R. Goldman

INTRODUCTION

The existence of the current volume on *Individual Differences in Cognition* and its diverse content is evidence that there has been a broad resurgence of interest in the assessment of cognitive abilities. This is true not only within the fields of psychometrics and education but also within cognitive and developmental psychology. The study of individual differences in cognition continues to have practical and theoretical significance. The practical significance lies within traditional instructional settings where much has been said about adaptive education and the individualization of instruction. If optimization through individualization is to be realized, then detailed diagnostic assessments are needed of the learner's current knowledge and skills relative

*The preparation of this chapter and portions of the research reported herein were supported by subcontract No. 4732–1 from the Learning Research and Development Center of the University of Pittsburgh which is supported, in part, by funds provided by the National Institute of Education, U.S. Department of Education.

to the knowledge and skills that define the short- and long-range goals of instruction. Traditional individual-difference assessment through aptitude and intelligence testing falls far short of these objectives since test scores are norm-referenced and lack theoretical interpretation with respect to cognitive processes and knowledge structure differences at various age levels. Attempts to match global aptitude scores to instructional treatments in Aptitude-Treatment Interaction (ATI) research have failed because of the lack of well-specified theories of both aptitude and instructional treatments. Thus, research has emerged aimed at specifying the cognitive structures and processes associated with (1) individual differences in aptitude; and (2) levels of expertise in various content domains and subject matters. In terms of Glaser's (1976) *Components of a Psychology of Instruction,* these represent attempts at specifying the initial state of the learner, the nature of competent performance, and the associated intermediate states.

The theoretical significance of research on individual differences in cognitive abilities stems from the fact that both experimental–cognitive and developmental psychology have largely ignored individual variation in their theories and models of cognitive performance. The goal has been to establish general laws of learning, memory, problem solving, developmental change, and so on with the assumption that individual variation is at a parametric–quantitative rather than qualitative level. Thus, the tendency has been to model group mean data, often with little concern about the adequacy of a given model at the level of the individual subject. Adequate theories of cognition and cognitive development must be able to encompass both the similarities and differences among individuals if they are to achieve breadth and explanatory power. Underwood (1975) referred to the study of individual differences in cognitive processes as a "crucible in theory construction."

In this chapter, we will review some of our own research on individual differences in cognitive abilities. The research represents an attempt to understand the cognitive components of developmental and individual differences as manifest on standardized aptitude and intelligence-test tasks. In the next section, we will sketch the general framework that has guided our research efforts. The bulk of what we subsequently present illustrates the application of such an approach to an understanding of developmental and individual differences in verbal and spatial reasoning ability. The final section of this chapter summarizes our results to date and considers some directions and issues for future research. In particular, practical difficulties associated with conducting and reporting research on developmental and individual differences in cognitive abilities will be discussed.

A *cognitive components* approach to developmental and individual-differences research attempts to directly identify the information processing components of performance on tasks used to assess general and specific aptitude. In this approach, performance on major psychometric test tasks becomes the object of theoretical and empirical analysis. The goal is to develop models of performance which can be used as the basis for specifying the sources of developmental and individual differences. Thus, tasks that have been shown to reliably differentiate among age groups and individuals within age groups are treated as "cognitive tasks" (Carroll, 1976) that can be approached and analyzed in the same way that cognitive and developmental psychologists have approached and analyzed memory search, visual scanning, sentence verification, and mental arithmetic tasks (to name just a few).

The initial step in a systematic analysis of verbal or spatial reasoning ability involves identifying the core or prototypical tasks associated with the aptitude factor of concern. This is based on a review of major factor-analytic studies and the content of widely used general intelligence and multiaptitude batteries. It must be noted that no single task uniquely defines an aptitude factor but that verbal reasoning or spatial-aptitude factors are typically defined by sets of tasks that show high levels of intercorrelation. An adequate understanding of developmental and individual differences in a cognitive aptitude cannot be based on an intensive empirical and theoretical analysis of only a single task with a high loading on an aptitude construct. Instead, it is necessary to pursue analyses that consider the various intercorrelated tasks that define more completely a set of processes or skills comprising aptitude. The analysis of multiple tasks permits the identification of general and specific cognitive-process differences and should help focus on a level of description where research can be pursued on process trainability and transfer effects. The latter are critical issues for instructional applications.

The obvious next steps in aptitude analysis are the development and application of process models of individual task performance. Theories and models of performance on verbal or spatial reasoning tasks can be derived from computer simulation programs and/or empirical studies of the effects of task properties on latency, solution protocols, and error patterns. The validation of such theories and models must be at two levels. First, they must be shown to be empirically valid at the group mean level. This is the standard approach within most cognitive research. However, the theories and models must also be shown to have validity at the individual subject level. Thus, we are explicitly proposing the idea that a model that serves to capture group performance must also be shown to be valid at the individual subject level. Developmental and individual differences can be investigated in terms of the parameters of a single model or in terms of the applicability of different models for the performance of different individuals. Part of such an analysis involves the investigation of the sources of interage and intraage individual differences. An approach combining developmental and individual-differences analyses is particularly important to the validation and application of models of task performance. Theories and models of aptitude should be able to account for overall developmental changes in a specific aptitude as well as the sources of individual differences within separate age groups. With respect to the latter issue, there is no reason to assume that the major sources of individual differences within one age group are necessarily applicable to individuals at a higher or lower maturational level.

Unfortunately, there has been very little integration of research on individual differences with research on cognitive development. This is surprising because standardized tests of intelligence or aptitude have been widely administered to children and used to make decisions that affect their educational opportunities. But little is known about the relationship between individual differences and developmental change. Consider how high-IQ children *might* differ from low-IQ children over the course of development. Some of the possible relationships are outlined in Figure 1. Proficiency on a particular information processing skill, such as mental rotation or retrieval from long-term memory, is plotted as function of age. The graph in the upper left corner represents the possibility that children who score poorly on a test of mental ability lag behind high scorers, but they share a single developmental course. This seems to have been the idea that guided Binet in construction of intelligence tests. Figures 1b and 1c are variations on this theme. Figure 1d represents the idea that a skill may show development without differentiating between high and low scorers, and Figure 1e illustrates that a skill may consistently distinguish between individuals without

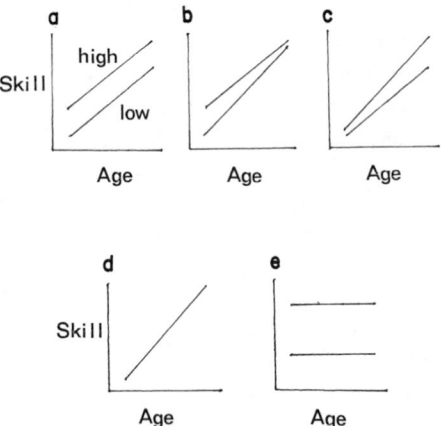

FIGURE 1. Examples of possible relationships between age and skill levels.

undergoing developmental change. These are just a subset of the possibilities. We would argue that theories about individual differences in childhood and theories about cognitive development would both be enhanced if the two lines of research were integrated.

In the remainder of this chapter, we will examine some of the ways in which age and skill differences are manifest on verbal and spatial reasoning tasks and some of the implications of this work for theories of individual differences and cognitive development.

DEVELOPMENTAL AND INDIVIDUAL DIFFERENCES IN VERBAL INDUCTIVE REASONING

Inductive reasoning problems have been a part of aptitude and intelligence tests almost from the inception of the testing movement. All such tasks have the same basic property: The individual must induce a rule governing a set of elements. This property is manifest in a variety of task forms ranging from simple classification problems to highly complex matrix items. One or more of these task forms can be found on virtually any standardized aptitude or intelligence test at any developmental level. As an example, the Cognitive Abilities Test (see Thorndike & Hagen, 1971) includes these item types in the multilevel battery intended for grades 3–12: verbal classification and analogy, number series, and figural classification and analogy. Multiple-aptitude batteries such as the Differential Aptitude Test (see Bennet, Seashore, & Wesman, 1974) and the Primary Mental Abilities Test (see Thurstone & Thurstone, 1949) provide separate inductive-reasoning scores.

The extensive use of induction items, and analogy in particular, in intelligence and aptitude tests was documented by Dawis and Siojo (Note 1); more recently, Sternberg (1977) has provided a detailed review and discussion of the importance of analogical reasoning within the field of differential psychology. Spearman (1923) and Raven (1938) both argued that inductive reasoning was central to the concept and measurement of intelligence. The only debate about the different task forms and content dimensions (letters, words, numbers, or geometric figures) is whether they represent a single aptitude construct or can be subdivided into separate aptitude factors that represent different relational types such as the induction of semantic as opposed to figural relations. The evidence favors the latter position. Correlational data involving classification and analogy performance indicate higher correlations for common content domains than common task forms. For example, on the Cognitive Abilities Test, the correlation between verbal analogy and verbal classification performance is higher than any other intertask correlations at the third-grade level. A similar correlational pattern emerges at grades 7 and 11 on this test.

Beyond being a psychometric curiosity, rule-induction tasks are relevant in the broader domain of cognitive and developmental research and theory. For example, Greeno (1978) has characterized rule-induction problems as instances of a major type of problem-solving task within a general problem typology. He has also suggested that, in many respects, comprehension can be viewed as a special instance of rule induction. Rule induction has also been discussed in the framework of semantic memory research. Egan and Greeno (1974) have pointed out that analogical reasoning, series completion, problem solving, and concept formation all require a search for relationships among elements resulting in new interconnections among the nodes of a network structure. Applying this notion to education, Norman, Gentner, and Stevens (1976) have argued for the essentially inductive nature of effective instruction. Structures of interrelated concepts are communicated to students by a teacher or through some other instructional medium. In order to comprehend and remember the material, the student must induce the structure of the presented information by detecting the relational pattern of the presented concepts and discover connections between the newly communicated material and the knowledge structures already in permanent memory. The importance of inductive thought processes and reasoning by analogy has been emphasized in science (Oppenheimer, 1956), mathematics, (Polya, 1965), and in the acquisition of information in the classroom (e.g., Bruner, 1957; Forehand, 1974).

Within developmental research and theory, there has been considerable emphasis on the importance of classification and categorization in cognitive development. Vygotsky's (1962) theory of conceptual development was based on the progressive refinement of the child's ability to classify objects. Nelson, Rescorla, Gruendel, and Benedict (1978) have argued that many of the child's early overextensions really reflect the attempt to categorize on the basis of similarities and to use analogy to express thoughts for which the child has no words. Anglin (1977) has found that preschool children, when presented with a category label, often show inconsistency between their intension and extension of the concept. The ability to coordinate the intension and extension of a concept develops as the child grows older and is needed for successful performance on classification tasks.

Researchers have also been interested in the development of analogical reasoning because of its potential relationship to different stages within Piagetian theory. It has been argued that true analogical reasoning does not emerge until the formal operational stage since it requires understanding a second-order relationship representing the relationship of first order relations (e.g., Piaget, Montangero, & Billeter, 1977). Studies of the development of analogical reasoning have attempted to determine if children in the concrete operational stage show evidence of such relationship coordination in solving verbal analogies.

MODELS OF CLASSIFICATION AND ANALOGY SOLUTION

As noted, inductive reasoning is a major aspect of cognitive development and plays an important role in both the development of a system of logical thought processes and in the acquisition of new information (e.g., Bruner, 1957; Gallagher, 1978). Verbal classification and analogy problems constitute the major types of verbal inductive reasoning tasks, occurring frequently on general aptitude and intelligence tests. The simplest classification tests involve nonverbal (pictorial) problems. Verbal items are first introduced in group tests at the third- or fourth-grade level. Classification problems are generally easier than analogy problems, having a wider set of possible correct completions. Analogical reasoning performance represents a prototypical measure of Spearman's g (e.g., Cronbach, 1970; Snow, 1980).

Recently, attention has been directed toward specifying the cognitive abilities associated with performance on analogy tasks and we have extended this effort to classification tasks (e.g., Pellegrino & Glaser, 1980; Sternberg, 1977; Sternberg & Nigro, 1980; Sternberg & Rifkin, 1979). Within the general theory of analogy solution described by Sternberg (1977), the terms of the analogy are encoded or represented internally. The relationship between the A and B terms is inferred, that information is applied to the C term, and a test for correspondence between the A–B and C–D pairs of terms is made. It may also be necessary to identify or map the relationship between A and C. Solution depends on accurate and efficient execution of these component processes. Successful process execution involves knowledge and use of rules and decision criteria that are consistent with constraints on analogical reasoning. The major constraint is that the relationship between A and B must parallel the relationship between C and D, and must not violate potential A–C and B–D relationship correspondence.

A general model for solution of classification problems can also be specified and includes a subset of the processes described by Sternberg (1977) for analogical reasoning. Specifically, solution of a forced-choice classification problem requires the following processes: (1) encoding each of the terms; (2) inferring the relationship(s) among the exemplars, and extracting a general class rule; (3) discriminating among alternative choices, evaluating each for consistency with the general rule to find the best answer; and (4) responding.

Although differences in testing format may serve to make the task more complex, classification is generally the easier type of inductive-reasoning task. The classification item is less constrained in its solution than the analogy item: Once a class rule has been induced, the task involves the identification of another exemplar consistent with the rule. However, the analogy problem requires mapping, application, and the identification of a very restricted completion term (Sternberg, 1977).

Process theories of the types outlined could be validated by constructing alternative models and testing their applicability to latency and error data. This approach has been taken by Sternberg (1977) in his studies of various reasoning tasks, including analogy. A complementary approach—which we have taken in our investigations of analogy and classification—is to apply the component-process theories to the prediction of individual differences in overall *accuracy* of forced-choice performance. We have developed a series of mathematical expressions that incorporate the probability of success on each component process involved in solving an analogy or classification item in forced-choice testing formats. Then, we compared these process-outcome measures in successful and less successful reasoners within different age groups, thereby isolating the component processes that contribute most to individual differences in overall performance. Estimates for each of the component processes are obtained by employing an incremental presentation methodology in conjunction with the more typical forced-choice format. The essence of this approach is to present the item so that, initially, only the relational inference process is required by presenting the first pair of stem terms in analogy and the three stem terms in classification. Subsequently, all of the stem terms are presented, and the task is to generate a correct completion term. Finally, the stem is re-presented along with an alternative set and the task is the typical forced-choice format.

The details of these mathematical expressions vary somewhat for analogy and classification items. First, we will present a relatively detailed discussion of the more complex analogy case, including the rationale for the various expressions in the equations, and then briefly, present the expressions appropriate to classification.

The typical psychometric format for analogy problems is forced choice in which a three-term stem is presented (i.e., A is to B as C is to ?) with four to five alternatives. The child must choose one of these alternatives. Another format is the generation task in which a three-term stem is presented but no alternatives are provided. In the generation task, choice of the completion term is not restricted to the alternative set. The individual may infer any possible A–B relationship and the probability of making a correct inference is p_i. Given the inference of an appropriate relationship, the individual must then attempt to apply that relationship to the C term to produce an ideal D' term. This constitutes a search of semantic memory for a term that satisfies the parallelism and directional constraints. The probability of success for the application process given correct inference is p_a. Thus, the level of correct performance in the generation task is given by

$$p_{gen} \text{ (corr)} = p_i p_a$$

The forced-choice task requires the same inference and application processes as the generation task plus discrimination-choice components that may facilitate performance. The alternatives define a restricted search space that may provide a chance to recognize a relationship and completion term that the individual's definition of the search space did not permit. Given the presence of a recognition process with probability of success p_r, the equation for correct performance in a K alternative forced-choice task is the following:

$$p_{fc} \text{ (corr)} = p_i p_a + p_r(1-p_i p_a) + 1/K(1- (p_i p_a + p_r(1-p_i p_a)))$$

This equation represents the separate and additive probabilities (proportions) that can contribute to the overall level of correct responding in a forced-choice task. If it is assumed that forced choice does not interfere with prior correct inference *and* application processes, then items that can be correctly answered in a generation task will also be correct in forced choice. The proportion of these cases is given by $p_i p_a$. The $p_r(1-p_i p_a)$ segment of the equation represents those cases where inference and/or application have failed; that is, items with incorrect generation responses. The proportion of such cases is $(1-p_i p_a)$ and this is multiplied by p_r, the probability of successful recognition or discovery of the correct response. The expectation is that p_r should be greater than or equal to zero, with positive values indicating the operation of a facilitating response-recognition process. The final segment of the equation represents those cases where inference, application, and/or recognition processes have failed and only random guessing leads to a correct response. The proportion of such cases is $(1-(p_i p_a + p_r(1-p_i p_a)))$ and the probability of successful guessing is $1/K$ in a K alternative situation.

The presence of the alternative set may also make certain items more difficult to solve. Certain kinds of distractors—salient-free associates to the C term—may cause the rejectlon of a previously generated analogically appropriate response. Research suggests that free-association distractors are a significant source of errors for young children and less skilled analogical reasoners (e.g., Achenbach, 1970; Gentile, Tedesco-Stratton, Davis, Lund, & Agunanne, 1977). Additionally, the distractor set may contain multiple alternatives that match the ideal D' term equally well. The individual may be unable to select the C–D pairing that yields the most precise matching relationship. Assuming the presence of an additional distractor-interference component, which has probability p_d of leading to an error, the complete equation for forced-choice performance is

$$p_{fc} \text{ (Corr)} = p_i p_a + p_r(1-p_i p_a) + 1/K(1-(p_i p_a + p_r(1-p_i p_a))) - p_d p_i p_a$$

The major difference between the analogy and classification expressions is that classification does not have the application (p_a) process. For a classification problem, the inference-rule generation process has probability p_i of success. The forced-choice testing format involves two types of discrimination components. The restricted set of alternatives can permit the recognition of the correct rule, given that it previously was not inferred; this occurs with probability p_r. Given that a correct rule has been induced previously, each of the alternatives must be evaluated for correspondence with the rule and the overall success of such an evaluation is p_e. The general equation for performance in a K alternative forced-choice classification task is

$$p_{fc}(\text{corr}) = p_i + p_r(1-p_i) + 1/K(1-(p_i + p_r(1-p_i))) - p_i(1-p_e)$$

The preceding analyses of performance components yield several possible sources of age and skill differences in analogical and classificatory reasoning. By obtaining estimates for each of the major components of forced-choice performance, the contribution of each component to age and skill differences can be determined. This represents a level of analysis that assumes an adequate task understanding and processing strategy since emphasis is placed on process-outcome measures associated with the necessary stages of item solution. Also, it assumes that the information available at each stage of processing remains available during subsequent stages and is appropriately coordinated within the general constraints of the task.

In addition, we have examined a second level of analysis in our investigations of classification and analogy performance. This other level of analysis considers the possibility that children differ in the extent to which performance reflects the presence of a processing strategy that is appropriate for classificatory or analogical reasoning. In our work on both types of problems, we have collected verbal justification data following the choice of a final answer for any given item. When individuals are asked to justify or explain their choice, they convey information about the interitem relationships governing their selection process. Thus, whether the answer is right or wrong, it is possible to determine if they have obeyed the constraints of analogy or classification problem solution. The use and interpretation of the verbal justifications as well as their implications for solution strategies are discussed in detail for each task in the next two sections where our empirical work on analogy and on classification is discussed.

DEVELOPMENTAL AND INDIVIDUAL DIFFERENCES IN VERBAL ANALOGY SOLUTION

The multilevel approach to investigating verbal-analogy solution was used in two studies conducted by Goldman, Pellegrino, Parseghian, and Sallis (1982). In the experiments, third- and fifth-grade children were presented either 50 (Experiment 1) or 20 (Experiment 2) verbal-analogy items selected from a variety of standardized tests. The incremental presentation procedure was used in both experiments. In Experiment 1, the child was presented the A:B::C: _____ stems and asked to generate completion terms for each item. Subsequently, the stem and alternative set were presented together, and the child was asked to select the best answer and verbally justify the choice. In Experiment 2, the child was first shown the A:B pair and asked to describe the relationship. This was immediately followed by presentation of the A:B::C:_____ stem and generation of a completion term was requested. Finally, the stem and option set were presented, and selection and verbal justification of the best answer for the item were requested. The first experiment involved 24 8-year-olds and 23 10-year-olds, whereas the second experiment involved a sample of 12 8-year-olds and 12 10-year-olds.

Both experiments yielded developmental differences in overall forced-choice performance. More importantly, however, there was substantial variability among individuals within each grade and considerable overlap between grades. As an example, the range of forced-choice performance in Experiment 1 was .18–.70 for the 8-year-olds and .22–.78 for the 10-year-olds.

Performance in the generation and forced-choice tasks was used to derive process-outcome values for each subject in Experiment 1. Table 1 identifies the three measures that were estimated and their mean value within each grade. All three measures showed significant differences. Thus, developmental differences in forced-choice performance are a function of the inference × application and recognition components as well as a reduced susceptibility to distractor interference. If the alternative set is viewed as a form of explicit countersuggestion, then the distractor–interference results are consistent with results obtained by Piaget et al. (1977). Specifically, they found that prior to full analogical reasoning, children are likely to change their responses in the face of experimenter-provided countersuggestion.

Correlation–regression analyses were done, using the values of the different-process-outcome measures as predictors of overall forced-choice performance. Table 2 shows the simple r values and the β weights for the different predictors. Grade was entered as a predictor and its contribution was negligible. All three process-outcome measures contributed to predict-

TABLE 1

Means and Standard Deviations for Process Components in Experiment 1

Process measure	Grade[a]	
	Third	Fifth
Inference × application ($p_i p_a$)	.30	.40
	(.10)	(.12)
Response recognition (p_r)	.10	.19
	(.11)	(.15)
Distractor interference (p_d)	.36	.27
	(.18)	(.15)

[a]All differences between grade means are statistically significant. Standard deviations are in parentheses.

ing individual differences in forced-choice performance. Components associated with the processing of information in the alternative set contribute substantially to predicting individual differences in forced-choice performance. The combined inference × application component is also an important performance component but its relative contribution to individual differences is less than the recognition and distraction components. The magnitude of the individual differences on these process components is illustrated in Table 3. Skilled groups within each grade comprise the top eight scorers on the forced-choice task and the less skilled groups the bottom seven.[1] Skill differences within and across age groups follow the overall developmental trends. Of interest is the fact that skilled third-graders perform at a level above that of less skilled fifth-graders.

TABLE 2

Simple and Multiple Regression Results Predicting Forced Choice Performance in Experiment 1

Predictor	Simple r	β
Grade	.41*	.02
Inference × application ($p_i p_a$)	.77**	.28**
Response recognition (p_r)	.91**	.58**
Distractor interference (p_d)	−.69**	−.35**

*$p < .01$.
**$p < .001$.

[1]The latter number was used to avoid an arbitrary choice among children with equal scores.

TABLE 3

Means and Standard Deviations for Process Components of Skilled and Less-Skilled Reasoners in Experiment 1

Process measure	Third grade[a]		Fifth grade	
	Skilled	Less-skilled	Skilled	Less-skilled
Inference × application $(p_i p_a)$	.37	.22	.52	.29
	(.11)	(.03)	(.07)	(.06)
Response recognition (p_r)	.21	.01	.34	.03
	(.10)	(.04)	(.10)	(.05)
Distractor interference (p_d)	.26	.52	.18	.41
	(.11)	(.15)	(.09)	(.16)

[a]Standard deviations are shown in parentheses.

In Experiment 2, performance in the inference, generation, and forced-choice tasks was used to derive process-outcome values representing four different components of analogy solution. The four process measures shown in Table 4 contain the results of correlation–regression analyses involving the prediction of forced-choice performance. Grade was entered as a predictor; its contribution was again minimal. All four process components were significant contributors to the multiple R. The least important factor was inference. Application, recognition, and distractor interference were, approximately, equal contributors to the regression. The major difference relative to Experiment 1 was the lower β value for the recognition component. Nevertheless, the two components that are unique to forced choice still make a larger total contribution to the prediction of individual differences than the combined inference and application components. This

TABLE 4

Simple and Multiple Regression Results Predicting Forced-Choice Performance in Experiment 2

Predictor	Simple r	β
Grade	.30	−.03
Inference (p_i)	.67**	.19*
Application (p_a)	.74**	.34**
Response recognition (p_r)	.82**	.36**
Distractor interference (p_d)	−.78**	−.40**

*p < .01.
**p < .001.

was the case even though the absolute level of performance in both the generation and forced-choice tasks was higher in Experiment 2.

Of the four process components examined, relational application, response recognition, and distractor interference were about equally important in predicting individual differences in forced-choice performance. Relational inference was a less important predictor but was, nonetheless, significantly related to individual differences. Thus, as in previous research, relational inference is a source of change in the development of analogical reasoning (e.g., Levinson & Carpenter, 1974; Lunzer, 1968). However, consistent with research that has examined relational inference independent of other components (e.g., Sternberg & Nigro, 1980), the present findings indicate that those processes associated with the coordination and comparison of pairs of relationships are more predictive of individual differences. All three components that involve the processing of relationships from more than a single pair of terms appear to be the primary factors producing individual differences in forced-choice performance. These results are supportive of the notion that a significant aspect of age and skill differences is the ability (and/or attempt) to coordinate sets of relationships relative to the constraints of the analogy task.

The importance of the distractor-interference process is consistent with previous conclusions regarding the role of associative responding in analogy tasks. A characteristic of younger and less-skilled reasoners is greater susceptibility to free associates of the C term (e.g., Achenbach, 1970) and to alternatives that have relatively high associative relatedness to the stem (Gentile, Kessler, & Gentile, 1969; Sternberg & Nigro, 1980). An additional aspect of our data is relevant to this point: less-skilled, in contrast to skilled, 8- and 10-year-olds, demonstrated a significantly greater tendency to choose personally dominant-free associates[2] when such terms were among the distractors.

The greater likelihood of distractibility for less-mature analogical reasoning may be related, in part, to a generally weaker understanding of the inherent nature of analogy and the constraints on this inductive-reasoning task, an example of the second level of analysis. Support for the presence of a weaker—or less-complete—understanding is provided by the relationship between verbal justification behavior and individual differences in forced-choice performance in both experiments.

It is possible to differentiate at least four response–generation (response–selection) strategies that might be used by children in an analogy task. The simplest solution strategy is one in which the A and B terms are

---

[2]Personally dominant free associates to individual C terms were determined from a free-association task given prior to the experiment.

ignored and the child chooses or generates an answer that is the highest free associate of the C term. A more complex strategy is one in which the child generates or chooses an answer that relates to any two or three terms, regardless of the way in which the terms go together. This strategy essentially reflects association to the group and relational and directional constraints are ignored, although more than just the C term is used to guide solution. The third strategy more closely approximates analogical reasoning. In this strategy, an answer is generated or chosen on the basis of a specific relationship to the C term and the child also is aware of and specifies a relationship between the A and B terms. However, relationships generated between the two pairs of terms need not match. They may be qualitatively different relationships or they may reflect reversal of direction of the same relationship as in "red is a color and fruit is a food" which is inappropriate for the item Color:Red::Fruit:_____. The highest level of solution is precise analogical reasoning in which all the terms and relational constraints are used to govern the generation or choice of answer.

What children say when they justify their responses estimates their

TABLE 5
Categories Used for Classifying Verbal Justifications

Example item:

Cat→Tiger :: Dog→ _____
1) Lion   2) Wolf   3) Bark   4) Animal   5) Horse

Categories	Example statements
Parallel relationships	
1. Standard relationship mentioned	
a. for A→B and C→D	1a. Cats and tigers are in the same family and dogs and WOLVES are too.
b. for C→D	1b. Dogs and WOLVES are in the same family.
2. Possible relationship mentioned	
a. for A→B and C→D	2a. Cats and tigers look alike and dogs and WOLVES look alike.
b. for C→D	2b. Dogs and WOLVES look alike.
Nonparallel relationships	
1. Relationships mentioned for A→B and C→D do not match.	1. Cats and tigers look alike and dogs and WOLVES run fast.
2. Relationships mentioned for C→D is irrelevant to analogy.	2. Dogs and WOLVES bark.
No Relationship	
No relationship mentioned. Statement refers to attribute or property of D term.	I like WOLVES. WOLVES scare me.

thinking about why a particular response is correct. Although it is a *post hoc* rationalization of a response and may not indicate how the child arrived at the answer, it does indicate constraints that she or he thinks the response satisfies. The categories used for classifying justification statements are shown in Table 5. In all the examples, the response being justified is the correct alternative. Those statements that indicated an understanding that the A–B and C–D relationships must match were scored in the parallel relationships category. All the statements in this category mentioned a C–D relationship that matched an A–B relationship. The nonparallel relationships category comprises statements that violate the requirement that the A–B and C–D relationships must match. Two types of statements were scored in this category: (1) when an A–B relationship was given and a different C–D relationship was also given; and (2) when only a C–D relationship was given, but it was irrelevant to the item since it was not a possible relationship for the A–B pair. The no-relationship category refers to statements in which the chosen response was not related to any of the stem terms. All statements were classified independently by two scorers. A third scorer classified a 50% random sample of the statements. Interscorer reliability was above 90%.

Table 6 shows the results of the statement classification for justifications of correct forced-choice responses in Experiment 1. In general, there are consistent but nonsignificant developmental differences in the type of understanding that children's statements reflect when justifying correct responses. The probabilities associated with the parallel and nonparallel relationships categories do not differ across grades. The only developmental difference is the tendency of younger children to make personal, idiosyncratic statements about the response more often than older children. In

TABLE 6
Verbal Justifications of Correct Responses in Experiment 1

Category	Grade[a]	
	Third	Fifth
Parallel relationship	.67	.76
	(.20)	(.19)
Nonparallel relationship	.08	.08
	(.05)	(.08)
No relationship	.20	.08
	(.21)	(.14)
Proportion of total	.95	.89

[a]Standard deviations are shown in parentheses.

contrast to the relatively minor developmental differences, there were substantial individual differences in justification behaviors within each grade. Consistent with Gallagher and Wright (Note 2), the probability of justifying correct responses in terms of parallel relationships was significantly correlated with overall forced-choice performance, r (45) = .73, p < .001. Less-skilled individuals in each grade justified only about half of their correct responses in terms of relational parallelism. Thus, a less-skilled individual often may not be able to verbalize why a correct answer that he or she has chosen is "analogically" correct. This finding was replicated in Experiment 2 where the probability that correct responses were justified in terms of parallel relationships was again significantly correlated with overall forced-choice accuracy r (18) = .74, p < .001.

Such results indicate that skill differences may result from faulty procedures and weak understanding of the analogy task. Even when explaining a correct response, less-skilled reasoners were just as likely to refer to no relationship or an irrelevant one as to refer to a parallel relationship between the pairs of terms. Weaker understanding of the task constraints may make such individuals more susceptible to countersuggestion, whether it comes from an individual (e.g., Piaget et al., 1977) or from the alternative set.

Weaker understanding in conjunction with the process-component differences observed in the present research provide support for the notion that different models of analogy solution are necessary to characterize the development of analogical reasoning (e.g., Piaget et al., 1977; Sternberg & Nigro, 1980). These models can be placed in a broader context. Analogy may be seen as a form of problem solving (Greeno, 1978) of moderate to high degree of complexity for children in midchildhood. A theory of performance for this task must explicitly deal with the child's problem space for the task. The problem space includes the child's representation of the task goals and constraints, relevant processes and declarative knowledge presupposed by the item content. Given vocabulary within one's range of competence, skill in analogy solution reflects an understanding of the parallelism and directional constraints on solution and the efficient and appropriate execution of inference, application, and discrimination-choice processes. Descriptions of developmentally prior models of analogical reasoning performance might assume the presence of a different set of constraints on solution and/or differences in the processes that are executed as well as the speed and accuracy of execution.

Our research (Goldman et al., 1982), as well as existing accounts of less successful analogical reasoning (e.g., Piaget et al., 1977; Sternberg & Nigro, 1980; Gallagher & Wright, Note 2), strongly indicate some type of simpler associative understanding of analogy. One factor contributing to the presence of an associative understanding may be the level of instruction or experience with this type of inductive-reasoning task. The instructions provided on many standardized tests are often minimal and the child may be forced to infer the task structure from a set of practice examples. Furthermore, the examples may be insufficient to discriminate between analogical and associative task constraints. Thus, many tests of inductive reasoning may well be testing induction of the task structure rather than the specific set of inductive-reasoning skills required by a given task form such as analogy, multiple classification, and so on. Another possible explanation for the presence of a simpler associative-solution strategy is that it may replace a weak or tentative analogical understanding when demands imposed by content and process execution exceed the child's capacity. Acquisition of skill may well coincide with the capacity to manage a solution requiring the coordination and comparison of multiple relations.

INDIVIDUAL DIFFERENCES IN VERBAL CLASSIFICATION

The multilevel approach was also used in an analysis of sources of individual differences in classification performance. Parseghian and Pellegrino (Note 3) examined performance on typical classification items, where three terms related by some rule are presented and a fourth term consistent with the rule must be chosen. The study was carried out in two stages. The first part involved group testing of children on a large set of items having different semantic characteristics. The group test was used to identify (1) individuals with high and low levels of skill; and (2) items that discriminated among skill groups. The children who were selected for the second part of the study were then tested on a subset of the items. The second phase involved an intensive examination of the outcomes of different solution components for individuals with varying levels of skill. Testing during the second phase was done individually and involved the collection of detailed protocols of the child's solution attempts. As with the analogy work, an incremental presentation and testing procedure was used to provide information about the outcomes of the various component processes required for solution.

The group testing involved 31 third-graders (8-year-olds) and 28 fifth-graders (10-year-olds). Twelve children at each grade level were then chosen to participate in individual testing sessions. Half of the children were selected to form a low-skill group and the remaining half represented a high-skill group. Table 7 compares the overall performance of the skill groups in each grade on the group administered test.

The items used for individual testing represented a subset of the items contained in the original group test. Thus, it was possible to contrast overall

TABLE 7
Mean Classification Performance on the Group Test of Skill Groups Selected for Individual Testing

	Mean proportion correct	Range
Grade 3		
Low skill	.39	.35–.43
High skill	.67	.64–.71
Grade 5		
Low skill	.40	.34–.46
High skill	.73	.64–.87

forced-choice performance on these items as a function of the different formats of subject testing. Figure 2 shows the interaction of skill by test administration, reflecting the dramatic improvement in performance across group and individual testing for the low-skill children. The lack of a change in performance in the high-skill groups indicates that we are observing more than a retesting effect and certainly more than regression to the mean. We will have more to say about this performance improvement shortly.

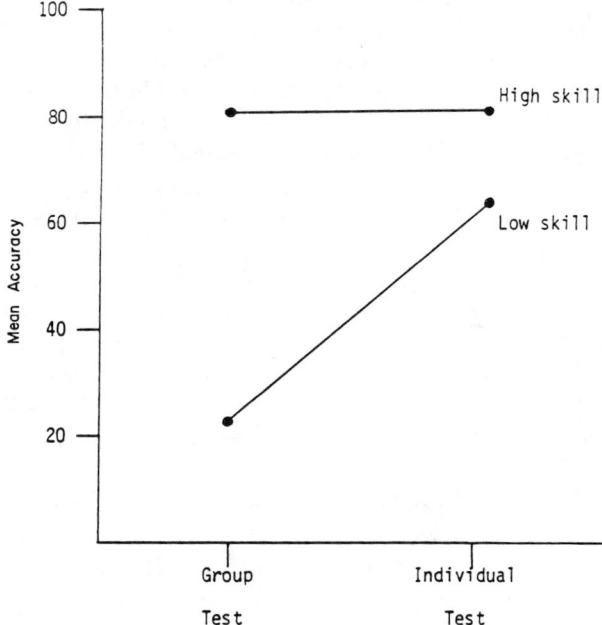

FIGURE 2. Classification performance as a function of skill and test administration.

TABLE 8

Mean Values and Regression Results for Process Components in Verbal Classification

Process measure	Low skill	High skill	Simple r
Inference (p_i)	.18	.47	.79**
Evaluation (p_e)	.64	.83	.43*
Recognition (p_r)	.62	.72	.13

$*p < .05.$
$**p < .01.$

The testing procedure used in the second phase of the study provided quantitative measures of the child's solution processes as defined by the model of solution outlined earlier. The principal process–outcome measures are summarized in Table 8. As shown in the table, the low-skill group has a lower probability of success for the relational inference process. Additionally, the low-skill individuals gave a relationship only 50% of the time while the high-skill individuals responded to over 90% of the items. The other two process measures in Table 8 relate to the discrimination components of the forced-choice task. Both the recognition component and the evaluation component also differentiated between the skill groups.

Simple and multiple regressions were carried out to assess the influence of different components of processing on the accuracy of final forced-choice performance and the results are also shown in Table 8. The most important predictor of final performance is the accuracy of inference made early in the course of solution. The performance of individuals on the group test was influenced most strongly by the accuracy of the inference process ($\beta = .79$), which alone accounted for 62% of the variance in performance. The failure of the recognition measure to contribute to prediction, coupled with the importance of the inference process, suggests that the alternative set does not provide a helpful clue for solution in less-skilled individuals when earlier inferences have failed.

Given the importance of the inference process in discriminating among individuals, an important question is how high- and low-skill individuals differ in their inference behavior. This was addressed by considering the characteristics of a child's behavior when a correct inference was not expressed. Skill differences did not appear in the proportion of cases where the child admitted a failure to find a solution. There was a marginal difference between skill groups in the proportion of statements falling into a "no content" subcategory.[3] Not only did more of the statements made by low-

---

[3]The "no content" category refers to verbal statements that failed to specify information about the semantic features of the individual terms.

skill children lack content, this subcategory represented the dominant mode of expression in the low-skill group. A third category of responses included cases where the stem words were related, but in a way that differed from the inference needed to solve the problem. The difference between the skill groups in the likelihood of expressing a relationship, even when wrong, was significant.

The verbal justifications of the final choice were augmented in this study by including a task in which the individual went through the nonselected alternatives and explained why each was not an appropriate response. Analysis of these data indicated that differences in inference behavior persisted throughout the course of solution. The child's approach to the set of alternatives was analyzed in terms of the use of a relevant, consistent rule. Four types of rule-governed behavior were typical: (1) use of a previously inferred relationship; (2) elaboration of a previously inferred relationship; (3) use of a new, different rule; and (4) identification and use of the correct rule. The child's behavior with the alternatives showed the same pattern as the inference behavior. High-skill individuals worked through the set of alternatives with a rule for evaluating each word 55% of the time, but low-skill individuals operated with rules only 29% of the time. This skill difference was also significant.

The data from this study indicate that processing failures occur at all stages of solution, and certain failures were observed more frequently among the low-skill children. These failures included misencodings (e.g., "Shine is like polishing your shoes and gleam is a toothpaste"), and inability to infer a relationship (e.g., "Radiator and scarf don't go together. You can't wear a radiator"). One processing factor that was systematically related to an individual's performance was the ability to infer a correct rule for the stem of the problem. Children who tended to choose the correct answer during the final forced-choice stage also tended to produce correct relational inferences and rules for the problem stem during the early stages of solution. Making a correct inference early in the solution process seems to enhance performance by providing an individual with information that is useful for all subsequent stages of processing. The correct inference provides the basis for a rule that will allow the unique acceptance of the choice word and the rejection of distractors in the alternative set. Analyses of the children's protocols support this interpretation. When a correct inference was not made, subsequent behavior was not rule-governed; alternatives were evaluated idiosyncratically. The implications of the importance of the inference process confirm the adequacy of the model of solution discussed earlier in this chapter. That model grew out of a task analysis that characterized performance on classification problems as the construction and utilization of a class rule for the evaluation of candidate class exemplars.

Solution processes cannot be considered independently of the child's approach to solution. Most of the low-skill children selected for individual testing had performed at essentially a chance level on the group-administered test. Such a low level of performance suggests that the low-skill child may be operating with no workable strategy for accomplishing the task. If this were true, one might expect that the structured format of the individual interview session would produce an improvement in performance among the low-skill children by providing them with an adequate plan for solution (see Dillon, 1980). If the high-skill children were solving the problem according to some strategic procedure, little change could be expected; the experimental procedure would either resemble the child's own plan very closely or at least be as effective. Both of these expectations were borne out in the data. The low-skill children showed a dramatic improvement in forced-choice accuracy from the group to the individual-testing sessions, while the high-skill children performed at the same level.

The interpretation for this change is that the structured format of the interview sessions essentially constituted the child's executive control over a set of processing stages adequate for solution. Sternberg and Rifkin (1979) have advanced a similar argument to account for the less-systematic problem-solving behavior of young children. In the present case, the argument is being developed more generally in terms of skill.

High-skill children tended to internalize the testing procedure quickly, requiring little intervention by the experimenter to carry out each stage of processing. For example, after choosing a best answer from the alternative set, high-skill children would often spontaneously explain why the two rejected alternatives were inadequate. Low-skill children required a greater amount of experimenter intervention both to elicit responses at each stage of processing and to maintain the structure of the task. The simple correlation between the number of interventions required during a testing session and performance on the individual test was significant, $r = -.60$, $p < .004$. Low-skill children required an average of 52 prompts by the experimenter to work through the solutions of 16 problems, whereas high-skill children needed 22 prompts on the average. Prompts were used to try to elicit a response after a long period of silence as well as to try to elicit an appropriate response (e.g., "You've told me what the words mean, but I'd like you to tell me how they go together.").

Prompting was one characteristic of the individual-testing procedure that ensured that the child would at least go through the motions of correct solution. The improvement in performance suggests that the low-skill children did benefit from the imposed structure. Analyses of their behavior showed that despite the additional prompting, low-skill children still produced fewer inferences and fewer correct inferences than high-skill children. Although performance improved, it was still difficult for the low-skill child to express his or her knowledge and to communicate the various stages of processing.

LATENCY AND ACCURACY OF SEMANTIC INFERENCES

Our studies of analogical reasoning and classification performance have shown that there are substantial developmental and individual differences in the induction of semantic relationships among concepts. Such differences contribute to overall task performance, and on any given item they influence the course of subsequent processing. This was most apparent in the analysis of classification skill. The Parseghian and Pellegrino (Note 3) study also yielded data indicating that item types differed in the relative difficulty of this process with conceptually related items involving easier inferences than items where the rule was based on common properties among the concepts.

The data that are available on inductive reasoning with verbal concepts emphasize the need to explore the inference process in more detail and to focus on "unpacking" it with regard to the processing of semantic features shared by concepts. This was attempted in a study conducted by Lairon, Goldman, and Pellegrino (Note 4) that examined developmental changes in semantic-feature processing. The majority of semantic memory–semantic processing research has focused on the performance of adults relative to the speed of verifying the truth of simple assertions about the class membership or properties of single concepts (e.g., E. E. Smith, 1978). Examples include studies of categorization speed for instances differing in prototypicality and studies showing longer times associated with verifying property as opposed to superordinate category information. The study conducted by Lairon et al. (Note 4) differs from past efforts by examining the speed and accuracy of semantic processing in a situation that does not constrain or predetermine feature processing and that focuses on the processing of several items presented simultaneously. The specific goals were to examine developmental similarities and differences in the speed and accuracy of inferential processes for item groups representing a diverse set of semantic relationship types.

The study involved the presentation of word triplets to 20 individuals representing three different age levels: 8-year-olds, 11-year-olds, and adults. The different items that were presented involved a contrast between two major item types, those involving categorical or class rules and those involving property rules. Within these two major item types, 40 separate instances were presented. The 40 class items represented a hierarchical scheme of animate versus inanimate, and within the animate portion, there was a subdivision of animals versus plants. Within the inanimate portion there was a subdivision of naturally occurring versus man-made objects. Thus, a contrast was possible between individual items and groups of items representing different categorical or class relationships. The 40 property items represented item groups with rules based on (1) color or shape; (2) texture or composition; (3) size, weight, or location; and (4) function. These different groups permitted a contrast within property items of the speed and accuracy of inferring different property relationships and could be compared with items involving categorical or class rules. All items were selected or constructed so that the vocabulary was within the third-grade range.

Each subject was presented each item triplet with the time to infer the item rule measured in milliseconds. Subjects responded to an item when they had determined the rule for the triplet, at which point, they pressed a response key and then verbally described the item rule. Thus, two measures of performance were obtained for each item, latency and accuracy of inference.

Mean-latency data were computed for each of the eight major item groups for each subject based upon correct responses only. All three age groups showed the same pattern with respect to inference latency for class versus property items. These data are shown in Table 9. Thus, the data are consistent with prior semantic memory studies with adults, showing that verification of item properties takes longer than verification of the category membership of an item. Moreover, the differences observed for adults increase in magnitude for both 11-year-olds and 8-year-olds.

The error data within each age group revealed a pattern that was different from that obtained for the latency data. These data are also shown in Table 9. The overall level of inference accuracy increased with age, but the pattern observed for class versus property items differed within age groups. For adults, there was no difference in inference accuracy for class versus property items. In the 11-year-old group class, items were responded to at

TABLE 9
Mean Latency and Accuracy of Semantic Inferences

	Latency (seconds)		Accuracy	
	Class	Property	Class	Property
Adults	1.88	2.53	.86	.86
11-year-olds	2.52	3.63	.87	.79
8-year-olds	3.72	5.56	.77	.76

adult accuracy levels and at a higher level than property items. The 8-year-olds showed a lower level of accuracy than the 11-year-olds on both class and property items and no difference in error rates on the two item types. Thus, the accuracy data support a gradual developmental trend in the ability to infer property relationships among concepts and a more rapid shift to asymptotic levels of performance on items involving class rules.

At each age level, mean latency and accuracy scores were computed for individual items. An important additional question is whether there are similarities over age groups in the items that produce long inference times and lower accuracy. This was examined by correlating item latency and accuracy scores across the separate age groups. The results of this analysis are shown in Table 10. As can be seen in the table, there were significant correlations involving each pair of age groups; but, in most cases, the correlations were lowest when adult performance was matched against the youngest age group. The 11-year-old group showed latency and accuracy patterns that were transitional in the sense that they sometimes were more similar to adult patterns; in other cases, they were more similar to the patterns shown in the youngest age group.

Up to this point, we have been focusing on group mean data and overall developmental similarities and differences in inference latency and accuracy. Another important issue concerns the magnitude of individual differences within each age group with respect to both latency and accuracy. For the adults, the average inference latency was 2.2 seconds and the average accuracy was .86. The corresponding standard deviations were .43 and .05. The correlation between latency and accuracy scores over individuals was only −.12, due in part to the restriction of range of the accuracy scores. A similar result appeared for the 11-year-olds where the average inference latency was 3.07 seconds and the average accuracy was .83. The corre-

TABLE 10
Item Latency and Accuracy Correlations across Age Levels

	Latency		Accuracy	
	Class	Property	Class	Property
Adults + 11-year-olds	.76**	.66**	.64**	.72**
11-year-olds + 8-year-olds	.56**	.73**	.76**	.65**
8-year-olds + adults	.42*	.71**	.50*	.61**

*p < .01.
**p < .001.

sponding standard deviations were .75 and .05. The latency–accuracy correlation over individuals was −.26. Thus, in the two older age groups, the most important individual-difference factor was speed of processing and there was little differentiation in accuracy leading to nonsignificant latency–accuracy correlations. A different pattern appeared for the youngest age group where the average inference latency was 4.64 seconds with a standard deviation of 1.45. The average accuracy was .77 with a standard deviation of .11. Both speed and accuracy were significant individual difference factors and they were significantly correlated, $r(18) = -.52$, $p < .01$. Higher accuracy was associated with faster response times with no evidence of a speed–accuracy trade-off. Thus, it would appear that, in a simple semantic inference task, there is a change in the factors associated with individual differences which parallel developmental trends. At younger age levels, individual differences exist in both speed and accuracy. Accuracy differences become attenuated and speed differences then become the primary individual-difference factor in older age groups.

Our examination of semantic inference has provided additional information about the types of relationships that are more difficult to infer and the nature of developmental change in this process. Classification problems that employ property relationships among concepts should pose particular difficulties for younger children as reflected by slower and less-accurate solutions. Given the substantial between-age and within-age variability in accuracy (and speed) of this process when applied to a triad of verbal concepts, it is not surprising that inference is the major contributor to individual differences in forced–choice verbal classification. The essence of the classification task is the extraction of a common rule that can be used to evaluate a candidate set of exemplars. The inference process is also a significant source of developmental and individual differences in analogy solution. However, its importance is diminished in this task; this may be attributed to two factors. First, inference in the analogy task is associated with a pair of concepts rather than a triad or larger group. Inference may be easier and more accurate when restricted to a smaller set of concepts. Second, analogy solution demands much more than the inference of a single relationship. Analogy requires the application of a relationship to a new semantic domain and the evaluation of the higher order relationship of relationships. Developmental and individual differences in analogical reasoning are a function of these application and coordination processes as well as the simple process of inferring the relationship between a single pair of concepts. Thus, the developmental and individual differences that exist in semantic inference become only one aspect of performance differences in more complex inductive reasoning tasks.

DEVELOPMENTAL AND INDIVIDUAL DIFFERENCES IN SPATIAL REASONING

Hierarchical theories of aptitude—such as those developed by Cattell (1971) and Vernon (1965)—based on procedures of factor analysis typically distinguish among verbal, general reasoning, and spatial-mechanical aptitude factors. In Cattell's theory, this is represented by the distinction among Gc, Gf, and Gv representing crystallized, fluid, and visualization intelligence. Vernon's hierarchy distinguishes between a verbal–educational construct (v:ed) and a practical–mechanical construct (k:m). The latter is then further subdivided into more specific aptitudes, some of which involve common spatial-processing tasks. Two reviews of factor-analytic research on spatial aptitude (McGee, 1979; Lohman, Note 5) have appeared. Both reviews have reemphasized points made by I. Smith (1964) in an earlier review of spatial ability. First, they were clear in noting that all major factor-analytic studies have identified mechanical–spatial factors that are distinct from other general and specific factors. However, both also point out that spatial aptitude is still an ill-defined psychometric construct after 70 years of psychometric research.

Lohman (Note 5) reanalyzed the data from several major studies in an attempt to isolate a common set of spatial factors. The result of these efforts was the delineation of three distinct factors, one of which is of direct concern in this chapter. That factor was labeled Spatial Relations and appears to involve the ability to rapidly and accurately engage in mental rotation processes that are necessary for judgments about the identity of a pair of stimuli. A common spatial-relations problem is shown in Figure 3. The problem is taken from the Primary Mental Abilities Space Test and requires the individual to identify those alternatives that are identical to the standard on the left. Identity is defined in terms of rotation in the picture plane while mismatches involve rotation plus mirror-image reversal.

Our research on performance in spatial-reasoning tasks has primarily focused on a single task—The Primary Mental Abilities (PMA) Space Test (Thurstone & Thurstone, 1949). This test was chosen for several reasons.

FIGURE 3.   Example of spatial item from the PMA.

First, the PMA is typical of many measures of spatial aptitude in which an individual must "mentally rotate" a stimulus in the picture plane in order to differentiate it from other similar stimuli and match it against some standard. Second, the PMA loads heavily on the Spatial Relations factor in factor-analytic studies of the structure of intelligence (Cattell, 1971; I. Smith, 1964; Thurstone, 1938; Lohman, Note 5). Third, the PMA is appropriate across a relatively broad developmental range, beginning at 10 or 11 years of age and continuing through adulthood (Thurstone & Thurstone, 1949).

In addition to the psychometric literature on spatial reasoning, there is a large literature in developmental psychology on spatial perspective-taking that originated with Piaget and Inhelder's (1956) work on the "three mountains" task. In this problem, a child is shown a model depicting three mountains, each with a distinctive object at the summit. The child is asked to imagine the appearance of the mountains to a doll who is placed in several positions around the model. The child responds by selecting the photograph that depicts the doll's view.

Piaget and Inhelder (1956) found that, prior to 7 or 8 years of age, children selected photographs corresponding to their own view of the mountains rather than that of the doll. Beginning at 7 or 8 years, children realize that the doll's view differs from their own but they will often select an incorrect photograph because they relate the doll's position to one mountain rather than to the entire group. Not until 9 or 10 years of age do children consistently select the appropriate photograph; in doing so, they demonstrate the knowledge that ". . . to each position of the observer there corresponds a particular set of left–right, before–behind relations between the objects constituting the group of mountains. These are governed by the projections and sections appropriate to the visual plane of the observer . . ." (Piaget & Inhelder, 1956, p. 241).

The literature stemming from Piaget and Inhelder's (1956) findings has attempted to reveal conditions that would facilitate young children's ability to coordinate perspectives (e.g., Liben, 1978); to determine the relationships between perspective taking, in which an array is stationary and the observer moves, versus rotation problems in which a stationary observer anticipates the appearance of an array after it moves (e.g., Huttenlocher & Presson, 1973); and research concerning rotation and perspective-taking skill in large-scale spaces (e.g., Hardwick, McIntyre, & Pick, 1976). Common to much of this research is an emphasis on spatial processing in young children. According to the Piagetian account, the critical developmental changes occur between 4 and 10 years of age—so adolescents and adults typically are not studied; when they are, it is primarily to provide a baseline against which to assess the performance of the younger children. The fact that there are consistent individual differences in spatial aptitude among adolescents and adults suggests that although all children may acquire the rudiments·of spatial processing by middle childhood, development in this realm continues, with individuals ultimately attaining different levels of skill.

Process Models for Spatial-Relations Problems

Performance on spatial-relations problems such as those found on the PMA can be related to a general model of the processes required for mental rotation problems that was proposed by Cooper and Shepard (1973). The process model was based on data obtained in a paradigm that required individuals to decide, as rapidly as possible, if two stimuli presented in different visual orientations were the same. This single trial comparison of a stimulus pair closely resembles the individual comparisons that must be made to solve PMA problems (see Figure 3). An example of the application of this paradigm is a study by Cooper (1975) in which she presented two nonsense shapes that differed in orientation from 0–300° and subjects judged whether they were identical or mirror images of one another. Response latencies in this task were a linearly increasing function of the difference in orientation (angular disparity) between the two shapes. Such a result has been interpreted as indicating that subjects mentally rotate the stimuli in a manner analogous to the actual physical rotation of the object. The greater the "mental distance" to be traveled, the longer it takes to solve the problem.

Cooper and Shepard (1973) presented evidence that response latency on these problems reflects four discrete stages of processing. The model that they proposed is illustrated in Figure 4. The first stage of processing requires encoding of the stimuli. Encoding involves representing the stimuli, that is, their identity and orientation, and storing this information in working memory. The second phase of processing involves rotation of the mental representation of the nonvertical stimulus to bring it into congruence with the vertical stimulus. This is followed by a comparison of the stimulus representations to determine if they are identical. The outcome of the comparison leads to a positive or negative response. As shown in Figure 4, only the second stage of processing (i.e., mental rotation) is affected by the orientation of the stimulus (Cooper & Shepard, 1973). Encoding, comparing, and responding take approximately the same amount of time, regardless of the orientation of the stimulus. Consequently, the overall equation for reaction time in this task is generally written as $RT = x(r) + (e + c + m)$ where x represents the angular disparity between the stimuli being com-

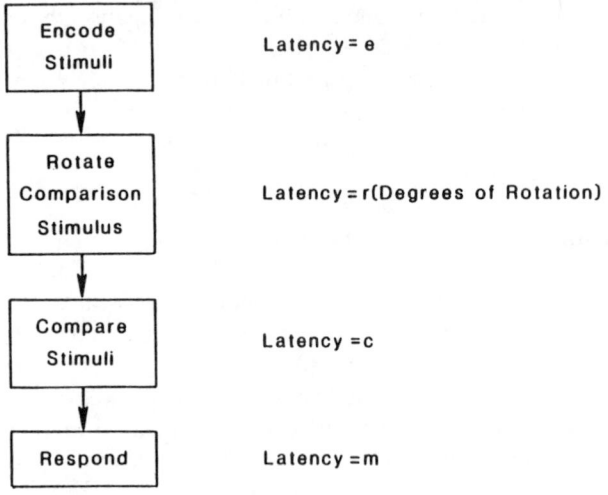

$$RT_{total} = r(\text{Degrees of Rotation}) + (e + c + m)$$

FIGURE 4.   Process model for mental rotation problems.

pared and r, e, c, and m represent the times for rotation, encoding, comparison, and motor response. The slope of the function relating response time
to stimulus orientation is used to estimate the rate of mental rotation whereas the intercept provides an estimate of the total time necessary for the
remaining processes that are constant over problems.

The process analysis of performance on a mental-rotation problem provides an obvious scheme for the analysis of individual and developmental
differences in simple spatial-relations performance. If the processes involved
in solving mental rotation problems can be reliably estimated for individuals then what remains to be determined is their respective contributions
to age and skill differences in this cognitive aptitude. Developmental and
individual differences in performance on a speeded test such as the PMA
may well be due entirely to speed differences in the cognitive process of
mental rotation. To estimate this process in its simplest form, one can
determine the slope value for the rotation of familiar stimuli such as alphanumerics. The intercept of the function for processing alphanumeric stimuli
is an estimate of the time to encode, compare, and respond to familiar
stimuli; it too may be related to individual differences in reference-test
performance. A potentially important aspect of performance on a test such
as the PMA may involve the capacity to encode, compare, and rotate stimuli that are not familiar, and lack representations and labels in permanent

memory. Previous studies have shown that it takes longer to rotate unfamiliar stimuli such as PMA characters than to rotate familiar alphanumerics. Similarly, there is a higher intercept for processing unfamiliar stimuli of the PMA type. Thus, it is necessary to consider the additional times associated with encoding, comparing, and rotating unfamiliar stimuli as potentially important aspects of skill differences on a reference test such as the PMA.

DEVELOPMENTAL CHANGES IN MENTAL ROTATION

All of the above-mentioned aspects of processing were considered by Kail, Pellegrino, and Carter (1980) in a study investigating the development of spatial processing in late childhood and adolescence. Kail et al. (1980) tested 37 8-year-olds, 22 9-year-olds, 44 11-year-olds, and 58 19-year-olds on various mental rotation problems. Two versions of a stimulus—a standard and a comparison—were presented on each trial. The comparison stimulus was rotated 0–150° from the standard. Subjects determined if the standard and comparison stimuli would be identical or mirror images (i.e., reflections) if the standard and comparison stimuli were to appear at the same orientation. On 72 trials, the stimuli were pairs of alphanumeric symbols; on 72, they were characters from the PMA.

Two types of data showed developmental invariance in the mental rotation task, and are of more than passing interest. First, errors were infrequent at all age levels, with values at 6, 8, 4 and 5% for 8-, 9-, 11-, and 19-year-olds, respectively. Consistent with the Piagetian position, by midchildhood, children are quite capable of anticipating the appearance of an object that is to be rotated. Similar developmental invariance was generally the case for r^2 values reflecting the goodness-of-fit of the Cooper and Shepard (1973) model to the mean-latency data. The r^2 values for alphanumerics based on group data were .91, .87, .91, and .94 for 8-, 9-, 11-, and 19-year-olds, respectively; corresponding values for PMA characters were .80, .97, .90, and .96. The r^2 values were smaller when derived from functions fit to individuals' data. Mean r^2s ranged from .68 to .78, with the exception of the 8-year-olds' mean r^2 for PMA characters, which was .52. Thus, with the exception of this one instance, the linear fit was also good for individuals, indicating that their performance was consistent with the expectations of the Cooper and Shepard (1973) model.

Developmental changes in the parameters of primary interest are depicted in Figure 5. Three features of the data are noteworthy. First, there was a regular developmental change in rate of mental rotation for alphanumerics, from approximately 7 milliseconds/degree among 8- and 9-year-

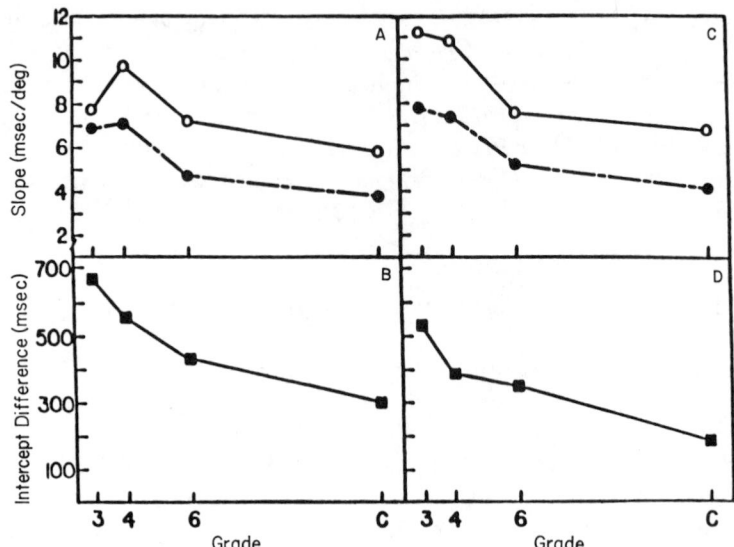

FIGURE 5. Mental rotation data as a function of age and stimulus type. O—O PMA,
●— - —● Alphanumerics. (A),(B) All subjects, (C),(D) well-fit subjects.

olds to somewhat less than 4 milliseconds/degree for adults. Second, unfamiliar PMA stimuli were rotated approximately 2.5 milliseconds/degree
more slowly than alphanumerics by all groups except 8-year-olds, for
whom interpretation of the parameters is problematic, due to the smaller r^2
values. Finally, the difference between the intercepts (i.e., PMA intercept–alphanumeric intercept) also declines systematically over development. Assuming that the response-time component of these two intercepts
is the same, then this decline reflects a developmental change in the speed
with which unfamiliar stimuli are encoded and compared.

These findings were based on slopes and intercepts computed for all
individuals. However, at each age level, there were some individuals whose
r^2 values were not significant. In these cases, interpretation of the slope and
intercept parameters is not straightforward; consequently, the analyses were
repeated but included only individuals with significant r^2 values for both
types of stimuli. The percentage of individuals who met this criterion increased developmentally, with values of 38, 50, 50, and 59% for 8-, 9-, 11-,
and 19-year-olds, respectively. However, the pattern of results is remarkably similar to that found when the data were analyzed for all individuals:
The mean slopes decline with development, as does the mean difference
between intercepts. The difference between slopes, in contrast, is essentially

constant developmentally, changing less than 1 millisecond/degree between 8 and 19 years of age.

What factors account for the developmental change observed in the various parameters? Age differences in the slope parameter might reflect a developmental shift toward a more efficient algorithm for mentally rotating stimuli, a suggestion we will examine in detail in the next section. Regarding the greater speed with which older individuals encoded and compared stimuli (i.e., the intercept difference), note that encoding of an alphanumeric stimulus presumably involves the activation of information already stored in long-term memory, while for PMA characters, encoding involves generating such a pattern anew for each trial. Thus, the age differences may reflect the greater speed with which older individuals construct such internal representations of unfamiliar stimuli.

Individual Differences in Mental Rotation

To this point, we have focused exclusively on change in the average speed with which individual processes are executed at different ages. An important related issue concerns the development of individual differences in spatial skill. We have been particularly interested in (1) the magnitude of within-age individual variation in the different processing parameters; and (2) whether such within-age individual variation is associated with psychometric performance differences.

Evidence regarding the first of these two issues comes from the Kail et al. (1980) study discussed previously. The standard deviations for each of the parameters were comparable for 9-, 11-, and 19-year-olds (8-year-olds are not considered here because of the interpretive problems associated with the low r^2 values). Yet, this similarity is somewhat misleading, due to the large developmental changes in the means associated with these standard deviations. A more insightful view of the range of individual variation is provided by the following analysis. We compared the performance of a hypothetical individual in the fifth percentile of his age group (i.e., $\overline{X} + 2$ sd, since superior performance is associated with smaller parameter values) with that of a person at the fiftieth percentile. Such comparisons were made for three parameters: the intercept for alphanumeric stimuli, the intercept difference (i.e., PMA intercept–alphanumeric intercept), and the slope for PMA stimuli. The results are shown in Figure 6 in which the parameter values for the hypothetical fifth percentile person are expressed as a percentage of the value for the fiftieth percentile individual (i.e., the group mean).

First, consider the alphanumeric intercept. Values for the fifth percentile

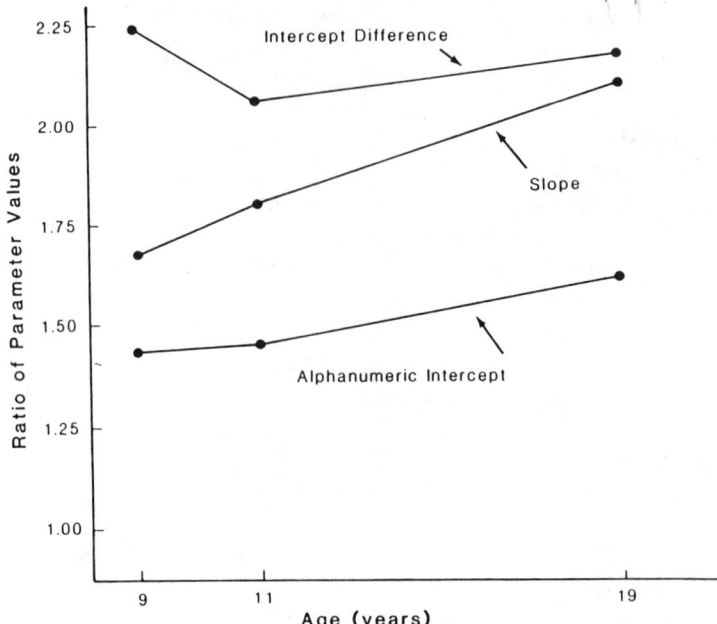

FIGURE 6.   Mental rotation-parameter ratios as a function of age.

are approximately 50% greater than the mean, for all age groups. The
intercept difference shows similar developmental invariance, but the fifth
percentile values are more than twice as large as the mean. Quite a different
pattern is found for the slope parameter: Among 8-year-olds, the fifth
percentile value is nearly 70% larger than the mean, but among adults, the
value is approximately 110% larger. In short, among young children, the
additional time to encode and compare unfamiliar stimuli is the source of
greatest individual variation; among adults, these processes plus the rate of
mental rotation are equally large sources of individual differences. Rate of
encoding, comparing alphanumeric stimuli, and responding has the smallest range of individual variation at all ages.

The Kail et al. (1980) data on individual differences within age groups
suggest that skill, as defined by reference-test performance, may be a function of different process components at different developmental levels. Two
additional studies support this hypothesis. In one of these studies, Pellegrino, Mumaw, Kail, and Carter (Note 6) tested 99 adults, who represented the entire range of performance on the PMA Spatial Relations test.
This included low scores near zero and high scores at the upper limit of 70.
Each subject was tested individually in experimental sessions involving the
presentation of over 275 stimulus pairs. As before, the pairs represented

actual PMA stimuli or asymmetric alphanumerics. Each trial involved the presentation of an upright PMA character or alphanumeric and a comparison stimulus rotated 0–150° from upright.

Least-squares regression lines were computed for each individual for both stimulus types and these were used to derive four specific parameters that formed the basis of the analysis of individual differences. The four basic parameters represent: (1) the time to encode, compare, and respond to familiar stimuli, Alphanumeric Intercept; (2) the additional time for encoding and comparing unfamiliar PMA stimuli, Intercept Difference; (3) the time to rotate familiar alphanumeric stimuli, Alphanumeric Slope; and (4) the additional time for rotating unfamiliar PMA stimuli, Slope Difference. The simple correlations and multiple regression results with PMA as the criterion are shown in Table 11. The simple correlations show that PMA test performance is most highly correlated with the speed of the mental rotation process for familiar stimuli and the processes associated with encoding and comparing unfamiliar stimuli, i.e., the intercept-difference parameter. The multiple-regression analysis shows that the slope-difference parameter, that is, the additional time to rotate unfamiliar PMA stimuli, is also a significant predictor of PMA performance.

Two additional points must be made relative to the results of the multiple regression analysis. First, the least important latency parameter for predicting performance is the intercept for alphanumeric stimuli. Such a result is of interest because this parameter accounts for approximately 50% of the total time to solve a typical rotation item. Second, errors are generally low on both PMA and alphanumeric rotation problems and individual differences in error rates on experimental items are not related to skill differences on the PMA. Thus, speed rather than accuracy differences seem to account for spatial-aptitude differences as measured by the PMA, a simple spatial-relations task. The particular speed differences that account for aptitude differences involve a basic mental rotation process and the speed of

TABLE 11
Correlational Results with PMA As Criterion

Predictor	Simple r	β
Error rate	−.18	−.15
Alphanumeric intercept	−.24	−.15
Intercept difference	−.41**	−.24*
Alphanumeric slope	−.42**	−.26*
Slope difference	−.14	−.20*

*$p < .05$.
**$p < .01$.

encoding, comparing, and rotating unfamiliar stimuli. Estimates of these components yield a multiple R of .57 when PMA performance is the criterion. Thus, the correlational results are consistent with the adult individual difference data of Kail et al. (1980).

In a subsequent study focusing on individual differences in younger age groups, Kail, Carter, and Pazak (Note 7) showed that individual differences in encoding–comparison and rotation processes are systematically and differentially related to individual differences in psychometric test performance. Slope and intercept measures were obtained for 26 9-year-olds and 42 13-year-olds who were first tested on the PMA Spatial Relations Test, then were given 100 trials in which pairs of PMA stimuli which differed in orientation by 0–135° in 15° increments were presented. Raw and corrected correlations are depicted in Table 12.

Consistent with the findings presented in Figure 6, the intercept parameter was significantly correlated with PMA performance for both younger and older children, while the slope was correlated only for the older group. Thus, some, as yet undetermined, combination of speed in encoding, comparison, and response processes is associated with superior spatial skill for both children and adolescents. Presumably, this is attributable to the special demands of encoding and comparing unfamiliar stimuli as is the case for adults. Rate of mental rotation, in contrast, is linked to psychometrically measured ability only for adolescents and adults. It would appear that individual differences in spatial aptitude are initially associated with basic encoding and comparison processes, that such differences persist over development, and are then accompanied by additional differences in the speed of mentally rotating or transforming the information that has been encoded. These developmental changes in the sources of individual differences are coincidental with overall developmental trends, indicating general improvement in the encoding, comparison, and rotation of unfamiliar stimuli. Thus, it seems that the overall developmental improvement in mental rotation speed is not uniform over individuals, and it may become a primary basis of individual differences in adolescents and adults.

TABLE 12
Correlations between Parameters and PMA Scores

Predictor	9-Year-olds	13-Year-olds
Slope	−.23 (−.31)**	−.40* (−.57)
Intercept	−.42* (−.53)	−.45* (−.57)

$^*p < .05$.
**Values in parentheses are adjusted for reliability of measures.

IMPLICATIONS AND ISSUES

Our research on developmental and individual differences in verbal and spatial reasoning represents an initial step toward understanding the processes and knowledge associated with aptitude. At the beginning of this chapter, we noted that traditional aptitude- and intelligence-test scores have limited diagnostic utility because they yield global, norm-referenced scores. Cognitive-components research of the type described herein circumvents this problem by moving from norm-referenced assessment to process-oriented assessment that identifies sources of developmental and individual differences on common verbal- and spatial-reasoning tests. Models are specified that permit the decomposition of a global test score into component scores representing the major factors producing intraage and interage variation.

With respect to understanding the development of specific cognitive abilities, it is possible to identify processes that show constancy and change. For example, evidence was provided of developmental changes in inference in both the speed and accuracy of executing this process. Speed differences are expected in the processing of verbal materials but accuracy differences for inferring relationships among common concepts are not necessarily an a priori prediction. Furthermore, evidence was provided of a differential-developmental change in the inference of category versus property relationships among concepts. The data on spatial-reasoning performance provide a complementary example. There is little evidence of a developmental change in accuracy but substantial changes in the speed of rotation (transformation) and encoding-comparison processes performed on unfamiliar stimuli. Adults executed mental rotation processes more rapidly than children for both familiar and unfamiliar stimuli, but there was no major developmental change in the additional time associated with transforming the unfamiliar stimuli.

The cognitive-components approach to performance assessment has also helped specify the magnitude and importance of specific-process differences within separate age groups. In the verbal-classification task, the accuracy of inference was the most important predictor of overall individual differences in the forced-choice performance. However, inference was a less important component of overall individual differences in the more complex analogy task. This can be understood by contrasting the demands made on coordinating separate sets of relationships in analogy and classification tasks. Analogy not only requires accuracy of inference for an initial pair of terms but the ability to search for concepts that have a coordinate relationship to a third concept that represents a new semantic domain. The coordination of relationships, reflected in application and discrimination-choice processes, is a major individual-difference factor in the analogy task.

Our studies of performance on verbal classification and analogy tasks have involved a limited age range; thus, little evidence has been obtained of changes in the importance of components of performance in different age groups. However, such a shift in the sources of individual differences has been obtained in the studies of simple spatial reasoning. Encoding-comparison processes are important sources of individual differences at three separate age levels. In addition, processes associated with rotating or transforming unfamiliar stimuli become increasingly important in older age groups. These data, as well as data obtained in the verbal-reasoning studies, show that individual differences within an age group may parallel overall developmental trends.

Although progress has been made in identifying some of the processes that contribute to developmental and individual differences in performance on analogy, classification, and mental rotation tasks, much remains to be specified. The component-process approach involves task decomposition and the generation of a set of individual-process scores rather than a global test score. Thus, a finer level of description is achieved. However, the processes themselves and the interpretation of latency or accuracy scores on individual processes remain largely unspecified. One might be tempted to argue that we have gone from a single "black box" to a whole series of smaller "black boxes." This criticism can be leveled at most process-oriented research and many of the current process models available in the cognitive and developmental literature. Individual-cognitive processes such as encoding, inference, rotation, and so forth need to be unpacked or specified more precisely. In some cases, this is realized through the development of computational models that are embodied in computer-simulation programs. Consensus exists that there may be a set of elementary information processes (see, e.g., Chase, 1978; Simon, 1976) that are the building blocks of most simple and complex cognitive performances. The specifics of these processes and the interdependency between processes and knowledge remain a major undertaking in cognitive science. To understand speed or power differences in a process such as simple inference, we will need to rely on models of the organization and activation of declarative knowledge. At this level, research on developmental and individual differences in cognitive processes can influence theory construction and evaluation. Detailed computational models must be capable of accommodating the types of speed and accuracy differences shown in cognitive components research.

Another issue that deserves consideration is the generality of our developmental and individual-differences results. The data on verbal analogy solution are consistent with other studies of the development of analogical reasoning ability (as discussed previously). This is also the case for the data on mental rotation. The results on individual differences in both verbal and spatial reasoning lack comparison data for the age and ability ranges studied.

A second point needs to be raised relative to the issue of generality. Earlier, we pointed out that an understanding of developmental and individual differences in verbal and spatial reasoning cannot be based upon analyses of single tasks in isolation. In the treatment of verbal reasoning, performance was examined on two highly correlated induction tasks. However, no studies have been undertaken examining the performance of the same individuals on related tasks. The studies of mental rotation are a step in that direction since the same individuals must process two different types of stimuli. In this regard, there are high correlations between individual subject latencies for rotating familiar and unfamiliar stimuli and lower, but substantial, correlations for encoding and comparison times on these two stimulus types. Nevertheless, performance differences have not been examined on other simple spatial-relations tasks nor have studies been conducted of the performance of the same individuals on two different spatial tasks.

Multitask analyses of sources of individual differences on related aptitude-test tasks need to be conducted. First, data would be available on the consistency of latency and accuracy values for identical processes executed under different task constraints. For example, one would expect that individual differences in the speed and/or accuracy of the inference component of verbal analogy solution would be correlated with individual differences in the same component when executed in the verbal classification task. Although this is predicted, it remains an unverified hypothesis. Second, not only can correlations between corresponding processes be verified, but analyses can be done of the process differences responsible for the general correlations between analogy and classification performance. In this way, general and specific sources of individual differences in verbal reasoning skill can be differentiated.

The analysis of process commonalities across tasks through the use of individual-difference data is also particularly important in the refinement of models of processing for sets of related tasks. The typical procedure in modeling performance on a given task is to designate some accuracy or latency measure, that is, slope, intercept, or a difference score, as an index of process X. A similar task is then modeled and, in an effort to achieve consistency of language, the same elementary process X is labeled and estimated in the new task. It may, in fact, turn out that the power scores or times associated with X are similar for the two tasks or they may be widely different. Whether X is, in fact, the same process can be determined only by reliably estimating it at the individual subject level and showing that there is at least relative consistency in the values obtained for X by different individuals. The magnitude of the correlation that is obtained indicates whether the measures of performance that are being considered reflect a complete, partial, or nonexistent process commonality.

Finally, the study of individual differences can affect cognitive theory by forcing greater precision in the description and measurement of individual cognitive processes. We mentioned earlier that current cognitive psychology embraces assumptions about a core set of elementary information processes that serve as the building blocks for all cognitive activity. Psychologists currently use the same limited set of process labels to describe performance in a wide range of simple and complex tasks. Examples include encoding, search, retrieval, decision, rotation, comparison, inference, and response. Thus, we appear to have a very powerful and general set of basic processing components. Unfortunately, little has been done to support or document the generality and existence of this set of basic or elementary information processes. Data on the duration and existence of specific mental processes comes from independent studies, using different stimuli, with different groups of individuals. All that appear to be common are the labels and the assumption that the processes are the same across tasks, subjects, and so forth. Individual-difference data can and must play an important role in validating some of our very basic assumptions about human cognition, that is, process invariance. By studying individual differences in cognitive processes, we can begin to verify some general assumptions about cognitive processing, while, at the same time, opening up possibilities for identifying elementary processes and higher-level strategies that contribute to general theory development.

Although it appears necessary to examine components of individual differences in performance on related tasks, there are severe practical limitations on conducting such research. The greatest problem is that the modeling of individual subject performance on a single task, particularly latency modeling, typically requires several hundred individual trials of individual subject testing. This is demanded if reliable process estimates are to be obtained at the individual subject level. Often, this can be achieved for a few subjects. It becomes very difficult to collect such data on a large and diverse enough sample of individuals for the results to be used in correlational analyses. Given such a logistic problem, it comes as no surprise that most individual-differences research focuses on adult samples, notably college students who represent a restricted range of skill on most reasoning tasks. The problems become more severe if one wishes to look at both developmental and individual differences in performance on related tasks. Not only are there difficulties in obtaining sufficient numbers of trials and reliable parameter estimates for a single task but the content of certain tasks changes as well. Classic examples of such changes in content are verbal reasoning tasks. The individual items administered to 8- and 10-year-olds may show no overlap with items that discriminate among adolescents and adults. By controlling content, that is, using items appropriate for the youngest age groups, individual differences in an older age group may be eliminated or become focused on speed rather than accuracy measures that bear little relationship to differences manifest on a test that is age-appropriate. Thus, although it is relatively easy to administer a battery of paper-and-pencil tests that yield reliable overall scores on verbal or spatial-reasoning tasks, it is considerably more difficult to conduct the process analyses that can help explain the meaning of such global aptitude scores.

Finally, some comment is merited on a general problem associated with conducting and reporting research on developmental and individual differences in cognitive abilities. In recent years, much has been said about the unification of the "two disciplines of scientific psychology," that is, experimental and correlational psychology. Commenting on an earlier symposium on this topic, Glaser and Pellegrino (1978) facetiously questioned whether there was evidence of a unification of psychometric, cognitive, and developmental research or whether the best that might be achieved is peaceful coexistence and détente.

The more serious issue involves fundamental differences in how research is conducted and theory evaluated within each of these disciplines. There is no problem as long as one does not try to cross party lines and communicate with all three groups. If we caricature each of these camps, then perhaps, the problem becomes obvious. The psychometrician requires that research on individual differences be based on a large N, preferably 75 or more, the measures show high reliability (validity is clearly less of an issue), and multiple measures be reduced by factor analysis to yield global scores that have convergent and discriminant validity. The developmentalist, on the other hand, requires that the research involve multiple developmental levels, that there is an emphasis on qualitative differences and that the results fall within theories of global stages of developmental change. Individual differences at a micro- or macrolevel—particularly quantitative ones—are eschewed. Finally, we have the cognitivist (of which there are many varieties) who cares about detailed computational models, specific hypotheses to be rejected, design and control that involve causal rather than correlational explanations, and descriptions that focus on global or general cognitive processes. At times, it is not clear whether research on developmental and individual differences in cognitive abilities effectively integrates all three disciplines or is simply a bastard child without a home.

ACKNOWLEDGMENT

The authors wish to acknowledge the assistance of David Alderton, Banu Oney, and Connie Varnhagen.

REFERENCES

Achenbach, T. The Children's Associative Responding test: A possible alternative to group IQ tests. *Journal of Educational Psychology*, 1970, *61*, 340–348.

Anglin, J. M. *Word, object, and conceptual development.* New York: Norton, 1977.

Bennet, G. K., Seashore, H. G., & Wesman, A. G. *Differential aptitude test.* New York: Psychological Corporation, 1974.

Bruner, J. S. Going beyond the information given. In H. Gruber (Ed.), *Contemporary approaches to cognition.* Cambridge, Mass.: Harvard University Press, 1957.

Carroll, J. B. Psychometric tests as cognitive tasks: A new "structure of intellect." In L. B. Resnick (Ed.), *The nature of intelligence.* Hillsdale, N.J.: Lawrence Erlbaum Associates, 1976.

Cattell, R. B. *Abilities: Their structure, growth and action.* Boston: Houghton Mifflin, 1971.

Chase, W. G. Elementary information processes. In W. K. Estes (Ed.), *Handbook of learning and cognitive processes* (Vol. 5). Hillsdale, N.J.: Lawrence Erlbaum Associates, 1978.

Cooper, L. A. Mental transformations of random two-dimensional shapes. *Cognitive Psychology*, 1975, *7*, 20–43.

Cooper, L. A., & Shepard, R. N. Chronometric studies of the rotation of mental images. In W. G. Chase (Ed.), *Visual information processing.* New York: Academic Press, 1973.

Cronbach, L. J. *Essentials of psychological testing* (3rd ed.). New York: Harper & Row, 1970.

Dillon, R. F. Cognitive style and elaboration of logical abilities in hearing-impaired children. *Journal of Experimental Child Psychology*, 1980, *30*, 389–400.

Egan, D. E., & Greeno, J. G. Theory of rule induction: Knowledge acquired in concept learning, serial pattern learning, and problem solving. In L. W. Gregg (Ed.), *Knowledge and cognition.* Hillsdale, N.J.: Lawrence Erlbaum Associates, 1974.

Forehand, G. A. Knowledge and the educational process. In L. W. Gregg (Ed.), *Knowledge and cognition.* Hillsdale, N.J.: Lawrence Erlbaum Associates, 1974.

Gallagher, J. M. The future of formal thought research: The study of analogy and metaphor. In B. Presseisen & D. Goldstein (Eds.), *Topics in cognitive development: Language and operational thought.* New York: Plenum, 1978.

Gentile, J. R., Kessler, D. K., & Gentile, P. K. Process of solving analogy items. *Journal of Educational Psychology*, 1969, *60*, 494–502.

Gentile, J. R., Tedesco-Stratton, L., Davis, E., Lund, N. J., & Agunanne, B. A. Associative responding versus analogical reasoning by children. *Intelligence*, 1977, *1*, 369–380.

Glaser, R. Components of a psychology of instruction: Toward a science of design. *Review of Educational Research*, 1976, *46*, 1–24.

Glaser, R., & Pellegrino, J. W. Uniting cognitive process theory and differential psychology: Back home from the wars. *Intelligence*, 1978, *2*, 305–319.

Goldman, S. R., Pellegrino, J. W., Parseghian, P. E., & Sallis, R. Developmental and individual differences in verbal analogical reasoning. *Child Development*, 1982, *53*, 550–559.

Greeno, J. G. Natures of problem-solving abilities. In W. K. Estes (Ed.), *Handbook of learning and cognitive processes* (Vol. 5). Hillsdale, N.J.: Lawrence Erlbaum Associates, 1978.

Hardwick, D. A., McIntyre, C. W., & Pick, H. L. The content and manipulation of cognitive maps in children and adults. *Monographs of the Society for Research in Child Development,* 1976, *41* (Serial No. 166).

Huttenlocher, J., & Presson, C. C. Mental rotation and the perspective problem. *Cognitive Psychology,* 1973, *4,* 277–299.

Kail, R., Pellegrino, J., & Carter, P. Developmental changes in mental rotation. *Journal of Experimental Child Psychology,* 1980, *29,* 102–116.

Levinson, P. J., & Carpenter, R. L. An analysis of analogical reasoning in children. *Child Development,* 1974, *45,* 857–861.

Liben, L. S. Perspective-taking skills in young children: Seeing the world through rose-colored glasses. *Developmental Psychology,* 1978, *14,* 87–92.

Lunzer, E. A. Formal reasoning. In E. A. Lunzer & J. F. Morris (Eds.), *Development in human learning.* N.Y.: American Elsevier, 1968.

McGee, M. G. *Human spatial abilities: Sources of sex differences.* New York: Praeger, 1979.

Nelson, K., Rescorla, L., Gruendel, J., & Benedict, H. Early lexicons: What do they mean? *Child Development,* 1978, *49,* 960–968.

Norman, D. A., Gentner, D. R., & Stevens, A. C. Comments on learning schemata and memory. In D. Klahr (Ed.), *Cognition and instruction.* Hillsdale, N.J.: Lawrence Erlbaum Associates, 1976.

Oppenheimer, J. R. Analogy in science. *American Psychologist,* 1956, *11,* 127–135.

Pellegrino, J. W., & Glaser, R. Components of inductive reasoning. In R. E. Snow, P.-A. Federico, & W. E. Montague (Eds.), *Aptitude, learning, and instruction: Cognitive process analyses of aptitude.* Hillsdale, N.J.: Lawrence Erlbaum Associates, 1980.

Piaget, J., & Inhelder, B. *The child's conception of space.* London: Routledge & Kegan Paul, 1956.

Piaget, J., Montangero, J., & Billeter, J. Les correlats. *L'Abstraction reflechissante.* Paris: Presses Universitaires de France, 1977.

Polya, G. *Mathematics and plausible reasoning: Induction and analogy in mathematics* (Vol. 1). Princeton, N.J.: Princeton University Press, 1965.

Raven, J. C. *Progressive matrices: A perceptual test of intelligence* (1938, individual form). London: Lewis, 1938.

Simon, H. A. Identifying basic abilities underlying intelligent performance of complex tasks. In L. B. Resnick (Ed.), *The nature of intelligence.* Hillsdale, N.J.: Lawrence Erlbaum Associates, 1976.

Smith, E. E. Theories of semantic memory. In W. K. Estes (Ed.), *Handbook of learning and cognitive processes,* (Vol. 6). Hillsdale, N.J.: Lawrence Erlbaum Associates, 1978.

Smith, I. *Spatial ability: Its educational and social significance.* London: University of London Press, 1964.

Snow, R. E. Aptitude processes. In R. E. Snow, P.-A. Federico, & W. E. Montague (Eds.), *Aptitude, learning, and instruction: Cognitive process analyses of aptitude.* Hillsdale, N.J.: Lawrence Erlbaum Associates, 1980.

Spearman, C. *The nature of intelligence and the principles of cognition.* London, Macmillan, 1923.

Sternberg, R. J. *Intelligence, information processing, and analogical reasoning: The componential analysis of human abilities.* Hillsdale, N.J.: Lawrence Erlbaum Associates, 1977.

Sternberg, R. J., & Nigro, G. Developmental patterns in the solution of verbal analogies. *Child Development,* 1980, *51,* 27–38.

Sternberg, R. J., & Rifkin, B. The development of analogical reasoning processes. *Journal of Experimental Child Psychology,* 1979, *27,* 195–232.

Thorndike, R. L., & Hagen, E. *Cognitive abilities test.* Boston: Houghton Mifflin, 1971.

Thurstone, L. L. *Primary mental abilities.* Chicago: University of Chicago Press, 1938.

Thurstone, L. L., & Thurstone, T. G. *Manual for the SRA Primary Mental Abilities*. Chicago: Science Research Associates, 1949.

Underwood, B. J. Individual differences as a crucible in theory construction. *American Psychologist*, 1975, *30*, 128–134.

Vernon, P. E. Ability factors and environmental influences. *American Psychologist*, 1965, *20*, 723–733.

Vygotsky, L. S. *Thought and language*. Cambridge, Mass.: MIT Press, 1962.

NOTES

1. Dawis, R. V., & Siojo, L. T. *Analogical reasoning: A review of the literature. Effects of social class differences on analogical reasoning* (Tech. Rep. No. 1). Minneapolis: University of Minnesota, 1972.

2. Gallagher, J. M., & Wright, R. J. *Children's solution of verbal analogies: Extension of Piaget's concept of reflexive abstraction*. Paper presented at SRCD, New Orleans, 1977.

3. Parseghian, P. E., & Pellegrino, J. W. *Components of individual differences in verbal classification performance*. Paper presented at American Educational Research Association, Boston, 1979.

4. Lairon, M. A., Goldman, S. R., & Pellegrino, J. W. Developmental changes in the speed and accuracy of semantic inferences. Unpublished manuscript, University of California at Santa Barbara, 1981.

5. Lohman, D. F. *Spatial ability: A review and reanalysis of the correlational literature* (Tech. Rep. No. 8). Stanford, Calif.: Stanford University, Aptitude Research Project, School of Education, 1979.

6. Pellegrino, J. W., Mumaw, R. J., Kail, R. V., & Carter, P. *Different slopes for different folks: Analyses of spatial ability*. Paper presented at the annual meeting of the Psychonomic Society, Phoenix, November 1979.

7. Kail, R., Carter, P., & Pazak, B. *Development of individual differences in spatial ability*. Presented at the annual meeting of the Psychonomic Society, Phoenix, 1979.

6

An Information-Processing Analysis of Mathematical Ability*

Diane J. Briars

INTRODUCTION

Why are some people "good" at mathematics while others are not? What underlying characteristics, if any, distinguish the former from the latter? In an attempt to answer these questions, researchers have examined a number of possible underlying factors and potential predictors of mathematics achievement, including affective variables such as attitude, motivation, and self-concept; nonintellectual variables such as sex, socioeconomic status, and ethnicity; and cognitive factors such as reasoning skills, spatial visualization, and so on. Although some noncognitive factors, such as sex (Fennema, 1974), have been found to be associated with mathematics achievement, studies including both cognitive and noncognitive variables indicate that cognitive variables, especially previous mathematics achievement, are the best predictors of mathematics achievement (Begle, 1979).

The most common cognitive analyses of mathematical ability are psychometric studies of its structure (Furneaux & Rees, 1978; Very, 1967;

*This work was supported by NSF grant number 1-55035. Any opinions expressed are those of the author and do not reflect the views of the National Science Foundation.

181

Werdelin, 1958).[1] In these studies, a battery of tests designed to tap the hypothetical components of mathematical ability is administered. Results are then factor-analyzed to determine the cognitive factors underlying the test battery. Factor analysis produces a characterization of mathematical ability in terms of various components, which usually include a numerical factor, a spatial factor, a verbal factor, and reasoning factors. These factors can be considered lower order abilities. For example, the numerical factor is interpreted to indicate proficiency in computation because arithmetic and algebra tests usually load reasonably high on that factor. Thus, research in this tradition tends to provide a finer-grain characterization of mathematical ability.

Though it is important to know what kind of subabilities contribute to general mathematical ability (e.g., that verbal reasoning is involved, which one might not suspect a priori), the resulting factor structure is somewhat unsatisfying as a characterization of mathematical ability. In some sense, the problem has just been taken down a level; now the question is, what underlies individual differences in each of these factors?

In this chapter, we take a different tack and attempt to describe mathematical ability in terms of underlying cognitive processes and knowledge structures. Our analysis is based on an information-processing model of cognition. Such models describe individuals as processors of information; as such, they take in, transform, and sometimes report information. (We describe the assumptions underlying this view of cognition more fully in the next section.) This view suggests that differences in mathematical ability may be related to differences in three components of the processing system: basic information-processing skills, content knowledge, and metacognitive knowledge. Basic information-processing skills involve cognitive processes that are independent of specific content knowledge; that is, processes that operate on representations of symbols independent of their referent (cf. Hunt, 1978). In contrast, content knowledge refers to the amount and organization of domain-specific knowledge, along with knowledge-dependent processes. Metacognitive knowledge includes general strategies that are both domain specific (e.g., heuristics for mathematical problem solving) and those that are not, along with general beliefs about a domain (e.g., a mathematics problem may take longer than 5 minutes to solve). Thus, our goal is to examine the research literature for evidence relating differences in mathematical ability to differences in these components.

Although a substantial body of research concerns mathematical ability,

---

[1]Interesting exceptions to this are several prominent mathematicians' analyses of mathematical ability based on reflections upon their own problem-solving processes. See Hadamard (1945) and Poincare (1948/1968) for discussions of these introspective analyses.

only a small portion of it has considered the cognitive-processing variables described above. Thus, a current limitation of our analysis is an apparent lack of empirical studies examining the relation of some cognitive processes to mathematical ability. As a result, at some points in our analyses we extrapolate from studies designed to examine a somewhat different question; at others, we can merely speculate about a potential source of difference without empirical support.

Our criteria for including studies in this review were that they examined the relation between a cognitive processing variable and performance on a mathematical task. We did not include factor-analytic studies; even though some of these studies have identified various memory and perceptual-processing factors to be components of mathematical ability, these factors tend to tap a number of different cognitive processes, and consequently, identify factors that cut across our three basic categories. Our review also does not include studies examining cognitive style variables such as impulsivity–reflectivity or field-dependence–independence. Indeed, these may be important sources of individual differences in mathematical ability; however, because their relation to the basic cognitive processes of interest here is unclear, they were not included in this analysis.

This chapter has four main sections. In the first, we present the fundamental notions underlying our analysis, including the basic assumptions of information-processing models of cognition, a definition of mathematical ability, and a description of mathematics as a subject-matter domain. In the following three sections, we examine mathematical ability in terms of basic information-processing skills, content knowledge, and metacognition about mathematics, respectively.

PRELIMINARIES

In this section, we discuss three basic premises underlying our analysis of mathematical ability. First, we describe the assumptions underlying information-processing models of cognition. Next, we define mathematical ability, and also describe dimensions along which individuals can be classified as more or less able. Finally, we describe the features of mathematics that make it unique as a domain.

INFORMATION-PROCESSING THEORIES OF COGNITION

Information-processing theories of cognition describe people as entities that mentally manipulate information, where information usually takes the form of some kind of symbol structure. The major difference between this view of cognition and those preceding it (e.g., behaviorism) is the emphasis on the transformation of information and the processes by which that occurs, rather than on inputs and outputs (stimuli and responses) (Estes, 1978).

Most information processing theories describe human memory as consisting of at least two kinds of memory structures: an unlimited (for all intents and purposes) long-term memory (LTM) and a limited short-term memory (STM). LTM can be thought of as an individual's relatively permanent store of knowledge; this includes both knowledge structures and associations among them. Potential sources of individual differences within a domain are thus the domain-related contents of LTM, how this knowledge is organized, and also, the accessibility of various pieces of information in LTM (i.e., how it is "indexed") (Simon, 1978).

STM, or active memory (Hunt, 1978), is the site of most infomation-processing activity. It contains the data the system is considering at the moment. The actual contents of STM are usually described as "pointers" to elements in LTM. In other words, STM represents current information by accessing concepts and relations that are in LTM. Thinking is then the transformation or manipulation of elements in STM.

Information is manipulated according to transformation rules that are also part of LTM. These rules are often represented as *productions* (Newell & Simon, 1972). A production is a condition–action pair (i.e., If A, then B). The condition side specifies one or more elements that must be in STM for that production's actions to be executed. The action side specifies one or more actions to be carried out. Actions can either be transformations of elements in STM, external physical actions (e.g., swinging a tennis racquet), or a combination of both.

A major part of cognition is, then, selecting productions to apply in particular situations. One thing that determines when a production is selected is the elements of its condition side. The condition elements associated with particular actions reflect knowledge about a situation or subject-matter domain. Hence, the elements of a condition side of a production are a knowledge-dependent aspect of production selection.

Another part of applying a production is actually matching elements in working memory to elements in condition sides of productions. Cognitive processes involved in this matching are assumed to be essentially content-independent in that they act on the representation of a symbol structure irrespective of its referent (Hunt, 1978). Hunt has termed these content-independent processes *mechanistic* processes. An example of such a process is decoding letters. Hunt argues that identifying the symbol "a" as a meaningful stimulus cannot depend on meaning since decoding is required to establish meaning. Hunt further distinguishes between mechanistic processes that require attention and those that do not. For example, retrieving context-dependent facts requires construction of a memory-search procedure which requires attention; in contrast, decoding (as in the letter example) appears to require little attention (Schneider & Shiffrin, 1977).

Mechanistic processes are a subset of what we will refer to as basic information-processing skills. These also include more complex processes composed of sequences of unspecified mechanistic processes, such as those required for tasks such as backward digit span and the sentence comprehension task described in a later section.

In summary, information-processing models of cognition suggest two sources of individual differences in performance. One is differences in relevant content knowledge—amount, organization, and accessibility (indexing)—and content-dependent processes. The other is differences in content-independent or basic information-processing skills.

DEFINITION OF MATHEMATICAL ABILITY

In the literature, mathematically able individuals (and mathematical ability) have been defined in a number of ways, including: creative mathematicians doing original mathematics (e.g., Hadamard, 1945; Poincare, 1948/1968); exceptionally talented or mathematically precocious youth; or students performing above grade level in school mathematics (or at grade level when compared to students below grade level). In some sense, all these individuals are more mathematically capable than some comparison group of individuals.

For our analyses, we adopt the very general definition of mathematical ability proposed by Kilpatrick and his associates, "mathematical ability [is] that ability which is inferred from a person's performance on a mathematical task" (Mason, 1979, p. 5). In most, but not all, studies we will be discussing, mathematical tasks are those found in the school mathematics curriculum.

According to this definition, correct performance on mathematical tasks is evidence of mathematical ability. Caution must be exercised with the converse implication, however. Lack of successful performance on a task may not imply lack of ability; poor performance may also be due to other variables like motivation, or poor prerequisite skills resulting from poor instruction (especially on school tasks).

The studies discussed in this chapter use a wide range of definitions of more and less able mathematics students. Most compare same-aged students with different levels of mathematics achievement, measured on the basis of standardized test scores and/or teacher ratings. IQ is statistically controlled in only some studies. In a majority of studies, gifted students or above-average-ability students are compared to average-ability students; few examine differences between average-ability students with different degrees of mathematical achievement (e.g., average-ability students who are performing at grade level with those who have not yet mastered a concept). Others define mathematically able and less able students on the basis of performance on the tasks in the specific study. Yet others are "expert–novice" studies, in which more capable and experienced subjects are compared with those having less expertise and experience. Admittedly, these differences make generalization across studies difficult if not impossible. In our subsequent discussion, care is taken to identify comparison groups for particular studies, so processing differences can be identified with respect to the appropriate group.

MATHEMATICS AS A FORMAL DOMAIN

Before attempting to analyze mathematical ability, it is useful to examine the nature of mathematics and what distinguishes it from other domains. Mathematics, along with most "hard" sciences is an example of what Larkin (1981) has called a formal domain, a domain "involving a considerable amount of rich semantic knowledge, but characterized by a set of principles logically sufficient to solve problems in the domain" (p. 311). The existence of this set of principles is what distinguishes the formal domain from other semantically rich domains (those for which successful problem solving requires domain-specific knowledge in addition to general problem-solving skill) like biology, psychology, and history. Further, due to the large number of principles involved, a considerable amount of additional knowledge is needed to use these principles to solve problems within the domain. In most formal domains, knowledge about applying principles is acquired by solving large numbers of problems within the domain; in other words, individuals become proficient problem solvers by solving large numbers of problems (e.g., Polya, 1957). Thus, individual differences in mathematics, as in most formal domains, may be a function of: (1) the amount of domain-specific knowledge acquired (Simon, 1979); (2) how this knowledge is organized (Simon, 1979); and/or (3) the amount of additional knowledge acquired about applying basic principles to solve problems (Larkin, 1981).

As a formal domain, mathematics is further characterized by its structure and its distinctive use of language and symbolism (Lesh, 1979). Mathematics has a distinctive hierarchical structure. Some of this structure is evident in the basic arithmetic algorithms, e.g., the division algorithm involves both the multiplication and subtraction algorithms. However, mathematics has a much more extensive and powerful structure than that. Mathematics is characterized by what Dienes (1960) called its "superimposed patterning"; that is, mathematical regularities or patterns noted at one level of analysis become the objects among which regularities and patterns are sought at the next level of analysis. For example, arithmetic operations, such as addition and multiplication, are initially operators in the system; as such, they act on whole numbers in a specific way. At a higher level, we look for regularities (properties) in the operations, such as, the order in which numbers are added is irrelevant (commutivity). Thus, now the operations themselves are the objects being analyzed. Finally, at an even higher level, we are concerned with finding commonalities among properties of operations on particular sets (e.g., addition on integers and multiplication on the rational numbers excluding 0) arriving at general algebraic structures like groups, rings, and so on. Dienes (1967) summarized this hierarchical structure with a grammatical analogy: "predicates become subjects for further predicates, which in turn become subjects for yet further predicates . . . " (p. 21). Thus, mathematical concepts become increasingly more abstract, in that they are regularities noted in previously acquired concepts. This suggests an additional source of differences in mathematical ability may be cognitive processes associated with learning increasingly more abstract concepts.

The other distinctive feature of mathematics is its language and symbolization. Mathematical language and symbolization and the processes by which it is taught differ greatly from that of natural language, the only other symbol system with which most children have contact. This difference is particularly important because mathematics is the first additional symbol system most children experience. Among the difficulties in learning this system are the following:

1. Mathematical symbols, terms, and concepts are usually introduced simultaneously (e.g., ½, "one-half," and "one of two equal parts"), whereas in natural language learning, children often have experience with a concept before knowing its label, and certainly learn the words before they learn the written symbols for them;
2. Mathematical symbols are flexible; e.g., variables can mean different things in different contexts;
3. Mathematical language and symbolization is not redundant, whereas natural language is (Dienes, 1967).

Thus, cognitive processes involved in acquiring and using an alternative symbol system may be another source of differences in mathematical ability.

BASIC INFORMATION-PROCESSING
SKILLS

Hunt and his colleagues examined the relation between verbal ability, measured by performance on group administered verbal aptitude tests, and three kinds of mechanistic processes involved in manipulating symbols in STM: decoding (accessing highly overlearned information in LTM, measured by the letter identification task of Posner et al.); detecting and maintaining information about stimulus order (assessed by a variant of the Brown–Peterson memory paradigm[2]); and scanning STM for particular elements (measured by a variant of the Sternberg paradigm). They also examined the relation between verbal ability and performance on a miniature comprehension task that is variant of the Clark and Chase paradigm.[3] Because this task involves only very simple pictures and overlearned vocabulary, individual differences in performance are thought to reflect differences in the underlying mechanistic process, rather than differences in knowledge. Results of a number of studies indicated that low verbal subjects have slower decoding processes than high verbal subjects. On the other hand, little relation was found between verbal ability and the other two tasks, which involve processes for holding information in STM, and assessing and manipulating information in STM, respectively. However, if the tasks were made much more difficult (i.e., attention demanding), high and lower verbal college students then performed differentially on the tasks. Differences were also found when extreme populations, like EMR, were used as the low verbal-ability comparison group.

From these results, Hunt concludes that decoding, which is an automatic mechanistic process "appears to be a stable and often limiting factor in processing verbal material" (p. 120). However, active memory, though a component of verbal ability as evidenced by differential performance by verbal ability groups under difficult task conditions, is not a limiting factor, as evidenced by nondifferential performance by ability groups under more "normal" (usual) task conditions. He suggests that these results are examples of the general principle that "tasks requiring attentional resources will yield stable individual measures only if tasks push the limits of a person's processing capacities (p. 120)." Thus, automatic mechanistic processes are more likely to be limiting factors in terms of an individual's verbal ability,

---

[2]Four letters were presented sequentially; subjects then shadowed from 1 to 36 digits, and then were to recall the letter sequence.

[3]Subjects were shown a sentence of the form "Plus above star." When a subject indicated he understood the sentence, he was shown a picture and was to indicate whether the sentence described the picture.

whereas mechanistic processes that require attention will not, unless the task taxes the limits of STM.

What role, if any, do basic information processing skills play in individual differences in mathematical ability? Do specific content-free processes vary with mathematical ability? Are there differences in the relation of automatic and attention-requiring processes and mathematics ability, as there are with verbal ability? Or is mathematics sufficiently demanding that processes require attention, erasing this distinction? Further, is there a unique set of cognitive processes related to mathematical ability, or is it the same set as related to verbal ability, suggesting that these processes are characteristic of smart people, not just the mathematically able?

As far as we can ascertain, the relation of mathematical ability and basic information processes has not been systematically studied as have the processes of verbal ability. Nonetheless, a few studies have examined the relation between mathematics achievement and two specific basic processing skills, processing speed and digit span. Interestingly, all but one of these studies have been interested in characterizing low-ability students, rather than high-ability ones.

Spiegel and Bryant (1978) examined the relation between speed of processing information and intelligence and reading and mathematics achievement of 94 sixth graders. Speed of processing was measured by three tasks: a sentence–picture comparison task similar to the one used by Hunt; a pictorial similarities-and-differences task, in which subjects are to select the picture that is different out of a set of four pictures; a matrix-analysis task, similar to Raven's Progressive Matrices. These tasks were thought to measure processing speed because errors could not be attributed to lack of knowledge or other difficulties with the tasks. Under untimed conditions, all subjects (actually a comparison sample of 20 subjects) had near-perfect performance on these tasks, yet made errors in the limited time condition. Under experimental conditions, mean processing speed for each measure was correlated about $-.4$ with mathematical concepts and mathematics computation scores. However, when IQ was controlled, the partial correlation coefficient between mean response times and mathematics achievement dropped to almost 0. Thus, the relation between processing speed and mathematics achievement appears to be attributable to general intellectual ability, suggesting that processing speed does not uniquely contribute to mathematical ability.

Performance on digit-span tasks, which test other basic information processing skills, has also been compared to mathematics achievement. Before looking at the results of these studies, it is useful to consider the tasks themselves. Digit-span tasks are usually assumed to measure capacity of STM; however, as Dempster (1981) argued, there are actually a number of sources of individual differences on such tasks, including speed of item identification, item ordering, and chunking (see Dempster, 1981, for a comprehensive analysis of what memory span tasks measure and a review of the relevant literature). Though there is considerable evidence that speed with which items can be identified is a major source of individual and developmental differences on these tasks, all other explanations cannot be eliminated. Thus, the best we can do at present is to recognize that individual differences in memory span may result from a variety of processing differences. However, this limitation does not make any less interesting the relation between performance on memory-span tasks and mathematics achievement.

Webster (1979) examined differences in memory span between a group of mathematically proficient (performing at or above grade level on the WRAT arithmetic subtest) and two groups of "mathematics disabled" (1 to 1½ years below grade level; 2 or more years below grade level) sixth graders. Memory span was measured with strings of seven digits and strings of seven nonrhyming consonants, presented both aurally and visually. Elements of each string were presented sequentially for 1 second exposure at 1 second intervals. Intelligence as measured by the Peabody Picture Vocabulary Test was a covariate in this analysis.

Even with IQ controlled, students two or more years below grade level had significantly lower memory-span scores that the mathematically proficient students; differences between other groups were not significant. In addition, there was a significant main effect of modality of presentation; students achieving below grade level had better memory-span performance in the visual condition, whereas those at or above grade level did somewhat better in the aural condition. These differences between means within achievement groups were not significant, however. One possible reason for the poor performance on the aural presentation condition was that the responses to the memory-span task were written; thus, students had to transfer from aural to written mode, which may be a more difficult translation than visual to written mode, both of which have visual components.

Carter, Spero, and Walsh (1978) examined differences in memory span and perceptual motor skills of 6- through 9-year-olds who were below average (9 months or more below grade level) and average (any other achievement score) in mathematics achievement. In this study, memory span was measured with the Visual Aural Digit Span test which tests digit span in four presentation–response conditions: aural–oral, visual–oral, aural–written and visual–written. Perceptual-motor skills were assessed with the Bender Visual Gestalt Test in which children are to copy various geometric forms, such as a circle, cross, diamond, and so on. WISC–R verbal intelligence was used as a covariate. Carter et al. found significant differences between both mathematics concepts and mathematics problem-solving achievement groups and the Bender Test, suggesting a relation between coordination of visual and motoric processing and mathematical achievement. The relation between mathematics achievement and digit span was more complex, however. Three subtests of the digit span task, visual–oral, aural–written, and visual–written, discriminated among below average and average groups in mathematics concepts; however, only the visual–oral subtest distinguished these groups on mathematical problem solving.

The Webster and Carter et al. studies share a methodological problem that adds ambiguity to their conclusions. Both Webster and Carter et al. not only separated performance groups, rather than using a regression procedure, but included students performing at or above grade level in their groups of "average" students. Thus, the scores of the average group really represent those of students with a wide range of mathematical skill. Admittedly, the goal of these studies was to distinguish potential low achievers from all others, so the methodology fit their purpose. However, such techniques may not provide an accurate picture of the relation of memory span to mathematics achievement (c.f., Hall & Humphreys, in press, for a detailed discussion of this and other methodological problems in research to characterize special populations.)

Romberg, Collis, and Buchanan (Note 1) examined the relation of 4- through 8-year-olds' cognitive capacity to performance on simple addition and subtraction word problems. Cognitive capacity was defined by a combination of M-space (Case, 1978) and cognitive processing capabilities:

> Cognitive Level 1 children operate on M-space Level 1, are capable of handling qualitative comparisons and transformations at a moderate level, and are incapable of dealing with quantitative tasks or logical reasoning. Cognitive Level 2 children operate at M-space Level 2, handle qualitative correspondence tasks, and cannot handle quantitative and logical skills (but were considerably better than Group 1 on all tasks). Cognitive Level 3 children also operate at M-space Level 2, are high on qualitative correspondence, have developed the specific counting skills of counting-on and counting-back, are inadequate in their use of those counting skills on transitive reasoning, and are inadequate on logical reasoning. Cognitive Level 4 children operate at M-space 3, are high on qualitative correspondence and all the quantitative tests, but are inadequate on the logical reasoning test. Cognitive Levels 5 and 6 are at M-space Levels 3 and 4. They reach the ceiling on the qualitative correspondence tests, have very high scores on all the quantitative tests, and also are high on logical reasoning.

Romberg et al. found a general trend of increasing performance with higher levels of cognitive capacity. When performance was collapsed across age, there were generally significant differences between all Cognitive levels, except 3 and 4; these two groups always performed very similarly. The same general pattern was observed to some extent within grades as well. In grades one and two, performance generally increased with cognitive level; however, in grade three, levels 3 and 4 had virtually identical performance on all tasks. The results from this study are equivocal with respect to the role of basic information processes in mathematical problem solving. Though performance generally increased with cognitive level, cognitive level was determined by a combination of knowledge based and basic information processes. That children at Levels 3 and 4 who have different M-space measures performed very similarly, and those at levels 2 and 3 who have similar M-space measures performed differently, suggests that M-space might at best marginally contribute to mathematics achievement when compared to knowledge-dependent processes.

Hiebert, Carpenter, and Moser (1982) found a small but consistent relationship between first graders ($N = 149$) performance on a backward digit-span task and ability to solve six types of verbal addition and subtraction problems, assessed under four conditions: large ($11 <$ sum < 16) versus small ($5 <$ sum < 9) addends crossed with availability versus nonavailability of concrete aids. Digit span was a significant predictor of both problem-solving ability and use of more sophisticated solution strategies (e.g., counting-on from the larger number versus counting all to solve addition problems). However, the size of the relationship was generally small, with digit span, coupled with other predictors, typically accounting for only 10–20% of the variance on these problems. Further, digit span was not a prerequisite for either ability to solve more difficult problems or for use of advanced strategies. Some children at all digit-span levels were able to solve some problems of each type and use advanced strategies on some problems. However, performance and tendency to use advanced strategies generally increased with increasing digit span.

Overall, these studies indicate that performance on digit-span tasks is related to mathematics achievement, even when IQ is controlled, but processing speed is not. However, because both mathematical ability and digit span are correlated with verbal ability, it is unclear whether this relation indicates that the basic information processes used in digit-span tasks are important components of mathematical ability, or whether it reflects the overlap between mathematical and verbal ability. Further, a particular degree of such processing skill, as measured by digit span, does not appear to be a prerequisite for skill in elementary mathematical tasks, at least not for solving simple word problems, though overall, those with lower digit spans did have poorer problem-solving performance. This suggests that even if these basic processing skills contribute uniquely to mathematical ability, their contribution may be relatively minor.

CONTENT KNOWLEDGE

A second aspect of cognition that contributes to individual differences in mathematical ability is content knowledge and content-dependent processes. Although one would expect more able students to have more mathematical knowledge, a number of recent studies suggest that more able students organize their knowledge differently than less able students as well. Evidence for this difference in organization comes primarily from students' judgments of problem similarity.

Chartoff (1977) investigated the dimensions used by junior and senior high school and college students to judge the similarity of mathematical problems and the generality of dimensions across age groups and types of problems. Approximately 500 students were asked to rate the similarity of algebra word problems from one of six specially constructed problem sets. Each problem set was constructed by taking two structurally dissimilar problems with similar context (e.g., problems about furniture) and the following variants of each: a structurally related problem with different context, a generalization, a reversal, and a specialization. An abstraction of one type of problem and a problem with insufficient data for solution were also included. Using a multidimensional scaling technique, he found that four dimensions were used by all age groups and on all problem sets: (1) how the problem is solved; (2) problem context; (3) comparison with a generic problem of the same type; and (4) the question posed by the problem. Dimension 1 was found to be the most important criterion for similarity in all age groups, with its salience tending to increase with age. The weight of this dimension also seemed to increase on similarity ratings made after seeing the solutions to the problems; however, no control groups were used, so it is not clear whether this increase was simply due to increased familiarity with the problems, or to seeing the solutions.

Using a card-sort task instead of a rating procedure, Silver (1979) identified four dimensions used by eighth-grade students in making similarity judgments: mathematical structure, contextual details, question form, and pseudostructure (the presence of measurable quantities such as weight, height, age, and time). These dimensions are virtually the same as those identified by Chartoff; Silver's pseudostructure can be considered a particular type of context. Since Silver's problem set did not contain generalizations, that dimension was not relevant to his study. The agreement in the dimensions found in the Chartoff and Silver studies strengthens the conjecture that older students use a few general dimensions to make judgments of relatedness among mathematical problems.

In a series of studies, Hinsley, Hayes, and Simon (1977) examined the role of categorization in solving typical high school algebra problems by high school and college students "known for their knowledge of algebra." They concluded that (1) people do recognize categories of algebra problems; (2) they can many times recognize a problem's category without completely formulating a solution; (3) people have a body of information about the problem categories which is useful in formulating problems of that type for solution; and (4) people use category identification to formulate problems in the course of actually solving them. From observations of students solving some standard and nonstandard algebra problems, they concluded that subjects have two ways of approaching algebra word problems. If they recognize a problem as an exemplar of a particular type of problem, they will use special heuristics useful in solving problems of that type; if the problem is not associated with a particular type, a more general, direct translation type of approach is employed.

The Hinsley, Hayes, and Simon study and the Chartoff study primarily established that (1) at least good algebra students categorize mathematical problems prior to their solution; (2) they seem to use these classifications in the process of solving the problems; and (3) students initially perceive mathematical problems as similar along four dimensions that seem to be general across problems and across older age groups. These studies did not directly assess the relationship between the nature of the classifications or similarity dimensions and mathematical ability.

In recent work, Krutetskii (1976) and Silver (1979) argue for a direct relationship between preference for mathematical structure as a similarity dimension and mathematical ability. In his 10-year study of mathematically gifted school children, Krutetskii identified a set of specific components which he claims are elements of the structure of mathematical ability. Among these are "the ability for formalized perception of mathematical material, for grasping the formal structure of the problems"; "the ability for rapid and broad generalization of mathematical objects, relations, and operations"; and "mathematical memory (generalized memory for mathematical relationships, type characteristics, schemes of arguments and proofs, methods of problem solving, and principles of approach)" (Krutetskii, 1976, p. 350). In this description, Krutetskii suggests that mathematical structure is very salient to capable mathematics students. This then implies that these students should be more likely to make similarity judgments on the basis of mathematical structure than on some other aspect of the problems, and that they should be more accurate in determining which problems are structurally related than those who are less talented.

Silver (1979) examined the relationship between students' perceptions of structural similarity among a set of mathematical problems and their mathematical ability in a more controlled experimental setting than that used by Krutetskii. Whereas Krutetskii relied on teacher rating to identify students' mathematical capabilities, Silver used standardized tests of mathematical concepts and computation along with several reading scores, and verbal and nonverbal IQ scores. In addition, he also considered students' problem-solving skill as judged by their ability to solve the set of problems used in the sorting task. His results supported Krutetskii's findings. The tendency to relate problems on the basis of structural similarities was found to be strongly correlated with standardized measures of mathematical ability. Furthermore, presolution and, not surprisingly, postsolution perceptions of problem structure were found to be significantly correlated with problem-solving performance on these problems, even when the effects of verbal and nonverbal IQ were controlled thought partial correlation analysis. When knowledge of mathematics concepts and computational skill were simultaneously controlled, however, the relationship between problem-solving performance and presolution perceptions of structure was not significant. Yet, a significant relationship remained between postsolution perception of structure and problem solution scores even when mathematics concepts and computation were controlled. Silver's results thus confirm Krutetskii's conclusion that good problem solvers are able to perceive a problem's structure before its solution. The strong relationship between postsolution sorting by structure and problem-solving performance suggests that good problem solvers are extracting information about problem structure from the solutions and are able to use that information in making future judgments of problem relatedness. Silver also found a significant increase in the extent to which structurally related problems were identified to be similar in the postsolution sorts compared to presolution sorts. This suggests that in solving the problems, students were becoming more aware of the mathematical structure of the problems.

The relationship between perception of problem structure and mathematical ability may not be as straightforward as presented in the Krutetskii study and Silver study. Both of these studies seem to suggest the following simple conclusion; mathematically capable students perceive the mathematical structure of problem and use this as a basis for similarity judgments while students of lower ability have difficulty perceiving mathematical structure and rely on problem context instead. However, both of these studies held one crucial variable constant—the familiarity of the students with the mathematical structure of the problems. It seems plausible that the ability to recognize the structure of a problem—at least partially—depends on whether the relevant system of mathematical operations and relations is already known to the student. If the mathematical relationships in a group of problems are beyond the range of a student's experience, a capable mathematics student may also have difficulty perceiving structural similarities among these problems and may resort to some other criterion, such as context, as a basis for similarity judgments.

Briars and Lesh (Note 2) examined the influence of familiarity of problem structure on second-, fourth-, and sixth-graders' perceptions of problem-relatedness. They found that although more capable students tended to group familiar problems according to mathematical structure, they did not do so for problems not yet included in their mathematical instruction. Instead, they placed the novel problems in categories already established by the familiar ones. After seeing the problem solutions, though, the novel problems were interpreted according to their mathematical structures to a greater extent, but still not as frequently as the familiar ones.

Schoenfeld and Herrman (in press) obtained a similar result. They compared novice (college students with one to three college mathematics courses) and expert (mathematicians) judgments of relatedness of a set of 32 nonstandard mathematics problems. Note that their "novice" subjects were probably fairly capable mathematics students; most incapable students would have dropped mathematics before this. Schoenfeld and Herrman found that mathematicians tended to classify problems on the basis of the general approach they would use in its solution (e.g., analogy, contradiction, induction), while novices tended to use surface features of the problems (e.g., geometric constructions, polynomials). However, the general approaches cited by the experts were probably not familiar to the novices, since such techniques are not explicitly taught as part of the mathematical curriculum. Thus, novices may have lacked the relevant knowledge structures to classify problems as the experts had. Half the students then participated in a problem-solving course in which they were instructed in these more general problem-solving techniques. The problem classifications of these students became more similar to the expert classifications following this instruction. Thus, the results of these two studies suggest that perception of mathematical problem structure can also depend on whether the relevant mathematical relationships are known to the student.

Through his detailed clinical interview studies, Krutetskii (1976) identified several other characteristics of the cognitive processes of the mathematically able: (1) the ability for logical thought in the sphere of quantitative and spatial relationships, number and letter symbols, and the ability to think in mathematical symbols; (2) the ability to curtail the process of mathematical reasoning and the system of corresponding operations, and the ability to think in curtailed structures; (3) flexibility of mental processes in mathematical activity; (4) striving for clarity, simplicity, economy, and rationality of solutions; and (5) the ability for rapid and free reconstruction of the direction of a mental process, switching from a direct to a reverse train of thought (reversibility of the mental process in mathematical reasoning). As far as we can ascertain, these processing abilities have not been investigated in any other studies. Thus, at this point, their role in mathematical ability is somewhat unclear. The major questions include: "Are these abilities independent of the ability to perceive mathematical structure or are they a consequence of that ability?" and "What effects do other variables, such as amount of content knowledge, have on these abilities?"

METACOGNITION

The third aspect of cognition that may affect mathematics achievement is metacognition. Metacognition refers to "knowledge and cognition about cognitive phenomena" (Flavell, 1979, p. 906). It includes knowledge of general cognitive strategies (e.g., rehearsal), awareness of ones own cognitive processes along with monitoring, evaluating, and regulating them, and beliefs about factors that affect cognitive activities (Flavell, 1979). Differences in such knowledge have been proposed as one factor underlying differences in intelligence (Baron, 1977); and in fact, comparisons of various groups differing in intelligence such as adults and children, normal children and retardates, and more and less educated adults, indicate that the more "intelligent" groups do show greater metacognitive knowledge, at least about memory and the memorial processes that have been assessed in these studies (see Baron, 1977, for a review). This suggests that metacognition may play an important role in mathematical ability as well.

The majority of research on metacognition has been done by developmental psychologists mainly interested in metamemory (knowledge about one's memory, memorial processes such as storage and retrieval, and memorial strategies). This research has focused primarily on three aspects of metamemory: awareness of the active nature of processing, knowledge of and use of various memory strategies, and analysis of task demands (Lawson, 1980; Silver, Note 3). Although these are important aspects of performance on memory tasks, they are of less relative importance for successful mathematical problem solving. Mathematical problem solving is a process, and often involves constructing an appropriate sequence of cognitive activities. Consequently, process-oriented aspects of metacognition such as strategy selection, monitoring, assessing, and evaluating progress in problem solving are of major importance (Silver, Note 3). Unfortunately, these topics have received little attention in the developmental literature.

Analysis of and research on mathematical metacognitions is just beginning (Silver, Note 3; Lester & Garofalo, Note 4; Schoenfeld, Note 5), with each researcher developing his own descriptive scheme. Three major categories of mathematical metacognitions emerge from all these schemes: (1) knowledge and selection of general mathematical problem-solving strategies, or heuristics, such as those described by Polya (1957) (e.g., think of a similar problem, simplify); (2) awareness of and monitoring, assessing, and evaluating one's problem-solving processes (i.e., guiding the problem-solving process); and (3) belief systems and expectations about mathematics and mathematical problem solving. Even though research about these aspects is in its infancy, recent exploratory studies are beginning to elucidate the important roles these types of metacognitions can play in mathematical achievement.

HEURISTICS

One type of metacognitive knowledge that influences mathematical problem-solving ability is knowledge of general mathematical problem-solving strategies (heuristics). These heuristics are general in that they are independent of particular mathematical content. They include fairly straightforward strategies, such as "draw a picture or diagram" and "look for a pattern," as well as ones that require more extensive mathematical knowledge to apply, such as "think of a related problem" and "consider special cases" (Polya, 1957).

Almost by definition, heuristics are characteristic of mathematical ability. They are problem-solving strategies that good mathematical problem solvers (mathematicians) typically use to solve nonroutine problems; in other words, they are techniques experts use when they do real problem solving. A number of studies indicate that most students, at least through the college level, do not spontaneously acquire any but the most elementary of these heuristics. In fact, there are some data that suggest that only elementary school students who are better problem solvers use even relatively simple heuristics such as keeping a written record of their work and planning (Branca, Adams, & Silver, 1980). However, if students are taught relevant heuristics along with cues identifying problems to which they may be benefically applied, and if students think to use them (which is not always the case), their problem-solving abilities significantly improve (Schoenfeld, 1979).

AWARENESS OF PROBLEM-SOLVING PROCESSES

A second category of metacognitive knowledge that seems to distinguish more and less skillful mathematical problem solvers is their awareness, monitoring, assessment, and evaluation of their own problem-solving behavior. For individuals with considerable mathematical knowledge (experts), solving routine exercise–type mathematical problems, such as high-school algebra problems, are pretty much a matter of recalling and executing the appropriate routine; little original problem solving takes place. Consequently, the solution process is very smooth, providing little opportunity for the emergence of metacognitive knowledge. In contrast, solutions to non-trivial mathematical problems appear much less smooth—solving such problems frequently involves false starts, hesitations, and decision points. It is precisely in attempting to solve these nontrivial problems that awareness of, monitoring, assessing, and evaluating cognitive processes plays a role.

Schoenfeld (Note 6) has identified two qualitatively different types of decisions involved in solving such nontrivial mathematical problems (and problems in other formal domains as well). Tactical decisions involve selecting the method to implement, such as a particular heuristic or algorithm. An example of such a decision is selecting an integration technique for evaluating a particular integral. Such decisions are part of the heuristic or content knowledge. *Strategic* or managerial decisions are ones that have a major impact on both the course of the solution and allocation of one's resources during the problem-solving process. One example of such a decision: given 20 minutes to solve a problem, deciding to spend 10 minutes (half the allotted time) calculating the area of a region. Although tactical decisions are important, Schoenfeld found that strategic decisions were the major difference between problem solving of experts (mathematicians) and novices with a fairly extensive mathematical background (college freshman mathematics students).

Schoenfeld compared the problem-solving performance of six pairs of college students with one to three courses of college mathematics (i.e., they all had good computational skill) to that of mathematicians on two nonroutine problems.[4] He found that the college students had very poor managerial strategies: They rarely, if ever, assessed the potential utility of a plan of action (e.g., one pair spent 10 minutes calculating the area of a triangle without ever asking what good it would do if they found it), they gave inadequate consideration to the utility of potential alternative methods to try, and in general, did not monitor or assess their progress toward solution, so had little way to end an unproductive line of reasoning. Even students with more awareness tended to make critical decisions very casually.

In contrast, the mathematicians seemed to be monitoring their progress almost continually, frequently indicating that "the entire solution process was being watched and controlled, both at the local and global levels" (Schoenfeld, Note 6, p. 36), and continually assessed their plan and its implementation, and acted accordingly. Thus, it seems that the expert problem solver engaged in cognitive monitoring behaviors, while less expert individuals did not.

BELIEF SYSTEMS

A third category of metacognition that may affect mathematical ability is one's belief system about mathematics and mathematical problem solving (Silver et al., 1980; Silver, Note 3; Lester & Garofalo, Note 4; Schoenfeld, Note 5). Expectations about mathematics and mathematical problem solving

---

[4]Students were asked to work in pairs because the student dialogue of the duo seemed to make problem-solving decisions more overt without being obtrusive.

should influence problem-solving behavior. Elementary school children's faulty beliefs present a clear example. Lester and Garofalo noted that third-graders typically believe that: (1) the difficulty of solving a mathematical problem is determined by the size of and number of numbers in the problem; (2) that all problems can be solved by the application of one (typically) or more (rarely) arithmetic operations; (3) the appropriate operation is determined by key words in the problem which usually appear in the last question or sentence (so there is no need to read the whole problem); and (4) decisions to check depend on the availability of time, and for story problems, one only needs to check the computation. In addition, Silver et al. (1980) identified other typical beliefs that can interfere with mathematical problem solving: (1) there is only one correct way to solve a problem; and (2) problems should take only a few minutes to solve. It is fairly easy to see how beliefs like these could interfere with children's problem-solving performance.

The most disturbing aspect of these results is that children's wrong beliefs are consistent with their experience with mathematics. In the primary grades, children do typically solve only problems that involve single operations, and each problem takes only a few minutes to solve. In an attempt to overcome this, Branca et al. (1980) implemented an instructional program for fourth-graders designed to develop children's problem-solving skills and provide them with an experience base to correct these wrong beliefs. Explicit goals of the program were to increase children's awareness that: (1) solving a mathematical problem may be a multifaceted complex of processes (i.e., more than one algorithm may be involved); (2) many problems permit multiple solutions; (3) planning is important; and (4) solving more difficult problems may take longer than a few minutes. Preliminary data indicated that indeed, children can acquire these modified beliefs through instruction, and thus improve their problem-solving performance.

Faulty beliefs and expectations are not confined to elementary school students. Again, looking at college students' problem-solving performance, Schoenfeld noted a number of typical beliefs about solving geometric construction problems held by college freshmen who have studied high school geometry:

1. One gains "insight into a problem situation in geometry by having a very accurate picture of it."
2. Verification is purely empirical. Hypotheses about constructions are tested by performing the indicated constructions. If the construction appears to work, it is correct..
3. "Proof" is irrelevant to discovery and verification. If absolutely necessary (i.e., the teacher asks for it), one can probably prove that constructions work. But this is simply "playing by the rules of the

game," verifying formally what one already knows (empirically) to be correct.

4. Candidates for solutions are tested seriatum. Hypothesis 1 is tested until it is accepted or rejected, then Hypothesis 2, and so on. Simple (intuitively apprehensive) hypotheses are tested first (p. 36).

In contrast, a mathematician has a different set of beliefs, including using proof as a means of discovery, rather than as a method of verification. These beliefs directly affect the approach taken, hence, success in solving geometric construction problems. Similar beliefs probably can be identified for other types of problems as well. Thus, it seems that at all levels, one's beliefs about mathematics will influence problem-solving performance.

Finally, beliefs about mathematics as a domain can influence how one organizes content knowledge in memory and what one determines is important. For example, one characteristic of the mathematically able individuals discussed is that they focus on the mathematical structure of situations and have acquired a rich store of problem schemata. As Silver (Note 3) suggests "A person who believes that there is an underlying structure to mathematics and that it is this structure that is important, not the surface details, is likely to approach the study of mathematical material quite differently than a student who does not hold this belief" (p. 8). Thus, more capable mathematics students may focus on mathematical structure precisely because they believe mathematics is a structured domain.

SUMMARY

In this chapter, we have analyzed mathematical ability within the framework of an information-processing model of cognition, examining differences in basic information-processing skills, content knowledge, and metacognition about mathematics as possible sources of individual differences in mathematical ability. We found few studies that have investigated the role of basic information-processing skills in mathematical ability; further, these studies have only examined processing speed and digit span. These studies indicate that digit span is related to mathematics achievement even when IQ is controlled, but processing speed is not. Because both mathematical ability and digit span are correlated with verbal ability, it is unclear whether this relation indicates that cognitive processes used in digit-span tasks are important components of mathematical ability, or whether it reflects the overlap between mathematical and verbal ability. A larger number of studies have investigated differences in content knowledge. The major conclusion from this work is that more able mathematics students not only have more mathematical knowledge, they organize their knowledge differently. Able students appear to have a rich network of knowledge structures reflecting the structure of mathematics. In addition, very able mathematics students exhibit some cognitive processes, such as curtailment of reasoning and generalization of mathematical structure from single instances, that may be unattainable by less able students. Metacognitive knowledge about mathematics is just beginning to be studied. However, the exploratory research on this topic does provide some evidence that skillful mathematical problem solvers know and use general problem-solving heuristics, are aware of and actively monitor, assess, and evaluate their problem-solving processes, and also have qualitatively different belief systems about mathematics than do less-skillful individuals. It is not known at present whether this metacognitive knowledge is a reflection of differences in basic information-processing skills and content knowledge, or whether it helps to create them.

REFERENCES

Baron, J. Intelligence and general strategies. In G. Underwood (Ed.), *Strategies in information processing*. New York: Academic Press, 1977.

Begle, E. G. *Critical variables in mathematics education*. Washington, D.C.: Mathematical Association of America and the National Council of Teachers of Mathematics, 1979.

Branca, N. A., Adams, V. M., & Silver, E. A. *Problem solving processes of ten and eleven year olds*. Berkeley: University of California Press, 1980.

Carter, D. E., Spero, A. J., & Walsh, J. A. A comparison of the visual and aural digit span and the Bender gestalt as discriminators of low achievement in the primary grades. *Psychology in the Schools*, 1978, *15*, 194–198.

Case, R. Piaget and beyond: Toward a developmentally based theory and technology of instruction. In R. Glaser (Ed.), *Advances in instructional psychology*. Hillsdale, N.J.: Lawrence Erlbaum Associates, 1978.

Chartoff, B. T. An exploratory investigation utilizing a multidimensional scaling procedure to discover classification criteria for algebra word problems used by students in grades 7–13 (Ph.D. thesis, Northwestern University, 1976). *Dissertation Abstracts International*, 1977, *37*, 7006A.

Demster, F. N. Memory span: Sources of individual and developmental differences. *Psychological Bulletin*, 1981, *89*, 63–100.

Dienes, Z. P. *Building up mathematics*. London: Educational Press, 1960.

Dienes, Z. P. *The power of mathematics*. London: Educational Press, 1967.

Estes, W. K. The information-processing approach to cognition: A confluence of metaphors and methods. In W. K. Estes (Ed.), *Handbook of learning and cognitive processes* (Vol. 5). Hillsdale, N.J.: Lawrence Erlbaum Associates, 1978.

Fennema, E. Sex differences in mathematics achievement: A review. *Journal for Research in Mathematics Education*, 1974, *5*, 126–139.

Flavell, J. H. Metacognition and cognitive monitoring: A new area of cognitive-developmental inquiry. *American Psychologist*, 1979, *34*, 906–911.

Furneaux, W. D., & Rees, R. The structure of mathematical ability. *British Journal of Psychology*, 1978, *69*, 507–512.

Hadamard, J. *The psychology of invention in the mathematical field*. Princeton, N.J.: Princeton University Press, 1945.

Hall, J. W. and Humphreys, M. S. Research on specific learning disabilities: Deficits and remediation. *Topics in Learning and Learning Disabilities*, in press.

Hiebert, J., Carpenter, T. P., & Moser, J. M. Cognitive development and children's solutions to verbal arithmetic problems. *Journal for Research in Mathematics Education*, 1982, *13*, 83–98.

Hinsley, D. A., Hayes, J. R., & Simon, H. A. From words to equations—meaning and representation in algebra word problems. In M. Just & P. Carpenter (Eds.), *Cognitive processes in comprehension*. Hillsdale, N.J.: Lawrence Erlbaum Associates, 1977.

Hunt, E. Mechanics of verbal ability. *Psychological Review*, 1978, *85*, 109–130.

Krutetskii, V. A. *The psychology of mathematical abilities in schoolchildren*. Chicago: University of Chicago Press, 1976.

Larkin, J. H. Enriching formal knowledge; A model for learning to solve textbook physics problems. In J. R. Anderson (Ed.), *Cognitive skills and their acquisition*. Hillsdale, N.J.: Lawrence Erlbaum Associates, 1981.

Lawson, M. J. Metamemory: Making decisions about strategies. In J. R. Kirby & J. B. Biggs (Eds), *Cognition, development, and instruction*. New York: Academic Press, 1980.

Lesh, R. A. Mathematical learning disabilities: Considerations for identification, diagnosis, remediation. In R. A. Lesh, D. B. Mierkiewicz, & M. G. Kantowski (Eds.), *Applied mathematical problem solving*. Columbus, Ohio: ERIC/SMEAC, 1979.

Newell, A., & Simon, H. A. *Human problem solving*. Englewood Cliffs, N.J.: Prentice-Hall, 1972.

Poincare, H. Mathematical creation. In J. R. Newman (Ed.), *Mathematics in the modern world*. San Francisco: Freeman, 1968. (Originally published, 1948.)

Polya, G. *How to solve it* (2nd ed.). Princeton, N.J.: Princeton University Press, 1957.

Schneider, W., & Shiffrin, R. M. Controlled and automatic human information processing. I. Detection, search, and attention. *Psychological Review*, 1977, *84*, 1–66.

Schoenfeld, A. H. Explicit heuristic training as a variable in problem-solving performance. *Journal for Research in Mathematics Education*, 1979, *10*, 173–187.

Schoenfeld, A. H., & Herrman, D. J. Problem perception and knowledge structure in expert and novice mathematical problem solvers. *Journal of Experimental Psychology*, in press.

Silver, E. A. Student perceptions of relatedness among mathematical verbal problems. *Journal for Research in Mathematics Education*, 1979, *10*, 195–210.

Silver, E. A., Branca, N. A., & Adams, V. M. *Metacognition: The missing link in problem solving?* Berkeley: University of California Press, 1980.

Simon, H. A. Information-processing theory of human problem solving. In W. K. Estes (Ed.), *Handbook of learning and cognitive processes* (Vol. 5). Hillsdale, N.J.: Lawrence Erlbaum Associates, 1978.

Simon, H. A. Information processing models of cognition. *Annual Review of Psycnology*, 1979, *30*, 363–396.

Spiegel, M. R., & Bryant, N. D. Is speed of processing information related to intelligence and achievement? *Journal of Educational Psychology*, 1978, *70*, 904–910.

Very, P. S. Differential factor structures in mathematical ability. *Genetic Psychology Monographs*, 1967, *75*, 169–207.

Webster, R. E. Visual and aural short-term memory capacity deficits in mathematics disabled students. *Journal of Educational Research*, 1979, *72*, 277–283.

Werdelin, I. *The mathematical ability: Experimental and factoral studies*. Copenhagen, Denmark: Lund, 1958.

NOTES

1.   Romberg, T. A., Collis, K. F., & Buchanan, A. *Performance on addition and subtraction problems: Results from individual interviews—Sandy Bay study* (Tech. Rep. 580). Wisconsin Research and Development Center, 1981.

2.   Briars, D. J., & Lesh, R. A. *Elementary school students' perceptions of relatedness among mathematical problems*. Paper presented at the annual meeting of the American Educational Research Association, April 1980.

3.   Silver, E. A. *Thinking about problem solving: Towards an understanding of metacognitive aspects of mathematical problem solving*. Paper presented at the Conference on Thinking, University of the South Pacific, Suva, Fiji, January 1982.

4.   Lester, F. K., & Garofalo, J. *Metacognitive aspects of elementary school students' performance on arithmetic tasks*. Paper presented at the annual meeting of the American Educational Research Association, New York, March 1982.

5.   Schoenfeld, A. H. *Beyond the purely cognitive: Metacognition and social cognition as driving forces in intellectual performance*. Paper presented at the annual meeting of the American Educational Research Association, New York, March 1982.

6.   Schoenfeld, A. H. *Episodes and executive decisions in mathematical problem solving*. Paper presented at the annual meeting of the American Educational Research Association, Los Angeles, April 1981.

7

INDIVIDUAL DIFFERENCES IN THE SOLVING OF SOCIAL SCIENCE PROBLEMS*

James F. Voss, Sherman W. Tyler, and Laurie A. Yengo

INTRODUCTION

This chapter is concerned with individual differences that occur in the solving of social science problems. Although in recent years cognitive psychol-

*Research reported in this paper was supported by the Learning Research and Development Center (LRDC) at the University of Pittsburgh, Pittsburgh, Pennsylvania. The LRDC is supported, in part, as a research and development center by funds from the National Institute of Education (NIE) and from the Advanced Research Projects Agency (ARPA), an office under the Secretary of Defense. The opinions expressed do not necessarily reflect the position or policy of NIE or ARPA, and no official endorsement should be inferred.

ogists have shown considerable interest in problem solving, the problems studied have almost exclusively been well structured, in effect, the initial state and the goal of the problem are clearly delineated and the steps required to reach the goal are well defined. The problems studied include puzzle problems such as the "Tower of Hanoi" problem (e.g., Simon, 1975) and the missionary–cannibal river crossing problem (e.g., Jeffries, Polson, Razran, & Atwood, 1977), as well as problems related to the subject matters of geometry (e.g., Greeno, 1978) and physics (e.g., Chi, Feltovich, & Glaser, 1981; Larkin, McDermott, Simon, & Simon, 1980). Conversely, problems that are poorly structured or ill defined have received little attention (Reitman, 1965; Simon, 1973). Since most problems in the social sciences are ill structured, the research reported here constitutes a specific extension of the study of individual differences, that is, to questions involving how individuals vary in solving ill structured problems in a particular subject-matter domain.

As noted, problem solving in social science domains has not been studied by cognitive psychologists and, in pursuing such a line of research, we have found it necessary to modify the existing problem-solving theory by extending the information-processing analysis of problem solving. The modification has consisted of incorporating a jurisprudence model into the information-processing framework. Thus, in order to discuss the nature of individual differences in social science problem solving, it is first necessary to provide an analysis of the problem-solving situation as found in the social sciences; only then can we move on to a detailed examination of the individual differences found in such problem solving. The first section of the chapter consists of a discussion of the information-processing framework of problem solving and our adaptation of this framework to the social science situation. Included in this section is an adaptation of Toulmin's jurisprudence model of argument (Toulmin, 1958; Toulmin, Rieke, & Janik, 1979) to social science problem solving. The latter sections then describe individual differences in such problem solving.

ADAPTATION OF THE INFORMATION-PROCESSING MODEL OF PROBLEM SOLVING TO SOCIAL SCIENCE PROBLEM SOLVING

INFORMATION-PROCESSING MODEL OF PROBLEM SOLVING

To begin, we summarize the information-processing model of problem solving. The reader is referred to Newell and Simon (1972) and Simon (1978) for a more detailed discussion of the model.

A problem is presented in a particular context or task environment. The problem statement is interpreted; in the course of interpretation, the solver establishes a representation of the problem and defines the problem space. The problem representation includes the initial state of the problem (the "givens") and the goal of the problem. The problem space includes the possible states of the problem and the operators that can be employed in moving from one state to the next. Thus, as Simon (1978) notes, arriving at a solution may be likened to going along a path from the initial state to the goal, the path consisting of a number of states through which the solver moves.

As the solver moves from one state to the next, he or she may evaluate whether or not the move to a particular state will, in fact, move him or her closer to the goal. Such evaluation often occurs through a process termed "means–ends analysis." This process consists of the solver examining the goal and looking backward to determine whether the particular move results in moving closer to the goal. Although means-ends analysis is used frequently (especially by individuals who are inexperienced with respect to a particular class of problems), experts often work forward from a given state without evaluating a particular move. The reason for this difference in novice and expert strategy is reasonably straightforward: Once an expert develops a representation of a problem, the solution path is often known and the expert needs only to execute the steps of the solution. The expert is, of course, able to do this with problems of known or easily derived solutions. However, for novices, the representation does not provide for the delineation of an appropriate and specific solution path, and the novice must evaluate one or more moves. The difference in evaluation techniques indicates not only an important distinction in the problem solving of experts and novices, but it also shows the critical role played in the development of an appropriate problem representation. We will return to this point later in the chapter.

The information-processing model also assumes a short-term or working memory system that is distinct from the long-term memory system. The problem-solving activity is assumed to take place in working memory, and long-term memory is used as a type of resource in the solving process. Working memory is considered to have a limited capacity, which means, in terms of the problem-solving model, that only a few states of the problem can be held in working memory at any one time. The problem solver is thus presumed to move from state to state without much backtracking, primarily because of the difficulty of going back to states that are no longer in working memory (Hayes & Simon, 1974). However, when a solver reaches a particular state and apparently cannot advance toward the goal from that state, the solver may return to the problem representation and define a new or modified problem space.

THE NATURE OF SOCIAL SCIENCE PROBLEMS

Insofar as we know, a taxonomy of social science problems (or even anything resembling a taxonomy) is not available. Moreover, it is clearly beyond the scope of this chapter to attempt to derive such a taxonomy. This chapter focuses on one type of problem which is, in fact, quite general. More specifically, the problem exists when there is an undesirable state of affairs that requires improvement. Problems of this type are common not only in social sciences but in fields such as medicine. Such problems arise in the social sciences when, for example, there is a poor import–export ratio, double-digit inflation, strained international relations, a poor voter turnout; in medicine, they arise when pain and discomfort occur.

A problem of this type that we have employed is the Soviet "agriculture problem." This problem essentially states that, in the Soviet Union, agricultural productivity has been quite poor in the last five years and, assuming that you are the head of the USSR Ministry of Agriculture, you must improve that productivity. The question is, How would you solve the problem?

The solution strategy typically pursued for this type of problem is to "Identify the cause(s) of the problem and solve by eliminating the cause(s)." For brevity, we shall refer to this strategy as the "Identify and Eliminate Cause(s)" (IEC) solution. In the social sciences, solutions are proposed to improve the import–export ratio, to reduce double-digit inflation, etc., and these solutions usually involve eliminating the causes of the specific problem. Incidentally, problems of this type were apparently recognized in Greek thinking (cf. von Wright, 1971).

In identifying the cause(s) of a problem and trying to solve it, an important characteristic of social science problem solving is that the solution usually cannot be implemented immediately or even within a reasonably short period of time. According to our data, what has happened is that in the evolution of the knowledge domains, the social science disciplines have developed criteria of evaluation that may be applied when a solution is proposed; this process was developed to deal with the issue of delayed evaluation. Our data also suggest that two of the means by which political science solutions are evaluated are (1) by determining whether a particular solution is feasible in relation to the constraints imposed by the problem itself; and (2) by determining whether a solution is tenable in light of the history of the problem. For example, in the aforementioned agriculture problem, solutions were often evaluated with respect to whether they were feasible within the framework of Soviet ideology. Also, occasionally solutions were evaluated with respect to what had been done in the past about the agriculture problem, such as comparing a particular solution to Khrushchev's "Virgin Lands" policy.

Finally, we note that a major characteristic of social science problems involves the question: What constitutes a solution? In puzzle problems such as the river-crossing problem, and in the problems of geometry, algebra, and physics, the solver usually reaches a particular solution. However, what constitutes the solution of a social science problem is an issue of considerably greater difficulty because, as previously indicated, solutions usually are not immediately testable. Thus, social science problems are usually "solved" only tentatively, with such solutions essentially being accepted if (1) implementation of the solution may be conducted without other-than-routine difficulty; and (2) such implementation will eliminate the undesirable state of affairs and thus solve the problem.

SOLVING SOCIAL SCIENCE PROBLEMS

The solving of social science problems, as considered here, distinguishes between the development of the problem representation and the subsequent solution process. As with experts in physics (Larkin et al., 1980), experts in social sciences spend a relatively large proportion of problem-solving activity in developing a problem representation. In doing so, experts delineate the constraints of the problem; subsequently they develop an orientation to the problem. The problem orientation typically involves a statement that the problem is political, technological, social, or some other type. The classification of the problem in terms of its orientation provides the expert with the problem representation from which the solution process may proceed.

Once the representation is developed, the solver proposes a solution. The solution proposed by the expert is usually abstract; generally, the expert offers only one or a few such solutions. However, an important point is that on proposing a solution, much of the subsequent solution activity goes into justifying and examining the solution that was proposed. This extensive development of argumentation in the solution process necessitated our adaptation of Toulmin's jurisprudence model to the solving of social science problems.

The difference in the solution process of solvers in physics and in social sciences is probably due to the fact that large classes of problems in domains such as physics are "understood," in the sense of having agreed upon solutions whereas in the social sciences, few problems have solutions that are "understood." Indeed, one could raise the question of whether "understanding" even means the same thing in reference to physics problems and social science problems (cf. von Wright, 1971).

ADAPTATION OF TOULMIN'S MODEL

Toulmin (1958) developed a model of argument which was later explained in greater detail (Toulmin et al., 1979). The model describes the components of a single argument. An individual is assumed to take some information, called "datum," D (or grounds), and makes a "claim," C, that is based upon the datum, this constituting a D–C unit. However, there must be certain information, beliefs, or other factors that permit the individual to make the claim, and this is called a "warrant," W. Two characteristics of warrants should be noted: First, warrants tend to be general statements; second, warrants are often implicit; that is, in stating the argument D–C the warrant is not explicitly mentioned. Quite often, however, an argument is supported by additional "backing information," B, and backing is explicitly stated. The backing thus provides, in a sense, a supportive statement for the warrant.

The remaining two components of Toulmin's model are the "qualifier," Q, and the "rebuttal," R. A qualifier indicates one or more particular constraining conditions under which a claim can be made, whereas a rebuttal is a statement which is essentially counter to the claim. In Figure 1A, these and the other main components of argument are shown as schematically depicted by Toulmin (1958) and Toulmin et al. (1979).

To adapt the Toulmin model to problem solving, it was necessary to account for the fact that social science problem solving involves the development of a series of arguments. We devised three rules to provide for the adaptation of the model to problem solving. The rules are (1) that a claim may be used as datum for a subsequent claim, denoted as D-C- - -D, the dashed line indicating an implied change in function of the claim, C, and (2) that backing may be an argument. We depict this by (B)-D-C, the parentheses indicating that the backing is implicit. Rules 1 and 2 are the most important as they provide a basis for describing argument development in problem solving. Rule 3 is that qualifiers and rebuttals may also be arguments. Figure 1B presents a diagram of these rules.

THE PROBLEM SITUATION

EXPERIMENTAL PROCEDURES

In our first study, we enlisted the help of four University of Pittsburgh faculty members (one of whom was just finishing his dissertation) whose field of expertise was the Soviet Union. In addition, we recruited six undergraduates who were taking a course on Soviet domestic policy. After providing instructions on "thinking aloud" during the solving of a problem, we presented each person with the previously mentioned Soviet agriculture problem and recorded, via tape, his/her verbal account. In the case of the undergraduates, we presented them with the problem both at the

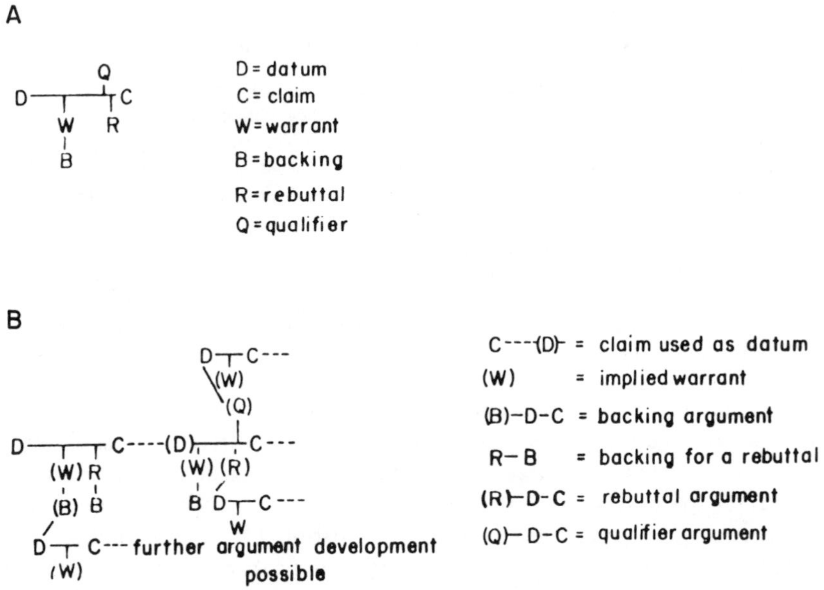
A
Q
D
C
W
R
B
D = datum
C = claim
W = warrant
B = backing
R = rebuttal
Q = qualifier
B
D C---
(W)
(Q)
D C----(D) C---
(W) R
(W) (R)
(B) B
B D C---
W
D C--- further argument development possible
(W)
C---(D) = claim used as datum
(W) = implied warrant
(B)–D–C = backing argument
R–B = backing for a rebuttal
(R)–D–C = rebuttal argument
(Q)–D–C = qualifier argument

FIGURE 1. Diagram of Toulmin's model of argument (**A**) and diagram of problem-solving adaptation of toulmin's model (**B**).

beginning and at the close of the domestic policy course. The problem was "Assume you are the head of the Soviet Ministry of Agriculture and assume crop productivity has been low over the past several years. You now have the responsibility of increasing crop production. How would you go about doing this?"

In using the contrastive procedure and comparing the performance of experts and novices, it is clear that experts and novices typically differ in ways other than their knowledge of a particular subject-matter domain. One important difference is that experts usually have received extensive academic training, whereas novices are usually individuals in the early stages of such training. Taking into account some of these differences, we also studied the problem-solving activity of two other groups, each consisting of four individuals. One group was composed of faculty members whose field of expertise was not the Soviet Union but some other field, namely, Latin America or the Third World. The second group was composed of members of the faculty of the Chemistry Department. Individuals of these two groups were presented with the agriculture problem and their solution performance was compared to members of the other groups.

In addition to this first study, a second study was run, again using experts and novices, but with a different problem. We shall refer to the second problem as the "policy problem," which was stated:

> Assume you are a foreign policy advisor to the President of the United States. The President asks you to draft a workable foreign policy with respect to the Soviet Union. He indicates that a number of factors must be considered in some way or another, including SALT talks, the military preparedness of the USA in relation to that of the USSR, cultural exchange with the USSR, the extent and nature of trade with the USSR, the mid-East, the relation to the Peoples Republic of China to the USA, the policies of the Western European countries, and current problems of the Eastern European countries. How would you go about developing such a policy and what would be the nature of the policy? In addition, possible Soviet involvement in the Western hemisphere is another factor. *Be sure to think out loud* as you consider the development of the policy.

This problem may be regarded as an "establish policy" type of problem. Whether this class of problems is fundamentally different from the previously described undesirable state of affairs problem is an open question. In one sense, the undesirable state of affairs in the foreign policy problem is that there is, by implication, either no existing US foreign policy with respect to the USSR or the current policy is probably not as good as it should be and it should be improved. In the following section, results from this study are mentioned, but because these results, as yet, have not been completely analyzed, these will not be discussed in great detail.

DATA ANALYSIS

After all of the protocols had been collected, the results were analyzed within the general information-processing framework, as modified by the use of the Toulmin model. All the protocols were first segmented into their basic constituent argument units, and the units were then classified into one of Toulmin's argument categories (i.e., datum, claim, warrant, backing, qualifier, rebuttal). These analyses were done by two raters and the interrater reliability exceeded .85 for both scoring steps. In addition, the connections among the argument components were determined and represented in the form of graphs.

Several other analyses were also conducted. To determine in a concrete way the knowledge base underlying participants' arguments, a close examination of the underlying warrants was made. It will be recalled that a warrant is the justification made for proposing a claim that is based on a certain set of data. For each individual, the warrants underlying each datum–claim pair were listed. After all warrants had been specified, a taxonomy was constructed in order to categorize the warrants into types. Table 1 lists these types, together with a definition and an example of each.

TABLE 1
Taxonomy of Warrant Types for Problem 1

Warrant type	Definition of type	Example
Meta	Based on the process of problem solving itself.	Solving a problem requires defining the constraints of the problem.
Governmental	Based on general knowledge of the way governments (especially the US) function.	Ministries of governments solve central problems slowly.
Logical	Based on general logical reasoning or common sense, independent of any specific knowledge domain.	If an approach is unsuccessful, it should be abandoned.
Soviet	Deriving from specific knowledge of the USSR and its institutions	The Soviet Communist Party chooses farm administrators based on their party loyalty.
Economic	Based on knowledge of economic principles.	Food subsidies can be used to increase incentive without increasing prices.
Agricultural	Using knowledge of farming principles (optimal growing conditions, harvesting techniques, etc.).	Nearly arable land can be made arable through irrigation.
Psychological	Deriving from general rules of human behavior, such as the typical human response to certain conditions.	People work harder when they are given incentives to work.
Analogical	Based on reasoning from what is known about a different system to conclusions about the target system.	In Latin America, the peasants find extralegal ways to obtain money; this is probably true in the USSR.
Historical	Based on knowledge of specific historical events (excluding events in the history of the USSR).	Nixon began the policy of friendship with China.

Finally, some numerical indices of the overall structure of argument development were derived, based on the graphic representation of the protocols. Since the top-level nodes in the graph represent the essential arguments (representation and solutions) of the protocol, the proportion of the total nodes which were top level was calculated for each protocol. Furthermore, the mean depth for each top-level node was measured. This was done by determining the deepest level of backing for each top-level node. For example, a claim and warrant backed by another claim and warrant, backed by a final claim and warrant, would have a depth of two. The average depth for a particular protocol could then be established. This calculation provided an indication of how extensively arguments were developed. In a similar vein, the average length for sequences of claims can be determined. In this case, length refers to the number of successive times that a claim became datum for the next claim. This measure thus provided an indication of length of argument chain or, in other terms, the extent to which a given line of argument was pursued. Finally, the nature of the backing statements was examined. In backing a particular warrant, one of three courses could be followed (1) Individuals could use a simple fact or logical principle (B); (2) They could use a simple argument (D–C); or (3) They could use a more elaborate argument chain (D-C-(D)-C-(D)-C. . .). These three types are listed in their order of complexity, the argument chain constituting the most elaborate and presumably most sophisticated form of argument backing. For each protocol, the relative proportion of each of these three types of backing was ascertained.

DIFFERENCES AMONG GROUPS

PROBLEM REPRESENTATION

As noted, a key aspect of problem solving concerns the problem representation that is developed by the solver. Especially for an ill structured problem in which the solver must define the initial state and the goal, the problem representation is of paramount concern. The nature of the representation developed by the individuals in the various groups is described below.

EXPERTS

For the expert problem solver, a relatively large proportion of the protocol was devoted to developing a representation of the problem (approximately 24% of the nodes were related to problem representation). The expert used constraints such as the nature of Soviet ideology and the outcomes of past solution attempts to develop a problem orientation. Additionally, experts often stated the existence of other constraints such as climate and the amount of arable land available. In fact, by the time the representation was developed, the expert had usually delineated the problem space sufficiently to be able to classify the problem in terms of some particular abstract cause. Although the chosen cause was generally different for the different experts (e.g., technological, social, political), its specification set the orientation from which all subsequent solution activity flowed. Experts thus followed the IEC strategy, but used a cause defined at an abstract level.

Figure 2 shows the problem representation of one expert. We have included the protocol statements from which the figure is derived, segmented according to their role in argument development, that is, according

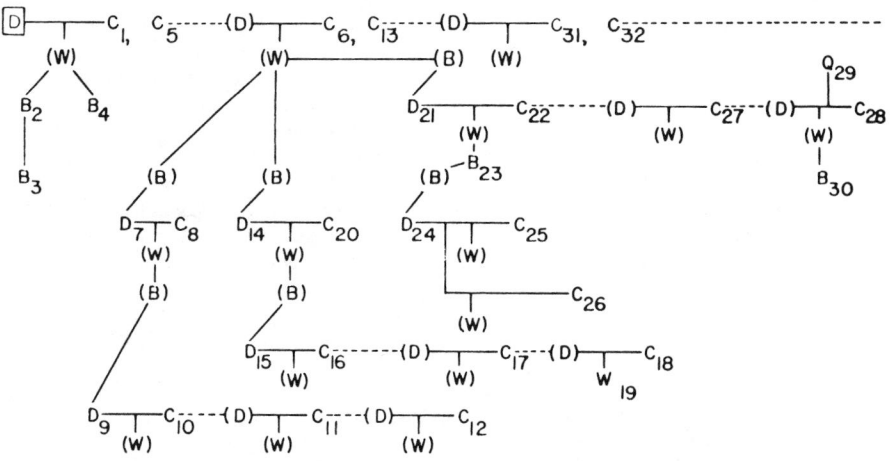

FIGURE 2. Diagram of problem representation of Expert A. D = datum, C = claim,
W = warrant, B = backing, Q = qualifier, R = rebuttal ( ) = implicit.

to our adaptation of Toulmin's model. The reader is asked to note especially
the initial delineation of constraints (geography and climate) and the use of
problem history. Problem history is used both to rule out possible solutions
(exhortation, D_{14}, and reorganization, D_{21}) and to generate the solution
finally accepted by A (mechanization and scientific advances, C_{32}). The
representation is thus of a problem caused by inadequate technology, and
the remainder of the protocol is a description of ways to eliminate this
shortcoming. A similar pattern of establishing the representation was found
for all four experts, although the contents of the protocols varied somewhat.

> I think that as minister of agriculture, one has to start out with the realization that
> there are certain kinds of special agriculture constraints within which you are going to
> work [C_1]. The first one, the most obvious one, is that by almost every count only
> ten percent of the land in the Soviet Union is arable [B_2]. This is normally what is
> called the Blackland in the Ukraine and surrounding areas [B_3]. And secondly, even
> in that arable ten percent of the total land surface, you still have climate for instance,
> problems over which you have no direct control [B_4]. Okay, so that is sort of the
> overall parameter in which we are working [B_5].
> Now we have traditionally in the Soviet Union used three kinds of policies to
> increase agricultural production [C_6]. Of course, agricultural production has been our
> "Achilles' heel" and something that we have inherited from the time the czars freed
> the serfs [D_7]. Even before then, the agricultural production was low [C_8] because
> historically the aristocracy had no need to fend for itself, as it turned to the czar for its
> support [D_9] and hence never, like the English aristocracy for instance, introduced
> modern methods of fertilization, never went to enclosures or consolidations of lands,
> never experimented with crop rotation [C_{10}]. That was passed on to the peasants

[C$_{11}$] and throughout the period when the peasant had been freed to do what he willed with the land, he's responding with the old, rather inefficient ways [C$_{12}$].

At any rate, we have had three different ways by which we have tried to increase agricultural production [C$_{13}$]. The first one might be labeled exhortation [D$_{14}$]. The Soviet approach to agricultural production is to mount campaigns continually to call for more effort on the part of the peasants and agricultural workers and put more effort into their labor activities for agricultural production [D$_{15}$]. Those things are mounted periodically [C$_{16}$], quite frankly, I think that they are a waste of time and energy [C$_{17}$] and they really, as minister of agriculture I must say, that they really do nothing more than give the party a sense of false importance [C$_{18}$] because it's normally incumbent upon the party to develop these ideological indoctrination campaigns and the notion of mind over matter in this case hasn't paid off and it leaves the party with the belief that ideological, and if you'll excuse the term, spiritual policies can overcome objective limitations [W$_{19}$]. So, I wouldn't emphasize very much exhortation [C$_{20}$].

It seems to me that the second way that we traditionally go about trying to increase agricultural production is through constant reorganization [D$_{21}$]. That leads to confusion, that leads to mismanagement and that has forced a mind set upon the peasant agricultural worker of sort of laying back and waiting because this too will also pass [C$_{22}$]. We've gone through collectives, state farms, and machine tractor stations, [B$_{23}$] the latest attempt at reorganization is through the development of what are called agroindustrialist complexes [D$_{24}$], which has knocked down, by the way, the number of collectives from about 250,000 to 30,000 in the last five years, [C$_{25}$] in which the former collective farmer becomes a wage earner [C$_{26}$].

So, I think we're going to have to tend, and I'm going to talk a minute, we have to tend to the nature of agricultural production [C$_{27}$]. I want to say one thing, and I have to recognize that this is clear as day, and that is, that in all of these cases more or less except for stringent ideological periods we've always allowed the private crop to exist [C$_{28}$] even though we take it to be a much more primitive, less historically progressive form of agricultural production [Q$_{29}$]. We must realize that in terms of some of our food staples, even until today, roughly forty percent of the food staples are grown on the private plots [B$_{30}$].

The third thing that we've done and this is where I'd like to start off in terms of turning around agricultural production, the third thing we've done is we've tried to mechanize, and I want to use that in the broad sense because it is not the word I want, we have tried to mechanize industrial production [C$_{31}$]. Not just mechanize it but also introduce scientific advances in Soviet production [C$_{32}$].

NOVICES AND POSTNOVICES

Novices spent little problem-solving time in developing their problem representations. Instead, their representations were simply embodied in a strategy of isolating possible causes of the problem. The causes mentioned were usually quite specific and the proposed solutions were stated in reference to the specific causes. Furthermore, the experience of being in a political science course related in content to the problem made little difference in development of a problem representation, for, as postnovices, the participants also spent little time in developing problem representations. Figure 3

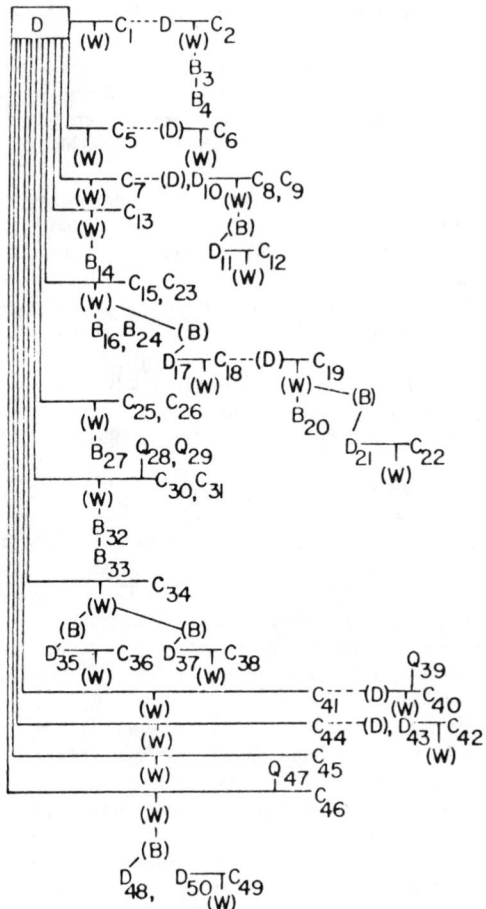

FIGURE 3. Diagram of protocol of Novice 1. (See Figure 2 legend for key.)

presents a graphic example of a novice protocol. The protocol statements of this novice are presented below. It can be seen that the novice begins discussing possible solutions to the problem without any consideration of constraints on, or orientations to, the solutions proposed.

Old-fashioned methods of farming [C_1]. So maybe what needs to be done is to introduce newer methods of farming [C_2] and obviously the people probably need to be educated on how to use these new methods [B_3], especially if they introduce new machinery [B_4]. I remember reading somewhere that on the land that the people own themselves, that crop production is much higher than it was on the state plots [C_5]. Perhaps if the people could be allocated more benefits from the state land, rather than giving it all to the state, crop production might increase [C_6]. Maybe the organization of how the crops are planted and harvested is not adequate [C_7]. Perhaps that should be changed [C_8]. What kind of system they use to plant the crops [C_9], if people from a certain town have to go out to a state plot and plant at a certain time [D_{10}]. Maybe if it has to be worked around their jobs and plus around their own little private ground [D_{11}], perhaps they are planting and harvesting at the wrong times [C_{12}]. It seems that just education in general may be a problem [C_{13}], like updating of methods [B_{14}].

[What about their machinery?] I think they would need new machinery [C_{15}]. When I think of the machinery they have, they probably have old rusting harvester machinery [B_{16}]. And if they got it [D_{17}], they'd probably import their new machinery [C_{18}], and they'd have to educate the people on how to use it [C_{19}], or there would probably be only a handful of people could use it [B_{20}], and if something should break [D_{21}], I doubt there would be very many people who would know how to repair [C_{22}], so maybe something on that line [C_{23}] maybe if their machinery is broken down [B_{24}]. Maybe soil fertilization methods [C_{25}] and maybe their horticulture isn't very good [C_{26}]. Maybe the people have been planting crops on this land year in and year out and they never fertilized land and its just really arid and not fertile [B_{27}].

[What about climate?] I'm not sure about their climate [Q_{28}]. I know its very wintery and pretty dry, a short summer [Q_{29}]. Maybe they're not planting the right crops for the climate [C_{30}]. Maybe they're trying to grow the wrong types of plants [C_{31}]. Maybe they should study the climate more and what types of crops grow better in that type of climate [B_{32}]. They're probably not growing pineapples [B_{33}]. Maybe their irrigation is bad [C_{34}]. If it's dry [D_{35}] maybe they have no irrigation system and the crops all just dry up and wither away [C_{36}], but maybe to have an efficient irrigation system, they would need better engineering [D_{37}]. Maybe they don't have that [C_{38}].

That's about it. [Can you think of anything else?] The government is probably very much involved in crop production anyway [Q_{39}], but maybe they would really study the problem of why crop production is lower [C_{40}], if they would get more people involved at the lower level where its happening rather than have like a bureaucratic overlook of the thing and maybe have a few foreman-type people supervise them [C_{41}]. The people who are doing the planting and who are deciding what needs to be planted and who are tending the crops—maybe people don't tend the crops [C_{42}], if it is state land [D_{43}]. Maybe they're tending their own crops on their own land [C_{44}]. Maybe weeds are overcoming them [C_{45}]. Maybe there's a way to get the people more incentive [C_{46}]. I think that's probably important [Q_{47}]. If they don't have any incentive [D_{48}], they're not going to take care of the crops very well [C_{49}], if they have to give them all away and have old machinery and no irrigation and dry land and grouchy overseers [D_{50}]. Thats about all I can think of.

POLITICAL SCIENTISTS AND CHEMISTS

As a subgroup, the political scientists (those four with specializations in fields other than the USSR) differed substantially from chemists in their representation of the problem. As was the case for experts, political scientists spent a considerable proportion of their problem-solving activity on problem representation (approximately 16% of their total nodes were thus involved). Although the constraints stated were often based on factors other than direct knowledge of the Soviet Union, such as knowledge of governmental operation in other political systems, the result was usually a representation similar to that of the experts, including a statement of an abstract cause.

For the chemists, the representations were quite different. Unlike the nonexpert political scientists, three of the four chemists devoted little effort to problem representation and thus performed more like novices. Overall, 1% of the nodes of the chemists were related to the development of a problem representation. Like novices, chemists tended to begin immediately with a list of specific causes and/or specific solutions, thus representing the problem only as a set of specific causes requiring solutions. The single exception was that of a chemist who developed a problem representation that essentially represented the problem as bureaucratic in nature. Although not showing much knowledge of the Soviet Union per se, the individual was, nevertheless, able to develop a representation more abstract than that of the novices and the other chemists, but not as extensive as the experts or even the political scientists.

SOLUTION PROCESS

EXPERTS

In broad terms, experts typically proposed relatively few solutions to the problem; however, those proposed were quite abstract. Considerable problem-solving activity went into argument development related to the solutions. On the average, only 4% of the experts' nodes were at the top level, that is, involved with the statement of a solution. When more than one such solution was offered, the solutions often were not closely related to each other. Instead, the expert seemed to return to the original problem representation to develop new ways of eliminating the problem cause. An excerpt of the solution process of an expert's protocol is stated below for the same expert whose representation process was previously described. The reader should note that the initial statement concerned the abstract solution of obtaining capital investment to modernize agriculture. A solution was also stated near the end of the protocol to deal with the problem of limited arable land, namely, increasing arable land through the development of irrigation.

> I think as a starting point as minister of agriculture, my first aim would be to get monies to invest in this further mechanization and further application of scientific techniques of agriculture, to agriculture situations [C$_{33}$]. Even though we have mechanized to some extent, it has been a rather crude form of mechanization. It's been rather low-level. It's not coherent, it's not consistent [B$_{34}$], it's—we have the same old problem that we, if we develop tractors or we produce tractors, we produce a thousand tractors [D$_{35}$], we have no parts to service them when they break down

[C_{36}]. We don't have adequate transportation supplies nor transportation networks to carry the produce we do have to the urban markets [B_{37}]. We have been woefully lacking in a methodical application of fertilizers to our agricultural sectors in society [B_{38}], we're much more like a third world than an industrial world country in terms of the way, the lack of use of fertilization [B_{39}]. We still don't have very scientific management in terms of crop rotation and because of all this, we still have a rather labor intensive agricultural production system [D_{41}] and therefore, production per unit is very marginal [C_{42}].

I would have to fight very strongly in the party and the government to redirect the investment ratio going to agriculture over heavy industry and even light industry in the way it's been in the past [C_{43}], though we have in the last ten years shifted investment policies so that more and more is coming into agriculture and away from industrial production per se [D_{44}]. It still is not anywhere near the break even point even though for international, political and domestic reasons, agriculture is our "Achilles' heel" [C_{45}]. If we simply don't produce enough [D_{46}] we will become more and more vulnerable to dependency upon the west for agricultural production [C_{47}] and we'll, if we don't have enough food stuffs internally, we'll develop a more unstable regime [C_{48}].

There'll be lack of support [C_{49}]. We've developed a program where the support from the people is going to come at least in some basic way from demand satisfaction [D_{50}] and yet we haven't been able to satisfy a lot of the basic food demands of large parts of our population [C_{51}].

So, I would first have to fight in the decision making circles to once and for all recognize that socialism is the construction of an entire society that is self-sufficient and does not have to depend upon, especially potential adversaries, for crucial parts of its basic resources [C_{52}].

That means that we have a high enough industrial base [D_{53}]. We have the war technology equivalent to the west [D_{54}], we must now redirect in a major way our investment policy towards agriculture, towards mechanization, towards the infrastructure around mechanization, towards the transportation program, towards the plastic bag program [C_{55}] so that whenever the damn fertilizer is packaged it doesn't sit out in the lot as it does [C_{56}]. We lose one-half of our fertilizers because it rains on paper packages [B_{57}]. What I mean by infrastructure, there is a whole series of secondary enterprises that we have to make [Q_{58}]. Secondly we have to develop an education program among the agricultural workers to teach them the more rational use of mechanization, mechanized planting and harvesting and fertilizer and crop rotation [C_{59}]. Even in this day and age, it's shocking how little and how backward many of our farmers are [D_{60}]. As minister of agriculture, I'd like to say as an aside, since I probably will be defecting to the west with the next ballot, that I blame the party for this [C_{61}]. The party has always insisted that the management of the state farms and even the collectives, be people who have strong party credentials and who quite frankly, don't know anything about agriculture [B_{62}]. So, I would like to see the development of a special, I want a special institute that trains managers of agricultural enterprises and trains them in the most up-to-date, modern techniques [C_{63}]. Even if we start with our investment policy [Q_{64}], we start to reap the benefits of fertilizing and mechanization if we have administrators in these three kinds of farms we have now: the agroindustrial enterprises, which are becoming the largest, the state farms and the smaller and smaller number of collectives [D_{66}]. If we don't have the right agricultural managers [D_{67}], all the most modern techniques and methods of farming will go out the window [C_{68}].

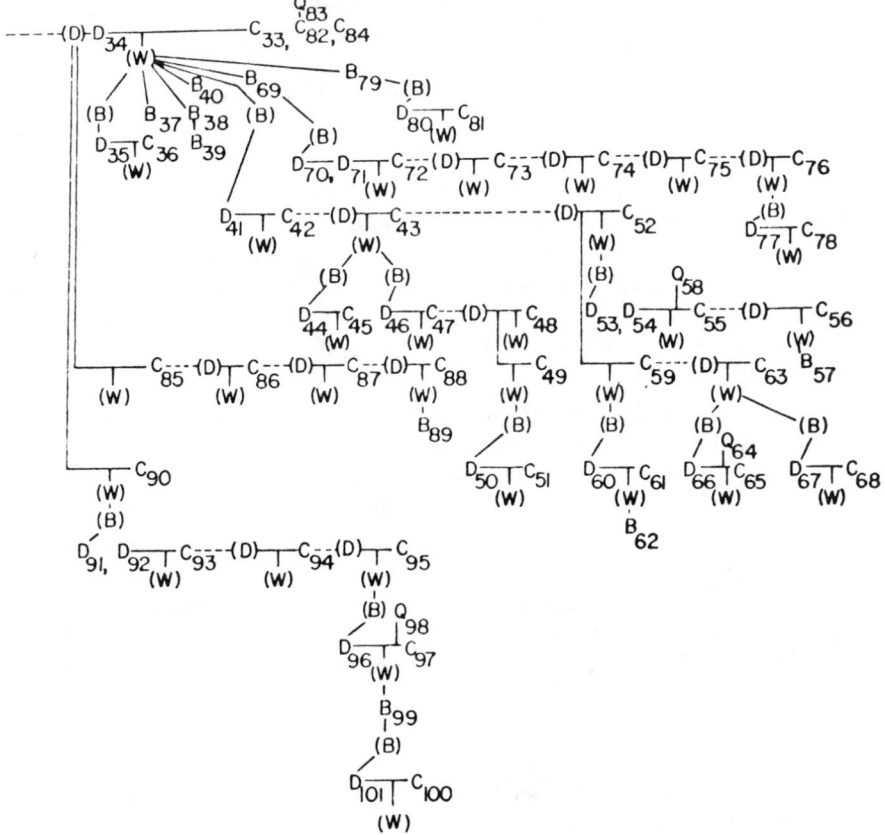

FIGURE 4. Diagram of problem solution of Expert A. (See Figure 2 legend for key.)

Figure 4 presents the sketch of the adaptation of Toulmin's model to the problem solving of the expert whose protocol was just presented. The reader is asked to note how the protocol contents are converted to the argument structure.

We turn now to the topic of argument development. Given the nature of problem solving in an ill structured situation such as in the present problem and given the abstract nature of the solutions experts proposed, argument development for the expert can be seen to achieve several purposes. One is simply to justify a solution to show that it is a good solution to the problem and that it can be achieved. A second purpose is to examine possible problems arising from the proposed solution, and determine how those, in turn, might be solved. A third purpose of argument development is to evaluate the solution in light of the problem representation, in effect, does the solution violate any of the constraints? Yet another purpose is to elaborate or state the proposed solution more clearly. Finally, argument development may aid in the retrieval of new information which may then suggest even more solutions.

Given these purposes of argument development, we performed a number of analyses on the protocols that were designed to provide quantification of some components of the argumentation process. The first tabulation considered is that of warrant classification. Table 1 presents the description of warrant categories. One would expect that a number of warrants indicated by experts would reflect knowledge of the Soviet Union. Indeed, 38% of the warrants were of this type, with the next largest category, economic warrants, constituting only 13%.

The next tabulations presented refer to argument development. The mean depth per top-level node was 8.8 per expert, indicating that each abstract solution was supported by almost nine levels of backing. In addition, the average D–C length was 7.1, thus showing that chains of arguments were developed by the expert. In terms of the nature of argument backing, experts employed a reasonably large number of the more complex D–C chains in their backing or warrant support. The mean proportions were as follows: simple backing, .50; simple D–C backing, .25; and D–C chain backing, .25. The reader is referred to the previously presented expert protocol for an explicit example of how the argumentation of experts is developed.

NOVICES AND POSTNOVICES

The novice protocols present a vivid contrast to those of the experts. Far more of the novice protocols consisted of top-level nodes (21%), and this changed little in the postnovice condition (25%). The reason novices have such a high percentage of top-level nodes is, of course, that their protocols contained a number of simple solutions with relatively little argument development. The experts, incidentally, often referred to the solutions mentioned by the novices, but the experts subsumed them under their more abstract solutions. The previously presented expert protocol provides an example of the subordination of specific solutions with respect to such issues as repair parts, fertilizer, and so forth. On the other hand, the diagram of Figure 3 represents a typical novice protocol in terms of style. This protocol is essentially a listing of possible solutions: newer farming methods, more benefits for farmers on state farms, better planting and harvesting techniques, education, new machinery, new fertilizer, and better irrigation.

With respect to the warrant types employed by novices, it was found that novices tended to rely greatly on their general logical and psychological knowledge in justifying the claims made. Although the reliance on Soviet Union knowledge was considerable (26% of all warrants), the combined categories of logic or common sense (24% of all warrants) and psychological knowledge (28% of all warrants) clearly point to the fact that novices were relying—for the most part—on their broader knowledge rather than on constraints imposed by the nature of the Soviet system.

In accord with their tendency to produce specific solutions, novices also demonstrated a relatively impoverished argument development in comparison to experts. The mean depth of argument backing per top-level node was only 2.3, and the mean D–C length was only 2.6. In addition, most of the backing provided for claims was simple in nature. The proportion of simple backing was .62; of simple D–C backing .29; and of D–C chain backing, only .09. Interestingly, there was some indication that the political science course novices took had some impact on their backing measures. There was a sizable change in backing of arguments after the course: for simple backing, .45; for simple D–C, .36; and for D–C, chain backing, .19. This was one of the few indications that the domain-relevant course work had any impact on the problem-solving behavior of novices.

POLITICAL SCIENTISTS AND CHEMISTS

Both political scientists and chemists were more like novices than experts in the proportion of nodes that were at the top level (25 and 38%, respectively). However, there was a difference in the abstractness and number of solutions proposed. For the political scientists, many of the top-level nodes were devoted to problem representation. The number of solutions offered, therefore, was on the same order as for the experts, and was similarly abstract. For example, one political scientist offered essentially only three solutions: investigating the source of the problem, getting more investment in the agricultural sector, and providing more incentives to farmers (the latter two solutions contingent on the result of the investigation). For the chemists, few nodes were centered on problem representation; instead, the top-level nodes represented fairly numerous and concrete solutions. For example, one chemist mentioned private ownership, better land use, developing better crop strains, increasing mechanization, use of more fertilizer and pesticides, farmer education, and better manpower distribution. This corresponds more closely to novice than to expert behavior.

Turning now to warrants, interesting differences appeared between the political scientists and chemists, differences that point in clear fashion to the differences in their domains of expertise. For the chemists, the largest category, by far, was agricultural warrants (35%), followed by Soviet Union warrants (21%) and logical warrants (16%). Given a chemist's training and the chemical nature of much agricultural knowledge (fertilizer manufacture and use, for example), the reliance of chemists on their general knowledge of agriculture is not surprising. The three largest categories for the political scientists, in contrast, were governmental (23%), logical (21%), and Soviet Union warrants (18%). Thus, trained in the nature and operation of governments, political scientists relied heavily on this general knowledge in supporting their claims. In essence, experts' background training was reflected in the knowledge they relied on in supporting their arguments.

In examining argument development, it is clear that both chemists and political scientists were more like novices than experts, with mean depths of backing per top-level node of 0.8 and 1.2, respectively; and mean D–C lengths of 3.6 and 2.6, respectively. In regard to types of warrant backing, chemists were again similar to novices, except for some tendency for chemists to use more D–C chains as backing. The proportions were: simple backing, .65; simple D–C backing, .13; and D–C chain backing, .22. For political scientists, there was a tendency to use more simple D–C backing than novices: simple backing, .41; simple D–C backing, .45; for D–C chain backing, .14. Overall, then, these subjects used slightly more complex backing for their warrants than novices, otherwise, their argument development was more novicelike than expert.

We have—to this point—discussed group differences with respect to solutions of the agriculture problem. Before considering within-group differences, we want to mention that the expert and novice differences reported for the agriculture problem generally hold for the data obtained from the previously described foreign-policy problem. Specifically, each of the experts solving the foreign-policy problem spent considerable problem-solving activity in representation development, and the solutions were then offered in relationship to the representation. Thus, one is reminded of Carbonell's (1978) simulation of political-science behavior which makes the solution offered to problems a function of the "hawk" or "dove" characteristics of the problem representation.

Novices, on the other hand, tended to have poorly developed representations and tended to consider each foreign policy item presented in the problem in a one-by-one, listlike manner. No novice attempted to develop an abstract representation of the problem from which the specific issues could be addressed. Thus, in a general way, the differences between experts and novices obtained with respect to the agricultural problem were shown to be characteristic for another type of problem in the same general subject-matter domain.

INDIVIDUAL DIFFERENCES WITHIN GROUPS

EXPERTS

One difference among experts was the extent and precision with which the problem representation was developed. This contrast can be seen in the difference between two experts whose protocols have not been presented. For one expert, the representation occupied nearly one-half of the total protocol; by the time the solution process had begun, the constraints had been so well defined that the solution was largely determined. The particular constraint on which this expert focused was Soviet ideology. For the other expert, less than 10% of the protocol was devoted to the representation and, seemingly as a consequence, the solution was very discursive, with frequent returns to old lines of argument and even new lines of representation intermixed with the solution process. The other two experts fell between these two. This difference in style of problem-representation development has important implications for the problem-solving skills of experts; further evidence will be cited in the next section that this difference is consistent in expert problem solving. Finally, we note that although experts used problem constraints to develop the problem solution, no expert focused on all constraints and the particular constraints considered varied somewhat from expert to expert.

We next examine differences in the knowledge base from which claim-justifying warrants were derived. Although for all experts Soviet warrants were substantial in number, two experts showed at least equivalent use of another warrant type. For one expert, this was the category of government warrants (39%); and for the other it was economic warrants (36%). These results indicate a difference among experts in the knowledge base relied upon in justifying (and formulating) arguments and is undoubtedly a large source of differences in problem representation and solution among experts. Such a difference can probably be traced to differences in background and training of experts, and provides an interesting key to the reasons experts' representations assume the orientations they do and to the way that disagreement of emphasis may arise among experts.

These two differences, in the extent and quality of problem representation and in the knowledge base for warrants were the two most apparent differences among the experts in addition to the variation in the nature of the representation previously mentioned (i.e., as a technological, economic, social, or political problem).

NOVICES AND POSTNOVICES

Within the novice group, one noteworthy difference was in the warrant categories employed. Most novices used a substantial number of Soviet Union warrants in their arguments, but two individuals were "extreme novices." These novices employed almost no Soviet Union-based warrants; instead, for both, most warrants were based on general logic (20% and 55%, respectively) and psychological knowledge (40% and 36%, respectively), although one of the novices also used general agricultural knowledge (40%). Thus, for both individuals, there was a reliance on only the most broad-based knowledge for argument justification, with no mention of information specific to the USSR, nor mention of the other major warrant categories. Interestingly, after taking the course in Soviet domestic policy, most individuals displayed roughly the same pattern of warrant categories as in their first problem-solving session. This was not true of the two individuals just considered, however. For them, a marked change occurred: Both displayed substantial use of Soviet Union warrants (27% and 38%, respectively) and the first-mentioned had a large number of economic warrants (20%).

A second difference among the novices was in the type of argument backing employed. Most of the novices showed a predominance of simple backings, with a small number of D–C and D–C chain backings. One, however, used primarily D–C backings (54%), and this persisted in the post-novice state (60%), despite the fact that these proportions changed for the other individuals following the domain-relevant course. Thus, there was evidence of a difference in argument development among novices; the individual who possessed the divergent approach was also more intransigent, being less likely to change that approach as the result of course experience.

POLITICAL SCIENTISTS AND CHEMISTS

Among political scientists and chemists, several differences were identified. The first involved problem representation of the chemists. Whereas most of the chemists did little problem representation, one was more like the political scientists in this regard. That chemist defined the problem as one tied to the bureaucracy of the Soviet Union, arguing that two general problem-solving approaches were possible, one a personnel approach and the other a scientific approach. For this individual, mean depth of backing was somewhat greater than the average (1.8 versus 0.8) and his average D–C length was substantially greater (10.4 versus 3.6).

Looking now at warrants, certain findings are noteworthy. Among the chemists, the same one stands out. Most of this individual's warrants were either logical (44%) or psychological (38%). This pattern is more like that of the extreme novices than any other groups of subjects. It suggests that there was something beyond specific domain-relevant knowledge contributing to the form of problem-solving activity engaged in by experts. The experience from which this derived must, presumably, be of a different sort, shared by a number of disciplines, and it was somehow the case that one expert, less fully indoctrinated in his own discipline, received just that experience. His behavior was expertlike in several regards, but lacked the apparent knowledge base to be expert in content.

Among the political scientists, there was also a deviant in the warrant pattern displayed. This individual did not use general governmental warrants as his dominant warrant type as the other political scientists did; instead, there was greater dependence on logical and agricultural warrants (27 and 20%, respectively). In most other respects, this individual's behavior followed the pattern of the group. Again, the underlying knowledge base did not seem to be the ultimate determinant of the form of the solution process.

WITHIN-INDIVIDUAL DIFFERENCES

Three of the experts who participated in the present study also provided solutions to other problems. Although an extensive discussion of this work is beyond the scope of this chapter, an interesting question is the extent to which the protocols generated by the same expert had consistencies or inconsistencies that could be determined. Whereas at the time of preparation of this chapter, we are still investigating this problem, the assertions presented here seem to have reasonable backing.

First, one expert tended to use problem history to develop the problem representation in a reasonably consistent manner. A second expert appeared to be inclined toward the development of relatively abstract problem representation (in the sense that he focused on a particular constraint and developed it at a high level). In the agriculture problem, he focused on the constraint of the Soviet ideology and how this would influence the representation as well as the solution of the problem; in the foreign policy problem, he focused on whether one thinks the Soviet foreign policy is aggressive or defensive (i.e., reactive). The specific policy solutions, he argued, then could be worked out based on how this fundamental issue is represented. This individual was the expert most inclined toward abstract thinking. Furthermore, it should be noted that this type of abstract thinking tends to lead to the most definitive problem solutions. The risk, of course, is that if one's particular abstract representation fails to take into account one or more important factors or if the representation is not correct (as the wrong representation about Soviet foreign policy), the solutions that follow could be disastrous.

The third expert tended to develop a similar representation in both problems in that the problem was viewed in a relatively pragmatic yet somewhat abstract manner. Whereas in the agriculture problem he represented the problem as economic and emphasized issues pertaining to incentives and capital investment, his approach to the foreign policy problem involved developing working procedures and interactions with the Soviet Union which would assure the development of a low-tension interaction. Within the experts' own protocols, the contents differ as a function of the problem. Although we have not yet completed analyses of intraindividual differences, the data do suggest that there may be consistencies that experts demonstrate across problems although the specific contents vary.

GENERAL DISCUSSION AND CONCLUSIONS

In this section, we will address three issues related to the contents of this chapter, namely, the nature of individual differences in social science problem solving compared to differences in other domains, methodological concerns raised by the present research, and some conceptual issues related to this research.

COMPARISON TO OTHER SUBJECT-MATTER DOMAINS

The subject-matter domains receiving the most attention in the study of problem solving are physics and geometry. Larkin and others (1980) have studied expert–novice differences in problem solving and their findings are similar to ours and also different from ours, each in one important way. The physics experts spend, on a relative basis, considerable time in representing a problem; once the representation is established, the solution is arrived at in a reasonably quick and straightforward manner. Novices in physics, however, spend relatively less problem-solving time on representation development and develop representations that are poor in terms of leading to a straightforward solution. Instead, novices try to fit more obvious equations (obvious in terms of the surface structure of the problem) to the problem without having an idea of the type of problem they are attempting to solve. The similarity of these findings to those reported in this chapter are clear in that the political science experts also spent considerable problem-solving activity in developing a problem representation.

The solution process of physics experts and political science experts differs considerably, however, once the representation is developed. Whereas the physics experts typically solve the problem by producing successive equations that lead to the solution, political science experts typically offer an abstract solution and then engage in extensive argument development. Phrased in terms of the information-processing model, the physics expert moves from state to state to reach the goal (solution) whereas the political science expert moves to a state and then develops justification for that move, evaluates the move, and explores subproblems that may be encountered with that move. Why does this difference occur?

Our argument is that problems used in physics research have well-established, generally agreed-upon solutions. The problems of political science, however, do not have well-established, generally agreed-upon solutions. Indeed, in some cases, the problems are not necessarily defined and solutions are matters of opinion. Given this state of affairs, one should not be surprised at the differences in the solution processes of the two groups of experts. The political science expert must indicate why the solution will work, what the problems of implementation may be, and so forth. The solution is, in the Toulmin (1958) sense, a lengthy argument regarding how the problem can be solved. Moreover, coupled with the lack of agreed-upon solutions, is the previously mentioned fact that solutions usually cannot be tested immediately or even in the immediate future. Thus, inspired test must give way to argument.

Although at first glance, one may conclude that the differences in the solution process used by experts in physics and in political science demonstrate fundamental problem-solving differences that are domain-specific, such a conclusion may not be warranted. How, one may ask, would a physics expert respond if presented with a problem for which the solution is not known? We are aware of no such data, but Tweney (Note 1) presented an interesting paper on the research of the physicist, Faraday. Having access to extensive notes of Faraday, Tweney made two points that are important in the present context. First, through many experiments, Faraday was testing only two basic hypotheses. Most of the experiments involved testing implications of these hypotheses. Second, Faraday developed lines of argumentation in his testing. These two issues are important in the present context in that the development of only two basic hypotheses as solutions to the problem under study strongly resembles the political science experts' statement of only one or a few relatively abstract solutions to the problem at hand. Whereas Faraday was able to test his notions by conducting experiments that provided results without much delay, the political scientist is typically unable to conduct experimental tests. The difference in the problem-solving process attributable to the domain is not that there is a basic difference in the process per se used by the experts in physics and in political science; instead it is due to the different means of evaluating solutions that are available in the two fields.

METHODOLOGICAL CONSIDERATIONS

As the reader is aware by now, studying individual differences in social science problem solving produces many methodological challenges. We will not dwell on the problems of contrastive (i.e., expert versus novice) research; we have mentioned this issue earlier in the chapter. Moreover, we did study the problem-solving behavior of political science experts who were not Soviet Union specialists, as well as chemistry experts, in an effort to deal with the expert–novice issue. A number of questions regarding expert behavior are, of course, unanswered; among the more important of these is how the novice becomes an expert, how the memory structure of the expert influences the problem-solving process, and the extent to which problem-solving strategies used on problems in one's general domain of expertise are acquired.

We have found our adaptation of the Toulmin (1958) model to be quite helpful. Not only does it provide for a description of the argument structure, it has enabled us to quantify particular characteristics of the protocol data. Specifically, it provides for obtaining measures of the depth and length of argument structure, and, through the analysis and classification of warrants, a means to determine the nature of the information used by the individuals in solving the problem.

Despite the methodological developments just mentioned, there is nevertheless, a need for developing other measures. For example, we need a better way to describe differences that may exist among experts in the same field. It would also be helpful to have some sort of structure containing a finite set of parameters—where the particular choice of parameters could depict individual problem-solving differences. Such a system would obviously be model-driven, so the issue really reduces to the study of the Toulmin adaptation or, perhaps, some other model to try to develop a more refined description of the problem-solving process. Certainly, if we want to study phenomena such as intrasubject differences in problem solving, further model development is necessary. Finally, we would note that there is a need to study problem solving via the use of "on-line" measures such as time to develop different phases of argument. In addition, measures such as eye movements and pupil dilation may be useful to suggest internal states occurring during the problem-solving process. Everything considered, the methodology used in the study of the type of problem solving we have addressed in this chapter should experience considerable refinement in the years to come.

CONCEPTUAL ISSUES

One of the more interesting findings of the present research relates to the differences obtained among the experts. What is apparent is that the previously discussed lack of agreement concerning the solution to problems of social science allows for considerable latitude in the problem-solving performance of experts. This variation leads to the question not only of how an expert becomes an expert, but why, in that transition one expert may develop a different way to approach problems than another expert.

The issue of interexpert differences becomes even more involved when one realizes that, in areas such as physics, there may be little difference between experts on problems that are well understood, for problems that are not well understood, there may be the same sort of wide range of difference as found in the social sciences. Shifting to psychology, which is of much greater familiarity to the present authors than physics, it seems apparent that different psychologists show definite investigative styles that remain reasonably constant throughout their careers. Although this matter is quite complex, that is, many factors may enter into why a person studies a particular phenomenon and why particular methods are employed, one is struck more by the consistency of investigators than by their variation. It is relatively easy to attribute such differences among experts to the way investigators were trained and to traditional modes of investigation of particular classes of problems, but one must not rule out the possibility that these are "hard-wired" cognitive differences which permit a particular investigator to "resonate" more with particular means of investigation. Indeed, it is, perhaps, the satisfaction of such predisposing tendencies that determines in part why a person chooses to become a political scientist and not an engineer.

Returning to a less peripheral area of the problem space, an important question raised by the present work is how experts store information in order to be able to retrieve it during the problem-solving process, and whether the problem-solving process itself aids in this storage. A number of the between-group as well as the within-group issues raised in this paper are related to this question. Certainly, much more needs to be learned before we can determine whether there are style differences in problem solving as a function of discipline, and how the differences among experts of the same discipline and even among the solutions to various problems offered by one individual relate to this question. We are hopeful that the approach offered in this chapter will be of assistance to investigators in their efforts to resolve this and other questions concerning the nature of social science problem solving.

In closing, we note that this chapter is essentially a progress report on our attempts to analyze the processes involved in social science problem solving. We feel that the primary deficiency of the chapter is that although the adaptation of the Toulmin model provides for studying a number of specific issues in the reasoning process, the analysis does not allow extraction of a general high-level problem solving structure which may be observed in the protocols, especially in the protocol of experts. We are currently working on this issue.

REFERENCES

Carbonell, J. G., Jr. Politics: Automated ideological reasoning. *Cognitive Science*, 1978, *2*, 27–52.

Chi, M. T. H., Feltovich, P. J., & Glaser, R. Categorization and representation of physics problems by experts and novices. *Cognitive Science*, 1981, *5*, 121–152.

Greeno, J. G. A study of problem solving. In R. Glaser (Ed.), *Advances in instructional psychology* (Vol. 1). Hillsdale, N.J.: Lawrence Erlbaum Associates, 1978.

Hayes, J. R., & Simon, H. A. Understanding written problem instructions. In L. W. Gregg (Ed.), *Knowledge and cognition*. Hillsdale, N.J.: Lawrence Erlbaum Associates, 1974.

Jeffries, R., Polson, P. G., Razran, L., & Atwood, M. E. A process model for missionaries-cannibals and other river-crossing problems. *Cognitive Psychology*, 1977, *9*, 412–440.

Larkin, J., McDermott, J., Simon, D. P., & Simon, H. A. Expert and novice performance in solving physics problems. *Science*, 1980, *208*, 1335–1342.

Newell, A., & Simon, H. A. *Human problem solving*. Englewood Cliffs, N.J.: Prentice-Hall, 1972.

Reitman, W. *Cognition and thought*. New York: Wiley, 1965.

Simon. H. A. The structure of ill structured problems. *Artificial Intelligence*, 1973, *4*, 181–201.

Simon, H. A. The functional equivalence of problem solving skills. *Cognitive Psychology*, 1975, *7*, 268–288.

Simon, H. A. Information-processing theory of human problem solving. In W. K. Estes (Ed.), *Handbook of learning and cognitive processes: Human information processing* (Vol. 5). Hillsdale, N.J.: Lawrence Erlbaum Associates, 1978.

Toulmin, S. E. *The uses of argument*. London/New York: Cambridge University Press, 1958.

Toulmin, S., Rieke, R., & Janik, A. *An introduction to reasoning*. New York: Macmillan, 1979.

von Wright, G. H. *Explanation and understanding*. Ithaca, N.Y.: Cornell University Press, 1971.

NOTES

1.   Tweney, R. D. *Confirmatory and disconfirmatory heuristics in Michael Faraday's scientific research.* Paper presented at the meeting of the Psychonomics Society, Philadelphia, 1981.

8

Learning Styles of College Students

R. R. Schmeck

LEARNING STRATEGY AND LEARNING
STYLE: AN INTRODUCTION

With the exception of a few studies (e.g., Biggs, 1970; Goldman & Warren, 1973), most early research concerned with individual differences and learning used traditional personality, attitudinal, cognitive style, and ability measures (e.g., Cowell & Entwistle, 1971; Cropley & Field, 1969). The research involving ability measures provided some useful data, but most of the early studies were not very definitive. This lack of clarity prompted Tallmadge and Shearer (1969, 1971) to state that *learning style* would be a more useful concept than traditional personality and cognitive style constructs in accounting for variance in academic performance. They further stressed the need to assess learning style from a behavioral-process orientation.

From my theoretical perspective, a learning style is a predisposition on the part of some students to adopt a particular learning strategy regardless of the specific demands of the learning task. Thus, a style is simply a strategy that is used with some cross-situational consistency. In turn, I

Copyright © 1983 by Academic Press, Inc.
All rights of reproduction in any form reserved.
ISBN 0-12-216401-6

define a *learning strategy* as a pattern of information-processing activities used to prepare for an anticipated test of memory. This definition of learning strategy is consistent w1th Craik and Lockhart's (1972) view that memory is simply a by-product of thinking: traces left behind by past information processing.

Some researchers have argued that a learning style (or predisposition) is less important than the immediate situation in determining which specific learning strategy a student will adopt. Within the university, the immediate situation includes characteristics of the course content, the instruction, and the test. For example, in one of Laurillard's (1979) studies, 19 of 31 students could not be classified as to their style of learning because they were thoroughly sensitive to situational demands, varying their strategies in response to the specific task requirements. Likewise, Ramsden (1979) has demonstrated that one source of variability in learning strategies is the students' perceptions of course requirements, and he has developed a way of measuring these perceptions. Battig (1979) has argued that the only individual difference worth studying in the field of learning is the ability to vary one's strategies and select those most appropriate for specific task requirements, and Flavell and Wellman (1977) have studied developmental changes in this skill under the label "metamemory" (cf. Chapter 4).

My own position on this issue is the same as that of Entwistle and Underwood. N. Entwistle, Hanley and Hounsell (1979) note that both consistency and variability can be seen in students' approaches to learning; either is a legitimate topic for study. One can focus on either so long as the existence and importance of the other is recognized. Indeed, although we may be using different paradigms, we are all interested in identifying basic behavioral processes (learning strategies in the present context). As Underwood (1975) has noted, a process or pattern of processes should be studied *both* by examining (manipulating) the situation that produces the process and by searching for unmanipulated, preexisting variability on the process dimension. Traditional individual-differences research aimed at establishing the construct validity of learning styles can provide a complement to experimental research aimed at isolating and delineating the causes of learning strategies. The two lines of research should converge. In my own research, I have tried to develop a technique for assessing unmanipulated variability on process dimensions previously studied by laboratory researchers (e.g., Craik & Tulving, 1975), but I have always assumed that I was studying the same processes that the laboratory researchers were studying.

Another issue concerns the question of the level of analysis that is appropriate in this area. It is probably true that an individual's learning style is the translation of personality and cognitive-style characteristics into study behavior. I defined learning style as a predisposition to display a particular pattern of information-processing activities when preparing for a test of memory, and Messick (1976) defines cognitive style as a general, habitual mode of processing information. Thus, one could argue that individuals' learning styles are simply the cognitive styles that they evidence when confronted with a learning task. Lewis (1976) has offered the convincing argument that we should always study the most basic individual differences that underlie more easily observable differences. If personality and cognitive-style differences underlie learning style, then Lewis would call for studies relating personality and cognitive style to learning. As I noted earlier, attempts in this area have not been very informative. If my primary interest was personality and cognitive style, I might have tried to develop some new, basic measures in these areas that *would* relate to learning. However, I am most interested in learning, and have chosen to custom-build a measure of individual differences in the predisposition to use certain learning strategies. I have no doubt that the differences I observe will ultimately be explained by more basic theories of personality and cognitive style (e.g., Kogan, 1976) and indeed, by some very basic theories of neurological functioning (e.g., Ornstein, 1977). However, as I noted earlier, we are all seeking to identify and delineate basic behavioral processes. I assume that my work will mesh with the work of others and will aid in the development of more basic theories.

In the remainder of this section, I will review research programs concerned with learning strategies and styles. This research is being carried out in different countries using different methodologies, but it seems to be converging on similar conclusions. Next, I will describe my own research in some detail and note how it relates to other research programs. Finally, I will describe some attempts to modify learning style. In keeping with my assumption that a style is simply a predisposition to favor a particular strategy, I feel that style is modifiable.

COMPREHENSION LEARNERS AND OPERATION LEARNERS

Pask and his colleagues in London have conducted extensive experimental research concerning learning style. In all of Pask's studies, the subject is instructed to understand and not simply to memorize the material. For example, in one study (Pask & Scott, 1972), students had to learn the principles of classification underlying the division of two species of "Martian animals" (the Clobbits and Gandlemullers). Students had to overtly request specific pieces of information and give reasons for each request. In addition, they had to "teach back" the classification system after they learned it. This teach-back method of measurement is one of the hallmarks of Pask's work.

In several studies, Pask (1976a, 1976b; Pask & Scott, 1972) has identified two different learning strategies and the associated learning styles demonstrated by subjects in the teach–back paradigm. In addition, Pask (1976b) has described two "pathologies" which result from the overuse (or misuse) of either of these two strategies. One strategy is labeled *holist,* and the person who shows cross-situational consistency in the use of this strategy is manifesting the style called *comprehension learning.* The associated pathology resulting from rigid adherence to this style is labeled *globetrotting.* Comprehension learners (who use a holist strategy) take a global approach to the task, liberally using anecdotes, illustrations, and analogies to arrive at an overall description. They tend to look further ahead than other subjects when working through a hierarchy of topics, have a wider focus of attention, and try to first build up the "big picture" before determining where any of the details fit. The pathology in this case (i.e. globetrotting) involves jumping to conclusions on the basis of too little evidence, using inappropriate analogies, and overgeneralizing.

The contrasting learning strategy is the *serialist* strategy and the accompanying style is *operation learning.* The pathology associated with overuse or misuse of this strategy is *improvidence.* Operation learners (who use the serialist strategy) progress linearly from one topic to the next. They are routinely concerned with operational details and procedures, working step by step through a series of topics, attending carefully to sequential details. The pathology to which an operation learner is most subject (improvidence) involves a failure to use analogies and to build up overall maps. Such an individual "sees the trees but misses the forest." However, if pathologies are avoided, both the comprehension and operation learners can arrive at comparable levels of understanding (cf. pp. 120–121).

Pask (1976b) notes that very consistent operation or comprehension learners are, in fact, likely to fall into the pathologies of either improvidence or globetrotting. Thus, the most competent student is one who Pask describes as having a versatile learning style. The versatile student uses a higher-order metacognitive strategy based on *both* the serialist and holist strategies, alternately employing analogy to get an overall model and then testing its applicability by examining details. The versatile learning style leads to a very high level of understanding.

DEEP AND SHALLOW APPROACHES TO READING

Marton and his colleagues at the University of Gothenburg, Sweden, have conducted a series of studies concerned with the approaches that students take to the task of reading academic articles. These researchers seem to have emphasized responsiveness to situational demands a bit more than styles, but their research has had a big impact on theorists in the learning styles area. Marton and Säljö (1976a, 1976b) used interviews to determine what different students do when they are instructed to read an article so that they might answer questions regarding its content. Unlike Pask, who specifically instructed subjects to achieve an understanding of the learning material, Marton and Säljö left their instructions vague so that variation in approach might be more observable. After subjects finished reading, they were asked questions designed to establish the *outcome* of the reading (what they had learned), their *intention* (what they expected to get from reading), and their *approach* to the task. It seems that the meaning of the term "approach" as it is used here is similar to that of strategy, but it is perhaps a bit broader. Marton describes a student's approach in terms of its "level of processing." Later, we will see that I use the similar term "depth of processing." However, I have tried to think only in terms of very specific cognitive processes or strategies and thus have not used general terms such as "intention" and "approach."

Marton and Säljö's (1976a) analysis of transcriptions of interviews revealed two general types of learning outcome: *conclusion-oriented,* and *description-oriented.* The conclusion-oriented outcome summarized the main argument and supporting evidence. This outcome resulted when the student's intent was to *understand* and when a *deep-level approach* was employed. This deep-level approach involved an evaluation of the relationship between the argument and the evidence and an attempt to relate the ideas to the student's past experience. The description-oriented outcome is a listing of the main points covered in the article. This outcome is the result of an intent to *memorize* and a *surface-level approach*. A surface-level approach focuses attention on specific facts and pieces of disconnected information which are rote learned.

Svensson (1977) noted deep- and surface-level approaches in students' normal studying and found superior examination performance by those who were using a deep-level approach. Marton and Säljö (1976b) noted that low-level examination questions unfortunately encourage a shallow-level approach. Also, Fransson (1977) demonstrated that students are more likely to use a shallow-level approach when the content of an article is not of interest to them, and in any situation which raises their level of anxiety. In one field study, Dahlgren and Marton (1978) examined the level of understanding of economic concepts demonstrated by students majoring in economics. They found a very low level of understanding and concluded that the stresses of the curriculum and the use of examinations that reward memorization were responsible.

In all of their work, the Gothenberg researchers emphasized the impact of contextual demands such as the content, instruction, and test. A student is not deep or shallow; the student's approach to reading within a given context is classified as such. Marton and his colleagues have been identifying the relationships between intention, approach, and outcome while minimizing the importance of stylistic consistency. Nevertheless, we will see below that Marton's work has had a profound effect on the thinking of researchers who study learning styles.

Meaning, Reproducing, and Achieving Orientations to the Learning Situation

In this section, I will describe two long-term research programs: one centered in England; the other, in Australia. Both have employed questionnaire methods of data-gathering; both seem to be reaching similar conclusions. The first program was begun by Entwistle and his colleagues at the University of Lancaster, England in 1968, with the aim of identifying the objectives of higher education and isolating student personality and motivational differences that would predict academic performance. Study method and motivation inventories were developed originally by N. J. Entwistle and Wilson (1970) and have been revised repeatedly since that time. One of the strengths of this work by Entwistle and his colleagues is that it incorporates the ideas and findings of other researchers. The most recent version of the Lancaster inventory (N. Entwistle et al., 1979) has been influenced by the work of Pask, Marton, and Biggs.

N. Entwistle et al. (1979) isolated three major *orientations* of students by factor analyzing the responses of 767 subjects obtained from three different universities. They obtained three second-order factors (orientations) that they labeled: *meaning* (search for personal understanding), *reproducing* (memorization), and *achieving* (doing whatever is necessary to earn high grades). According to the authors, each of these orientations involves a different source of motivation. The student seeking meaning is intrinsically motivated and is somewhat autonomous and independent of course syllabi. The student with a reproducing orientation is extrinsically motivated by fear of failure, dependent on course syllabi, and prone to memorize information verbatim. The achieving student is extrinsically motivated by hope for success and is said to be "stable, self-confident, and ruthless."

Each of the orientations predisposes the student to adopt a certain approach to studying. The student seeking meaning tends to adopt a deep-level approach (Marton's concept) or a holist strategy (Pask's concept). However, the person with a meaning orientation who uses only the holist strategy is prone to achieve a limited understanding because of his or her proneness to the globetrotting pathology. The individual with a reproducing orientation tends to adopt either a surface-level approach (Marton) or a serialist strategy (Pask). The former leads to memorization and overlearning without true understanding. On the other hand, the serialist strategy can produce a greater degree of understanding; more frequently, it leads to the pathology of improvidence and a very incomplete level of understanding.

The achieving orientation leads the individual to use any approach or strategy that earns high grades. Such an individual is very sensitive to the contingencies present in the situation. If the instructor wants understanding, the achieving student will use a deep-level approach. If the instructor rewards reproduction, the achieving student will use a shallow-level approach. Thus, we see that Entwistle has a way of accounting for both variability and consistency in approach to the learning task.

Entwistle's meaning, reproducing, and achievement orientations seem to resemble personality types. As I noted earlier, with a few exceptions (e.g., H. J. Eysenck, 1972), studies that have tried to relate traditional personality measures and learning outcomes have not been very enlightening. However, Entwistle's work is unique in that he is—in a sense—starting within the learning situation itself and "working backward" to develop typologies that might relate to the learning outcome. This approach contrasts with that of trying to predict learning outcome with traditional personality measures developed outside of the learning context.

A similar analysis has been proposed in Australia by Biggs (1979). Like the Lancaster studies, Biggs' research has been aimed at the development of an inventory for assessing learning styles. His original inventory (Biggs, 1970) was called the Study Behavior Questionnaire, but it has been revised and relabeled the Study Processes Questionnaire. Biggs (1979) reports the results of a factor analysis of his inventory producing three second-order factors that closely parallel those reported by N. Entwistle et al. (1979).

The three factors reported by Biggs (1979) contain both cognitive and motivational components. The first, *utilizing,* includes a fact-rote cognitive strategy and an extrinsic, fear-of-failure motivational component. The utilizing individual would, presumably, be a shallow-level processor. The second factor, *internalizing,* contains a meaning-assimilation cognitive component and an intrinsic source of motivation. An internalizing individual would be a deep-level processor. The last factor, *achieving,* has study skill and organization as cognitive components and need for achievement as a source of motivation (cf. Biggs, in press).

Biggs (1979) also reports the development of a performance, learning-outcome-based measure of Marton's deep-level approach to learning that can be used with large groups of subjects (recall that Marton interviewed subjects one at a time). Biggs was originally interested in assessing Piaget's stages of cognitive development in college students. However, after conferring with Marton and his colleagues in Sweden, Biggs decided that levels of processing might be more relevant to college instruction than distinctions between concrete and formal reasoning.

Biggs' outcome-based measure is called the Structure of the Observed Learning Outcome (or SOLO). It requires that subjects be presented with a display of information (e.g., a paragraph) and a rather open-ended question to which they respond in writing. These essay answers are then scored by trained raters using the scoring system developed by Biggs. The scoring system consists of five categories of response running from "1" (prestructural), which indicates an answer that is not logically related to the display, through "3" (multistructural), which contains several bits of information taken directly from the display, and ending with "5" (extended-abstract), which tends to go "beyond" the information in the display to reach a logically supportable conclusion. Biggs' procedure is similar to the method used by Marton in that it is based on the quality of the learning outcome, however, it is less time-consuming to administer and more standardized; thus it could be applied to larger groups of subjects. Schmeck and Phillips (in press) report good reliability for the rating system but note that they found it necessary to give raters a considerable amount of training.

Biggs (1979) studied the relationship between his Study Processes Questionnaire and SOLO. He found partial support for his prediction that "utilizing" students develop a more shallow level of understanding, and "internalizing" students develop a deeper level of understanding. Surprisingly, students with an "achieving" orientation demonstrated a shallow learning outcome even under conditions that should have encouraged a deep-level approach. Later in this chapter, I will describe studies that examined the relationships between my own inventory and both Biggs' Study Behavior Questionnaire and his SOLO rating system.

OTHER APPROACHES TO THE STUDY OF LEARNING STYLE

Working within the framework of his "experiential learning model," Kolb (1971, 1981) developed yet another learning-style-assessment device. According to his model, the learning process is both active and passive, concrete and abstract. It can be conceived of as a four-stage cycle: (1) concrete experience; (2) observation and reflection; (3) the formation of abstract concepts and generalizations; and (4) hypotheses to be tested by active experimentation which may then lead to new concrete experiences. His

Learning Style Inventory assesses the extent to which a learner emphasizes the importance of each of the four stages (relative to the others). Using the Learning Style Inventory to assess the learning-style profiles of managers in different functional departments of a firm (e.g., research, marketing, personnel (Kolb, 1974), and of students in different academic majors, as well as at different educational levels; Kolb, 1971), Kolb has found support for his four-stage model of learning styles.

Similarly, Gregorc (1979) proposed four learning styles based on his observations and interviews of students. Like Kolb, Gregorc concluded that learning is based on both concrete experience and abstraction, but Gregorc also found it to be either random or sequential. *Concrete sequential* learners work best in structured settings that present information in step–by–step fashion, and they prefer direct, hands–on experience. The *concrete random* learner similarly prefers direct experience but takes an experimental attitude, preferring to explore freely and make intuitive leaps. The *abstract sequential* learner prefers symbolic input to hands–on experience and likes logical step–by–step presentations. Lastly, *abstract random* learners are again sensitive to symbolic input, but they are more holist and prefer less-structured presentations, such as group discussions. The learning strategies of the random learner seem quite similar to the holist strategy described by Pask (1976a;b). Similarly, the strategy of the sequential learner seems similar to Pask's serialist strategy. Perhaps Pask's comprehension and operation learners could be subdivided into concrete and abstract types similar to Gregorc's (1979) subdivisions.

Chickering (1976) emphasized the need for students to alternate between the two basic cognitive processes of differentiation and integration. *Differentiation* is the analytic process of noting the "interacting parts of something formerly seen as unitary." *Integration* is the synthetic process whereby the relationships among parts are "perceived or constructed so more complex wholes result" (Chickering, 1976, pp. 81–82). It seems likely that some individuals would be predisposed to engage more in the process of differentiation than integration. Perhaps we could call them "analyzers" and we would have yet another learning style. Likewise, others would be predisposed to favor integration and they might be labeled "synthesizers" (cf. Ornstein's, 1977, views on cerebral dominance).

INTERACTIONS BETWEEN LEARNING STYLES, ABILITIES,
AND DEVELOPMENTAL LEVEL

In addition to studying the construct validity of various learning style dimensions, future research should be aimed at determining the ways in which learning style interacts with developmental level and cognitive abilities. Perry (1970) described nine positions through which the most thoroughly developed students at Harvard University passed during their four years of college education. Students tended to begin in a *dualistic* phase in which they saw all information as falling into one of two categories: true or false. The learning task during this phase is seen as one of storing truth in memory. Presumably, students at this phase of development would be processing information at a surface level. Next, Perry's students seemed to enter a *relativistic* phase in which they saw information as ephemeral and maintained that any idea was as valid as any other since there was no such thing as "truth." Finally, the most developed students entered a phase of *commitment* in which they recognized that any issue has more than one legitimate, defensible stand, but it is pragmatically important to make a rational commitment to one of these stands. One then operates under the *assumption* that his or her position is "true" while recognizing the legitimacy of other positions. Students in the relativistic and commitment phases would presumably be processing information more deeply than those in the dualistic phase. Thus, the probability that a student will process deeply may increase as he or she progresses from the freshman to the senior level in college.

It seems likely that future research will uncover relationships between the stages of cognitive development described by Jean Piaget (1963) and learning style. Perhaps there are limits to the learning strategies that an individual can employ and these limits depend on stage of cognitive development. For example, it seems unlikely that one could process information very deeply before attaining the stage of formal operations. Biggs (1980) provides considerable support for this conclusion. Furthermore, research has shown that people do not necessarily reach the level of formal operations by the end of adolescence (e.g., Neimark, 1975) and even when they reach that level in one content area, they may not have reached it in other areas (e.g., Vu, 1977). Thus, some adults may be incapable of using a deep processing learning strategy, and those that can use it in one content area might be incapable of using it in some other area. Also, most individuals may be forced to process at a shallow level when beginning a new content area. To use N. Entwistle's (1981) terminology, these individuals would begin with a reproducing orientation toward the content and only later be able to move on to an understanding orientation.[1]

[1]With regard to his own extensive research program, Watkins (Note 1) comments, "The data to date, supported by interviews, suggest that the younger students do not have the requisite cognitive structures into which they might assimilate their tertiary learning, and they have had little experience in having to provide such structures for themselves due to overreliance on parents and teachers."

It seems likely that aging would have an impact on learning style. La-
bouvie–Vief (1977, in press) seems to view the elderly as more conclusion-
oriented and less description-oriented in their information processing.
Based on research concerned with the effects of aging on memory, one
might expect the elderly to be especially susceptible to the pathology of
globetrotting, emphasizing global ideas to the exclusion of episodic details
and using past experiences to reason analogically about some present situation even when the analogy is inappropriate.

Future research should also examine the possibility that cognitive abilities place limits upon learning strategies. Schmeck and Ribich (1978) obtained support for their argument that individuals must demonstrate a minimal amount of critical thinking ability before they are capable of deep-level
processing. Later in this chapter, I will discuss attempts to modify learning
style by teaching people how to use new learning strategies. We will see that
one of the studies in this area (Snowman, Krebs & Kelly, Note 2) reported
that the more intelligent subjects benefited most from training. This finding
suggests that individuals with lesser ability might be incapable of learning to
use some strategies. Perhaps intelligence is related to school learning *not*
because it indicates a limited storage capacity but rather because it places
limits on the learning strategies that an individual can employ, that is, *by
limiting thinking,* it limits learning. (Recall that I am regarding learning
simply as a by-product of thinking.) Goldman and his colleagues (Goldman
& Hudson, 1973; Goldman & Warren, 1973) found that learning strategies
were more fundamental than abilities in determining learning outcome.
This result would support the assumption that intelligence limits strategies
and strategies, in turn, limit learning (cf. p. 126).

As I noted earlier, I have tried to limit my review to research concerned
with the learning processes or strategies of college students. If I expanded
the review to include learning research concerned with cognitive style (e.g.,
Hill, 1971; Letteri, Note 3) or personality (e.g., H. J. Eysenck, 1972; H. J.
Eysenck & Cookson, 1969; Hunt, 1979), and if I added studies specializing
in primary and secondary school students (e.g., Dunn & Dunn, 1978), I
would fill several books rather than a single chapter. For some excellent
reviews, the reader is referred to Dunn, DeBello, Brennan, Krimsky, and
Murrain (1981), and Keefe (1979).

The studies that I have reviewed suggest that there is both consistency
and variability observable in students' use of learning strategies. The models
proposed by Entwistle (1981) and Biggs (1979) each include two styles of
learning that account for intraindividual consistency: one labeled a meaning
orientation (Entwistle) or internalizing dimension (Biggs) and another labeled a reproducing orientation (Entwistle) or utilizing dimension (Biggs).
Similarly, both theorists propose a third "style" that may account for *vari-*

ability in students' learning strategies (i.e., Entwistle's achieving orientation, and Bigg's achieving dimension). Thus, they suggest that some people
are more consistent or stylistic in their strategy usage while others are more
opportunistic, or sensitive to the demands of the immediate situation. Perhaps I should comment that the similarities between the theories should not
blind us to their differences. Each makes a unique contribution to our
understanding of learning style. For example, although Pask's versatile style
and the achieving styles of Entwistle and Biggs seem similar, they are quite
different in terms of outcome. The versatile style alternately uses serialist
and holist strategies to generate a high level of understanding. However, the
achieving styles are basically game playing strategies, paying special attention to course contingencies in order to earn higher grades. The only objective of an achieving style is high grades. I turn now to a description of my
own work. Once again, we will see that it has much in common with the
work I have reviewed, but I feel it also makes a unique contribution which I
will try to illustrate in the course of describing it.

THE INVENTORY OF LEARNING
PROCESSES

This section will describe the development and validation of a self-report
inventory derived through both rational and empirical procedures for the
purpose of assessing learning style. The instrument was developed under
the assumption that learning style is a pattern of information-processing
activities used with some consistency to prepare for future test events. Such
elements as attitudes, personality, cognitive style, or preferences for time of
day, physical environment, or social climate were not considered when
preparing items for the inventory.

DEVELOPMENT AND VALIDATION OF THE INVENTORY

The Inventory of Learning Processes was originally developed by
Schmeck, Ribich, and Ramanaiah (1977). It was derived by factor analyzing
responses to a pool of 121 items. Since the interpretation of such an analysis
is aided by knowing the source of the items, and since my approach is
somewhat unique in this regard, I will begin by describing the manner in
which the items were prepared. The pool was developed by three experts in
the areas of human learning and memory with the objective of representing
the findings and theoretical processes of their area of expertise.

The group of experts first prepared a list of the processes uncovered by research or advocated by major theories in the areas of human learning and memory. Then, each author wrote behavioral descriptions of these processes by phrasing them in terms of the environment and activities of the typical college student. For example, *encoding* can be defined as a process whereby the learner transforms new information into a form that can be related to the old information already stored in memory. An inventory item that might assess this process is: "I learn new concepts by expressing them in my own words," or "I learn new words or ideas by visualizing a situation in which they occur." *Organizational processes* are stressed by most theories of learning and memory. These include such processes as *clustering* and *subjective organization*. Some inventory items that might assess organization are: "I have trouble organizing the information that I remember"; "I generally prepare a set of notes designed to integrate the information from all sources in a course"; and "I have no trouble seeing the difference between apparently similar ideas."

The group of three experts met regularly to critique each other's items and settle upon a final item pool. One hundred and twenty-one items derived in this fashion were administered to 503 undergraduate students at Southern Illinois University. Intercorrelations among the items were first subjected to a principal components factor analysis, and a scree test was used to determine the number of factors. This number was then rotated to the Varimax criterion, using the principal factor method with squared multiple correlations as estimates of communalities. Only those factors were retained which had five or more items with loadings of .25 or more. The final Inventory of Learning Processes contains 62 items grouped into four scales assessing dimensions of learning behavior and conceptual processes characteristic of college students. The items are displayed in Table 1.

The first scale, called "Deep Processing," contains 18 items which assess the extent to which students critically evaluate, conceptually organize, and compare and contrast the information they study. In my previous writings, I labeled this scale "Synthesis Analysis," but subsequent research has convinced me that Deep Processing is a more appropriate label. Depth of processing is a concept first proposed by Craik and Lockhart (1972). As stated earlier, these authors maintained that memory traces are simply by-products of information processing activities. They further stated that these activities vary along a continuum from shallow (in which the physical stimulus is the sole object of attention) to deep (in which meanings and conceptual associations are processed). Craik and Lockhart assumed that deeper processing laid down more enduring memory traces. I should note that I am well aware of the criticisms of the "depth of processing" metaphor (e.g., M. W. Eysenck, 1978), and I have taken them into consideration when developing my own model (cf. Lockhart & Craik, 1978).

TABLE 1
Description of the Four ILP Factors in Terms of Their Salient Items[a]

Factor I: Deep processing (18 items)		Factor II: Methodical study (23 items)	
Item	Loading	Item'	Loading
I find it difficult to handle questions requiring comparison of different concepts	−53	I cram for exams	−47
I have trouble making inferences	−51	I have regular weekly review periods	46
I have trouble organizing the information I remember	−47	Getting myself to begin studying is usually difficult	−45
Even when I know that I have carefully learned the material, I have trouble remembering it for an examination	−46	I review course material periodically during the term	45
I find it difficult to handle questions requiring critical evaluation	−46	I maintain a daily schedule of study hours	44
I do well on essay tests	46	I carefully complete all course assignments	41
I often have difficulty finding the right words for expressing my ideas	−43	I generally write an outline of the material I read	39
I have difficulty learning how to study for a course	−43	I spend more time studying than most of my friends	36
I have difficulty planning work when confronted with a complex task	−41	I prepare a set of notes integrating the information from all sources in a course	36
I get good grades on term papers	41	I generally read beyond what is assigned in class	35
I often memorize material I do not understand	−37	I usually refer to several sources in order to understand a concept	34
I have trouble seeing the difference between apparently similar ideas	−35	Toward the end of a course, I prepare an overview of all material covered	33
I can usually state the underlying message of films and readings	34	I increase my vocabulary by building lists of new terms	32
I think fast	32	I make frequent use of a dictionary	32
Most of my instructors lecture too fast	−31	Even when I feel I have learned the material, I continue to study it	32
I can usually formulate a good guess even when I do not know the answer	26	I make simple charts and diagrams to help me remember material	30
I ignore conflicts between the information obtained from different sources	−25	I always make a special effort to get all the details	28
I read critically	25	I work through practice exercises and sample problems	28

TABLE 1 (*Continued*)

Factor II: Methodical study (*continued*)		Factor IV: Elaborative processing (14 items)	
Item	Loading	Item	Loading
I have a regular place to study	27	I look for reasons behind the facts	51
When necessary, I can easily locate		New concepts usually make me	
particular passages in a textbook	25	think of similar concepts	46
I would rather read the original arti-		While studying, I attempt to find	
cle than a summary	25	answers to questions I have in	
I frequently use the library	25	mind	44
When studying for an examination, I		I am usually able to design	
prepare a list of probable questions		procedures for solving problems	41
and answers	25	After reading a unit of material, I sit	
		and think about it	38
Factor III: Fact retention (7 items)		I learn new words or ideas by	
I do well on examinations requiring		visualizing a situation in which	
factual information	57	they could occur	33
I am very good at learning formulas,		When learning a unit of material, I	
names, and dates	53	usually summarize it in my own	
I do well on tests requiring		words	33
definitions	44	I learn new concepts by expressing	
I do well on completion items	38	them in my own words	32
I have trouble remembering		I daydream about things I have	
definitions	−34	studied	27
My memory is actually pretty poor	−33	When I study something I devise a	
For examinations, I memorize the		system for later recalling it	26
material as given in the text or		I learn new words and ideas by	
class notes	26	associating them with words and	
		ideas I already know	26
		I learn new ideas by relating them to	
		similar ideas	25
		I try to convert facts into "rules of	
		thumb"	25
		While learning new concepts	
		practical applications often come	25
		to mind	

[a]Note that decimal points are omitted. Items with a positive loading are keyed "True" and those with a negative loading are keyed "False."

This is a good place to note that "depth of processing," as I use the term, is not identical to the "levels-of-processing" concept of Marton and his colleagues. My own work was begun independently of Marton's, and I was operating within the framework of cognition and information processing with its emphasis on detailed description of cognitive processes. Deep processing in my analysis is an information *process* of verbal classification and categorical comparison. The analysis of Marton and his colleagues is more general, describing the *intention* and resulting *approach* of the student to the task of reading, with deep processing being a matter of attending more to the argument made and shallow processing involving greater attention to the main points listed. Marton's description of deep processing includes relating information to personal experiences, however, my own research has suggested that conceptual understanding and personalization of knowledge, although correlated, are actually *separate* learning strategies (see below).

Another scale revealed by the factor analysis (Factor IV in Table 1) contained 14 items which assess the extent to which students translate new information into their own terminology, generate concrete examples from their own experience, apply new information to their own lives, and use visual imagery to encode new ideas. My colleagues and I have chosen to call this scale "Elaborative Processing." Once again, we borrowed the concept from Craik and his colleagues. Craik and Tulving (1975) assumed that elaboration, or spread of processing, was another way in which more intricate and enduring memory traces were formed. Spread of processing refers to more extensive processing at any given level of depth. As my colleagues and I use the concept, elaboration can involve the processing of more concrete associations, or examples, from the person's actual experience without any change in depth of processing. In our system, elaboration is an exercise in applying information to one's own life or personalizing it, whereas deep processing is a more "academic" exercise in verbal classification and categorical comparison (cf. pp. 96–97).

We have labeled the third scale on the inventory "Fact Retention." Although this scale contains only seven items, it has been a useful predictor of performance. People who score high on the Fact Retention scale carefully process (and thus store) details and specific pieces of new information regardless of what other information-processing strategies they might employ. The strategy assessed by the scale seems similar to the operation-learning strategy described by Pask (1976a, 1976b). Students who earn high scores on the scale perform well on any test calling for names, dates, places, and other details. Schmeck et al. (1977) reported some data suggesting that people who score high on Fact Retention tend to classify information into narrower (more precise) categories.

The last scale on the inventory we have called the "Methodical Study" scale. In my previous articles, I used the term "Study Methods" to refer to this scale, but I believe that the label "Methodical Study" is more appropriate for reasons that will become apparent. Students who earn high scores on this scale claim to study more often and more carefully than other students, and the methods that they claim to employ are the systematic techniques recommended in all of the old "how to study" manuals (e.g., "type your notes, outline the text, study everyday in the same location, make up practice tests, etc."). Later, I will describe some research which suggests that these students have high-achievement motivation but may lack the skill or ability necessary to engage in deep or elaborative processing. These students seem to compensate by engaging in very frequent drill-and-practive study. It is interesting to note that Schmeck and Spofford (in press) found a small but significant positive relationship between the methodical study scale and the dissimulation scale of the Eysenck Personality Inventory. This suggests that students who score high on the scale are "eager to please" (perhaps desperately so). It may be the case that the person who scores high on methodical study is using the achieving style described by Entwistle (1981) and Biggs (1979).

After some additional work designed to balance the number of true- and false-keyed items on the inventory, Schmeck et al. (1977) examined the intercorrelations among the four scales and then determined their reliabilities. This information is presented in Table 2. One can see that the internal consistencies are acceptable, although slightly low for Fact Retention and Elaborative Processing. Nevertheless, temporal stability (i.e., test–retest reliability) of all of the inventory scales measured over a 2-week interval was quite acceptable, ranging from .79 to .88.

The intercorrelations reported in Table 2 indicate that the scales on the inventory are not completely independent of one another. The largest relationship exists between the Deep and Elaborative Processing scales. The work of Craik and Tulving (1975) suggests that deep and elaborative processing are the two most powerful ways of improving the durability of a memory trace. Thus, one might expect some overlap between these two scales. It should be pointed out, however, that research reported indicates that the Deep and Elaborative Processing scales have differential validity.

TABLE 2
Intercorrelations, Internal Consistency, and Test–Retest Reliabilities of the Four ILP Scales[a]

	Deep processing	Methodical study	Fact retention	Elaborative processing	Test–retest reliability
Deep processing	(82)				88
Methodical study	26	(74)			83
Fact retention	39	20	(58)		79
Elaborative processing	45	44	13	(67)	80

[a]Note that intercorrelations and internal consistencies were based on a sample of 434 subjects, and test–retest reliabilities were based on a sample of 95. Internal consistencies are listed on the diagonal. Decimal points have been omited.

We will see that the Deep Processing scale is related to critical thinking ability (Schmeck & Ribich, 1978), reading comprehension (Schmeck, 1980), verbal ability (Tracy, Schmeck, and Spofford, Note 4; Mueller & Fisher, Note 5), attention to the semantic attributes of words (Schmeck & Spofford, in press), ability to build conceptual tree structures (Ribich, 1977), and the WAIS digit-span subtests (Mueller & Fisher, Note 5). The Elaborative Processing scale is related to writing performance (Meier, 1981), use of mental imagery (Schmeck & Ribich, 1978), subjective organization of re-called word lists (Ribich & Schmeck, 1979), and the tendency to organize word lists around rhymes (Mueller & Fisher, 1980).

Schmeck et al. (1977) included two validity studies in the initial development of the Inventory of Learning Processes. In one study, subjects watched a videotape of an introductory psychology lecture while supposedly trying to "judge its complexity." Afterward, they were administered an unannounced 30-item multiple-choice test composed of 15 knowledge-level items and 15 comprehension-level items (Bloom, 1956). Subjects were not informed of the test because we wanted to determine whether style would have an impact when situational demands were at a minimum. The results indicated significant positive correlations between performance on the test and both Deep Processing ($r = .42$) and Elaborative Processing ($r = .51$). In addition, the two scales were somewhat more related to performance on higher-level comprehension questions than lower-level knowledge questions.

As one would expect, based on Craik and Lockhart (1972) and Craik and Tulving (1975), those who used deep and elaborative strategies for processing information during the lecture retained more of that information even though they were not instructed to learn it. Thus, "intent to learn" seemed to be less important than information-processing activities in determining the permanence and retrievability of stored information. Also, the fact that deep and elaborative processors retained more information in spite of the fact that they were not instructed to learn the information suggests that predisposition to favor a particular learning strategy (i.e., a learning *style*) can have an impact even when situational demands are minimized.

Another validation attempt reported by Schmeck et al. (1977) was a traditional memory study employing a list of 15 concrete and 15 abstract nouns. Half the subjects were told to study the list and the other half were given a cover task which, presumably, caused them to read the list but not actively study it. Then, all subjects were given both recall and recognition tests of memory. The relationships that were observed between the scales of the Inventory of Learning Processes and performance on the memory tests occurred only on the recall test and only with concrete material. Since recall tests are especially sensitive to retrieval processes and recognition tests simply reflect what is held in storage, the data indicate that retrieval processes are assessed by the scales of the inventory.

The results further indicated significant relationships between memory for the word list and both Deep Processing ($r = .50$) and Elaborative Processing ($r = .35$). These relationships appeared mainly in the conditions in which subjects were not specifically instructed to learn. The Methodical Study scale was related to recall when subjects were instructed to learn. Thus, once again, it appeared that subjects can form durable memory traces regardless of their intent to learn as long as they process deeply and elaboratively. In addition, this study suggested that when intent to learn was stimulated by instructing subjects to learn the material, it was those who scored high on the Methodical Study scale who performed best. Apparently, instructions to learn elicited intense study behavior (probably repetitive rehearsal) in some subjects—at the expense of deep and elaborative processing.

In another validity study described by Schmeck and Ribich (1978), we examined the relationships between the scales of the Inventory of Learning Processes and other known measures of individual difference. These included measures of critical thinking ability, preference for fact versus theory, two types of achievement motivation (conforming and independent), academic curiosity, anxiety, and two measures of visual imagery. The Deep Processing scale was positively related to critical thinking ability, to curiosity, to both independent and conforming achievement striving behaviors, and was negatively related to anxiety. Thus, the person who scored high on Deep Processing appeared to be a calm and skilled critical thinker who could achieve in an academic setting either by following instructions or by performing independently. Hunt (1979) considers the ability to function independently in an unstructured situation to be an indication of a higher level of personality development. Also, Parlett (1970) distinguishes between *syllabus-bound* students, who need deadlines and course guides, and *syllabus-free* students who like autonomy. It would appear that students who score high on the Deep Processing scale can be syllabus-free.

The Methodical Study scale was positively related to curiosity and conforming types of achievement striving and negatively related to critical thinking ability. The fact that critical thinking ability was related positively to the Deep Processing scale and negatively to the Methodical Study scale suggested that students with low critical thinking ability and high achievement motivation might substitute traditional "study skills" for deep processing because they find it difficult to engage in deep processing. The fact that their achievement motivation is of the *conforming* sort suggests that these students are eager to please and are bound by the course syllabus. I will describe a study shortly which showed that the Methodical Study scale related negatively to actual performance in a school setting.

Schmeck and Ribich (1978) also reported that fact retention related positively to conforming achievement-striving behaviors and negatively to anxiety, while elaborative processing related positively to curiosity and mental imagery ability. These findings suggest that the person who scores high on Fact Retention is prone to follow instructions carefully, to be bound by the course syllabus, and to process details, while the person who scores high on Elaborative Processing is able to elaborate and personalize information verbally as well as through imagery.

Schmeck and Grove (1979) conducted an extensive study of the relationship between the scales of the Inventory of Learning Processes and the academic performance of 790 college students from all grade levels and majors. Their measures of performance included both college grade-point average and the college entrance-examination scores of the American College Testing (ACT) Assessment. The results were analyzed, using both multivariate analyses of variance and path analyses. The profiles of successful and unsuccessful students that emerged from the study are presented in Table 3 together with the results of multivariate analyses of variance.

Students with high grade-point averages and high ACT scores tended to score high on Deep Processing, Fact Retention, and Elaborative Processing. Thus, they were processing deeply and encoding elaboratively while still retaining specific details. The path analysis suggested that the effects of fact retention and elaborative processing upon GPA were direct while the effect of deep processing was mostly interpreted by ACT scores. Since ACT assessed *prior* achievement (e.g., high-school performance), this result suggests that deep processing is already having a major impact at the high-school level. This finding also suggests that any intervention program designed to affect depth of processing really should begin *prior to* entrance into college. Table 3 also demonstrates that the students with high ACT scores actually scored *lower* on the Methodical Study scale, suggesting once again that people who score high on the Methodical Study scale may lack the skills necessary to engage in deep and elaborative processing. This conclusion is supported by Hudson (Note 6) who found that seventh graders who earned the highest scores on the Methodical Study scale had not yet attained the formal operations stage of cognitive development.

Moss (in press) replicated Schmeck and Grove (1979) using the specialized population at a college developmental reading and writing center. The center was designed to provide catch-up training in the basic skills of reading and writing. Moss found scores well below the norm for the campus on the Deep Processing, Elaborative Processing, and Fact Retention

TABLE 3

ILP Means and Standard Deviations of High and Low Achievers Classified First on the Basis of GPA, Then on the Basis of ACT

	n	Deep processing	Methodical study	Fact retention	Elaborative processing
GPA groups					
Low GPA	395				
M		10.40	10.15	4.26	9.80
S.D.		4.03	4.35	1.81	2.55
High GPA	395				
M		12.58	10.57	5.11	10.53
S.D.		3.83	3.94	1.58	2.66
F ratio		57.79**	2.04	54.08**	15.60**
ACT groups					
Low ACT	395				
M		10.46	10.74	4.48	9.97
S.D.		4.15	4.29	1.77	2.66
High ACT	395				
M		12.49	9.97	4.88	10.36
S.D.		3.75	3.97	1.71	2.59
F ratio		51.05**	7.04**	10.54**	4.35*
All subjects	790				
M		11.49	10.36	4.68	10.17
S.D.		4.08	4.15	1.75	2.63

*$p < .01$.
**$p < .001$.

scales of the Inventory of Learning Processes. She found *above*-average scores on the Methodical Study scale. In addition, the negative relationship between the Methodical Study scale and academic performance was the only one predicting success in this restricted group (i.e., there were no significant relationships between achievement and any of the other scales on the Inventory of Learning Processes in this restricted population).

There is evidence that the relationships between learning style and performance are not attributable to simple differences in intelligence. Ribich (1977) demonstrated that relationships between performance and the scales of the Inventory of Learning Processes remained even when intelligence was statistically extracted from the relationship. Furthermore, Ribich (1977) reports that the strongest relationship obtained between intelligence-test scores and the scales of the inventory was $r = .39$ between IQ and Deep Processing, suggesting that the two dimensions are related but far from equivalent. In another study, Tracy et al. (Note 4) administered the inventory along with the space relations and verbal reasoning subtests of the

Differential Aptitude Tests (Bennett, Seashore & Wesman, 1974). For males, Fact Retention related positively to verbal and negatively to spatial ability. All subjects showed a positive relationship between Deep Processing and verbal ability. Thus verbal ability is vital, but note that "verbosity" is not since Ribich and Schmeck (1979) found that deep processors can routinely express *more* ideas with *less* words.

Tracy et al. (Note 4) also administered the Bem Sex Role Inventory (Bem, 1974). The study demonstrated significant positive relationships between the Deep Processing, Elaborative Processing, and Fact Retention scales and both the masculinity and femininity subscores on the Bem, suggesting that androgyny is characteristic of people who score high on those three Inventory of Learning Processes scales. People classified as androgynous are generally assumed to be more adaptable, healthy, and stable than individuals with more rigid sex-role orientations.

Mueller and Fisher (1980) included the Inventory of Learning Processes in a traditional memory study using word lists as stimuli. The study was designed to examine the relationships between recall organization and individual-difference measures. Ribich and Schmeck (1979) found greater subjective organization in subjects who scored high on the Elaborative Processing scale. Similarly, Mueller and Fisher (1980) provide evidence that subjects who scored high on Elaborative Processing had more organized recall. Interestingly, their data suggest that the recall of these subjects was organized around rhyming relationships more often than semantic relationships. Mueller and Fisher (Note 5) also reported positive relationships between the WAIS digit-span subtests and both the Deep Processing and Fact Retention scales, suggesting superior working memory (attention and short-term storage) for those who scored high on these two scales. This latter relationship might account for the superior reading comprehension of those who score high on Deep Processing (cf. Chapter 3, this volume). Superior working memory could also account for greater retention of details and specifics by those who score high on Fact Retention in that they may have greater rehearsal capacity (cf. Chapter 2, this volume).

McDaniel (Note 7) administered the Deep Processing and Elaborative Processing scales to 44 high school sophomores enrolled in a special advanced-placement English course. He reports that both scales were positively related to verbal ability while neither scale was related to numerical ability. In addition, both were positively related to teacher ratings of student verbal expression and ability to relate ideas from literature to real life. This latter rating included both the ability to go from the abstract to the concrete (presumably elaborative processing) and the ability to go from the concrete to the abstract (presumably deep processing). I should add that McDaniel also reports that his own measure of "cognitive preference" was actually a better predictor of the criteria than were the two scales of the Inventory of Learning Processes.

Watkins and Hattie (1981a) provided some cross-cultural data in a recently published evaluation of the Inventory of Learning Processes. They looked at the internal structure and predictive validity of the inventory using 255 Australian and 173 Filipino college students. They reported good internal consistency for the Deep Processing and Methodical Study scales but less internal consistency for the other two scales. The factor structure for the Australian sample did not replicate the four current scales, but the Filipino data provided two factors equivalent to deep processing and methodical study. Discrepancies between the results of the factor analysis carried out by Watkins and Hattie (1981a) and my own earlier work are probably due to cultural and linguistic differences between their population and mine. Indeed, I find it reassuring that the inventory demonstrated good predictive validity with populations that differ so greatly from the one used to develop the instrument.

With regard to validity, Watkins and Hattie (1981a, 1981b) report that the inventory scales were good predictors of academic achievement for their Australian sample. Watkins and Hattie (1981a) report multiple r values ranging from .60 in the Arts to .75 in the Sciences. Deep processing was related to achievement in all fields of specialization. Elaborative processing also tended to relate positively to performance in all fields, but the relationships were significant only in the case of liberal arts and economics. Fact retention was a significant predictor of performance in the sciences and in economics. Methodical study was positively related to performance in liberal arts and economics. Watkins, Hattie, and Astilla (Note 8) report that academic achievement of a Filipino sample is similarly predicted by the Deep Processing and Elaborative Processing scales but, with the Filipino sample, the Elaborative Processing scale is clearly the best predictor.

Watkins and Hattie (1981b) also report that older Australian students earned significantly higher scores on the Deep and Elaborative Processing scale of the Inventory of Learning Processes. This supports my earlier suggestion that developmental stage might impose limits on the level of information processing that an individual is capable of demonstrating. With regard to college major, Watkins and Hattie (1981b) report that students in the Arts generally score higher on Deep Processing. Also, it is interesting to note that, although the Deep Processing scale was the most powerful predictor of grades in the sciences, most students in the Sciences scored relatively low on this scale indicating that they were not aware of the best strategy for success in their own college. Finally, sex differences indicated that females generally scored higher than males on the Methodical Study scale.

Further cross-cultural data are provided by Joseph Weinbaum (Note 9) who developed a Hebrew version of the Inventory of Learning Processes. A preliminary study involved administration of the inventory to 95 male Israeli high-school graduates (ages 18–19). The means and standard deviations obtained by Weinbaum are comparable to those my colleagues and I have obtained with American college students—with the possible exception that the Israelis were a bit higher and less variable on the Deep Processing scale. Weinbaum (Note 9) also found that the Deep Processing and Methodical Study scales were negatively correlated with his own measure of "school aversion" ($r = -.47$ and $-.32$, respectively).

DEPTH OF PROCESSING AS A DIMENSION OF LEARNING STYLE

Ribich and Schmeck (1979) administered three self-report assessments of learning style: the Inventory of Learning Processes, Kolb's (1974) Learning Style Inventory, and Biggs' (1976) Study Behavior Questionnaire. They also collected extensive data with 13 word-list and prose-learning measures, including both immediate and delayed retention tests. Canonical correlational analyses of the pairs of learning-style instruments and performance measures provided an opportunity to determine whether the learning-style measures were assessing common dimensions of learning style. There was a small-to-moderate amount of overlapped variance. Inspection of the canonical variates revealed that what overlap existed between the learning-style measures was generally due to the common factor, "depth of processing."

Canonical analyses of the relationships between each of the measures of learning style and the set of performance measures indicated that the Inventory of Learning Processes and Kolb's Learning Style Inventory each shared some variance with the performance measures. Once again, the analysis suggested that the overlap between the self-report inventories and performance was due to the common factor, depth of processing. Overall, the Ribich and Schmeck (1979) study indicated that the Inventory of Learning Processes showed the strongest relationships with the 13 performance measures and the variable of major interest assessed by the learning-style inventories was depth of processing.

As part of a large unpublished study, Ribich (1977) examined the extent to which subjects were able to organize lecture information into theoretically ideal conceptual networks. (This would require that the information be processed to considerable depth.) We will see later in this chapter that Dansereau, Collins, McDonald, Holley, Garland, Diekhoff, and Evans (1979) have devised a learning-strategy training program that improves student learning by teaching them to organize information into networks similar to those studied by Ribich. However, Ribich's subjects received no training in the use of such a networking strategy. Subjects were asked to structure the concepts of behavior analysis both before and after listening to the lecture. In addition, they filled out the Inventory of Learning Processes, the Otis–Lennon Mental Abilities Test (Otis & Lennon, 1968), and the Watson-Glaser Critical Thinking Appraisal (Watson & Glaser, 1964). Ribich found that those who scored high on Deep Processing were better at structuring the information both before and after the lecture. Furthermore, regression analysis showed that the relationship between the Inventory of Learning Processes and ability to structure or organize information was independent of intelligence (as measured by the Otis–Lennon test) and critical thinking ability (as measured by the Watson-Glaser).

Schmeck and Spofford (in press) were interested in determining whether a deep-processing style of learning might counteract an effect originally demonstrated by Schwartz (1975), who found that subjects who scored high on a measure of emotional arousal made more errors when interference was produced on a paired-associates task by making the words phonetically similar. Those low on arousal made more errors when the words were semantically similar. This greater susceptibility to phonetic interference among highly aroused individuals suggested that they were processing information more shallowly than individuals low on arousal. Schmeck and Spofford suspected that this negative relationship between arousal and depth of processing would be attenuated in subjects who had developed a deep-processing *style* of learning. We administered both the Eysenck Personality Inventory (H. J. Eysenck & Eysenck, 1964) as a measure of individual differences in arousal and the Inventory of Learning Processes as a measure of a deep-processing learning style. The learning task was composed of two types of paired associates: word pairs that used response words semantically similar to one another and pairs that used phonetically similar responses.

The results indicated that arousal and learning style interacted with regard to their effects on performance on the paired-associates task. The three-way interaction is illustrated in Figure 1. The figure shows that the two-way interaction that Schwartz (1975) obtained, that is, greater susceptibility to semantic interference with low arousal and phonetic interference with high arousal, occurred only when Deep Processing scores were low. In other words, emotional arousal tends to produce shallow processing unless the individual has developed a well-practiced, deep-processing style of learning. If the chronically aroused individual can manage to adopt such a deep-processing style, it apparently attenuates the negative effects of emotional arousal on depth of processing.

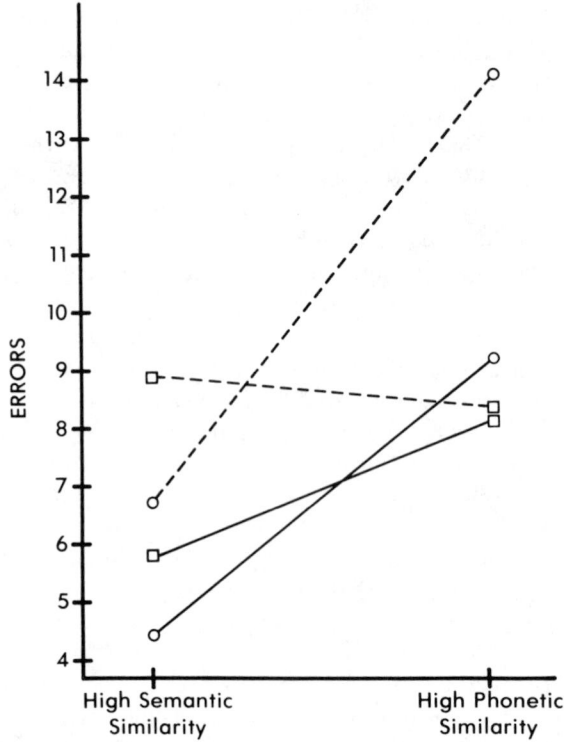

FIGURE 1. Mean errors of the four groups formed via independent median splits on neuroticism and deep processing, performing under two different conditions of response similarity. O--O High N–low DP (N = 25); □--□ low N–low DP (N = 13); O—O high N–high DP (N = 11); □—□ low N–high DP (N = 25). From Schmeck and Spofford, with permission. N, neuroticism; DP, deep processing.

Schmeck and Phillips (in press) examined the relationship between a measure of Marton's levels of processing and the Inventory of Learning Processes. I noted earlier that Biggs' (1979) measure is called the SOLO taxonomy and is designed to classify the answers to open-ended essay questions (the learning outcome) on the dimension of levels of processing as defined by Marton and Säljö (1976a). Phillips and I administered the Inventory of Learning Processes along with a widely used measure of reading comprehension (the Iowa Silent Reading Test; Harcourt, Brace, Jovanovich, 1973). We attached to the end of each comprehension test two essay questions concerned with the last reading passage on the test. The answers to these questions were scored by four trained raters using the SOLO taxonomy. The reliability of the SOLO ratings was acceptable (r = .88), and the intercorrelations among the three measures provided some support for the validity of both the self-report inventory and the performance measure.

The Deep Processing scale and SOLO were positively correlated ($r = .37$), and both were positively related to the standardized reading comprehension test. The Deep-Processing scale was actually more highly related to the standardized comprehension scores ($r = .51$) than was the SOLO performance measure ($r = .36$). Since Wittrock (1974) essentially defines reading comprehension as a product of deep processing, the relationships between learning style and comprehension support the construct validity of the depth (and Marton's "levels") of processing dimension of individual difference. It is worth emphasizing the fact that a comprehension test such as the one that Phillips and I used is different from the memory tests that my colleagues and I have used in other studies. The comprehension test allows the student to have direct access to the original source of information while answering questions. Thus, such a test is assessing process variables more than memory variables.

The magnitude of the relationship between SOLO and the deep-processing scale ($r = .37$) suggests overlap between the depth and levels constructs, but it certainly does not indicate that the two constructs are identical. Furthermore, Marton and his colleagues include a search for personal meaning in their description of deep processing, but Phillips and I found very little relationship between SOLO and the Elaborative Processing scale ($r = .12$). The absence of expected relationships might be due to the use of different methods of measurement, or it may indicate that the strategy suggested by the levels construct is different from those assessed by the scales of the Inventory of Learning Processes. The issues should be resolved as we continue to gather data regarding the construct validity of the various learning style dimensions.

In another study of reading comprehension, Schmeck (1980) administered the Nelson-Denny Reading Test (Brown, Nelson, & Denny, 1973) and the Inventory of Learning Processes to 162 students. For comparison purposes, the study also included a classic measure of study skills called the Survey of Study Habits and Attitudes (Brown & Holtzman, 1967). This is probably the most widely used study skills inventory on the market (cf. Bray, Maxwell, & Schmeck, 1980). The Inventory of Learning Processes was clearly the best predictor of reading comprehension and the deep-processing scale was clearly responsible for this predictive power. This study also provided evidence of differential validity with the Deep Processing scale relating to the comprehension ($r = .37$) and vocabulary ($r = .27$) subscales on the Nelson-Denny but showing no relationship to reading rate ($r = .07$).

Several studies have provided a personality sketch of the "deep processor." *Calmness* is indicated by the fact that scores on the Deep Processing scale relate negatively to neuroticism (Schmeck & Spofford, in press), manifest anxiety (Schmeck & Ribich, 1978), test anxiety (Schmeck & Ribich, 1978), and writing anxiety (Meier, McCarthy, and Schmeck, in press). *Confidence* and *responsibility* are indicated by positive relationships between scores on the Deep Processing scale and both self-efficacy and internality on the locus of control dimension (Meier et al., in press). *Flexibility* is indicated by the fact that deep processing was positively related to both independent and conforming achievement striving (Schmeck & Ribich, 1978), to androgyny (Tracy et al., Note 4), and to the accuracy of students' ratings of their own cognitive skills (Meier et al., in press).

In the introduction to this chapter, I mentioned Battig's (1979) position that the most basic individual difference in the area of learning and memory is the insight and cognitive flexibility involved in selecting the best strategy for a given task. The label "metamemory" (Flavell & Wellman, 1977), seems appropriate for this dimension. My colleagues and I assume that students who score high on the Deep Processing scale have greater metamemory, that is, more insight into their own cognitive processes and more ability to select processes for given tasks. N. Entwistle et al. (1979) similarly suggested that Marton's deep approach to learning might be comparable to Pask's versatile learning style with students alternately attending to both overall ideas and detailed evidence. Meier, et al. (in press) provided some relevant data. They had subjects estimate their abilities to perform the various functions necessary for effective writing, then they collected actual writing samples. They found that the overall correlation between subjects' estimates of their own competence and their actual performance was $r = .36$. However, when they did a median split on the Deep Processing scale they found that this correlation coefficient increased to $r = .51$ for deep processors and dropped to $r = .20$ for shallow processors. This suggested that deep processors were more accurate in their estimates of their own competence. Meier, et al. (in press) also noted that a median split on the Elaborative Processing scale produced similar results, with the correlation between the subjects' estimated and actual competence being $r = .44$ for persons high on elaborative processing and $r = .15$ for those low on the scale. This suggested the possibility of combining the Deep and Elaborative Processing scales to obtain a single score. A median split on the sum of the two scores produced $r = .64$ for high scorers and $r = .08$ for low scorers.

Schmeck (1981) has suggested the possibility of summing scores on these two scales as a way of assessing a learning-style dimension that would have deep-elaborative learners on one end and shallow-reiterative learners on the other. There are several similarities between deep and elaborative processing. For example, we just collected data that indicate that deep and elaborative processors are equally high on sensation seeking (Zuckerman, 1971). Students who score high on the two scales indicate a need for new experiences and a susceptibility to the aversive effects of boredom. I have kept the two scales separate for several reasons. Of course, the original factor-analytic development of the inventory yielded two separate factors, but Craik and Tulving (1975) also concluded, on the basis of laboratory research, that the two processes were separate. Furthermore, I have an intuitive recognition after 17 years of teaching that certain students really do operate in one of the other of these two modes. On the one hand, we have the academic, conceptual, formalistic type of person who categorizes, compares, and contrasts at the highest possible levels of abstraction. On the other hand, we have the practical, applied-concrete type who operationally defines and relates all material to personal experience. Obviously, the two types of activity are not mutually exclusive, and the most effective students would do both in a manner similar to that suggested by Pask's (1976a, 1976b) versatile learning style.

New Data Concerning the Deep Processing Scale

My intention in this section is to provide an extensive example of the type of research that both my colleagues and I have been doing. The study was designed and conducted by Mark Spofford to provide some previously unpublished data for this chapter. The study was concerned with the validity of the Deep Processing scale of the Inventory of Learning Processes and was set in a fairly traditional memory paradigm. The encoding-specificity principle states: "Specific encoding operations performed on what is perceived determine what is stored, and what is stored determines what retrieval cues are effective in providing access to what is stored" (Tulving & Thomson, 1973, p. 369). Fisher and Craik (1977) manipulated encoding operations by giving subjects either deep or shallow (i.e., semantic or phonetic) orienting tasks to be performed during acquisition. In support of the encoding-specificity principle, they report that, when subjects were given both semantic (deep) and phonetic (shallow) retrieval cues on a cued recall test, those who were given a semantic-orienting task during their initial exposure to the items profited most from the semantic cues and those given a phonetic task during the initial period profited most from phonetic retrieval cues.

The present study was a partial replication of the Fisher and Craik (1977) study, but instead of manipulating depth of encoding, subjects were divided into deep or shallow encoders on the basis of their scores on the Deep Processing scale. It was reasoned that if the results paralleled those of Fisher and Craik, they would serve as evidence that the Deep Processing scale is, in fact, assessing a stylistic predisposition to use the same learning strategy that Fisher and Craik produced by experimentally manipulating the situation. Thus, subjects scoring above and below the median on the Deep Processing scale of the Inventory of Learning Processes were given a word list to learn and a subsequent cued recall test containing half semantic and half phonetic retrieval cues. In light of the Fisher and Craik (1977) study, an interaction was predicted, with those subjects above the median on Deep Processing profiting most from semantic (deep) cues, and those below the median profiting most from phonetic (shallow) cues.

METHOD

The subjects were 31 female and 35 male undergraduate students enrolled in an introductory psychology course that required their participation in five experiments during the term. Our subjects were recruited in the final weeks of the semester. The basic design was a 2 × 2 mixed design with a between-subjects comparison of deep versus shallow information processors (formed via a median split on the Deep Processing scale) and a within-subject comparison of retrieval cue type (semantic versus phonetic). As noted below, sex was added later as a third factor in the analysis because of a significant correlation between sex and the dependent measure. A 36-word recall list was constructed from one-syllable words selected from Cluster 8 (high meaningfulness, familiarity, and imagery) of Toglia and Battig (1978). The words were selected on the basis that each did not rhyme with or belong to the same semantic category as any of the others. Each word was assigned at random to the rhyming-retrieval cue condition ("This word rhymes with _____") or the semantic-retrieval cue condition ("This word is a type of _____"). Following list presentation, the 36-item cued recall sheet was given to each subject who had as much time as necessary to recall the words.

RESULTS

The initial correlational analyses revealed no significant correlation between overall performance on the cued recall test and scores on the Deep Processing scale, but there was a significant relationship between sex and performance on the cued recall test ($r = .45$, $p < .001$). Thus, the original 2 × 2 design (cue type × deep processing) was modified to include sex. The Deep Processing scores of subjects classified as shallow processors ranged from 1 to 11, and those of deep processors ranged from 12 to 18. Since the addition of sex as a factor produced unequal cell sizes, the data were analyzed using a least-squares approach to deal with the unequal n values (Jennrich & Sampson, 1977; Program P2V).

TABLE 4

Mean Number of Words Recalled As a Function of Sex, Scores on the Deep Processing Scale (DP), and Retrieval Cue

Retrieval cue	Males		Females	
	Low DP ($n = 12$)	High DP ($n = 23$)	Low DP ($n = 19$)	High DP ($n = 12$)
Rhyme	8.2 (2.2)	8.3 (3.2)	11.3 (2.3)	9.2 (3.6)
Category	9.7 (2.2)	9.7 (3.5)	12.3 (3.1)	13.1 (2.2)
M	9.0	9.0	11.8	11.1

[a]Note that standard deviations are in parentheses.

The predicted interaction between cue type and deep processing did occur [F (1,62) = 4.56, p < .05, MS_e = 3.59]. However, the analysis also revealed a three-way interaction between sex, cue type, and deep processing [F (1,62) = 4.45, p < .05, MS_e = 3.59], and a significant main effect for sex [F (1,61) = 13.82, p < .005, MS_e = 13.55]. Table 4, which presents the results separately for males and females, suggests that the interaction between cue type and deep processing occurred only with female subjects. Analyses performed separately for males and females indicated, that, indeed, the interaction between cue type and deep processing was significant for females [F (1,61) = 31.96, p < .001, MS_e = 3.43] but not for males [F (1,61) < 1.00].

DISCUSSION.

Fisher and Craik (1977) found that subjects given a deep (semantic) orienting task during encoding recalled more when given deep (semantic) retrieval cues on a cued recall test, while those given a shallow (phonetic) task recalled more when given shallow (phonetic) retrieval cues. In the present study, instead of manipulating encoding strategy, the Deep Processing scale was used to group subjects according to whether they were expected to routinely engage in deep processing or shallow processing. The significant interaction between retrieval cue type and deep processing suggests that the results are in agreement with Fisher and Craik (1977) and thus in support of the view that the Deep Processing scale is a valid assessment of depth of processing. However, the inclusion of sex as a factor in the analysis complicated the results somewhat, and separate analyses for males and females indicated that the retrieval cue by deep–processing interaction occurred only with the female subjects.

An admittedly post hoc explanation for the three-way interaction involving sex concerns the fact that the study was conducted in the very last week of an academic term using students whose participation in 5 experiments, while technically optional, was demanded by a system which makes alternate means of meeting course requirements more difficult and time consuming. Evans and Donnerstein (1974) report data suggesting that, under such recruitment conditions, samples of females are essentially the same in terms of important personality and performance variables regardless of whether they are obtained early or late in the academic term, but early and late males are different in several respects. In their study, late-term males tended to have lower GPAs, less achievement orientation, and a less positive attitude toward research participation. Each of those variables would be expected to correlate negatively with the dependent measure in the present study and thus result in lower overall performance for males as well as the suppression of the cue type by deep processing interaction.

Ribich and Schmeck (1979) argue that, in addition to the usual experimental technique of manipulating the orienting tasks given to subjects, researchers should study natural variation on the depth of processing dimension. They also present data which suggest using the Deep Processing scale for this purpose; the results of the present study would add further support to their recommendation. Additionally, past research has shown the Deep Processing scale to relate positively to measures of educational achievement (Schmeck & Grove, 1979). Thus, the behavioral description of deep processing provided by the Deep Processing scale would seem to be ideal for use as the basis of a training program for students who are academically weak because of deficiencies in their information processing abilities. In the next section, I will describe such a program.

ATTEMPTS TO MODIFY LEARNING STYLE

The material in this section is based upon the dissertation of Edward Reid, one of my doctoral students (Reid, 1981). Reid attempted to design a learning-strategy training program based on the Inventory of Learning Processes. Although the program was not very successful, the review of the literature and the techniques that Reid used for designing the training program are instructive.

LEARNING-STRATEGY TRAINING PROGRAMS

Haslam and Brown (1968) designed a program to improve students' motivation, efficiency, organization, reading, writing, and examination--taking skills. The training group showed a gain in GPA from 2.37 to 2.63

while a control group showed no significant change, 2.33 to 2.37. Van Zoost and Jackson (1974) pretested 43 subjects on the *Survey of Study Habits and Attitudes* (Brown & Holtzman, 1967), and then exposed them to an eight-session group study skills program with goals similar to those of Haslam and Brown (1968). Upon completion of the program, students demonstrated significant improvement in knowledge of effective study methods and test-taking skills. However, a problem with both of these studies is that they failed to describe the specific nature of their training programs.

Briggs, Tosi, and Morley (1971) taught the SQ3R (Survey-Question-Read-Recite-Review) method to 10 students who entered college on probation; a similar group of 10 students served as the control group. The SQ3R method (Robinson, 1946) is basically an encoding strategy, but it also forces students to practice retrieval. Students are taught to *survey* the headings and summaries of a chapter, convert them to *questions, read* to find answers, *recite* the question–answer combinations, and *review* periodically. The SQ3R technique was taught step by step, and only after mastering one step could the student go on to the next. This required an average of three weeks of training. At the end of the term, the experimental group GPA was 2.25 whereas the control group's was 1.83.

Driskell and Kelly (1980) taught the SQ3R method to 14 first-term students who had been identified as potential failures—based on SAT scores, and who voluntarily agreed to participate in a study-skills class. Forty-seven students in the poor-risk category who refused the opportunity to participate in the study-skills course constituted a no-treatment control group. In addition to training in the SQ3R method, the students received instruction in notetaking and Bloom's (1956) taxonomy which they used to critique examinations they had taken in other courses. At the end of the term, it was found that the treatment group obtained a GPA of 2.55 compared to a GPA of 1.70 for the control group.

Whitehill (1972)·described his "Information Organization Program" wherein students organize information into conceptual matrices, develop informational flow charts, and then study these notes. Whitehill used the Minnesota Study Habits Blank (MSHB) to identify students who were most in need of the training program. Those students who scored high on the MSHB or indicated that they were already using good organizational techniques showed very little GPA gain whereas those who scored low on the MSHB showed an average gain of .75 on a four-point scale. It seems likely that the Information Organization Program was forcing students to process more deeply.

Malin and Malin (Note 10) gave 18 students a prose-learning pretest followed by 6 hours of instruction in the use of one of two learning strategies. One group of 9 subjects was trained to use the SQ3R method while the other nine received training in Malin and Malin's "IDEA method," a multiple-pass approach in which the passage is read three times. The first reading is designed to reduce the information to short statements of gist; the second involves diagraming the relationships between these statements; and the third arranges them into heirarchical networks. The technique should increase the depth to which students process the information being read. On the posttest, all students using the IDEA method and only five of the nine students using the SQ3R method showed a significant gain.

A similar training program has been developed by Dansereau and his colleagues (1979) at Texas Christian University. They gave students detailed training in the use of one of three methods designed to facilitate recall of prose. The "paraphrase/imagery strategy" required students to rephrase material in their own words then imagine essential concepts. This would be a form of elaborative processing. The "networking strategy" has the student diagram text with node–link maps that illustrate the interrelationships between concepts. The third method, "analysis of key ideas," was similar to the networking strategy, but the student specified interrelationships by writing them out rather than constructing diagrams. These last two strategies would involve deep processing.

Dansereau et al. (1979) had 38 students enrolled in a 15-week learning-strategy course take a pretest, a midterm, and a posttest consisting of short-answer and multiple-choice questions over three different 3000-word passages. A possible weak point in the design concerns the fact that students selected which of the three strategies they wished to learn. Scores obtained by these students were compared to a no-treatment control group composed of 28 students recruited from a general psychology class. Subjects using the networking strategy showed a large gain on the midterm examination and a further gain on the post-test compared to the control group. The key-ideas group showed a large gain on the midterm examination but no further improvement, and the paraphrase/imagery group actually suffered a decline in advantage over the control group from the midterm examination to the post-test.

In an extension of the Dansereau et al. (1979) research, Holley, Dansereau, McDonald, Garland, and Collins (1979) gave 5½ hours of network-ing-strategy training to 17 general psychology students. At the end of the training period, the students spent 1 hour constructing node–link maps for a 3000-word prose passage. Five days later, the students were given 3 minutes to review their notes, were asked to summarize the passage by writing an essay, and then to take a test consisting of 18 multiple-choice questions, 10 short-answer questions, and seven cloze questions. Cloze questions are measures of comprehension which have subjects fill in gaps in a prose passage. A no-treatment control group was given one session to use their normal methods in studying the same passage, and 5 days later, took the same test as the experimental group. A factor analysis revealed that the data from the multiple-choice and short-answer items formed a "details" (shallow processing?) factor and the data from the cloze and essay questions formed a "main ideas" (deep processing?) factor. The results indicated that the networking group significantly outperformed the control group on the main ideas but not the details measure. A further analysis in terms of GPA indicated that the training benefited students with low GPAs more than those with high GPAs, presumably because students with high GPAs already possessed effective learning strategies before participating in the experiment.

Ribich (1977) found that subjects who earned high scores on the deep-processing scale of the Inventory of Learning Processes were better at constructing concept networks of the type used by Dansereau et al. (1979), and this relationship was independent of intelligence and critical thinking ability. It may be the case that Dansereau's training program is teaching students a technique that will force them to process information deeply. However, we have no data as to whether or not the program produced any change in predisposition (or *style*) of processing in addition to teaching students a new *strategy*.

Snowman et al. (Note 2) studied the effect of four different learning strategies on the recall of 96 college students. The students had signed up for a 15-week course in memory-improvement skills and were randomly assigned to treatments. In one condition, the students were taught a networking method of prose analysis, based upon the work of Meyer (1975), followed by instruction in the method of loci (an imagery mnemonic). In two additional conditions, the method of loci and prose analysis were presented alone. Prior to training, subjects were administered the Wonderlic Personnel Test (Wonderlic, 1961) as a measure of general mental ability. Subjects were tested for recall of main ideas on three passages prior to training, during the sixth and eleventh weeks. The training program was found to be effective, with the group receiving *both* prose analysis and loci training showing the greatest improvement in recall. Snowman et al. (Note 2) also report that subjects with high mental ability benefited most from the training program, suggesting that ability may place limits on the learning strategies that an individual is capable of mastering.

Weinstein (1975) taught elaboration strategies similar to those presumed to be assessed by the Elaborative Processing scale of the Inventory of Learning Processes. The training group was compared to placebo and post-test-only control groups. Subjects were 75 ninth-grade students randomly assigned to groups. The experimental group was exposed to 20 serial, paired-associate, and prose-learning tasks with the aim of teaching subjects to match their elaboration to the material. Imagery might facilitate paired-associate learning, whereas creating logical relationships might work better for prose learning. Weinstein did not supply specific elaborators to subjects, but she did give general hints as to the type of elaborators that might be effective. A test was given in the sixth week followed, four weeks later, by a delayed post-test. The experimental group outperformed the two control groups on all tests, but of 16 planned comparisons, only one was significant. Pooling the data for the control groups increased the number of significant comparisons to five.

The training materials used by Weinstein consisted of exercises a student might expect to encounter either in school (e.g., learning the difference between arteries and veins) or daily life (e.g., learning a grocery list). In contrast, the post-test contained no measure of prose learning, and the serial lists and paired-associates were devoid of obvious practical relevance. The use of novel materials is essential for the demonstration of positive transfer since it rules out practice effects due to rote memory. However, if Weinstein had selected postexperimental material similar to the training exercises, it is possible that a greater number of significant comparisons would have been obtained with no decrement in internal validity (cf. Weinstein, in press).

Weinstein, Underwood, Wicker, and Cubberly (1979) compared the effectiveness of (1) instructing students in the method of loci; (2) giving instructions in the method of loci and development of a story line; (3) giving instructions in the method of loci and story-line development plus an additional 1-hour practice session prior to the test session; and (4) giving all the treatments in the first three groups received plus additional instructions in the method of loci. A fifth group of students was employed as a no-treatment control group. The information to be learned consisted of six lists of 20 nouns—either high or low in concreteness. The findings of most theoretical importance was that groups 2, 3, and 4 significantly outperformed the loci group (#1 above) and the control group (which did not differ significantly from the loci group). Thus, the three groups forced to process meanings (i.e., process *deeply*) outperformed those that were not.

Pask and his colleagues have designed "learning to learn seminars" in which students are given feedback regarding their own learning styles (cf. N. Entwistle, 1981). The pathologies associated with their styles are discussed and an attempt is made to develop a more versatile style by teaching students to use strategies different from their preferred strategies. One of Pask's techniques is to teach students to build and use *entailment graphs* that heirarchically arrange topics and subtopics and show the various ways in which they can be synthesized and analyzed. Like Weinstein, Pask has emphasized the necessity of having students *apply* knowledge to novel problems in order to demonstrate their *understanding* of the material.

A TRAINING PROGRAM BASED ON THE INVENTORY OF LEARNING PROCESSES

Reid (1981) reasoned that, since the Deep and Elaborative Processing scales of the Inventory of Learning Processes relate positively to academic achievement (Schmeck & Grove, 1979), these scales might be used as the basis for constructing a learning-strategy training program. From these two scales, Reid selected 11 items that seemed to provide the most useful suggestions for training exercises; the skills specified in an item were selected from various published sources. I will present one example of the way in which Reid used the inventory items to derive exercises. Item number six says, "New concepts rarely make me think of many other similar concepts" (keyed "false"). This suggests the usefulness of processing associative links between concepts. To teach students to be sensitive to associative links that might not be immediately obvious, Reid (1981) used items from the Remote Associates Test (Mednick, 1962, 1967). The test was used as a training device, not an assessment device. The items on the Remote Associates Test provide three words that are in some way related and ask subjects to specify a fourth word that would provide an associative link between them all. For example, the three words coffee, derby, and coal could be associated by specifying the word "black." Subjects were given extensive training (with feedback) designed to teach them to solve items such as these. Eight exercises were developed in this manner. The average time required for completion of an exercise is 45 minutes. Total training time is approximately 6 hours. The materials are bound into a booklet that students can work through at their own rate.

Reid's (1981) initial attempt to implement and evaluate the program was somewhat disappointing. Ninety-eight students from an introductory psychology class were randomly assigned to an experimental (training) group and a placebo control group. Subjects were administered the Inventory of Learning Processes, the Otis-Lennon Mental Ability Test, a prose-learning pretest, and a prose-learning post-test. Data was also collected concerning the critical thinking ability of subjects. The relevant comparisons provided no indication that the training program had been effective.

In retrospect, I feel that Reid's (1981) program did not include a sufficient attempt to teach students the *relevance* of the training with regard to their everyday study behaviors. The exercises provided operational definitions of the learning strategies assessed by the Inventory of Learning Processes, but it was not clear to the student how to actually *use* those strategies when studying. We are currently trying to design an improved version of this intervention which I hope will be more successful.

CONCLUSIONS

Let me begin by reiterating my position. I agree with Craik and Lockhart (1972) that the memory trace is a by-product of information processing, and I regard a learning strategy as the processing that occurs when preparing for a test of memory. I use the term "learning style" to refer to any predisposition to use a particular strategy, and I feel I have identified four such styles. The first presumably is assessed by the Deep Processing scale of the Inventory of Learning Processes. The student who earns a high score on this scale appears to be very conceptual, spending time categorizing, critically evaluating the appropriateness of the categorizations, and comparing and contrasting categories with one another. The second style is that assessed by the Elaborative Processing scale. It is the tendency to personalize and concretize information by translating it into one's own terminology and life experiences and by searching for practical applications. The third style is that assessed by the Fact Retention scale. It is a predisposition to process details and specifics and is assumed to vary independently of the extent to which one processes deeply or elaboratively. The fourth style is assessed by the Methodical Study scale. It is a strategy of organization, planning, scheduling, and meticulous performance of study skills of the type specified in the old, classic how-to-study manuals.

Schmeck and Grove (1979) provided evidence that the most successful college students were deep, elaborative, fact retainers. There was no evidence that methodical study contributed to success in college. Students who score high on the Deep Processing, Elaborative Processing, and Fact Retention scales would seem to be what Pask (1976a, 1976b) has labeled "versatile learners." By the same token, those who score high on fact retention but low on deep processing would be operation learners in Pask's system, and those who score high on deep processing and low on fact retention would be comprehension learners. Of course, this should not be taken to imply that the dimensions of the two models are identical. Further research is needed to determine whether the learning-style measures derived in different laboratories are accounting for common or unique portions of the variance in learning outcomes.

The researchers discussed in the introduction to this chapter made no distinction between deep and elaborative processing. Marton's "deep-level processing," Entwistle's "understanding orientation," and Biggs' "internalizing dimension" all have the student placing emphasis on the meanings of symbols and not just on the symbols themselves. However, I maintain that one can establish meaning in two distinct ways, that is, by conceptually analyzing (deep processing) or by translating into personal experiences and images (elaborative processing).[2] Nevertheless, I have admitted (Schmeck, 1981) that, sometimes, there is value in summing scores on the Deep and Elaborative Processing scales. Such a combined score would serve as an indication of versatility on the part of the learner, and it would assess a continuum with "deep-elaborative learners" (those who "think" while they study) on one end and "shallow-reiterative learners" (those who rely on sheer repetition) on the other end.

The mention of shallow-reiterative learners brings me to another difference between my own model and the models of other researchers. Several of the models seem to suggest that shallow processing is a separate style comparable to memorization. These models seem to suggest that one can have a deep or shallow style. However, in my own conceptual framework, shallow processing is simply the low end of the depth-of-processing continuum. On the shallow end of the continuum, the student is processing the symbols used in the communication. As depth increases, the number of conceptual associations increases, giving the material more and more meaning. Everyone processes shallowly since it is only through shallow processing (attending to symbols) that one can get to deep processing (conceptual associations). Shallow processing is not a separate style, nor does it necessarily lead to retention of facts and details. In order to retain facts and details, one has to specifically *process* facts and details as indicated by high scores on the Fact Retention scale.

One can retain facts by processing deeply and attending to facts (i.e., having high scores on deep processing and fact retention) or by processing shallowly and attending to facts (i.e., having low scores on deep processing and high scores on fact retention). Schmeck and Grove (1979) found that the former student was more successful academically than the latter student. The latter student is the only one who could be said to be a memorizer in the traditional sense of retaining information verbatim with little understanding of meanings. Also, it should be noted that Table 2 shows a substantial *positive* relationship between the Deep Processing and Fact Retention scales. The person who is best at retaining facts and details is not a shallow processor. The best fact retainers tend to score high on *both* fact retention and

[2]Pask does not use the levels-of-processing concept in his theoretical analyses, but in some ways, his holist strategy is comparable to deep processing; he has described a type of holist (the "redundant holist") who does personalize information in a manner similar to the individual who scores high on the elaborative–processing scale.

deep processing. Some theorists (e.g., Morris, Bransford, & Franks, 1977) have argued that shallow processing is best when preparing for a low-level (e.g., fact retention) type of test. However, Schmeck and Spofford (Note 11) argue that deep processing is always better than shallow processing regardless of the test. Using a laboratory manipulation to vary depth of processing, Schmeck and Spofford (Note 11) reported that deep processing produced superior memory performance regardless of whether subjects were given shallow (rhyme) or deep (associate) retrieval cues during the test.[3]

The Methodical Study scale seems to assess the orientation labeled "achieving" by Entwistle and Biggs. Both these authors assume that high grades result from such an orientation to study. Indeed, Watkins and Hattie (1981a) found a significant positive relationship between scores on my Methodical Study scale and academic achievement with Australian students in liberal arts and economics. However, very little relationship between methodical study and achievement has been found with American students (Schmeck & Grove, 1979). The small relationship that we did find was negative. Also, Schmeck and Ribich (1978) found a negative relationship between critical thinking ability and methodical study; Mueller and Fisher (Note 5) reported a negative relationship between verbal ability and methodical study; Hudson (Note 6) observed a negative relationship between cognitive developmental level and methodical study; and Schmeck and Spofford (in press) found a small positive relationship between methodical study and dissimulation. We have just completed the collection of some data that indicate a negative relationship between Zuckerman's (1971) disinhibition subscale and methodical study. This suggests that students high on methodical study carefully avoid violating any social norms. The items on the scale do seem to be high on social desirability (in the sense that they mention skills that appear certain to improve memory at least on the surface). It may be that in the United States *some* of the students who subscribe to the activities listed in the Methodical Study scale are low on the abilities necessary to process deeply and are groping for a solution to their repeated academic failures by engaging in the activities listed in the scale or by pretending to engage in them. In this regard, Biggs (1979) reported that achieving students produced shallow-learning outcomes even when given

---

[3]Biggs (1978) studied the retention of details contained in meaningful discourse (rather than lists of words) and found that, if you give a meaningful (deep) task to someone who is prone to memorize, their memory for details is greatly decreased. Although this does not detract from my assumption that combining the styles of deep processing and fact retention improves recall for details, it does conflict with the findings of Schmeck and Spofford (Note 11) using word lists.

instructions that should have encouraged a deep approach to learning the material.

Abilities and development would, presumably, set limits on the range of learning strategies (and styles) that an individual can employ. It may be the case that abilities (including general intelligence) actually impact learning and memory *indirectly* by limiting learning strategies rather than by directly limiting storage capacity. Also, we need more research designed to determine the extent to which learning-style measures are independent of general abilities measures such as intelligence and more specific verbal and spatial abilities. The assumption at this point is that learning-style measures are not simply self-report measures of abilities. However, studies in this area should routinely include ability measures to test this assumption. Also, more of the studies in this area should include learning-outcome measures rather than simply examining the interrelationships among various self-report measures. In this regard, more research should provide an opportunity to observe attribute-by-treatment interactions (cf. Cronbach & Snow, 1977). In this manner, we may find that certain instructional procedures counteract the negative influence of certain styles or take advantage of the strengths of other styles.

An important question for future research concerns the extent to which learning styles affect writing in the same way they affect studying. If individuals process deeply when reading, do they also process deeply when writing? Is there a particular combination, or sequence, of strategies that is best for good composition? What learning styles are demonstrated by the most effective writers? Meier (1981) found that the Elaborative Processing scale was the only one that predicted creative writing performance. Lockhart and Schmeck (in press) found that deep processing predicted writing performance on a research paper that required use of theory to explain and predict data. Is this generally the case? While reading, I find that I am a comprehension learner using a holist strategy. However, in writing this chapter, I began as an operation learner using a serialist strategy. I added the higher-level (holist) conceptualizations in the process of reworking the original serialist product. I would like to know whether other writers demonstrate similar stylistic consistencies (cf. p. 99).

Also, it is my bias that we need more research concerned with the modifiability of learning style. This research, too, would have to take into account ability and developmental level. The studies that I have reported seem to agree on the very general conclusion that there is a positive relationship between the *amount* of thought given to an idea and the *probability* that the idea will be recalled, and there is a relationship between the *type* of thought and the *quality* of the recall. All thoughts are not created equal. Thoughts which lead to categorization and comparison of the chosen category with other potential categories are more likely to improve recall. Thoughts which translate ideas into personal terminology and operationally define it with personal experiences will, similarly, contribute more to recall. We need more attempts to develop training programs based on empirically derived learning-style measures. Pask has developed such a program and so has Reid (1981). The problem with such programs is that they are carried out at the college level; however, Schmeck and Grove (1979) concluded that learning style is already partially developed and affecting performance at the high-school level. Thus, we need to devise short-term interventions or routine instructional procedures that can be used to influence learning-style development *prior* to entrance into college.

REFERENCES

Battig, W. F. Are the important 'individual differences' between or within individuals? *Journal of Research in Personality*, 1979, *13*, 546–558.

Bem, S. L. The measurement of psychological androgyny. *Journal of Consulting and Clinical Psychology*, 1974, *42*, 155–162.

Bennett, G. K., Seashore, H. G., & Wesman, A. *Manual for the differential aptitude tests.* New York: Psychological Corporation, 1974.

Biggs, J. B. Faculty patterns in study behavior. *Australian Journal of Psychology*, 1970, *22*, 161–174.

Biggs, J. B. Dimensions of study behavior: Another look at ATI. *British Journal of Educational Psychology*, 1976, *46*, 68–80.

Biggs, J. B. Levels of processing, study processes, and factual recall. In M. M. Gruneberg, P. Morris, & R. Sykes *Practical Aspects of Memory*. London: Academic Press, 1978.

Biggs, J. Individual differences in study processes and the quality of learning outcomes. *Higher Education*, 1979, *8*, 381–394.

Biggs, J. B. Developmental processes and learning outcomes. In J. R. Kirby & J. B. Biggs (Eds) *Cognition, Development, and Instruction*. New York: Academic Press, 1980.

Biggs, J. B. Learning strategies, student motivation patterns, and subjectively perceived success. In J. Kirby (Ed) *Cognitive Strategies and Educational Performance*. New York: Academic Press, in press.

Bloom, B. S. *Taxonomy of educational objectives: Cognitive domain*. New York: McKay, 1956.

Bray, J. H., Maxwell, S. E., & Schmeck, R. R. A psychometric investigation of the survey of study habits and attitudes. *Applied Psychological Measurement*, 1980, *4*, 195–201.

Briggs, R. D., Tosi, D. J., & Morley, R. M. Study habit modification and its effect on academic performance: A behavioral approach. *Journal of Educational Research*, 1971, *64*, 347–350.

Brown, W. F., & Holtman, W. H. *Survey of study habits and attitudes*. New York: Psychological Corporation, 1967.

Brown, W. F., Nelson, M. J., & Denny, E. C. *Nelson-Denny reading test*. Boston: Houghton Mifflin, 1973.

Chickering, A. The double bind of field dependence/independence in program alternatives for educational development. In S. Messick (Ed.), *Individuality in Learning*. San Francisco: Jossey-Bass, 1976.

Cowell, M. D., & Entwistle, N. J. The relationship between personality, study attitudes, and academic performance in a technical college. *British Journal of Educational Psychology*, 1971, *41*, 85–90.

Craik, F. I. M., & Lockhart, R. S. Levels of processing: a framework for memory research. *Journal of Verbal Learning and Verbal Behavior*, 1972, *11*, 671–684.

Craik, F. I. M., & Tulving, E. Depth of processing and retention of words in episodic memory. *Journal of Experimental Psychology: General*, 1975, *104*, 268–294.

Cronbach, L. J., & Snow, R. E. *Aptitudes and instructional methods: A handbook for research on interactions.* New York: Halsted Press, 1977.

Cropley, A. J., & Field, T. W. Achievement in science and intellectual style. *Journal of Applied Psychology*, 1969, *53*, 132–135.

Dahlgren, L. O., & Marton, F. Students' conceptions of subject matter: An aspect of learning and teaching in higher education. *Studies in Higher Education*, 1978, *3*, 25–35.

Dansereau, D. F., Collins, K. W., McDonald, B. A., Holley, C. D., Garland, J., Diekhoff, G., & Evans, S. H. Development and evaluation of a learning strategy training program. *Journal of Educational Psychology*, 1979, *71*, 64–73.

Driskell, J. L., & Kelly, E. L. A guided notetaking and study skills system for use with university freshmen predicted to fail. *Journal of Reading*, 1980, *1*, 4–5.

Dunn, R., DeBello, T., Brennan, P., Krimsky, J., & Murrain, P. Learning style researchers define differences differently. *Educational Leadership*, February, 1981, pp. 372–374.

Dunn, R., & Dunn, K. *Teaching students through their individual learning styles: A practical approach.* Reston, Va.: Reston Publishing Division of Prentice-Hall, 1978.

Entwistle, N. *Styles of learning and teaching.* New York: Wiley, 1981.

Entwistle, N., Hanley, M., & Hounsell, D. J. Identifying distinctive approaches to studying. *Higher Education*, 1979, *8*, 365–380.

Entwistle, N., & Wilson, J. D. Personality, study methods and academic performance. *University Quarterly*, 1970, *24*, 147–156.

Evans, R., & Donnerstein, E. Some implications for psychological research of early versus late term participation by college subjects. *Journal of Research in Personality*, 1974, *8*, 102–109.

Eysenck, H. J. Personality and attainment: An application of psychological principles to educational objectives. *Higher Education*, 1972, *1*, 39–52.

Eysenck, H. J., & Cookson, D. Personality in primary school children. I. Ability and achievement. *British Journal of Educational Psychology*, 1969, *39*, 109–122.

Eysenck, H. J., & Eysenck, S. B. G. *Manual of the Eysenck personality inventory.* London: University of London Press, 1964.

Eysenck, M. W. Levels of processing: A critique. *British Journal of Psychology*, 1978, *69*, 157–169.

Fisher, R. P., & Craik, F. I. M. Interaction between encoding and retrieval operations in cued recall. *Journal of Experimental Psychology: Human Learning and Memory*, 1977, *3*, 701–711.

Flavell, J. H., & Wellman, H. H. Metamemory. In R. V. Kail, Jr., & J. W. Hagen (Eds.), *Perspectives on the development of memory and cognition.* Hillsdale, N.J.: Lawrence Erlbaum Associates, 1977.

Fransson, A. On qualitative differences in learning. IV. Effects of motivation and test anxiety on process and outcome. *British Journal of Educational Psychology*, 1977, *47*, 244–257.

Goldman, R., Hudson, D. J. A multivariate analysis of academic abilities and strategies for successful and unsuccessful college students in different major fields. *Journal of Educational Psychology*, 1973, *65*, 364–370.

Goldman, R., & Warren, R. Discriminant analysis of study strategies connected with college grade success in different major fields. *Journal of Educational Measures*, 1973, *10*, 39–47.

Gregorc, A. F. Learning/teaching styles: Their nature and effects. In J. W. Keefe (Ed.), *Student learning styles: Diagnosing and prescribing programs*. Reston, Va.: national Association of Secondary School Principals, 1979.

Harcourt, Brace, Jovanovich. *Manual for the Iowa test of silent reading*. New York: Harcourt, Brace, Jovanovich, 1973.

Haslam, W. L., & Brown, W. F. Effectiveness of study skills instruction for high school sophomores. *Journal of Educational Psychology*, 1968, *59*, 223–226.

Hill, J. *Personalized education programs utilizing cognitive style mapping*. Bloomfield Hills, Mich.: Oakland Community College, 1971.

Holley, C. D., Dansereau, D. F., McDonald, B. A., Garland, J. C., & Collins, K. W. Evaluations of a hierarchical mapping technique as an aid to prose processing. *Contemporary Educational Psychology*, 1979, *4*, 227–237.

Hunt, D. Learning style and student needs: An introduction to conceptual level. In J. W. Keefe (Ed.), *Student learning styles: Diagnosing and prescribing programs*. Reston, Va.: National Association of Secondary School Principals, 1979.

Jennrich, R., & Sampson, P. Analysis of variance and covariance including repeated measures. In M. B. Brown (Ed.), *Biomedical computer programs*. Berkeley: University of California Press, 1977.

Keefe, J. W. (Ed.). *Student learning styles: Diagnosing and prescribing programs*. Reston, Va.: National Association of Secondary School Principals, 1979.

Kogan, N. *Cognitive styles in infancy and early childhood*. Hillsdale, N.J.: Lawrence Erlbaum Associates, 1976.

Kolb, D. A. *Individual learning styles and the learning process*. Cambridge, Mass.: MIT Press, 1971. (Sloan Working Paper No. 535-71)

Kolb, D. A. On management and the learning process. In D. A. Kolb, I. M. Rubin, & J. M. McIntyre (Eds.), *Organizational psychology: A book of readings*. Englewood Cliffs, N.J.: Prentice-Hall, 1974.

Kolb, D. A. Disciplinary inquiry norms and student learning styles: Diverse pathways for growth. In A. Chickering (Ed.), *The modern American college*. San Francisco: Jossey-Bass, 1981.

Labouvie-Vief, G. Adult cognitive development: In search of alternative interpretations. *Merrill-Palmer Quarterly*, 1977, *23*, 227–263.

Labouvie-Vief, G. Individual time, social time, and intellectual aging. In T. K. Hareven (Ed.), *Life course transition in interdisciplinary and cross-cultural perspectives*. New York: Guilford Press, in press.

Laurillard, D. The processes of student learning. *Higher Education*, 1979, *8*, 395–409.

Lewis, B. N. Avoidance of aptitude-treatment trivialities. In S. Messick (Ed.), *Individuality in Learning*. San Francisco: Jossey-Bass, 1976.

Lockhart, R. S., & Craik, F. I. M. Levels of processing: A reply to Eysenck. *British Journal of Psychology*, 1978, 69, 171–175.

Lockhart, D., & Schmeck, R. R. Learning styles and classroom evaluation methods: Different strokes for different folks. *College Student Journal*, in press.

Marton, F., & Säljö, R. On qualitative differences in learning. I. Outcome and processes. *British Journal of Educational Psychology*, 1976, *46*, 4–11. (a)

Marton, F., & Säljö, R. On qualitative differences in learning. II. Outcome as a function of the learner's conception of the task. *British Journal of Educational Psychology*, 1976, *46*, 115–127. (b)

Mednick, S. A. The associative basis of the creative process. *Psychological Review*, 1962, *69*, 220–232.

Mednick, S. A. *The remote associates test*. Boston: Houghton Mifflin, 1967.

Meier, S. *Self-efficacy theory and students' writing performance.* Master's thesis, Southern Illinois University at Carbondale, 1981.

Meier, S., McCarthy, P., & Schmeck, R. R. Validity of self-efficacy as a predictor of writing performance. *Cognitive Therapy and Research* (in press).

Messick, S. Personality consistencies in cognition and creativity. In S. Messick (Ed.), *Individuality in learning.* San Francisco: Jossey-Bass, 1976.

Meyer, B. J. F. *The organization of prose and its effects on memory.* Amsterdam: North-Holland Publishing Co., 1975.

Morris, C. D., Bransford, J. D., & Franks, J. J. Levels of processing versus transfer appropriate processing. *Journal of Verbal Learning and Verbal Behavior,* 1977, *16,* 519–533.

Moss, C. Academic achievement and individual differences in the learning processes of basic skills students in the university. *Applied Psychological Measurement,* 1982, *6,* 291–296.

Mueller, J. H., & Fisher, D. M. Field independence and input grouping in free recall. *Bulletin of the Psychonomic Society,* 1980, *16,* 397–400.

Neimark, E. D. Longitudinal development of formal operational thought. *Genetic Psychology Monographs,* 1975, *91,* 171–225.

Ornstein, R. E. *The psychology of consciousness* (2nd ed.). New York: Harcourt, Brace, Jovanovich, 1977.

Otis, A. S., & Lennon, R. T. *Otis-Lennon mental ability test and manual for administration: Advance level, Form J.* New York: Psychological Corporation, 1968.

Parlett, M. R. The syllabus-bound student. In L. Hudson (Ed.), *The ecology of human intelligence.* Harmondsworth, England: Penguin Books, 1970.

Pask, G. Conversational techniques in the study and practice of education. *British Journal of Educational Psychology,* 1976, *45,* 12–25. (a)

Pask, G. Styles and strategies of learning. *British Journal of Educational Psychology,* 1976, *46,* 128–148. (b)

Pask, G., & Scott, B. C. E. Learning strategies and individual competence. *International Journal of Man-Machine Studies,* 1972, *4,* 217–253.

Perry, W. F. *Forms of intellectual and ethical development in the college years: A scheme.* New York: Holt, Rinehart, & Winston, 1970.

Piaget, J. *The origins of intelligence in children.* New York: Norton, 1963.

Ramsden, P. Student learning and perceptions of the academic environment. *Higher Education,* 1979, *8,* 411–427.

Reid, E. *Training Higher-Level Cognitive Skills.* Unpublished doctoral dissertation, Southern Illinois University, Carbondale, 1981.

Ribich, F. D. *Memory for a lecture: Effects of an advance organizer and levels of processing on semantic and episodic memory.* Unpublished doctoral dissertation, Southern Illinois University, Carbondale, 1977.

Ribich, F. D., & Schmeck, R. R. Multivariate relationships between measures of learning style and memory. *Journal of Research in Personality,* 1979, *13,* 515–529.

Robinson, F. P. *Effective study.* New York: Harper, 1946.

Schmeck, R. R. Relationships between measures of learning style and reading comprehension. *Perceptual and Motor Skills,* 1980, *50,* 461–462.

Schmeck, R. R. Improving learning by improving thinking. *Educational Leadership,* February 1981, pp. 384–385.

Schmeck, R. R., & Grove, E. Academic achievement and individual differences in learning processes. *Applied Psychological Measurement,* 1979, *3,* 43–49.

Schmeck, R. R., & Phillips, J. Levels of processing as a dimension of difference between individuals. *Human Learning,* 1982, *1,* 95–103.

Schmeck, R. R., & Ribich, F. D. Construct validation of the inventory of learning processes. *Applied Psychological Measurement*, 1978, *2*, 551–562.

Schmeck, R. R., Ribich, F. D., & Ramanaiah, N. Development of a self-report inventory for assessing individual differences in learning processes. *Applied Psychological Measurement*, 1977, *1*, 413–431.

Schmeck, R. R., & Spofford, M. Attention to semantic versus phonetic verbal attributes as a function of individual differences in arousal and learning strategy. *Contemporary Educational Psychology*, in press.

Schwartz, S. Individual differences in cognition: some relationships between personality and memory. *Journal of Research in Personality*, 1975, *9*, 217–225.

Svensson, L. On qualitative differences in learning. III. Study skill and learning. *British Journal of Educational Psychology*, 1977, *47*, 233–243.

Tallmadge, G. K., & Shearer, J. W. Relationships among learning styles, instructional methods, and the nature of learning experiences. *Journal of Educational Psychology*, 1969, *60*, 222–230.

Tallmadge, G. K., & Shearer, J. W. Interactive relationships among learner characteristics, types of learning, instructional methods and subject matter variables. *Journal of Educational Psychology*, 1971, *62*, 31–38.

Toglia, M. P., & Battig, W. F. *Handbook of semantic word norms*. Hillsdale, N.J.: Lawrence Erlbaum Associates, 1978.

Tulving, E., & Thomson, D. M. Encoding specificity and retrieval processes in episodic memory. *Psychological Review*, 1973, *80*, 352–373.

Underwood, B. J. Individual differences as a crucible in theory construction. *American Psychologist*, 1975, *30*, 128–134.

Van Zoost, B. L., & Jackson, B. T. Effect of self-monitoring and self-administered reinforcement on study behaviors. *Journal of Educational Research*, 1974, *67*, 216–218.

Vu, V. N. *Piaget's formal operations and the acquisition of the probability and correlation concepts of graduate students*. Unpublished doctoral dissertation, Southern Illinois University, Carbondale, 1977.

Watkins, D., & Hattie, J. The internal structure and predictive validity of the inventory of learning processes: Some Australian and Filipino data. *Educational and Psychological Measurement*, 1981, *41*, 511–514. (a)

Watkins, D., & Hattie, J. The learning processes of Australian university students: Investigations of contextual and personological factors. *British Journal of Educational Psychology*, 1981, *51*, 384–393. (b)

Watson, G., & Glaser, E. M. *Watson-Glaser critical thinking appraisal manual*. New York: Harcourt, Brace, & World, 1964.

Weinstein, C. E. *Learning of Elaboration Strategies*. Unpublished doctoral dissertation, University of Texas at Austin, 1975.

Weinstein, C. E. Training students to use elaboration learning strategies. *Contemporary Education*, in press.

Weinstein, C. E., Underwood, V. L., Wicker, F. W., & Cubberly, W. E. Cognitive learning strategies: Verbal and imaginal elaboration. In H. F. O'Neil & C. D. Speilberger (Eds.), *Cognitive and affective learning strategies*. New York: Academic Press, 1979.

Whitehill, R. P. The development of effective learning skills programs. *Journal of Educational Research*, 1972, *65*, 281–285.

Wittrock, M. C. Learning as a generative process. *Education Psychologist*, 1974, *11*, 87–95.

Wonderlic, E. F. *Wonderlic personnel test manual*. Northfield, Ill.: E. F. Wonderlic, P. O. Box 7, 1961.

Zuckerman, M. Dimensions of sensation seeking. *Journal of Consulting and Clinical Psychology*, 1971, *36*, 45–52.

NOTES

1. Watkins, D. Personal communication, April 16, 1982.

2. Snowman, J., Krebs, E. W., & Kelly, F. J. *Enhancing memory for prose through learning strategy training*. Paper presented at the annual meeting of the American Educational Research Association, Boston, March 1980.

3. Letteri, C. A. *Cognitive profile*. Paper presented at the major conference on student learning styles and brain behavior, New Orleans, 1981.

4. Tracy, K., Schmeck, R. R., & Spofford, M. *Determiners of vocational interest: Sex, spatial-verbal abilities, and information processing style*. Paper presented at the Midwestern Psychological Association Convention, St. Louis, 1980.

5. Mueller, J. H., & Fisher, D. M. Personal communication, January 10, 1980.

6. Hudson, T. Personal communication. April 24, 1982.

7. McDaniel, E. *Cognitive preference and student performance*. Paper presented at the American Psychological Association Convention, Washington, D.C., 1982.

8. Watkins, D., Hattie, J., & Astilla, E. *Learning processes and academic achievement: A Filipino investigation*. Unpublished manuscript, Australian National University, 1982.

9. Weinbaum, J. Personal communication, January 7, 1982.

10. Malin, J. T., & Malin, D. H. *Text comprehension and study skills: Final report*. Unpublished manuscript, University of Houston, 1976.

11. Schmeck, R. R., & Spofford, M. *Levels of processing and encoding specificity: Does processing depth make a significant independent contribution to recall performance?* Paper presented at the Midwestern Psychological Association, Minneapolis, 1982.

9

Individual Differences in Children's Play: Selected Theoretical Analyses*

Thomas D. Yawkey

INTRODUCTION

Play is defined as the cognitive ability of children to change themselves and things about them into other individuals, objects, or events as observed through their motoric and/or verbal actions and activities (Curry & Arnaud, 1974; J. L. Singer, 1973). This change or cognitive transformation has been of interest from historical, contemporary, and more recently, from individual differences perspectives.

The long tradition and current history of interest in child's play provide a background for viewing and understanding it. However, psychological research on individual differences in areas such as child's cognitive play is a fairly new phenomenon (Carroll, 1978; pp. 1–106; Rubin, Fein & Vandenberg, in press). That is, psychological differences in child's play have been of some direct, but largely marginal, interest to researchers. Accordingly, the following discussion in child's play focuses exclusively on those selected research studies which are limited to the examination of individual differences in child's play. The focus and results of these research studies are

*The author's research and writing on constructivist play, cognition, and communication in young children is supported, in part, by grants from the United States Department of Education, Margaret M. Patton and Spencer Foundations, and the Research and Development Division of The Economy Company Educational Publishers, Inc. He gratefully acknowledges and appreciates their support and assistance. The ideas expressed are those of the author and not of the funding agencies.

grouped for purposes of discussion into the following sections: (1) sex differences; (2) playfulness and imaginativeness; (3) symbolic play styles; and (4) handicapped differences. First, however, selected early and contemporary theories of child's play are described to provide a foundation for understanding selected roots of individual-differences research in child's play.

EARLY AND CONTEMPORARY THEORIES OF CHILD'S PLAY

The early theories of child's play, for example, surplus energy (Schiller, 1954; Spencer, 1873), recapitulation (Hall, 1921), and the more contemporary—ludic theory (Piaget, 1962)—rest on the nature of organisms, their evolution from immaturity to maturity, and the role of play in this developmental continuum. Individual differences from the early mainstreams of thought on play are not exclusively considered or studied. The emphasis is on global play processes and patterns of same-stage and same-age. The ludic theory developed by Piaget (1964) to describe and account for the child's growth of symbolic play—generally viewed in stage and age relationships (Flavell, 1963)—can and has generated considerable information in the empirical study of play and the phenemonon of individual differences.

As a backdrop, the first of the early theories of child's play is the surplus-energy theory. Developed by Spencer (1873) and Schiller (1954), it characterizes child's play as nothing more than a "release" of pent-up energies. Throughout his writings, Schiller's primary interests were aesthetics and aesthetic education. Mature humans and animals, Schiller writes, are driven to work by their primary need or "formal" impulses. Formal impulses are characterized by physical necessity, reason, and objective thought. Another set, called "material impulses," are associated with man's sensuous nature and are characterized by subjective and egocentric thought. Schiller writes that these two impulses are in constant imbalance, with the result that the human organism is controlled by one impulse, and in alternative fashion, by the other. Sometimes, these two impulses are in equilibrium. Man's formal impulses are used primarily in his day-to-day struggle for survival—that is, obtaining food, shelter, and clothing. When these primary needs are realized, the remaining residual or superfluous energy can become the fuel for material impulses, and this surplus of energy can be worked off.

Of particular interest is Spencer and Schiller's distinction between formal and material impulses and their relationships to varying forms of play. Formal impulses, according to theory, gave rise to aesthetic play. This form of play showed man's attainable balance between matter and form and between sensuousness and reason. Spencer and Schiller felt that through aesthetic play, human organisms are made complete and imagination develops and becomes "unbounded." For Spencer and Schiller, aesthetic play ultimately resulted in dramatic and/or sociodramatic play. The human organism in dramatic and sociodramatic play transcends reality and develops new aesthetic appreciations or symbolic actions and activities. Rubin, Fein & Vandenberg (in press) feel that the roots of symbolic or make-believe representation as cognition are embedded in Spencer–Schiller's concept of aesthetic play. In turn, this view is currently seen in contemporary "play" theorists, such as Piaget (1962) and J. L. Singer (1973).

Material impulses, the second kind of impulse innate in human organisms, according to theory, lead to physical play. The surplus energy remaining after the human organism has struggled for survival is worked off through physical play. The human organisms in physical play have specific ends which result in immediate gratification and fulfillment. This particular view of working off residual energy through physical play reappears according to Rubin et al. (in press) as sensorimotor play in writings of Piaget, Singer, and others.

Initially, Spencer and Schiller's surplus energy theory identified play as an important set of actions and activities, especially noting the value of aesthetic or symbolic play to individuals and society. Second, this early theory of child's play explained and described different forms of play. Both the value and the varying forms of play provide a foundation for selected contemporary theories of cognitive play as well as for the phenomenon of individual differences.

The second early theory of play selected for discussion was developed by Hall (1921) and called the recapitulation theory of play. Similar to Spencer and Schiller, Hall also based this theory on instincts. Hall's emphasis theory was placed on hereditary factors—which he elaborated at great length. This theorizing went far beyond those of Spencer and Schiller in the nature of and need for child's play. Suggesting the simultaneous importance of the contributions of both heredity and instinct, Hall (1906) notes that every affective mood and physical movement used in play is instinct with heredity (Hall, 1906). Recapitulation theory is based on the assumption that skills learned culturally by one generation can be inherited by the next (Millar, 1968). Defining play in terms of biological inheritance, Hall (1921) explains that play exists as motor patterns and spirits of the biological and historical pasts of the race that persist into the present through rudimentary functions resembling rudimentary organs.

In child's play, Hall (1906) sees the activities of past generations exhibited and transmitted by heredity through a stage-by-stage reenactment in the lives of human organisms. Hall's stages are actually sequences in the child's play that are similar to and parallel with the growth and development of ancestral activities. The child progresses through these stages and recapitulates the historical evolution of the human race. Accordingly, those activities characteristic of the extreme or most distant past of human evolution are the same ones which the child reenacted in the very first stages of play. In sequences and through the child's play, later evolutionary advances in ancestral development followed. In addition, the adult activities of past generations could be most clearly seen in the spontaneous, instinctive play of the very young child. The make-believe content of the children's play activities in each of the stages conform to these sequences and are derived from ancestral patterns of evolution.

According to theory, play united body and soul. Since this was an ultimate and much desired state, play had become immensely important. Hall views play as the best of activities for children, youth, and adults because it enhances both their bodies and their minds. In addition, it provides for development and growth, a specific yet all-encompassing provision. For example, play is purported to provide strength, courage, and confidence to children. In addition, play helps human beings simplify life habits and provides them with physical energy. Hall also noted that play brought out individual characteristics in human organisms.

Interestingly, the pleasure the child finds in and through play was always in direct relationship to the intensity of the hereditary factors exhibited. Those activities that are most necessary for the survival of the race in past generations would then, logically, be the most enjoyable in child's play. Some ancient or past activities in child's play were little in evidence— some appeared imperceptibly; other activities became extinct. Those activities needed for survival, although basically useless in contemporary society, still require expression for the complete development of the human organism to occur. Furthermore, children found some activities more enjoyable and pleasant than others because they were the ones most necessary for the growth of the race. For instance, Hall (1906), in observing a child performing and enjoying a fishing activity, noted that this play transposition is characteristic of the time when man's food source was supplied by fishing. Also, Hall felt that child's play helped socialization because it provided for releases of those nonprimitive and primitive activities which, conceivably, could be detrimental to individuals in an adult society. He thought that those hereditary tendencies which were most freely exhibited and expressed in childhood would, by their expression during that period, become weakened and would not be exemplified strongly in later life. For example, if the youngster repeatedly and strongly demonstrates a "fighting" instinct, then he would, in later life, not show this fighting trait to such a great degree (Mitchell & Mason, 1934). Here, Hall writes that play purges the child of unpleasant instincts and actions in childhood which, in maturity, could be shown in ways inappropriate.

Recapitulation essentially emphasizes the serious nature of play; children work very hard at their play to points of physical and mental exhaustion. However, Hall cautions strongly against distinguishing between work and play in childhood. He notes that children often complete work in form of play because of their instinctual interests. Conceivably, work could become enjoyable if there were an interest or element of imagination involved within it. For Hall, the differences between work and play are actually functions of the quantity and quality of "psychophysic" motivations used by the child at play.

Recapitulation made several significant contributions to more contemporary theories of play and to explanations of the individual differences involved. First, play is valued for the contributions it can make to emerging areas of the child's growth and development. Several of the specific growth areas contributed by recapitulation, as play, are imagination, creativity, and other forms of aesthetic appreciation. Rubin, et al. (in press) feel that regardless of empirical and theoretical limitations of Hall's recapitulation theory, it has made an impact on contemporary theories of play as developed by Lieberman (1977) and J. L. Singer (1973). Second, child's play as recapitulation provided an age and stage element to theorizing about these activities.

In sum, Hall's recapitulation theory, like Spencer–Schiller's surplus-energy model, described play as a fundamentally important and valued set of actions and activities. The impact of Hall's recapitulation theory is especially significant from the perspective of Lieberman (1977) relative to individual differences in creativity and imagination which is discussed in a later section.

Developed within the twentieth century, the ludic theory of play, developed by Piaget (1962), is more contemporary than the two former theories of play. In addition, his theory of cognitive development fueled a great amount of the research on individual differences. In similar fashion, the breadth and depth of Piaget's theory of ludic play provides substantive foundations for research on individual differences. The process of play for Piaget emphasizes its significance and relationships to cognitive growth. This aspect of human behavior is viewed as "instrumental" in explaining the organization of experience rather than as inherited biological tendencies.

Piaget (1962) adopts a broad view of play not confined to the previous early theories of play. In distinguishing ludic from nonludic activities, play is not a specific behavior or all-encompassing set of behaviors. Rather, ludic play becomes a polarity of (and for) thought. Each behavior is characterized by its proximity to the pole; whether the polarized behaviors are in equilibrium is fundamental to ludic theory.

The two kinds of behavior possible for a human organism with a developing intellectual capacity are assimilation and accommodation. According to Piagetian theory, assimilation is the process of taking in all forms of information and stimulation from the environment. Assimilation also implies categorizing and utilizing this information in accord with understood or known patterns of behavior. Accommodation is the process of recognizing new aspects of the environment and arranging conditions in it. It also implies adjusting existing mental structures to this new reality. These two twin behaviors are present in play activities. Play is the domination of assimilation. Essentially, play through assimilation distorts reality to fit existing cognitive structures. Logical aspects of stimuli are ignored and others are favored. Still other aspects are altered to conform to the immature schemata of the developing individual.

Assimilation and accommodation are in relative equilibrium with respect to the young child's physical motor actions; they are in imbalance in regard to ludic, representational, or symbolic actions. The imbalance of the two processes and the dominance of assimilation over accommodation leads to play—a purely functional flow of stimuli which the organism adapts to self, relative to the degree of imbalance between reality and self. Accordingly, the assimilative quality or tonality of an activity is the basic criterion used in determining whether it is ludic or nonludic behavior (Flavell, 1963).

Like the development of intelligence or intellect, Piaget divides the growth of ludic, symbolic or make-believe play into stages. Piaget sees three main stages and one transitional level which span the age ranges of birth through maturity. They are (1) practice play; (2) symbolic play; (3) games with rules; and (4) constructional and creative transitional play.

Practice play is the repetition of a movement that the child has performed before. It has no meaning and the only purpose it serves is to allow the child to refine this movement. An example of practice play may be a young child interacting with a mobile over the crib. The child unknowingly moves his arm in such a way that it strikes the mobile. The sudden movement of the mobile startles the child and attracts his attention. The child repeats the previous action and strikes the mobile again. Practice play begins when the child strikes the mobile over and over again. Since practice play is simple repetition, no new information is gained. Accordingly, practice play does not modify thinking structures. The main result of practice play is the pleasure the child receives from performing the movements. Practice play ends when a child first pretends, for example, to eat a block and calls it an orange. The child is now participating in symbolic play.

Symbolic play evolves from practice play once a symbol having been developed is reproduced by the child through action. At the most primitive level, children practice motoric skills used in daily living such as "sleeping," "eating," "washing," and so forth. But they practice sleeping without a pillow, eating without food, or washing without a bar of soap. Here, none of these objects are present; therefore, the play is symbolic.

According to theory, there are a number of cognitive characteristics basic to "true" ludic play. Several of these include (1) projection of symbolic schemata onto new objects; (2) projection of imitative schemata onto new objects; (3) simple identification of one object with another, (4) simple combinations; and (5) liquidating combinations, and others. First, in "projection of symbolic schemata onto new objects," the child uses a familiar action but applies it to a new object such as a doll. Here, the doll "sleeps" or "washes." The child, by using his own actions with other objects, has dissociated the ludic symbol from the level of sensorimotor actions and related it to other objects as independent representations of the concept.

Second, in "projection of imitative schemata onto new objects," the symbolic schemata originate with models which the child imitates. Essentially, the symbolic schemata, acquired by imitation, are neither a part of nor do they arise from the child's own involvement activities; rather, they stem from activities of others, which the child witnesses and imitates. Illustrations of symbolic play with this second characteristic include a child imitating other people in the family telephoning, reading the newspaper, washing dishes, or shaving. The "symbol" here is the mother, father, or grandparent, or other family member. The example is still considered play (accommodation predominating over assimilation) because the child uses familiar objects as "symbolizers" such as toy telephone, picture book, toy dishes, or plastic razor. However, the child does not imitate the model directly because he employs movements in conjunction with objects.

The third characteristic, "simple identification of one object with another," is one of a series focusing on games of imitation and complete dissociation of the symbolizer from the symbolized. Here, the child merely imitates his own familiar actions with new objects; the identification of one object with another is inseparable from his actions which gave rise to it. With "simple identification of one object with another," symbolic identification precedes the imitative action and becomes dissociated from the child's own activity. An example of "simple identification with other objects" is the child who begins stroking his mother's hair and then says the name for the family cat, "Poco," "Poco." Symbolic identification of the mother's hair with the cat's fur, for example, spontaneously occurred and preceded the imitative actions of "stroking."

The fourth and fifth examples of cognitive characteristics of ludic play are more complex symbols, for they have developed into varieties of combinations Piaget calls "symbolic combinations." Accordingly, the fourth characteristic is called the "simple combinations" in which the ludic symbol takes on greater and greater complexity and depth. The child's symbolic play showing simple combinations involves construction of whole play episodes in contrast to isolated imitations or simple assimilations. A more advanced form of simple combinations is when a child builds, connects, and interrelates cycles of play episodes to form whole scenes which are related to other scenes.

The fifth characteristic is "liquidating combinations," wherein the child is faced with difficult or unpleasant situations that he refuses to accept. Instead, he symbolically transposes situations which become dissociated from their unpleasant contexts and incorporated into other ongoing activities. For example, pretending to be a doctor in symbolic play is a much safer way of reenacting an unpleasant episode faced in the hospital or doctor's office.

As the child develops and shows ludic characteristics from "projection of symbolic schemata onto new objects" through liquidating combinations, pretend play begins to diminish in quality and quantity. The ludic symbol, having evolved through the developmental continuua shows greater and greater adaptations to reality. According to Piaget, ludic play has lost much of its distorting symbolic character and begins to approximate reality. Here, the ludic play shows some additional cognitive characteristics of orderliness, exact imitation of reality, and collective symbolism. According to theory, orderliness refers to symbolic play episodes that show greater order, more logical sequence, and display more coherence than previous play transpositions. With exact imitation of reality, the child shows increasing concern and desire for verisimilitude in symbolic play. The cognitive characteristic of collective symbolism is shown in symbolic play transpositions as the children in a group setting decide, divide up, and adapt their roles and actions to present and ongoing cues of individual players.

According to Piaget's theory of ludic play, Stage 3, "game with rules" begins on the average at 7 or 8 years of age through 11–12 and continues to increase in quantity and quality or level of sophistication—both absolutely and relatively with age. Rules of the game are rules of socialized groups. As such, they involve the cognitive characteristics of socialization, regularity, self-discipline, codes of honor, and sanctions against players who violate the rules. The characteristic of socialization, according to theory, means game structure based on two or more same-age children. Regularity implies the players developing, coming to know and practicing the rules of their game.

Self-discipline requires the player to subordinate his or her individual and personal impulses and behaviors to the collective actions permitted by the rules of the game through the social peer group. Finally, both codes of honor and sanctions are those behaviors (and rules of behavior) that are considered respectable and those viewed as disreputable (with penalties for transgressing them imposed by peer group members). These characteristics of the rule-governed game arise from social groups through collective discipline and efforts of same-age children.

The transitional level or phase in the ludic play theory is labeled by Piaget "creative and constructional play." It indicates development from internal transformations of symbolic representation to adapted representation. As such, it occupies a position halfway between the poles of assimilation and accommodation or what Piaget calls play and "intelligent" work. It can occur at any stage of ludic play. The transition from play to intelligent work, for example, implies greater use of adaptive thought processes to perceive means–ends relationships than the transition from intelligent work to play. In the case of the former, ludic play to some extent becomes constructional; in the case of the latter, it becomes more personal and ideopathic.

The theory of ludic play as formulated and tested by Piaget has generated many research studies on cognitive and social developmental changes within and across these stages and in the various forms of play (Rubin et al., in press). Rubin et al. (in press) note that Piaget's view of ludic play provides a remarkably coherent description and analysis of symbol making relative to play.

In sum, Piaget's ludic theory of play illustrates several fundamental approaches to symbolic play which have provided rich foundations for continued research in this area. First, it has spawned research on the relationships between play as assimilative functions and more mature expressions of cognition as per practice, symbolic, and rule-governed games (Rubin et al., in press). Second, it has spurred investigations of representational forms and their development from the child's onset of symbolization (Rubin et al., in press). Third, Piaget's theory of ludic play has aided in the study of individual differences in cognition and symbolic play. Relative to the latter phenomena, Piaget's theory of ludic play has aided investigators interested in observing, identifying, and describing individual differences in child's play and then explaining the sources and causes of these variations.

In the following sections, selected research studies that directly focus on and examine selected dimensions of individual differences relative to child's play are explained. The basic dimensions and limits of individual differences are described relative, to the research populations, procedures, and analyses used in the studies. These sections are discussed in consecutive order: (1) sex differences; (2) playfulness and imaginativeness; (2) symbolic play styles; and (4) handicapped differences (Rubin et al., in press).

SEX DIFFERENCES

Although sex differences are group rather than individual differences, the findings in this area are enlightening. Of the selected studies on sex differences and child's play, the majority focused on examining play-object preferences at varying ages. Another group of studies examined sex differences and child's play in infants and toddlers. The third and final group of two investigations studied cross-setting generalities and solitary play of young children.

The results of the individual studies within the first group follow. The initial study was conducted by Benjamin (1932). With 100 participants, 50 boys and 50 girls—ranging in age from 2 to 6 years—the study examined toy preferences. The children were tested individually in their homes with their parent(s) but no siblings present. Procedurally, each child was asked to play with a set of toys. The six selections were a car, an airplane, a cowboy figure, powder (in a cylindrical vanity case), and boy figure, and a girl figure. Presented consistently in a row, the amount of time used by the child in playing with each of the toys and their preferences were recorded. The mean time across these procedures was 30 minutes per participant. In determining statistical differences between choices of boys and girls, the results show that a significantly greater number of boys than girls preferred to play with the car, and a significantly greater number of girls than boys choose to use the girl and boy figures. There were no differences between boys and girls on their preferences for the airplane, cowboy, and powder toys. Boys spent more time than girls playing with the car; girls spent significantly more time than boys playing with the boy and girl figures. There was no significant relationship between the number of siblings and choice of toys or between age "decidedness" (i.e., the length of time playing with one toy longest and selecting it as the choice) and choices.

The next study was conducted by Farrell (1957) and examined sex differences in choices of blocks as play materials. The sample consisted of 376 children, 187 boys and 189 girls. They ranged in age from 4½ to 7½ years. Procedurally, the children were located in the 13-year-old or grade-level groups. The groups self-selected whether to play with blocks when given the opportunity in inside play sessions. A behavioral questionnaire was developed and trained observers recorded responses to such questions as: the number of boys and girls playing with blocks, the length of time they played with them, and so on. Ninety-two observations were recorded. The percentage of boys and girls who played with blocks and the percentage of time at block play was determined. At the .01 level of confidence, the results of the analyses showed that (1) a significantly greater number of boys (24%) than girls (5%) played witb blocks; and (2) significantly more time was used in block play by boys (99%) than girls (55%).

The third study in this group was conducted by Goldberg and Lewis (1969). The study examined the existence of sex differences in children's behavior toward toys, mother, and a frustration episode at 13 months of age. Sixty-four infants, in two samples of 16 girls and 16 boys each, were observed individually with their mothers in a standard free-play situation. Procedurally, the infant was placed by the mother in an observation room and observed in a free-play situation with nine simple toys: a set of blocks, a pail, a stuffed dog, an inflated plastic cat, a "lawnmower," a set of quoits, a wooden mallet, a pegboard, and a wooden pull bug. The infant's behavior was recorded by dictation during the 15-minute session; an event recorder documented the location of the child and the duration of each contact with the mother who remained seated in one corner of the room.

Results indicated that (1) for responses to mother, girls showed significantly greater dependence, more crying, and more requests to mother for help on the barrier-frustration task, and less exploratory behavior than boys; (2) for toy preferences, there were no significant sex differences in overall toy preferences; (3) for individual toy preferences, girls spend significantly more time than boys playing with blocks, pegboard, and the dog and cat; and girls chose significantly more toys that required gross motor movements; (4) boys spend significantly more time than girls playing with nontoys (e.g., doorknobs, covered outlets); and (5) girls spend significantly more time sitting and playing with combinations of toys than boys, whereas boys evidenced significantly more movement and made a greater number of banging noises than girls.

The fourth study was conducted by Fein, Johnson, Kosson, Stork, and Wasserman (1975). The study explored infants' toy preferences at 20 months, whether these preferences show cross-sex asymmetry, whether toy preferences could be changed in a specific modeling situation, and whether an infant's familiarity with toys is related to his or her toy preferences. Twenty-four first-born children, 11 boys and 13 girls, were enrolled in the study. The children were individually observed in a free-play session in their homes with mothers present. Procedurally, the youngster played with six toys, each rated as "male" or "female" toys by college students.

The set was composed of three "male" toys (i.e., hammer, truck, gun) and three "female" toys (i.e., bead bracelet, iron, doll). Each infant played with the objects for 5 minutes and the number of 10-second toy-contact intervals was recorded. A 10-second adult-toy modeling session followed, and the infant was given 1 more minute to play with each toy.

Using a 2 × 2 analysis of variance (ANOVA) with repeated measures on sex of toy–contact scores, the results indicated that (1) boys played with boy toys more than girls did; (2) girls played with girl toys more than boys did; (3) boys and girls played more with girl than boy toys; (4) girls touched and contacted girl toys more than boy toys, but for boys, toy preferences were not significant; and (5) girls spent a greater amount of time at play with the bracelet and doll and boys spent a greater quantity of time with the hammer than with all other toys. In addition, a 2 × 2 ANOVA on the total number of imitations showed that: (1) girls imitated more with girl than boy toys; and (2) boys modeled more with girl than boy toys. And mothers' responses showed that their identification of the kinds of toys owned matched the toy preferences of their children.

The fifth study (Harper & Sanders, 1975) explored the use of space and sex differences in outdoor play. Over a 2-year period, two different groups of 16 girls each, and 16 and 17 boys, respectively, were observed. They ranged in age from 3 to 5 years. Procedurally, each child's free play was individually and continuously recorded in 15-second intervals for 35–50 minutes once a week for three 10-week periods. The children were observed for uses of space within designated play areas. The results indicated that (1) boys spent more time than girls in outdoor play areas across both years; (2) girls spent more time than boys in the indoor areas but significant differences in the second year were not observed; (3) boys spent much more time than girls in play out of doors regardless of season and entered a significantly greater number of play areas over both years; (4) boys spent more time playing in sand, on the tractor and climbing structure, and at the toy shed than girls; and (5) girls were more involved indoors, and at craft tables, and in the kitchen than boys.

The sixth study was completed by Honzik (1951). The investigation examined sex differences in the occurrences of materials in play constructions of children 11–13 years old. The play constructions of 272 preadolescents were observed and analyzed for types of objects used. Procedurally, after completing the play construction, the youngster was asked to describe it, and the data were recorded. The results indicated that (1) regardless of age, a significantly larger percentage of boys than girls used blocks, vehicles, and persons in various uniforms (e.g., cowboy, police official); and (2) a significantly larger percentage of girls than boys, regardless of age, used doll furniture, family people, and a dog figure in their play transpositions.

PLAYFULNESS AND IMAGINATIVENESS

Research on playfulness, a characteristic basic to child's play, conducted by Lieberman (1965) evidenced a unique personality dimension in 5-year-olds. Lieberman (1977) defines playfulness as the behavioral characteristic of "lightheartedness" found in young children's play activities and in combinatorial play. Lieberman (1977) notes that playfulness is an innate behavior and personality trait, that goes beyond the early years of the child. Along with Lieberman's (1965) classic study that initially identified this personality dimension basic to individual differences in child's play, the results of investigations conducted by other researchers also support the existence of this behavioral trait. Reviewed in this section, these selected studies were conducted by J. L. Singer (1973), D. G. 'Singer and Singer (1976), D. G. Singer (1978), D. G. Singer and Rummo (1973), and Tower & Singer, Singer and Biggs (1979).

Lieberman's (1965) classic study in 5-year-olds identified and rated their qualities of playfulness and examined the relationship between playfulness and divergent thinking factors of ideational fluency, spontaneous flexibility, and originality. In the study, each of the 93 children, 52 boys and 41 girls, was individually administered a playfulness scale, a divergent thinking interview, and the Peabody picture vocabulary test (PPVT). For the dimension of playfulness, the results of the factor analyses indicated that a single factor accounted for the majority of common variance, among the five playfulness traits examined in the study. The traits were physical, social, and cognitive spontaneity; manifest joy; and sense of humor. Thus, playfulness seems to be a unitary behavioral dimension. For the relationship between playfulness and divergent thinking, the results indicated that each of the playfulness traits correlated significantly with ideational fluency, with spontaneous flexibility, and originality. The results also showed that chronological age correlated significantly with each of the playfulness traits. And, mental age correlated significantly with four playfulness traits, but not with physical spontaneity. Both chronological and mental ages correlated with all three of the divergent-thinking factors. In reanalyzing parts of her data from this study, Lieberman (1977) initially found a high positive correlation between playfulness and creativity; after the effects of intelligence were partialed out, the magnitude of the association was substantially reduced.

In a second but related study, D. G. Singer and Rummo (1973) reinvestigated the relationships between playfulness and creativity found by Lieberman (1965). Procedurally, of the 79 children employed in the study, 27 were boys and 52 were girls, ranging in age from 4⅓ to 6½ years. The youngsters were individually administered several assessments: behavioral styles, creativity, and IQ (using the Peabody picture vocabulary test). First, the results of the factor analysis yielded a major dimension of playfulness similar to the finds of Lieberman (1965). This factor contained several selected behaviors such as curiosity, novelty seeking, imagination, and emotional expressiveness. Second, there was a significant relationship between playfulness and creativity for boys but not for girls.

The third, fourth and fifth studies were conducted by J. L. Singer (1973), D. G. Singer and Singer (1976), and Tower et al. (1979), respectively. The studies explored individual differences in imaginativeness of children's play. J. L. Singer (1973) explored the variables of imaginative predisposition and creative storytelling in young children and the amount of time the children spent with their parents. Preschool children were rated, using the Singer Interview for Imaginative Predispositions and their responses scored to the Baron Ink Blot Test. The results of the study suggested that children with high scores on the Singer interview also had less impatience compared to those with lower scores on imaginativeness. Furthermore, children with higher scores were rated as more creative storytellers and spent more time with their parents.

Using J. L. Singer's (1973) results on individual differences in imaginativeness, D. G. Singer and Singer (1976) explored the impact of television on the youngsters' imaginations. The experimenters randomly assigned 276 preschool children to one of four experimental conditions. One condition exposed the children to a model who taught them make-believe games. Children in another condition saw Mister Rogers' TV program with an adult interpreting events and focusing their attentions on salient elements in the programs. The children in the third condition were exposed to Mister Rogers' show without the mediational attributes; those in the fourth condition were the controls. The children were given tests for imaginativeness and rated on 13 other variables. The ratings on the latter variables were made during free-play settings. With pretest and posttest data collected and 10 treatment sessions over 2 weeks, the results indicated that children exposed to the modeling condition yielded significantly higher scores on imaginativeness than those in the other conditions.

In a final study, Tower et al. (1979) explored the effects of television programming on imaginativeness and other selected variables. Interactions between IQ and imaginativeness were also of interest. Procedurally, 58 preschool children were randomly assigned to one of three viewing conditions. Children in Condition 1 saw Mister Rogers' "Neighborhood House." Those in Condition 2 viewed "Sesame Street," and those in the third condition saw films about nature, animals, and health. Before the beginning of the treatment conditions, the children were assessed for IQ, imaginativeness, and other measures. The results showed that (1) high IQ children scored significantly better than average and low IQ children on correct answers to both inferential and recognition questions based on content of the respective programs; and (2) children in the Mister Rogers condition who were more imaginative remembered significantly greater content on inferential and recall questions than those in the same condition but who were less imaginative.

SYMBOLIC PLAY STYLES

Symbolic play styles indicating individual differences in children's play is a relatively new area of investigation (Rubin et al., in press). Symbolic play style is a dimension of cognitive understanding of reality and fantasy. These categories in turn, are used by children to assess aspects of their social and physical worlds.

The first study representative of symbolic play styles as individual differences in children's play was conducted by Morison and Gardner (1978). With 20 participants each in kindergarten, second, fourth, and sixth grades, this study examined the children's cognitive capacities to distinguish between fantasy and reality. Procedurally, children were given two experimental sessions. In the first session, a child explained pairings of three-picture items, some of which illustrated fantasy and nonfantasy characters. In the second session, the youngster was asked to sort the pictures into groups of "pretend" and real figures used in the first session and then to explain the classification. Using ANOVA designs, the results showed that (1) as children's age increased, their ability to use fantasy, classifications, and explanations also increased; (2) the use of fantasy responses is a function of the competing mode of response (e.g., category–functional) and salient cues signaling fantasy (e.g., potency, source of characters); and (3) children, regardless of age, made significantly more fantasy pairings than fantasy explanations even when they were asked for description.

The second study, conducted by Jennings (1975), explored the preference or orientation of preschool children to interaction with people versus objects and its relationship to intellectual abilities. There were 38 children, 22 boys and 16 girls, used in the study; they ranged in age from 4¼ to 5⅓ years. Procedurally, the children were rated in free play on a number of measures and then were given a battery of tests. Using correlational and t-test analyses, the results indicated that (1) children who spent more time at play with objects performed much better on tests of ability to classify and organize physical materials; (2) those who spent more time in play with people did not perform better on object-oriented tests of social knowledge;

and (3) social knowledge was associated with sociometric popularity with peers and to elements of social competency such as peer leadership.

HANDICAPPED DIFFERENCES

Differences between handicapped and nonhandicapped children in play behaviors has been considered as a dimension of individual differences in child's play. The studies conducted by Switzky, Ludwig, and Haywood (1979) and Weiner and Weiner (1974) represent investigations that compare handicapped with nonhandicapped on play and play-related behaviors.

Switzky et al. used 12 nonretarded and retarded children who were 3⅓ years old and 12 nonretarded and retarded who were 4⅓ years old. The study examined play, exploration, and the variables of object complexity and age across these two populations. The children were given individual intelligence tests and divided into these groups: young retarded, young nonretarded, older retarded, and older nonretarded. Procedurally, the youngsters were given objects varying in complexity and were asked to play with them. They were observed individually for the amount of time they spent with the objects in exploration and play; the kinds of behaviors they used were scored in 5-second intervals. The results indicated that (1) total exploratory time decreased, but total play time increased as linear functions of the amounts of exposure to the objects across these two populations; (2) retarded youngsters spent significantly greater amounts of exploratory time compared to nonretarded with objects of different levels of complexity; (3) nonretarded children did not differ significantly in the amount of exploration time across levels of complexity; (4) retarded youngsters explored less complex objects significantly longer than more complex ones; and (5) older retarded children explored less complex objects significantly longer than older nonretarded youngsters.

Weiner and Weiner (1974) examined handicapped and nonhandicapped populations on toy–play measures. There were 20 retarded and 40 normal children employed in the research; of the 20 retarded children, 9 were girls and 10 were boys; of the 40 normal youngsters, 21 were girls and 19 were boys. Procedurally, the toy behavior of each child was recorded independently during an 18-minute period; 20-second intervals were used for scoring. Included in the toys were a ball and a bear; several of the toy–play behaviors observed involved combinational use and separation of parts. Discriminant analyses were used. The results were (1) six-year-old normal children spent significantly more time than 6-year-old retardates in the toy–play behaviors of combinations, separations, manipulation of parts and pushing and pulling of toys with retarded children showing more person-alized uses of toys than the normal children (in this age comparison); (2) the best single toy–play behavior that distinguished retarded from normal children was combinations; (3) normal 3-year-olds showed a significantly greater number of combinations and throws than the retarded; (4) the best predictors of toy–play for the normal children were separations, manipulating parts, and undefined; and (5) the 6-year-old normal youngsters spent significantly more time in separating and manipulating parts of toys contrasted with 3-year-old normal children exhibiting more undefined usage.

The following research studies concern play behaviors of autistic, severely mentally retarded children. Black, Freeman, and Montgomery (1975) investigated how play behaviors in autistic youngsters are affected by differing settings: stark environment, theraplay unit, playroom, and outside yard. The children were also scored on their interaction with peers or objects in these environments. Procedurally, each child was observed for 3 minutes for each of the four environments and at three different times. Using mean percentage of time for each of the variables of (a) environment, (b) model, and (c) objects, the results follow: (1) With some youngsters, the environment, had little or no effects on the quantity of play; (2) autistic children spent a greater amount of time relating to objects than peers when using multiple objects; (3) play with objects more frequently occurred during the manipulation stage together with repetitive and negative behaviors; (4) autistic children primarily used solitary repetitive behaviors in stark environments with no objects present; and (5) autistic children modeled, imitated, and were involved together in large motor play in theraplay environments.

The article by Wing, Gould, Yeates, and Brierley (1977) explored symbolic play in severely mentally retarded children. In the research, there were 108 children ranging in chronological age from 5 to 14. Procedurally, the children's parents were interviewed in home settings and the children observed and tested on several instruments (e.g., the Illinois Test of Psycholinguistic Abilities). Based on the interviewing and observing of the parents and their children, respectively, the participants were divided into 3 groups: no symbolic play (with 42 children); stereotyped, repetitive, and copying play (with 23 youngsters); and flexible and varied symbolic play (with 43 children). In analyzing test data and group placement on quality of symbolic play, the results showed that (1) in retarded children below the mental age of 20 months, symbolic representational play did not occur; (2) stereotypic play is largely found in retarded children whose language comprehension behaviors are 19 months and above as determined by standardized assessment; (3) retarded children who scored below the mental age of 20 months on language comprehension and other selected skills (examined in the study) do not show any symbolic play.

Knapczyk and Yoppi (1975), the fifth study in this section, focused on the development of cooperative and competitive interactions which are high level social skills in the continua of development. All five subjects, four males and one female, were classified as educable mentally retarded with language and/or social–behavioral problems. The children ranged in chronological ages from 8 to 10. Procedurally, measures of base rate were taken per each subject during a 30-minute observational period. Treatment 1 consisted of teaching the children to play together in terms of cooperative and competitive social play based on positive social and token reinforcement (e.g., praise, model car). Reversal procedures were used; Treatment 2 was reinstated, and it paralleled those in Treatment 1. The latter three conditions lasted for 10 days while the baseline lasted 5 days. Using percentages, the results of the study show that: (1) in baserate, children showed no competitive play and very low levels of cooperative play; (2) during Treatment 1, the frequency of cooperative play increased and some small increases in competitive play were observed; and (3) during Treatment 2, the frequency of competitive play substantially increased and there was no change in the quantity of cooperative play compared to Treatment 1.

In a sixth study, Peck, Apolloni, Cooke, and Raver (1978), examined the generalities of social–behavioral changes through peer imitation between retarded and normal children under free-play conditions. In the first experiment, three retarded children, one girl and two boys were used; these children were diagnosed as having Down's syndrome. Of the three normal children employed as peer models, two were boys; one was a girl. All participants ranged in chronological age from 3 to 5 years. Throughout Study 1, peer imitation and social interaction (i.e., vocalizing and sharing) were monitored by time sampling across all six children. Procedurally, the pretraining phase consisted of observations of all six children together in the same room for 30 minutes. In the first training period, one retarded child's imitative behavior was reinforced by an adult in free play, but in close proximity to the nonretarded peer who was observing. In the second and third training periods, the procedures were repeated, but in conjunction with retarded and nonretarded subjects 2 and 3. A generalization period followed. The results indicate that the retarded children's imitative and social interaction behaviors across the training periods increased. Furthermore, the modeling of the retarded by the normal children did not occur.

In the second study, two retarded children, one normal child, and the peer model, a normal youngster, were used. The retarded children's IQs were 46 and 74; they demonstrated low rates of parallel and solitary social play behaviors. The children ranged in age from 2 to 5. Procedurally, in the pretraining phase, base rates of imitation of child-to-child and negative and positive social interactions were observed. During training, the adult introduced toys (e.g., modeling clay) and prompted the subject and peer model to play simultaneously with them. The trainer also introduced songs and the retarded were socially and physically prompted to imitate the peer model. The generalization phase followed. The results of this study showed that imitative and positive social interaction from the retarded subjects to the peer model and from the peer model to the retarded subjects rarely were observed.

CONCLUSIONS

Individual differences in cognition as it relates to child's play is a promising area for empirical investigation. The precursor to child's play research rests in the early theories (essentially surplus energy and recapitulation). These are the two primary theories that provide some understanding of individual-difference phenomena in child's play. Both theories emphasize the significance of child's play from cognitive (and social) developmental perspectives. However, recapitulation theory more than surplus-energy contributes directly to one of the mainstreams of research on individual differences in child's play. The roots of research on playfulness and imaginativeness are planted firmly in recapitulation theory's emphasis on imagination and creativity (Rubin et al., in press). Although the early theories valued child's play because of its purported connection to cognitive (and social) development, Piaget's ludic theory, a contemporary perspective, established not only salient connections and relationships between play and cognition, but also provided a rich structure of theory whence the majority of research in individual differences in child's play has emanated. The Piagetian influence is rooted primarily in the contemporary mainstreams of individual differences in child's play which include sex differences, playfulness and imaginativeness, symbolic play styles and to a lesser extent, handicapped differences (Rubin et al., in press). The selected studies reviewed and summarized within each of the four contemporary areas of individual-difference research in child's play are simply representative of contemporary research and illustrate the continued viability of investigation in the field of individual differences in child's play.

The four mainstreams reviewed were: (1) sex differences; (2) playfulness and imaginativeness; (3) symbolic play styles; and (4) handicapped differences. From the results of studies on sex differences, Benjamin (1932) and Farrell (1957) found sex differences for toy objects. Benjamin's results show that more girls than boys preferred to play with the miniature girl and boy figures; more boys than girls desired to use the toy car. The amount of time spent with these objects were in a similar direction by gender and by toy. In reference to playing with blocks, the results of Farrell (1957) show that a greater number of boys than girls prefer "unit" blocks (relative to choosing or not choosing them).

With the two selected studies reviewed using infants, the results of Goldberg and Lewis (1969) with 13-month-olds and Fein et al. (1975) with 20-month-olds are noteworthy and show individual toy preferences by gender. Girls spent significantly more time than boys playing with blocks, pegboards, miniature animals, and used more fine vis-à-vis gross motor movements (Goldberg & Lewis, 1969). And, at 20 months, Fein et al. report that of the objects available for selection, girls spend a greater amount of time playing and selecting girl toys and more time touching and contacting girl toys than boy toys. Boys used more time in playing and selecting boy than girl toys; whereas, boys touching and contacting preferences with toys were not significant. Interestingly, results from interviewing children's mothers indicate that their identification of toys found in the home was consistent with the toy preferences made by their children.

In addition, the results of Harper and Sanders (1975) suggest that preschool boys spend significantly more time than preschool girls in outdoor areas, whereas girls use a greater amount of time in indoor areas. Further, the boys in outdoor settings preferred to use sand as a play medium, tractors, and climbing apparati relative to the number of "outdoor" choices available to them. In indoor environments, girls preferred to play with crafts and use the kitchen. Honzik (1951) observed play constructions of preadolescents. The results show that even with 11-, 12- and 13-year-olds, gender differences are consistently observed in their play choices and materials. For example, more boys than girls chose and used blocks, vehicles, and miniature people figures in uniforms, whereas more girls than boys used doll furniture, miniature family figures, and a miniature figure of a dog for their play materials.

Halverson and Waldrop (1973) examined generality of play behaviors and activity levels of preschool boys and girls. Their results show that boys were able to generalize their play behaviors from indoor to outdoor environments and vice versa; girls did not evidence this generality across settings. And, boys were physically active in play compared to girls (as determined by adult ratings). Observational studies of sex preferences in child's play in home settings are another area of potential investigation relative to individual difference phenomena. For example, Smith and

Daglish (1977) observed infants' behaviors in home settings; their results show that boys evidenced more active play than girls. And, boys used more transportation toys and attempted and practiced significantly more play forbidden them by adults. These and other areas are open for additional fruitful research on sex differences in cognitive child's play.

From the mainstream of research on playfulness and imaginativeness in child's play, the results of Lieberman (1965, 1977) suggest that playfulness, composed of physical, social, and cognitive spontaneity; manifest joy, and sense of humor, is an individual difference variable. D. G. Singer and Rummo (1973) in support of Leiberman's findings note the playfulness dimension as a unitary variable. However, additional research will need to be conducted on the relationship between playfulness and divergent thinking to determine whether Leiberman's findings of a strong, positive relationship are robust. Further, Meehl, Lykken, Schofield, and Tellegen (1971) in a factor procedure labeled "recaptured-item technique" noted that playfulness may not be a unitary factor in adults as it appears to be in preschoolers. A great number of contemporary research methodology and longitudinal investigations are needed to further explore this and other individual difference variables in child's play.

Related to playfulness is the individual difference variable of imaginativeness. Research studies (e.g., D. G. Singer, 1978; D. G. Singer & Singer, 1976; J. L. Singer, 1973) on imaginativeness show it to be a significant variable, particularly in the modes which the child uses to interact with his milieus. Children who scored high on imaginativeness as determined by the Singer interview were also those who were rated low on impatience (J. L. Singer, 1973). Imaginativeness warrants further cross-sectional and longitudinal research to determine the consistency of its unitary dimension across additional selected variables.

With the mainstream on symbolic modes in child's play, selected research results (Morison & Gardner, 1978) appear to suggest an individual-difference dimension. The way humans perceive reality and fantasy may rest on their symbolic modes and styles (e.g., Morison & Gardner, 1978). In support of this individual-difference dimension, the results of Jennings (1975) also support differences in symbolic play styles between those she labeled "people versus object-oriented individuals." Further research should highlight the significance of symbolic play styles as a potential and fruitful variable of individual differences in child's play.

Handicapped differences between normal and retarded children in the field of individual differences and child's play is a very intriguing, and conceptually stimulating area of research. For example, in differentiating between play actions and activities of retarded versus normal children, the research of Switzky et al. (1979) and Weiner and Weiner (1974), illuminate cognitive differences. Retarded preschoolers compared to normal pre-schoolers spend more time exploring toy objects of differing levels of com-plexity; older retarded children compared to normal youngsters spend more time exploring less complex objects (Switzky et al., 1979). The best single predictor of toy–play behaviors in normal children was separations, manip-ulating parts of toys, and an undefined or miscellaneous category of behav-ior; the best single predictor that distinguished normal from retarded chil-dren was toy–combinations (Weiner & Weiner, 1974).

Black et al. (1975) and Wing et al. (1977) investigated play behaviors in autistic and severely mentally retarded children. Autistic children, for in-stance, spend more time with objects than with peers when playing with many objects (Black et al., 1975), in severely mentally retarded children, symbolic representational play does not occur below the mental age of 20 months (Wing et al., 1977). With educable mentally retarded children, the results of Knapczyk and Yoppi (1975) illustrate that they can be trained to demonstrate cooperative and competitive play interactions. Peck et al. (1978) results indicate that peer imitation of normal by retarded children can develop imitative and social interactive play behaviors in the children.

Child's play may be a particularly effective tool in attempting to remedi-ate certain kinds of handicapping conditions in retarded children as well as in training them in types of prosocial behaviors. For example, child's play may help schizophrenic children to demonstrate greater flexibility of behav-iors (Rutter, 1972).

Exploration of handicapped differences in child's play as an individual-differences variable is just beginning. To determine whether the foci of these mainstreams of research remain unitary dimensions of individual dif-ferences in child's play requires additional longitudinal endeavors and use of several allied types of research methodologies and paradigms (Yawkey, under editorial review).

REFERENCES

Benjamin, H. Age and sex differences in toy preference in young children. *Journal of Genetic Psychology*, 1932, *41*, 417–429.

Black, M., Freeman, B. J., & Montgomery, J. Systematic observation of play behavior in autistic children. *Journal of Autism and Childhood Schizophrenia*, 1975, *5*(4), 363–371.

Carroll, J. B. On the theory-practice interface in the measurement of intellectual abilities. In P. Suppes (Ed.), *Impact of research on education: Some case studies*. Washington, D.C.: National Academy of Education, 1978.

Curry, N., & Arnaud, S. Cognitive implications in children's spontaneous role play. *Theory Into Practice*, 1974, *13*(6), 173–177.

Farrell, M. Sex differences in block play in early childhood education. *Journal of Educational Research*, 1957, *51*, 279–284.

Fein, G., Johnson, D., Kosson, N., Stork, L., & Wasserman, L. Sex stereotypes and preferences in the toy choices of 20-month-old boys and girls. *Developmental Psychology*, 1975, *11*(4), 527–528.

Flavell, J. H. *The developmental psychology of Jean Piaget*. Princeton, N.J.: Van Nostrand-Reinhold, 1963.

Goldberg, S., & Lewis, M. Play behavior in the year-old infant: Early sex differences. *Child Development*, 1969, *40*, 21–32.

Hall, G. S. *Youth*. New York: Appleton, 1912.

Hall, G. S. *Aspects of child life and education*. New York: Appleton, 1921.

Halverson, C. F., & Waldrop, M. F. The relations of mechanically recorded activity level to varieties of preschool play behavior. *Child Development*, 1973, *44*, 678–681.

Harper, L. V., & Sanders, K. Preschool children's use of space: Sex differences in outdoor play. *Developmental Psychology*, 1975, *11*, 119.

Hartup, W. W., Moore, S. G., & Sager, G. Avoidance of inappropriate sex-typing by young children. *Journal of Consulting Psychology*, 1963, *27*, 467–473.

Honzik, M. P. Sex differences in the occurrence of materials in the play constructions of preadolescents. *Child Development*, 1951, *22*(1), 15–35.

Jennings, K. D. People versus object orientation, social behavior, and intellectual abilities in preschool children. *Developmental Psychology*, 1975, *11*, 511–519.

Knapczyk, D. R., & Yoppi, J. O. Development of cooperative and competitive play responses in developmentally disabled children. *American Journal of Mental Deficiency*, 1975, *80*(3), 245–255.

Lieberman, J. N. Playfulness and divergent thinking: An investigation of their relationship at the kindergarten level. *Journal of Genetic Psychology*, 1965, *107*, 219–224.

Lieberman, J. N. *Playfulness: Its relation to imagination and creativity*. New York: Academic Press, 1977.

Lovell, J., Hoyle, W., & Siddall, M. Q. A study of some aspects of the play and language of young children with delayed speech. *Journal of Child Psychology and Psychiatry*, 1968, *9*, 41–50.

Manosevitz, M., Prentice, N. M., & Wilson, F. Individual and family correlates of imaginary companions in preschool children. *Developmental Psychology*, 1973, *8*, 72–79.

Meehl, P. E., Lykken, D. T., Schofield, W., & Tellegen, A. Recaptured-item technique (RIT): A method for reducing somewhat the subjective element in factor naming. *Journal of Experimental Research in Personality*, 1971, *5*, 171–190.

Millar, S. *The psychology of play*. Harmondsworth, England: Penguin Books, 1968.

Mitchell, E., & Mason, B. *The theory of play*. New York: A. S. Barnes, 1934.

Moore, N. V., Evertson, C. M., & Brophy, J. E. Solitary play: Some functional reconsiderations. *Developmental Psychology*, 1974, *10*(6), 830–834.

Morison, P., & Gardner, H. Dragons and dinosaurs: The child's capacity to differentiate fantasy from reality. *Child Development*, 1978, *49*, 642–648.

Nahme-Huang, L., Singer, D. G., Singer, J. L., & Wheaton, A. B. Imaginative play training and perceptual-motor interventions with emotionally-disturbed hospitalized children. *American Journal of Orthopsychiatry*, 1977, *47*(2), 238–249.

Peck, C. A., Apolloni, T., Cooke, T. P., & Raver, S. A. Teaching retarded preschoolers to imitate the free-play behavior of nonretarded classmates: Trained and generalized effects. *Journal of Special Education*, 1978, *12*(2), 195–207.

Pederson, F. A., & Bell, R. Q. Sex differences in preschool children without histories of complications of pregnancy and delivery. *Developmental Psychology*, 1970, *3*, 10–15.

Piaget, J. *Play, dreams and imitation in childhood.* New York: W. W. Norton, 1962.

Rubin, K. H., Fein, G. G., & Vandenberg, B. Play. In P. Mussen (Editor-in Chief), *Carmichael's manual of child psychology: Social development* (E. M. Hetherington, Ed.). New York: Wiley, in press.

Rutter, M. Childhood schizophrenia reconsidered. *Journal of Autism and Childhood Schizophrenia,* 1972, *2*(4), 315–337.

Schiller, F. *On the aesthetic education of man.* New Haven, Conn.: Yale University Press, 1954.

Singer, D. G. Television and imaginative play. *Journal of Mental Imagery,* 1978, *2*, 145–164.

Singer, D. G., & Rummo, J. Ideational creativity and behavioral style in kindergarten aged children. *Developmental Psychology,* 1973, *8*, 154–161.

Singer, D. G., & Singer, J. L. Family television viewing habits and the spontaneous play of preschool children. *American Journal of Orthopsychiatry,* 1976, *46*, 496–502.

Singer, J. L. (Ed.) *The child's world of make-believe.* New York: Academic Press, 1973.

Singer, J. L., & Streiner, B. F. Imaginative content in the dreams and fantasy play of blind and sighted children. *Perceptual and Motor Skills,* 1966, *22*, 475–482.

Smith, P. K., & Daglish, L. Sex differences in parent and infant behavior in the home. *Child Development,* 1977, *48*, 1250–1254.

Spencer, H. *Principles of psychology* (Vol. 2, 3rd ed.). New York: Appleton, 1873.

Strain, P. Increasing social play of severely retarded preschoolers with socio-dramatic activities. *Mental Retardation,* 1975, *13*, 7–9.

Switzky, H. N., Ludwig, L., & Haywood, H. C. Exploration of object complexity and age. *American Journal of Mental Deficiency,* 1979, *83*(6), 637–644.

Tower, R. B., Singer, D. G., Singer, J. L., & Biggs, A. Differential aspects of television programming on preschoolers' cognition, imagination, and social play. *American Journal of Orthopsychiatry,* 1979, *49*(2) 265–280.

Weiner, E. A., & Weiner, B. J. Differentiation of retarded and normal children through toy-play analysis. *Multivariate Behaviorial Research,* 1974, *9*(7), 245–252.

Wing, L., Gould, J., Yeates, S. R., & Brierley, L. M. Symbolic play in severely mentally retarded and in autistic children. *Journal of Child Psychology and Psychiatry,* 1977, *18*, 167–178.

Yawkey, T. D. Sociodramatic play tutoring and sex effects on selected cognitive-academic and play-related behaviors in five-year-olds. *Contemporary Educational Psychology,* under editorial review.

Author Index

Numbers in *italics* refer to the pages on which the complete references are listed.

Subject Index